FORBIDDEN ARCANA

CATALYST
game labs™

CONTENTS & CREDITS

INTRODUCTION	**5**
A WALK IN THE PARK	**6**
SEEING THE INVISIBLE WORLD	**10**
The Magic of Mundanes	11
Sibling Magic	11
ArjuanGuit241, Tenochtitlan	11
down4mojo2, Seattle	11
canuslingit4me, Indianapolis	12
wiresoverwiz4life, Detroit	12
cathater4real, Bone City	12
feartheunseen, Butte	13
NoSpellsHere, Raleigh	13
LostChild708, Palos Hills	14
Shadowrunner Encounters	15
HotSouthernNight, Atlanta	15
PugetOldTimer, Seattle	15
MilesAboveYou, Denver	16
ToughTexan, Dallas/Fort Worth	16
Law Enforcement and Security	16
SeeingIsBelieving, St. Louis	16
ForRosa, Amarillo	17
LostintheMix, Seattle	17
Trid and Stage	18
MageMuse9000, Atlanta	18
WestCoastWills, Hollywood	18
Corporate Usage	18
Jane Doe, Pyramid Arcane Supplies	18
The Magic Show	19
The Will of the Manasphere	25
MAGIC MASTERY	**30**
Adept Healer	31
Alchemical Armorer	31
Alchemical Bomb Maker	31
Animal Familiar	31
Apt Pupil	32
Arcane Bodyguard	32
Arcane Improviser [Chaos]	32
Archivist	32
Astral Bouncer	32
Astral Infiltrator	32
Barehanded Adept [Buddhism]	33
Blood Necromancer	33
Chain Breaker [Shaman]	33
Chakra Interrupter	34
Charlatan	34
Chosen Follower	35
Close Combat Mage	35
Dark Ally	35
Death Dealer	35
Dedicated Conjurer	36
Dedicated Spellslinger	36

Dual-Natured Defender	36
Durable Preparations	36
Elemental Master [Wuxing]	36
Flesh Sculpter	37
Healer	37
Illusionist	37
Items of Power	38
Mage Hunter	38
Missile Deflector	38
Mystic Foreman	38
Mystic Pitcher	38
Pacifist Adept	39
Potion Maker	39
Practiced Alchemist [Islamic]	39
Puppet Master [Black Magic]	39
Reckless Spell Master	39
Renaissance Ritualist [Chaos]	40
Revenant Adept	40
Shock Mage	40
Skinwalker [Sioux]	40
Spectral Warden [Hermetic]	40
Spell Jammer	40
Spirit Hunter	40
Spiritual Lodge	41
Spiritual Pilgrim [Buddhism]	41
Sprawl Tamer	41
Stalwart Ally	42
Taboo Transformer [Wicca]	42
Vexcraft	42
Worship Leader	42
FOCUSED AWAKENED	**42**
The Elementalist	43
The Hedge Witch/Wizard	43
The Null Wizard	43
The Seer	43
NEW METAMAGICS	**43**
Paradigm Shift	43
Paradigm Shift: Insect Shaman	43
Paradigm Shift: Toxic	44
Spirit Expansion: UMT	44
Spirit Expansion: Shedim	44
Improved Astral Form	44
Astralnaut	44
Structured Spellcasting	44
Tarot Summoning	45
Reckless Necro Conjuring	45
Noble Sacrifice	46
Harmonious Defense	46
Harmonious Reflection	46
EXPANDED ASPECTS	**46**
The Apprentice	47

The Enchanter (Optional)	47
The Explorer	47
The Aware	49
NEW SPELLS	**49**
Branch	49
Vines	49
Thorn	49
Rosebush	49
Growth	49
Lash	49
Slash	49
Claw	50
Barrage	50
Multiply Food	50
Comet	50
Gravity	50
Gravity Well	50
Evil Eye	50
Alter Ballistics	51
List of Effects	52
NEW RITUALS	**52**
Forest Transformation (Anchored)	52
Necro Summoning	52
(Minion) Ritual	52
Necro Spirits	52
Carcass Spirit	52
Corpse Spirit	53
Rot Spirit	53
Palefire Spirit	53
Detritus Spirit	53
TEA & SYMPATHY	**54**
TRADITIONS	**58**
TRADITION UPDATES	**60**
BLACK MAGIC (UPDATE)	60
Related Mentor Spirits	60
The Buddhist Tradition (Updated)	61
Related Mentor Spirits	62
Christian Theurgist Tradtition (Updated)	63
Order of St. Sylvester	63
New Knights Templar	63
Vigilia Evangelica	63
Westphalian Theurgists	63
Orthodox Exarchs	63
Related Mentor Spirits	63
The Druidic Tradition (Updated)	65
Celtic Druids	65
Wild Druids	66
English Druids	66
Related Mentor Spirits	66
Traditional Druid Rules	66
Wild Druids (Optional)	67

English Druids (Optional)	67	**MENTOR SPIRITS**	94	Ordo Maximus	122
The Norse Tradition (Updated)	67	**Dove**	94	NAN	122
Related Mentor Spirits	67	**Planar Entity**	95	Wicca	123
Norse Magician Rules	68	**Arcana**	95	Theurgy	123
Berserkers (Adept Only)	68	**Holy Text**	95	DIMR	124
Islam (Updated)	69	**Death**	96	**BLOOD IN, BLOOD OUT**	125
Islamic Alchemists	69	**War**	97		
Licit Qur'anic Magic	69	**Tohu Wa-Bohu**	97	**Blood Spells**	125
Related Mentor Spirits	69	**Green Man**	98	**Combat**	125
Islamic Magician Rules	70	**Sun**	98	Boil Blood	125
Djinn	70	**Dark King**	98	Corpse Explosion	126
Shamanism (Updated)	73	**Moon**	98	Embolism	126
Traditionalist Shaman	73	**Oak**	99	Giger Spit	126
Ancestor Shaman	73	**Stag**	99	Ice Veins	127
Related Mentor Spirits	73	**Great Mother**	99	Pyrohemetics	127
Alternate Shamanic Path Rules	74	**Globalization and Mentors**	99	Rupture	127
NEW TRADITIONS	75	**Spider (alt)**	100	**Health**	127
		Wolf (alt)	100	Clot	127
Cosmic	75	**Rat (alt)**	100	Share Damage	127
Related Mentor Spirits	75	**MAGICAL ODDITIES**	101	Somatic Healing	127
Cosmic Mage Rules	76			Sympathetic Reprisal	128
Draconic	76	**Hybrid Traditions**	101	**Manipulation**	128
Restrictions	77	Awakened Martial Arts	101	Blood Puppet	128
Related Mentor Spirits	77	Way of Unified Mana (Hapsum-Do)	101	Corpse Spikes	129
Elder God Magic	78	**MAGICAL DEMOGRAPHICS**	102	Corpse Lash	129
Related Mentor Spirits	78			Blood Whip	129
Elder God Mage Rules	79	**Traditional Demographics**	104	Blood Blade	129
Green Magic	80	**BLOOD MAGIC**	**106**	Viscera Web	129
Related Mentor Spirits	80			**Blood Rituals**	130
Green Mage Rules	80	**WORDS FROM THE CONTRIBUTORS**	106	Blood Bath	130
Missionists	81	**Netcat**	106	Blood Oath	130
Related Mentor Spirits	82	**Red**	106	Death Curse	130
Missionist Mage Rules	82	**Frosty**	106	Guardian Bond	131
Necro Magic	82	**Glitch**	106	**Metamagic**	131
Related Mentor Spirits	83	**THE PULSE OF MAGIC**	107	Predator Feast	
Necro Mage Rules	84	**What It Is**	107	(Adepts Only)	131
Olympianism	84	**What It Isn't**	107	Soul Tether	131
Related Mentor Spirits	85	**How It Works**	107	Spiritual Sacrifice	131
Path of Pariah	85	Theory	107	**Blood Crystal Qualities**	132
Related Mentor Spirits	86	History	109	Crystal Breath	132
Pariah Rules	86	The Benefits	110	Crystal Eye	132
Planar Magic	87	The Risks	110	Crystal Gut	133
Related Mentor Spirits	88	Conclusion	112	Crystal Jaw	133
Planar Mage Rules	88	**The New Shit**	112	Crystal Limb	133
Red Magic	88	So What Is It?	113	Crystal Spine	133
Related Mentor Spirits	89	Self-Sacrifice	114	Crystalline Blade	133
Red Mage Rules	89	Greed Pays, But Caution Stays	115	Crystalline Claws	133
The Romani Tradition	90	Blood, Sweat, and Murder	116	Crystalline Diver	133
Related Mentor Spirits	90	Painting in Scarlet	118	Crystalline Grace	134
Romani Mage Rules	91	Riding the Tide	119	Crystalline Reflexes	134
Tarot	91	**Crimson Crystals**	119	Crystalline Shards	134
Related Mentor Spirits	92	**Rivers of Power**	121	Crystalline Vision	134
Notable Feature	94	Aztlan (Aztechnology)	121	**New Spirits**	134
Tarot Mage Rules	94			Bone Spirit	134
				Blood Shade	135

THICKER THAN WATER	135
Blood Magic and Addiction	135
BREATH OF THE WILD	**138**
WHERE THE WILD THINGS ARE	**142**
UNIVERSAL MAGIC THEORY	142
Where Does Magic Come From?	143
Where Does Magic Go?	147
WILD SPIRITS	149
NATURE SPIRITS	151
Domains	151
Spirits of the Land	151
Spirits of the Winds	152
Spirits of the Waters	153
Spirits of Man	155
Wild Beast Spirits	157
Wild Urban Spirits	158
Spirits of Ceramics	159
Spirits of Metal	160
Spirits of Energy	161
Spirits of the Airwaves	161
Vehicle Spirits	162
Vehicles of the Sea	162
Vehicles of the Land	163
Vehicles of the Air	164
Awakened Vehicles	165
Hermetic Elementals	165
Elementals in General	166
Elementals in Particular	167
Four Out of Five Ain't Bad	167
Platonic Concepts	167
In Closing ...	169
WILD SUMMONING RULES	175
Wild Reputation	175
Accruing Wild Index	176
Wild Reputation	177
Calling Wild Spirits	177
Dealing With	
Wild Spirits	177
Wild Spirit Rules	178
Wild Nature Spirits	179
Wild Beast Spirits	179
Beast Traits	179
Wild Spirits of Man	179
Wild Urban Spirits	180
Ceramic Spirits	180
Metal Spirits	180
Energy Spirits	180
Airwave Spirits	180
Vehicle Spirits	180
Vehicle Spirit Powers	180

Ship Spirits	180
Train Spirits	181
Automotive Spirits	181
Aircraft Spirits	181
Awakened Vehicles	181
Hermetic Elementals	181
Spirits as Contacts	181
OPTIONAL RULES	182
The Mentor's Mask	182
Spirit Leashing	182
Testing the Leash	182
ADVANCED ALCHEMY	**184**
LIFE OF A CORPORATE ALCHEMIST	184
MANATECH: RISKS AND REWARDS	185
NEW REAGENTS OF THE SIXTH WORLD	187
Harvesting Reagents	187
Overharvesting Reagents	187
NEW WAYS TO LEVERAGE REAGENTS	187
Raw Reagents	188
Refined Reagents	188
Radical Reagents	188
NEW RARE REAGENTS	188
Reagent: Bone or Hair from a Baobhan Sith	188
Reagent: Drop Bear Saliva	189
Reagent: Ghost Orchid Petals	190
Reagent: Ground Killdeer Antlers	190
Reagent: Kayeri Mushroom	190
NEW EXOTIC REAGENTS	190
Reagent: Drake Scales	191
Reagent: Organ of Insect Spirit Host	191
Reagent: Veins of an Adept	191
ALTERNATIVE USES FOR ORICHALCUM	192
NEW ALCHEMICAL TOOLS	192
Atomizer	193
Alembic	193
Athanor	193
Crucible	193
Vault of Ages	193
NEW COMPOUNDS	194
Alchemical Duct Tape	194
Astral Increase	194
Astral Bond	195
Baobhan's Tears	195
Drain Away	195
Dulled Edges	195
Feel No Pain	195
Force of Personality	196
HMHVV II Inhibitor	196

Laminate	196
Perfect Sight	196
Sharpshooter	197
Unstoppable Vigor	197
Water Breathing	197
NEW ALCHEMICAL PREPARATIONS	198
Abandon All Hope	198
Barricade	198
Burn, Baby, Burn	198
Do Your Best	198
Get Away from My Ride	198
High as a Kite	199
Noise on the Line	199
NOMW (Not on My Watch)	199
Lightning Blade	199
Spirit Zapper	199
Stink Bomb	199
Stop Thief!	199
Truth Serum	200
Up and At 'Em	200
Watch Your Step	200
THE SYNERGY OF ALCHEMY AND DARK TRADITIONS	201
Blood Magic	201
Insect Magic	201
Toxic Magic	202
RESEARCH, RUMORS, AND LEGENDS	203
Philosopher's Stone	203
Harvesting the Court of Shadows	204
INFECTED ALCHEMY	205
Ancient Secrets in Modern Hands (Corporate Alchemy Crackdown)	206
Toxicity	208
THE ALCHEMIST'S GUIDE TO SHADOWRUNNING	209
Finding the Sweet Spot: Planning for Drain	209
Selecting the Best Spells for Alchemy	209
Dirty Deeds and Tricks: Watching the Dominoes Fall	210
INDEX	211
Alchemical Tools	211
Compounds	211
Mastery Qualities	211
Mentor Spirits	211
Metamagics	211
Preparations	212
Reagents	212
Rituals	212
Spells	212
Spirits	212
Traditions	212

First Printing by Catalyst Game Labs, an imprint of InMediaRes Productions, LLC
PMB 202 • 303 -91st Ave. NE, E-502
Lake Stevens, WA 98258

Find us online:
info@shadowruntabletop.com
    (*Shadowrun* questions)
http://www.shadowruntabletop.com
    (Catalyst *Shadowrun* website)
http://www.shadowrun.com
    (official *Shadowrun Universe* website)
http://www.catalystgamelabs.com
    (Catalyst website)
http://shop.catalystgamelabs.com
    (Catalyst/Shadowrun orders)

INTRODUCTION

The world of magic is infinite. For everything you know, there are a hundred things, a million things, that you don't. You learn how magic works, you learn how mana is ordered, then you learn that everything you had been taught was wrong. That if you just look at it from a different angle, the whole system of magic becomes something entirely different. And maybe it isn't even a system, or at least not an orderly one.

Forbidden Arcana is all about exploring the back roads and dark corners of magic, discovering the hidden truths that tell you how little you knew in the first place—and how much more power is waiting to be grabbed. It starts with **Seeing the Invisible World**, a guide for both Awakened and non-Awakened about what magic looks like in practice. If you want to geek the mage first, this is your guide to recognizing who is doing the casting. And if you're a mage, here are some of the tells people will be looking for if they want to recognize what you're up to.

Next is **Magical Mastery**. While it would be great to live long enough to be a master of all forms of arcane arts, very few of us are dragons or immortal elves, so we are often best served by choosing an area to master, becoming better at it than anyone else. This chapter is your guide to selecting where to excel and how to do it.

Then we have **Traditions**, one of the most notable ways the Awakened differentiate themselves from their peers. With both new and updated traditions, this provides info on how to shape magic with your beliefs—or have your beliefs shaped by magic. New mentor spirits are also included here.

The book then truly delves into the realm of the forbidden with **Blood Magic**. Most mages know about the dark paths of those who would inflict pain on others to gain power for themselves, but this chapter paints the art in a different light, showing those who practice blood magic with aims that might be called "good"—insofar as that label can be applied to anything in the Sixth World.

Where the Wild Things Are dives into the realms of wild spirits, untamed and unruly beings whose power may be tapped by brave conjurers—if they can bear the possible cost to themselves.

Finally, **Advanced Alchemy** offers tools, ideas, reagents, compounds, and more to make alchemy more effective and more dangerous.

All these are secrets available to those who have put in the effort to learn them, and who have paid whatever price is asked of them. They may have come to a new awareness of how much they have left to learn, but they possess one precious truth: No matter how much they don't know, they now know a little than the people they'll be running into on the streets.

FORBIDDEN ARCANA CREDITS

Writing: Jason Andrew, Raymond Croteau, Kevin Czarnecki, Jeff Fowler, Alexander Kadar, Adam Large, O.C. Presley, Scott Schletz, Dylan Stangel, Thomas Willoughby, Evans, Andre Garcia, Michele Giorgi, Phil Hilliker, David Hovey, Brian McCranie, Allen Morris, Alex Stone, Takashi Tan, Kim Van Deun

Art Direction: Brent Evans

Cover Art: Victor Manuel Leza Moreno

Cover Layout: Maxwell "Matt Heerdt" Lamé

Iconography: Nigel Sade

Interior Art: Bruno Balixa, Brent Chumley, Tyler Clark, Daniel Comerci, Álvaro Calvo Escudero, Brent

Interior Layout: Maxwell "Matt Heerdt" Lamé

Shadowrun Line Developer: Jason M. Hardy

Playtesting & Proofing: Natalie Aked, Rob Aked, Adam Bruno, Chuck Burhanna, Karlene Dickens, Bruce Ford, Timothy Gray, Mason Hart, Francis Jose, Kendall Jung, David Dashifen Kees, Dave Lundquest, Chris Maxfield, Suzanna Powell, Lindsay Riessen, Richard Riessen, Carl Schelin, David Silberstein, Mark Somers, Jeremy Weyand, Leland Zavadil

A WALK
IN THE PARK

A light snow covered the ground and tumbled gently from the sky, painting a picturesque scene of peace and tranquility over the streets. It was a rare thing. Snow in Seattle was not common, and peace in Redmond was even rarer. The snow was keeping trouble indoors for now and left Abby to stroll the streets on her way home from another late night at Stacy Sweets' Diner.

The peaceful scene lightened her heart, but her mind was still Redmond Barrens born and raised. She saw the snow on the ground as a way to mark the passage or presence of people. The snow was a mixed blessing, as it muffled noise, making it both harder to be heard and hear others. The chill air and slippery streets kept go-gangers in their garages and cooled the heads of thrill-gangs for the night.

She enjoyed the peace of the streets and the false beauty that was laid out over the urban decay and detritus of Redmond, but the quiet night presented a rare opportunity for her to take a different route home. She cut down an alley, checking for tracks or signs of life before taking the darkened path that would lead her towards BI Park, known as Bought Park to most locals. The BI stood for Brackhaven Investments, the former governor's financial firm, that had funded the revitalization of the park as a bit of PR during the governor's tenure in office. The effort had benefited Brackhaven far more than the local community because his construction contracts raked

in the money from the high-cost urban redevelopment project while locals were hassled and abused by the increased Knight Errant presence during construction.

Regardless of local opinions, the final result was a wide expanse of grass, trees, and bushes built within a patch of rolling ground, with winding paths and a beautiful open fairway at the center that might actually have local children gliding down it tomorrow on anything slippery enough to sled on. For now that space would be a massive field of white within a winter wonderland of the type that Seattle rarely saw.

Minutes later, Abby was not disappointed as she stood at the mouth of another alley staring across the street at the white-topped wall of evergreen bushes that ringed the park. The metal archway with the script BI at its peak was covered in a thin layer of white, contrasting beautifully with its dark wrought iron. Beneath the archway, the footpath leading into the park was devoid of any marring prints.

Abby changed that quickly. Once inside the maze of tall evergreen shrubs, her senses opened to the cold and snow rather than the possible dangers of the streets. She laid her head back and opened her mouth wide. Tongue out, she enjoyed the combined sensations of snow gently landing and melting on her face and in her mouth. Her stroll was filled with moments that would stay with her forever, but the cold, combined with too many cups of soykaf, threatened to cut it short.

BY SCOTT SCHLETZ

The night was late, but she was enjoying it far too much to end it sooner than needed. She quickened her step toward the open central plaza of the park—not to get to the beautiful open scenery faster, but because she knew there was a restroom there that she could use and extend her stay in wintery dreamscape.

The warmth of the restroom was a welcome change from the cold. After relieving her strained bladder, Abby decided to take a few minutes to warm up before heading back out for more snowy fun. The lady's restroom actually had a sitting area separate from the stalls. It was a strange throwback to another day and time when the restroom was a social stop for women. She sat down and distracted herself by clearing her inbox of old messages while checking on a few of her favorite P2.0 streams. She uploaded a few pictures she had taken before leaving work of the peaceful falling snow. She wanted to load some pics of the park, but her Redmond upbringing taught her it was better to post about where you've been than where you are. Instead she dug her trodes out from her bag and stuck them around her head before replacing her knit cap to hold them in place—and, of course, keep her head warm. She linked her commlink to her cloud storage and started the sim recording through the trodes. Later on, everyone could upload her experience and enjoy a moment of peace in Redmond.

As she bundled back up to return to the joyous cold, she caught a murmur of what sounded like a voice. She lifted the hat from her ears and moved a little closer to the door. The sound was distant but carried the distinctive rhythm of speech. When it stopped, there was another similarly cadenced reply, perhaps with a jovial bounce.

Curious about who was speaking, Abby slipped out the door with appropriate Redmond caution. As she slowly guided the door closed, night flashed to day. The sudden brightness startled her, and the door slipped from her grasp. As it connected with the frame, there was a crash like thunder. It took Abby a moment to realize the crash was related to the flash, not the door. It was like lightning and thunder at a distance.

The voices returned. She froze. This time she could understand them.

"Did your Wiccan grandmother teach you that one?" The voice was jovially mocking.

"If you have better, gutter slinger, toss away." The response had far less joviality, along with an air of pretentiousness.

"In fact we do! Sickle!" Seemed like the first voice was calling an ally.

Curiosity bubbled up in Abby. The words Wiccan and slinger tickled her mind with thoughts of magic. Real magic. And it sounded like it was going on nearby. This wasn't some trid snow—this was going to be the real thing. Right in front of her. The bubbles of curiosity inside her began to burst into excitement.

Despite the danger of discovery, she crept to the edge of the building to get a look. Peeking a single eye around the corner, she gazed upon the scene before her in awe.

The sloped central fairway of the park was an open expanse of unmolested white. Small groups gathered at the high and low ends of the slope.

Wiz-gangs!

At the high end, Abby could see a half-dozen figures unified by the shades of red they all wore on their gutter-chic garb. She watched as one figure rose into the air, a swirl of snow spinning beneath his feet. His red was a jacket the shade of fresh blood with an uncountable number of zippers. Abby thought of it as infinite pockets for his wizardly materials, a flaw in her views based on too many *Dawn of Atlantis* references by her little brother. Hovering several meters in the air, the man—obviously Sickle—began waving his arms in a swirling circular pattern. Wispy white clouds of smoke formed around his waving hands that coalesced into white orbs as Sickle shifted his swirling hand motion above his head.

In a flurry of motion, Sickle shot his hands forward. The orbs sailed in a high arc across the open space between the rival wiz-gangers.

Abby's gaze followed the orbs. She didn't even notice that she had shifted further past the corner, her whole head potentially exposed to their view. The orbs sailed high toward the collection of gangers with accents of blue and silver on their Trés Chic clothing, the starkest contrast between the gangs.

As the orbs fell, a blonde woman in a sky-blue pantsuit cried out, "Aster, I've got this!" She swung both arms in wide arcs, then held them over her head. The orbs impacted an invisible shield, flattening into white lumps.

Abby laughed to herself at the sight of magic being used to have a snowball fight.

The gang in red laughed raucously at the panicked protective shield defending against the arcane practical joke. "Hey Aster, you're lucky she protected you from all those snowballs! Wouldn't want a a little snow messing up your fancy suits!" the leader called out over the distance.

Abby glanced back and forth between the groups, waiting to see what came next. The laughs on the red side dwindled, while the frustration and anger grew among the azure-clad gangers.

A mild squabble cascaded through the ranks of the blue gang. Abby heard one yell, "Nobody treats the Washington Wizards like some common street gang!" So she knew the identity of one of the gangs. Abby knew a lot of Redmond's gangs—it was part of surviving in the city—but the Ancients was the only wizzer gang she knew, and they weren't really a wizzer gang. They were a go-gang with a lot of magic. Wizzer gangs just weren't common, and they definitely weren't big. She counted a total of fourteen people out in the park, and that was probably the entirety of both gangs.

The rumblings among the Wizards grew steadily worse, fed by the laughter of the other gang that grew as their rivals

failed to respond to their last spell. Abby was still rapt. She had heard tales of wizard's duels but never seen anything of the sort. She'd never even seen real magic until now. She waited with bated breath for the next spell.

Abby's attention was on the wrong gang when it started. She was watching the red gang laugh and commiserate when from the corner of her eye she saw a flash of white. Snow swirled where the Wizards once stood, but they abruptly were gone.

She heard the red gang yell, "Arcanists, prepare to play!" The laughter stopped immediately as the gang took up a defensive posture.

Abby's eyes darted back and forth between the swirling snow and vigilant Arcanists, two of whom rose up into the air, lifted by unseen forces.

When the action came, it was fast and violent. Arcs of neon-purple lightning shot down from above the snowswirl, their unnatural color contrasting sharply against the snow-white scene.

The fire followed quickly. Not the orange, red, and yellow of natural fire, this flame shot out and exploded in hues of green and blue. It flowed through the air and across the ground like burning water.

The attacks hit sparking shields erected by the Arcanists through rapid, flicking hand gestures. The colors flowed into and off the shields, not touching the gang of motley mages.

Abby watched the arcane fireworks with childlike excitement. Her eyes darted everywhere, taking in everything, including seeing what the Arcanists missed.

A figure in a black suit accented with top hat and cane appeared in the air above and behind the cluster of red-clad gangers. None of them noticed him, as they were too focused on their efforts to repel the onslaught from the front. He spread his hands wide to the sides and then clapped them together. The force of the spell blasted into the Arcanists on the ground. All four tumbled forward. Their defenses broken, the raining lightning and fire found targets. Flames exploded on the ground and sent the tumbling gangers flying through the air. Arcs of lightning connected, stiffening flying figures as voltage tensed muscles. Their landings were hard, awkward, and painful-looking.

One of the hovering Arcanists, a woman with a short-cropped mop of bright-red hair, was quick to react. She spun, arms flaring wide. The move sent a wave of energy, made visible by its effect on the falling snow, through the air. The wall of force smacked hard into her hovering foe. The blow sent him sailing towards Abby, top hat and cane left behind to tumble to the ground. She lost sight of him as he passed over the building she was crouched behind. She looked up and caught sight of his continued flight after she heard him hit hard on the roof above. He moved on, skipping over the hedge wall and into the hedge maze adjoining the pathways of the park.

Abby's attention was now split in three. She wondered what had become of the sailing, suit-clad spellcaster but couldn't bring herself to follow him while the action on the fairway continued. The Arcanists had recovered from the sneak attack, returning the attack with a ferocity fueled by anger and rage. The anger in their faces would have been visible at any distance. Their first massive assault of mana forced the Wizards to drop their invisibility in order to better protect themselves. Every spell thrown by the Arcanists was tinged in fiery red light. The air around all of them filled with a faint red haze that flared bright when struck by enemy spells. Arcane energy dissipated into the light, doing little to harm the intended targets. On the other side, the Washington Wizards were panicking. Their plan had failed to break the rival gang and instead had fueled them to strike with abandon. Purple lightning and blue and green fire were traded for shimmering white armor, electric purple shields, and massive yellow walls of crackling energy.

The perfect smooth field of snow was quickly turned to a pockmarked mess of green patches at the center of snowy craters. Abby was surprised by the lack of scorching from the fire, not sure if it was because of the cold or some aspect of real magic as opposed to what she saw on the trid. From her distant vantage, Abby began to spot a real color gaining small footholds on the white scene.

Red.

Droplets of warm blood dripped from noses as casters pushed themselves past their limits.

The scene before her was exciting, like an action trid in real life, but the hedge maze kept calling to her. The ganger that had been cast off the field had not returned. She had expected him to fly back onto the field of battle, healed of his injuries, but nothing emerged.

Abby crept away from the edge of the bathroom building and back onto the park path. The sound of the raging battle became muffled and distant. She hadn't even realized just how loud it had become while watching the scene unfold. But now that it was behind her and her senses were focused on finding the missing mage rather than catching every detail of the arcane duel, the cracking lightning and booming fireballs were a nuisance—and a rather loud one at that.

With her ears unable to catch even the slightest hint of her cast-off quarry, Abby relied on her eyes. The snow was still falling gently but had picked up in volume over the past handful of minutes, muffling sights and sounds. She wasn't certain how far the ganger had been flung, but she knew he had to be within the square spiral, a section of hedges off the main path that had only one entrance and a path that turned in on itself at every corner. It eventually led to a small central court with several benches where people could sit before returning the same way they came. As Abby stepped off the main path, she noticed that no one else had traversed the snow within the square, in or out. It didn't mean much, since all these mages seemed to be able to fly, but it was a detail her mundane brain picked up.

Walking the path, she quickly noticed signs of the ganger's passage. Dots of red signaled his injury before she saw him. Ridges in the snow had formed from the force of the wind generated as he passed over the hedges. Snow was cleared and shaken loose from the first hedges he clipped. Broken branches and more displaced snow showed where he hit and broke through a single circuit before she found his wracked and twisted form draped over a bench in the central square.

Abby stopped at the archway signifying the end of the spiraling path. From there she could see his body, long and lanky, sprawling from the bench he had crawled to. Blood pooled on the bench, melting the snow away in a river of red warmth, crystals of icy blood lining the banks where the escaping life finally succumbed to icy death.

Despite the freezing blood, the unnatural angle at which his left knee bent, the jagged tears ruining the fine lines of his suit, and the growing layer of snow covering his splayed form, Abby could tell he was alive. His chest heaved slightly, and small huffs of cloudy breath puffed into the air. It looked to be a struggle for each one, but he still drew breath.

Abby dared a step forward. She half-expected an illusion to drop as she passed the threshold and reveal the healed and healthy ganger-mage waiting for her arrival as if this had all been a trap for her, but her step brought nothing but the further realization that the man before her was just that. A mortal man. Death was not held at bay by simple possession of the Talent.

Another step, and she was close enough to see the man was not really much more than a boy. He may have had a year or two at most on her sixteen. He was no wizened wizard; he was a mystic mageboy.

His head shifted slightly, eyes meeting Abby's through the heavy falling snow, one bloodied and swollen but still open and gazing at what must seem the apparition of death in a diner uniform. He looked as if gathering every milligram of strength he had as he stretched an arm toward her. She cringed inside, unsure what power he was about to unleash as he died.

But nothing came. Instead the arm fell, the eyes opened wider as they pled for help, and Abby stepped closer. Fear cast aside, she saw the powerful wizard who had so recently been hovering in the air and hurling lightning and balls of force as nothing more than the teenage boy whose sense of invincibility had been shattered.

Abby took the hand that lay outstretched, lifted it from the marble seat where it lay, and cupped it between her own. She felt fingers weakly clench before falling slack.

She sat for several more minutes watching the lights flash in the sky from the direction of the fairway, holding the hand of the dying—or already dead—ganger the entire time. She didn't know if he lived, but she didn't know what she could do besides offer the scant comfort of her presence.

The frequency of flashes decreased, and Abby felt it was time to go, thinking it best to not rely on the sentimentality of gangers for her health and well-being. She gently laid the hand back to the bench, placed two fingers to her lips and then his forehead, and slipped back out into the maze of hedges.

Not sure of the route the gangs would take, Abby returned the way she came. She tried to retrace her steps only to find her stride was longer than normal, pulling her away from the park. She had seen beauty and she had seen terror. And as was often the case in the Barrens, they had arrived in the same package.

SEEING THE INVISIBLE WORLD

UNIFIED MAGICAL THEORY: A MUNDANE VIEW

What is UMT? That's a great question and of utmost importance when considering whether or not you may be witnessing arcane talents in use. Let's start with the basics.

UMT was first proposed in the 2030s by Dr. Ava Nickson, Th.D. Originally met with nearly universal opposition, it took almost three decades and a presentation on a different continent to finally be accepted. Once it was accepted, it began leading an entire generation of Talented individuals into following its formulaic patterns and style. Dr. Nickson isn't even the one who ended up with the bulk of the credit, though. That distinct honor went to two universities—one in Prague, the other in Boston (may it rest in peace). In Prague, the University of Prague, working with the University of Erfurt, brought the principles to Europe. The Arcane Research and Thaumaturgical Division of MIT&T in conjunction with (read that as "funded by") Mitsuhama Computer Technologies brought it to North America. Their work created an alignment of magical theories and belief systems that bridged traditions and reshaped the very nature of the magic in the Sixth World.

No matter whether your fundamental magical beliefs were hermetic, shamanic, Aztec, Egyptian, chaotic, or even just some tricks learned on the streets, magic changed. It took time. Those three decades I mentioned above passed, and in the mid-'50s through the early '60s, when the philosophies worked their way into the magical schools and the cultures of the world, UMT slipped into the minds and views of the everyday Joe. This changed the face of magic in the world—the views of mundanes made Unified Magical Theory work.

Unified Magical Theory is about belief. But not always the belief you think.

POSTED BY: GLITCH

All magic in the Sixth World is not the same. Shaped by the will of its wielders and the forces of the manasphere, the same arcane cantrip can look very different when slung by a chaos mage as opposed to spells cast by one who believes in magic as a psionic gift. The scientists try to place rules and formulae on every spell like chemical equations for mana, but that is not how everyone understands mana. The shaman believes, with every ounce of their being, that their power is a gift from their totem. They earn the power—they do not control it and wield it at will, they wield it because their mentor wills it, and their mentor favors them. This belief shapes their power. The same belief that will strip them of a gift that no hermetic ever fears losing as long as they have their wits. These differences mean that the same spell cast by two different spellslingers, the same spirit called up by two different summoners, or the same alchemical creation developed by different enchanters can have the same effects and abilities while having absolutely zero similarities in appearance.

So how do we know when something is magic, or what kind of magic something is, without the ability to see the forces behind it? The truth is, we can't. It's a cold, hard truth for the mundane that you will never know with one hundred percent certainty what mojo is being slung at you. That's not to say you can't come up with a damned good idea of what's going on, and that's what this little JackPoint piece is going to be about. I've taken a couple of different angles with this and built up a thorough—though far from comprehensive—view of magic these days, focusing on the UMT methods that most standard wageslaves learn, but calling on those with a wider viewpoint for some real street-slinger styles. Because in the shadows, most of the magic that's learned is figured out, not taught in a college class.

THE MAGIC OF MUNDANES

Welcome to the Mundane Corner! This forum is specifically intended for individuals born without the Talent to talk about their experiences with magic in the real world. This is a place to talk about the magic you've seen, whether spell, spirit, or flaming spin kick out on the streets—or even at home. Remember this is all about metahumans, so keep the dragon sightings and paracritter encounters to the forums where they belong. Try to keep your specific posts within the headers where they belong to keep this all nice and organized. Standard Matrix etiquette rules apply; keep it civil. You never know when the guy you've decided to flame happens to have a hacker pal (or be one themselves) who will work to make your life miserable.

SIBLING MAGIC

ARJUANGUIT241, TENOCHTITLAN

They say magic is in the genes, but my twin brother—yes, we're identical—is an adept, and I'm not. It's not fair. He has to suffer from all the phobes, mana clingers, and scam artists out there. Bet you weren't expecting that, were you? Being an adept was great for him, and I was jealous for all of about two years. They were rough. He was popular, and I was his weirdo twin who didn't get any powers. There were even rumors that he had extra magic that he'd stolen from me in the womb. It was stupid. But then, the shine wore off and people started to get jealous of him, sometimes violently. He got into fistfights almost every day, and while he won most of them, it wasn't without getting hurt. He transferred out of our high school during his sophomore year. I made it to junior year, but we didn't go to the same place. He went to a special corporate school for adepts, sponsored by Aztechnology. I had to transfer to a new public school when our parents moved us closer to his corporate campus. It didn't make it easier to see him. They rarely let the students leave, and after a while his loyalties were much more with corp and country than family and friends.

In the end, it was a mixed bag. He barely survived being a teenage adept, and now he works for a megacorp doing ghost only knows what, ghost only knows where, to ghost only knows who.

DOWN4MOJO2, SEATTLE

My cousin lived with us from the age of four, when both his parents died in a "car accident" that I later learned was a shadowrun gone bad. He was the trid-trope son of runners, born with magic. He had it young, too. My parents didn't realize, but I knew. He could float things around and light small fires. Even had "imaginary" friends that I later figured out weren't imaginary.

His magic was pretty wild when he was young. He stared intently, wiggled his fingers, even muttered rubbish when he was casting.

Until he saw a documentary on the Hermetic Order of the Auric Aurora. He became obsessed, and that obsession focused him. His belief in magic went from wild and free with rubbish incantations to specific and focused with a right and a wrong way to do things. He learned certain hand shapes and motions to focus certain forms of energy and spent hours each day learning Latin so he could read old texts on magic.

By the age of thirteen, he had serious skills, and he found himself sought after by several corporations. The problem was, they wanted to know his lineage. My parents only knew some basics about my aunt and uncle, but it was enough to lead them to the dossier the megacorp had on these former runners.

Mom was a Dog shaman, with the full-on belief that her power was given by Dog and her loyalty to her totem was the only way to keep her gifts.

Dad was a devout Roman Catholic. He learned his magic as prayers to God and considered spirits the embodiment of the forces of good and evil.

Neither of them was anything like their son. The mana didn't care about their genes, just their belief.

My cousin belted out Latin phrases and chants, posed his hands in a series of strict patterns, and slung mojo that could melt steel.

CANUSLINGIT4ME, INDIANAPOLIS

My mom's got the Gift. She runs a small magic shop in Indianapolis. I've watched her do some enchanting and helped prep a few poultices when I was a kid. I remember watching in amazement as she pulled together swirling threads of smoky energy that came from nowhere, bound them together around the objects she had prepared, and then seemed to push them inward and trap them inside.

I've never seen her sling a single spell. All of her magic goes into things. Things I could manage to use even though I don't have a whit of magical Talent.

I've met a lot of her friends, too, people who come into the shop and buy things from her or sell her materials for her work. I've seen them cast in the store, and I've gotten pretty good at spotting the "rifts," as I call them. That spot where the mana changes places and goes from surrounding us as an unseen force on another plane to manifesting as some form of spell in our physical world. Most of the mages that come in use a basic set of rules for casting set forth by the various magic colleges using hermetic traditions as their foundation, but I've seen screamers, shamans, psions, voodoo priests, religious types of all sorts. Magic has a million mysteries.

WIRESOVERWIZ4LIFE, DETROIT

I hate being mundane. I'm the only child of six who doesn't have any magical abilities. My oldest brother is an adept. He got a job with Lone Star before he even left high school. He got the nickname Thunder growing up because every one of his abilities comes with a crack like thunder when he uses it.

My other brother, still older, got the mixed thing. A mystic adept, as he tells it. He's got some

abilities similar to our eldest brother, though without the sound effects, and he can do stuff like turn invisible and shoot lightning. I'm sure he knows other tricks, but all he talks about is how secretive he has to be about his talents because of the society he joined. Sounds like a fraggin' cult to me.

I have twin older sisters whose claim to fame is splitting their magic between them in the womb. Or so they say. One can cast spells, the other summon spirits, but neither can do both. They used to play that the abilities passed back and forth between them, but switching places to fool people all the time got old. Well, that and one of them decided to actually sleep with the other's boyfriend to sell the switch. That was a fun Christmas.

My last sister is the family's pride and joy, a full mage. She can do it all. Well, she doesn't have any adept powers, but she has plenty of spells and friends that help her mimic most of them, and she's got a great trick that pretty much shuts both of my brothers off. I like that one. She got a full ride through Ares and now works somewhere in their upper ranks. She was actually the nicest to me growing up. When we'd play, she'd give me little boosts here and there to make me more like my siblings. My parents always got excited when she did that, thinking I was Awakening. Then they'd yell at her for wasting her talents on me.

Oh yeah, my parents are both mundane, too, but it made them feel like they were better than a lot of other people because they had magically talented children. Then they had me, and I burst their special bubble.

My chrome does me just fine now.

CATHATER4REAL, BONE CITY

My sister is a shaman. Everything she does is reflective of her totem—I think that's what she calls it. When she does any kind of magic, even the most minor tricks, her appearance shifts in some aspect. The smallest change is usually her eyes. She follows Cat (she told me it's capitalized if I ever talk about it), and her eyes turn catlike (or Catlike?), with narrow vertical pupils, with the slightest magical effort. When she really tries hard—man, it's crazy! She was showing off to her friends once, and I happened to be around when she used magic to make her beat-up junker look all yerzed out. Her eyes went into slits, but then this illusion(?) popped up all around her head and body that totally made her look like she had a cat head and a tail. She called it a shamanic mask and

said that only shamans who were truly devoted to their totems got them, and only when they really channeled their energy.

It's strange. Even when she casts spells and summons things, she makes purring and meowing noises. Sometimes it makes me really happy that I'm not magical. Until she does things that I don't have a hope in the world of ever managing. Then I hate her.

FEARTHEUNSEEN, BUTTE

The only thing my brother can do is view the astral plane, but it's still so cool to think about. He's tried to explain what it looks like, but I just didn't understand. Then he introduced me to a friend of his who knows a spell to make the astral visible, like creating a window where mundane folks like me can look into the astral plane. I was jealous of my brother until then. When the guy cast the

spell and I saw all the dark spots and veins running through people, I was appalled. I could see spirits all around. They were everywhere. I don't think I could live knowing how much activity is going on around me, unseen by me—or if I could see it, knowing how much is going on that I can see. It's scary either way, but at least now I can pretend it isn't going on.

NOSPELLSHERE, RALEIGH

My dad is a conjurer and has, for years, been trying to teach me how to conjure spirits, even though I was tested and don't have a lick of magical talent in my body. He's convinced anyone can do it, like magic in the dark ages and throughout history was just people who had enough will and the right formulas to make it happen. I keep trying, not because I think it will work, but because, first off, it lets me connect with my dad, but also because watching him do it is so interesting. He uses a lot of stuff to make his magic work. Incense, candles, powders, chalks, feathers, sound machines, instruments, and the occasional pile of dirt. He chants when he's summoning and when he talks to the spirits, it's always in Latin because that's the language the spirits he calls understand.

LOSTCHILD708, PALOS HILLS

Sorry, this might get long. I've seen a lot of magic. My parents are both instructors at ArcanArts. Yeah, I know it's a magic tutor corp scam and tons of parents send their mundos in, but a lot of actually talented kids have come through. My parents screen them all early on, and they tailor the program to each kid, trying to find the certain focus, activity, or style that's most likely to help ignite the spark. Man, I sound like the ads, but it was true with my parents, they cared a lot more about that place than they ever cared about me. Sorry, sob story done. The Magic. Top five most interesting.

Billy Rhodes loved sports. He dreamed of being an adept. It was the only thing he wanted to be. He didn't care about spells or spirits, he wanted to run, hit, and jump, faster, harder, and farther than anyone else. His focus was so intense that he mistook his real gifts for the abilities of an adept early on. My parents knew better but in order to get him to practice and push himself they let him continue to think and perform his magic in ways that seemed adept-like, but were in truth, cast and sustained spells.

Billy did focusing mantras before running jumps, used the hisses and shouts of martial arts to focus, and did extensive stretching motions, all as a means to boost his natural talent in different fields, but none of it was permanently ingrained, as are the gifts of an adept. After each use he would feel the wear and tear of the exercises. The harder he performed, the more it hurt. It all made sense most of the time—work out hard, get sore—but even when he would perform singular acts to show off, he was getting tired. Drain, as my parents called it.

Now, when he does little things, things that stay within the realm of normal expectations for a human boy, his magic is barely noticeable. But, when he does stuff that no one should be able to do, like hurdle a two-meter fence or make a punching bag explode, that's when you can see the magic. The world around him almost seems to waver, like heat waves over a hot summer street, or his punches

actually create light when they hit. The best was a standing jump I saw him take where he left a trail, like a retro AR mouse cursor or an anime trid.

Next up, Emily Bhutan. She sent everyone running for the street on her first day when she lit a wall of papers on fire. Not by accident. She came in knowing she was gifted but hiding it from her parents. She wasn't the most pleasant little girl to look at, and a few of the older kids, who were still hoping for a magical miracle but filled with hate and anger for themselves for failing, made themselves feel better by picking on Emily. Bhutan is an easy name for even the dim to mock. She lashed out, her entire body wreathed in hazy white flames an instant before she cast gouts of orange fire at her tormentors. She hit the board behind them (I think intentionally), and the place cleared out fast. My parents let her come back, but she only lasted about two weeks before she got picked up by a mega. Once real Talent was discovered, it usually didn't hang out in ArcanArts for long.

Derrick Byrd didn't like me because I was the child of the teachers, and he somehow thought that meant I got special treatment. We've been over how they treated me, so we'll let that lie. Instead we'll focus on the purple-and-black energy that swirled around Derrick's fingers as he cast spells. Sometimes it was just wispy threads, barely noticeable; other times it was massive swirls that he seemed to shape before releasing them out into the world. The energy didn't usually travel far—most of the time it just dissipated into the ether once it left his reach, but it was always cool to watch, whether he liked me or not.

Ignatius Pasdenelli spent way too much time reading fantasy novels. He took all that belief in magic (with the help of my parents who thought it was a good focus) and formed his own style and method. He turned out to be one of those mystic adepts, as they call them in the texts. He used this inner-void mental-focus thing to "power" the abilities he channeled within, and then cast his spells like a blade-slinging wizard, complete with Elvish incantations (and I mean Tolkien Elvish, not Sperethiel). Power made his hair flare, his cloak billow, and his eyes occasionally glow when he cast. The power of the mind to create delusions and shape them into power with access to mana is a field I think I should study further, what with all my experiences in my younger days.

Scott Hyvinson couldn't cast, summon, or channel mana into himself worth a lick, but he was able to sit in class, shape modeling clay into little people, and infuse them with a little mana so they'd walk around and do funny things. He was an outcast when I was young—no one was huge into the enchanting concept yet because mass reagent manufacture hadn't become the lucrative business it is now. My parents pushed Scott to try to use the gift from a distance to animate the clay but it never took. He became disheartened, as did his parents, and Scott left ArcanArts. We kept in touch, and I've sat and watched him shape that same boring clay into flat discs that can heal cuts, rolled up balls that explode, and pieces of clay that he could hand to people to make them forget he was even around. Last time I talked to him, he was actually sculpting a replica of Michelangelo's David to see if he could animate it.

Meegan Foster had more invisible friends than any other kid that ever came to ArcanArts. They were only invisible to me, but you get the point. She summoned them by singing Gaelic folk tales that her grandmother, an exile from Tír na nÓg, taught her. It was beautiful to hear her sing. A little eerie—creepy if you were the only one around, and there was always a slight shrillness to it—but still, the girl had an amazing voice. The fact that it called beings to our plane is just another aspect of her musical talent.

This was all before UMT became all the rage. Now, the ArcanArts studios use tested, tried, and true UMT techniques to pump out more wagemages each week than they used to manage in a month.

SHADOWRUNNER ENCOUNTERS

HOTSOUTHERNNIGHT, ATLANTA

I was sitting in a café across the street from the Ares offices in Atlanta when all hell came flying out the front door. I saw this massive troll carrying something that looked like one of those DocWagon stabilization units. He had it up on one shoulder while he hoisted a massive gun in his other hand. Anyway, that's not the magic. Not exactly. I know trolls are strong, but those units are supposed to weigh a metric fragton, literally. Three more armored-up runner types came out close behind, but they weren't the magic, either.

The mage was actually the guy sitting next to me, sweating bullets. I thought at first that it was because of the heat, but the real reason was that he was sustaining some serious mojo. The troll ran full tilt toward a roach coach—one of those food

trucks—at the curb when the thing shimmered and shifted into a straight-up trid-real, black runner van, complete with a mini gun that opened up on the front of the HQ. The mage stood up and started walking toward the drama, unlike everyone else who was ducking for cover, standing around like a dunce (me), or running like hell. He did this little flick of his wrist and the air around him shook (that's the best way to describe it) and then coalesced into a field of blue lightning. By day the field was visible, though barely in open sun, but by night it would have been quite the spectacle. The troll made the van, dropped the giant pod inside, and then started taking chunks out of the side of the building with the cannon he carried.

The mage yelled something, and the troll switched up his grip to two hands as I watched a white streak of arcane energy slide off him and snap back to the mage. The troll went from gargantuan to simply massive in an instant. The mage jumped in the back of the van, and the shimmering blue field dropped off. I was totally focused on him as he drew his hands together in a little swirling motion in front of his face and then blew outward. I remembered seeing a wispy white cloud blow out from his hands before I blacked out.

When I woke, they were gone, Knight-Errant was questioning witnesses, Ares had a full AR screen up along with some of their own spellslingers recreating the façade, and everyone around was waking up from a serious sleep spell.

It was like a trid, but real.

PUGETOLDTIMER, SEATTLE

I worked at a sec company for almost twenty years, through plenty of magical discoveries, and I can count the number of times I encountered magic on one hand. It's memorable, but it doesn't happen every day.

Top moment:

I was working the dock gate for a private contract in Fort Lewis. A delivery van pulled up, and I stepped out to check credentials. Paperwork said the driver was human, average Joe type. As the window rolled down, I found myself staring at an ork, cyber-eyes gleaming, bulky body armor way out of standard for the delivery company, and no chance of talking his way past me.

Out leaned this slender elf woman from the back. She told me he was the new driver and there was no need to confirm it with anyone. Told me to just let us roll by.

I saw the world wobble around her, and I knew to the depths of my being she was lying, and letting them through was the wrong move, but I let him go right through because no matter what I thought, she was right.

Investigations go on afterwards and they told me it was some sort of spell. I certainly didn't *think* it was anything else but it *felt* totally natural to just believe her. It'd be scarier if it weren't so rare.

MILESABOVEYOU, DENVER

I'm not sure it was magic, but I'll describe what I saw as best I can, and you guys tell me.

I was inside the Rock Shop in Denver's UCAS sector. It was packed that night, and I was there trying to have a good time. DJ Carbon was spinning, drinks were flowing, and the dance floor was one massive grinding mass. It was a great spot to slide into the crowd, get a little grind on, and strike up an AR dialogue. The problem was, by the time I went to slide out into the crowd it was all sausage. The ladies were all clustered at the center around this elf who looked like something out of a bad Outlaw Murder Hobos trideo. He wasn't even grinding his gears. He had like a meter around him with nothing, and then a nice clear look at all the fine ladies dancing up a storm.

I was watching close at this point, but from a distance as I had no desire to push through the meat market, and every few moments I swore I saw a little thread of smoke zip from the dancing clown to a lady walking through the door. Every time it happened, the chick ditched her man, ground her way through the man mass, and joined the center cluster.

That's part one. Part two was happening at the back line of ladies. They had a crowd of guys sliding up for a groove and grind, but every time the guys slid up, they almost made contact and then slid off to move back into the crowd and start the cycle of pushing to the front again.

Guys around the rim were pissed, there was a bunch griping about the clown, but every one that hopped out on the dance floor just joined the crowd of crashing waves. It was fragging nuts.

Magic?

TOUGHTEXAN, DALLAS/FORT WORTH

The worst place to be when runners come rolling through the door is between them and their in-tended paydata. I was working as a receptionist at a corp office tower—I'll keep the details to myself—when this guy just walks right into the turnstiles like he's going to get right through. I look up and it's Mr. Collins, one of our junior executives, but he's dressed different than Mr. Collins usually does and Mr. Collins had already passed the security station an hour earlier to head up to his office. Normally I would have referred him to the security officers I work with, but they were off dealing with some unruly ork ganger who decided today was the day to make his way into corporate life.

It was all a setup.

The guy who came at me, who I'll call Faux Collins, just slides out of the turnstile and sidles up to the desk. The ork has everyone else in the room looking at the ruckus while this guy lines up on me and feeds me the lamest line about his gym bag getting left at home. I'm ready to hold him and just wait on the security guys when he smiles, cocks his head slightly to the side, and tells me it's a one-time thing and will never happen again. I let him through. I even do a quick check-out/check-in mock-up for him to make it all legit.

Mr. Collins was sitting in his office the entire time. Faux Collins was a runner with some subtle mojo that had me doing everything I was trained not to do and even helping cover the whole thing up. All while his pal, the ork, kept the attention of my co-workers.

When I think back, I can tell there was a little something off in his head cock and the smile, almost like it was more ritual than real. Needless to say Mr. Collins was extracted, and I ended up getting transferred over to manufacturing while my two pals from security got demoted to correctional services.

LAW ENFORCEMENT AND SECURITY

SEEINGISBELIEVING, ST. LOUIS

My sister got kidnapped when we were younger. My dad had serious clout with the corp, and they put a mage on the case. He was the first spellcaster I'd ever met; I was only twelve and a corp kid through and through. "Sheltered" was an understatement. Anyway, this mage showed up and trashed all the stereotypes I'd seen on the trid. No mystical jacket, no bones, no magical accoutrements at all. He wore a suit like the other detectives, had a perpetual cop grimace, and when it came time to sling mojo, he wasn't loud and big with all his motions and incantations.

He checked my sister's room and asked my parents a couple of questions, then went into her room again. He didn't like what he found because he came out and asked me what her favorite thing was. I told him, though it was way more personal than my parents would have known about. My room shared a wall, and I could always hear her. Still got scars to this day.

He went back in and had a bunch of her furniture taken out of the room. He had her bed moved to the center of the room and then set up candles and incense while marking her floor with powders and chalk. He didn't make a big ritual out of it. No chanting, no dim lights, no dancing, nothing but walking the room and doing things like he was setting the table for dinner or any other mundane task. When he was done he laid on the bed for about an hour.

Things were frantic afterward, because he'd found her while she was being subjected to a ritual of some kind that would have ended with her sacrifice. He issued directions while stumbling from exhaustion. I was panicked, but the adults took over. By the next morning her room was back to normal and she was sleeping off the traumatic event.

FORROSA, AMARILLO

I don't mess with the police. When they ask me to do something, I do it. Not because it's my civic duty, but because I know that if I don't, they have every right to stomp me until I follow their commands, or physically can't move. And sometimes they keep stomping you even then. The problem is, there are some people who don't change their ways, no matter how often you stomp them, or who are just too big to stomp. To gain obedience with these types, our local Lone Star precinct brings out Mikey. Mikey, a.k.a. Officer Abraham Michaels, isn't the most talented spellslinger around, but he knows a lot about spells that affect people's minds. Around the neighborhood they call him the "perp whisperer." Whenever there's a disturbance, Mikey comes along, has a conversation with the angry citizen in question, and off they go, quietly, with the authorities.

I can't see auras or any of that, but I see whatever mojo Mikey is using. Whenever he starts to talk,

I can see this wispy smoke seem to reach out and wrap around the head of the person he's talking to. Others can see it too, not just me, so it must be the spell. When he talks slow, the spell seems to slowly build up around the other person, but it can happen fast. I remember seeing Mikey arrive while Gil Two-Ravens was in the middle of hoisting an officer in the air by the neck. Mikey just yelled "Stop!", the wispy whiteness flashed out at Gil's head, and he just set the cop down. The cop yanked out his baton and pulled his arm back for a big swing, and Mikey did it again. Just yelled, and the white bolt hit the cop. The two were both standing there in front of each other for a few minutes while Mikey took a seat on a nearby park bench and dealt with the bloody nose he must have got from slinging so much mojo so fast.

LOSTINTHEMIX, SEATTLE

My sainthood ain't never getting granted. I spent four years doing time at the Kick—Killingsworth Corporate Incarceration Complex—up in Seattle. They don't use mages very often, too costly, but when they did it was a show and a half. Two biggest reasons they brought them in was to bring down another of their kind or to search entire cell blocks for weapons in massive sweeps.

The sweeps were pretty standard fare, timing-wise, and all the inmates knew to get the tools off the block ahead of time, but occasionally they'd catch a guppy who didn't know better or lacked friends. We'd all go into lockdown, and the guards would bring in the black coat. They all wore long black coats and all black clothes. Maybe to look intimidating, maybe to stick out in a riot, I dunno, but the black coat would take a spot near the center of the block and start chanting. Never loud enough to understand, more of a mutter. He'd get into a rhythm and then the "smoke" formed, white tendrils that whipped out across the whole block. It slipped through every cell and all the inmates. I always felt a chill, but some guys said they felt nothing. A lot of them slept through it.

Just so you know, there are criminals who either: A) actually have magic and manage to hide it; or B) Awaken in the joint. It's a high-stress environment, and a lot of guys there that are really just kids. Once the black coats find them, though, they take them off the block. I've never seen one come back. Probably recruiting, since everyone thinks they're so valuable, but I'm sure a few get the brain scrambler or "nuyen solution."

TRID AND STAGE

MAGEMUSE9000, ATLANTA

I went to see *Elfstrike* in Atlanta and they use a lot of spellcasting in their shows. The casting itself is often as much a part of the show as the actual effect—probably more. All of them use Sperethiel, but the actual chants aren't some ancient code or text. Most of it is just their lyrics.

"I'll bring the winds of fate to bear" creates a swirling tornado effect on stage. The words are the focus, but the flapping of Gallowglee's black mane occurs before the wind ever picks up.

"'Til sight is no more mine to bear the burden of your stare" strikes fans blind across a swath of the audience. Those affected, and everyone else, see a flash of white light from Arinscar. The blinded are blind; the rest recover from the glare quickly. It's all part of the show.

WESTCOASTWILLS, HOLLYWOOD

The set crew for *The Scrolls of Elfwind* get to see real magic all the time. The show uses real mages for the effects instead of CGI or pyrotechnics. They get slammed for their lack of realism a lot, but that's the problem with real magic—it's not the same as the stuff they show on the trid in every other show. I loved me some Sukie Redflower when I was ten. The show made magic seem awesome. It was obvious when they wanted flash, but she could hide even the most powerful of castings.

On *Scrolls*, every spell can be seen being cast. It's true to life. Spells are pulling power to our plane from another, and when it comes through it leaks a little—or a lot.

CORPORATE USAGE

JANE DOE, PYRAMID ARCANE SUPPLIES

I love reading all these exciting magic posts, but that's not life inside the corps. I've seen real magic, lots of it, but it's not exactly flashy. Most of the corp mages I know do boring stuff, like audits and inventories. They summon spirits for the company to use on security. They work basic security gigs running weapon checks over swaths of guests visiting the arcology. Now, I hear everyone talking about how rare the Talent is and how

these people are worth more because they're rare, but they're not once you're in a megacorporation. We gather them up and concentrate them in our population. Sure, maybe well under one percent of the world's population are born with some kind of magical potential, but once you focus inside the corps, where they identify and exploit every possible arcane resource that pops up its head, that number goes up. The megacorps have more Talent than the rest of the world, and they use it all.

Don't believe me? Here are a few examples I've run across in my boring everyday corp life.

I've seen an executive pop into the bathroom for a little social boost from their staff mage. A few waves of the hands and flashes of light later, and the exec's teeth are gleaming, his hair is perfect, and suddenly there's just something about him that makes you want to like the guy. Even if most of the time you think he's a complete fragbag.

I know that the warehousing department puts in special requests around inventory time to get a few specially trained mages down into the warehouse to help get through the counts fast. The mages block off sections that must pertain to the limit of their ability and then sit at the center. They mumble a few words, lift up their datapad or log in their trodes and begin magically counting everything around them. The ones I've seen create a sort of haze in the air around the objects to be counted as the spell progresses. Larger areas, or more dense counts, usually push the haze all the way to the point of fog. I have to say it isn't always about saving time. The worst is when they do this not to count the items in the first place but to audit the counts performed by the mundane employees.

I know an executive who has a personal mage. He gets a little reflex boost in the locker room before he goes out to compete against his fellow executives. They use the locker room because the casting process looks like a white fire cascading over his body that gets drawn inside or seeps into his skin. It would be really obvious to do it midgame, so the mage has to sustain it the whole time.

Then there's the obvious healing spells. I've seen those all over the place. Everything from closing a cut with a little glow, to repairing a broken bone or large injury in a blinding flash. Similar, but different, are the executives who use the corp's mages to detox them after a hard night of drinking and partying. Depending on just how much fun the exec had the night before, the process can look like everything from cold-weather steam breath to their whole body smoking and steaming.

I've seen the scary parts, too, like the corporate lie detectors. The mages who sit in the room behind you while someone from personnel asks you questions. You don't know how they are communicating with the questioners, but you can feel and see the line of energy that is wreathing your head and sliding through your brain with every question, scanning for any hint of falsity.

My division has a high-security wing that is staffed solely by spirits. The corp mages summon them and set them to work on whatever assignments we have. It's strange, but it means theft is unheard of, the turnover rate doesn't matter, and none of them are a concern for security breaches, because when they're done they just get released back to their regular home metaplane.

We get a lot of security scans, too. Mages come along, most of them chant some form of incantation, and then splash us with white light. I've been told it's a security scan for weapons, dangerous chemicals, or explosives on our person, but as I've never tried to bring any of those three into a meeting where they are using these guys to scan, it could all just be one giant show.

I see magic often enough to know when it's being cast. Most of the mages have similar incantations, as do the shamans, and many of the shamans get what they call a "shamanic mask," which is basically an illusory image that resembles their totem, appearing over their head when they cast.

I've never seen a completely invisible spell. I know a few mages who do everything without the pomp and circumstance of hand-waving and incantations, but then they get lights, sounds, smells, and other visual effects. Hide-able, yes, but still detectable.

- It's things like this that make working against megacorps fraggin' scary. I've never even thought about the math, but she's probably right. They cultivate arcane talent, and with that concentration they definitely boost the risk.
- Mika

- I've seen enough extractions of magical assets to know that corps target one another's mages. "Geek the mage" is often replaced with "sleep the mage," and runner teams have been known to gather opposing mana-wielders in order to sell them off to the highest bidder.
- Thorn

THE MAGIC SHOW

- Time to talk about spotting mojo when you aren't a slinger yourself. I pulled the starter over from a MagickNet blogger who seems to have a clue, but my expectation is for our Awakened members to pop in with their views and opinions.
- Glitch

- The blogger should have a clue. He's a veteran face that runs the East Coast shadows under the name C.J. He's well-known for working with low-magic teams against high-magic targets.
- Icarus

I hate to say it, omae, but no matter how many times you wish upon a star, order that at-home gene therapy program, or visit the local alchera, you aren't going to be slinging spells, summoning spirits, or running on walls in this lifetime. If you don't have the Talent, you don't have the Talent. But that doesn't mean you need to fear the Talent. What you need to do is understand it, learning how to identify its use and counter it with mundane means.

Today we're going to focus on identifying it. First off, it's not always like the trids. But it can be. Magic is shaped by the will of its wielder, not by some mysterious series of arcane rules. There are a few general principles we'll need to cover, but let me repeat that crucial point: Magic is shaped by the man, not the mana.

Principle #1: The shifting of mana from the astral to the physical plane is always detectable. It's energy, and while you may lack the precise mental software to see this particular kind of energy, you can use the subtle or not-so-subtle shifts it creates on our plane to spot it. I equate this to the "seeing" of black holes. Even if you can't see it because light doesn't escape, you see the effects it has on the space around it.

- True, but avoidable, and in the heat of battle, who can tell the difference between cordite smoke and the haze created by a spell being cast?
- Haze

- Hey, the point here is to help, not nitpick, bitch, or boast. Get helpful.
- Bull

Mana is greatly affected by the efforts of the caster and their mindset, but no one has yet mastered the mindset of the perfect manashift. Even when channeling small quantities, it's still like opening a floodgate to fill a few cubic centimeters of a test tube. You'll fill it, but spillage will result. That spillage is the physical manifestation of the casting, not the spell, that's the fireball, bent light, sticky hands, etc. We're talking solely about opening the door to give you something to shape.

- ⊙ That's well put. It also explains why often the little sideshows that pop up from our casting don't care about our mental paradigm. It's mana spilling over that shapes itself by its own rules, not necessarily our world views.
- ⊙ Arete

Principle #2: The more mana that's shifted, the greater effect it has on the physical plane at the time of casting. Using our floodgate analogy, the more you pull through fast, the wider you need to open the gates to fill it at a fast rate. That means you get a greater volume of spillage.

When someone tries to pull across enough mana to throw deadly lightning or fire, or weave a large enough illusion to cover a van, they need to draw a lot of mana, but they don't change the rate of the draw. The "adverse manifestation," a term coined by Dr. Andrew Bollman, Th.D., is directly proportional to mana quantity required to fuel the spell, mitigated by the aptitude of the caster. Those who have trained and understood the principles of manashift involved in powering spells are better able to control their draw.

- ⊙ This part is where the shamanic mask comes in as a merged belief of the caster and the general population as influenced by the media. Powerful shamans are expected to manifest this totemic overlay and thus, in many cases, the overflow of mana manifests in that form.
- ⊙ Lyran

Principle #3: The manifestation of mana in the form of spells, the abilities of adepts, the forms of spirits, or the appearance of alchemical preparations does not obey a single paradigm of sensory characteristics. No matter how much UMT anyone forces into the world, mana will always be free to take on other forms, because it is a substance shaped by belief and, in some fashion, imagination.

I offer you Arien Neal. Blind since birth, Arien has no concept of what fire or lightning look like, yet he has learned to cast spells that allow him to control these forces. Not blind to the astral, Arien was only able to study the shaping of the mana and not the actual physical appearance. When cast, Arien's fire and lightning spells are both black, because it is the only thing he knows. The black fire still burns and the black electricity still shorts things out. Others who have tried to mimic this effect, based on studying Arien's spellcasting, have had no luck recreating the effect. It's not totally unique; there are others who cast their fires in other shades, as well as their lightning, but his blindness makes his forms unique.

Sight is not the only sense. Scents related to some individuals' spells are different based on their own sculpting and belief. The same with sounds and even taste.

- ⊙ The taste part is especially key for enchanters. Creating potions intended to be ingested, it's good to have someone who believes that taste is important. Too often the belief is that potions are intended to taste unpleasant, so the spell creates an unpleasant taste.
- ⊙ Ethernaut

- ⊙ Smelling a spell being cast is a strange thought, but I know it can be done. The mana coming through takes on aspects from every sense, even smell, so it is quite possible to smell a spell. My sleep spell actually smells like chamomile tea. I never really noticed, but a chummer pointed it out on a job once; he and I notice it every time now.
- ⊙ Lyran

Principle #4: All magic does have a few immutable rules.

A. Line of sight: A spellcaster needs to be able to see the target of their spell. If they can see you, you can usually see them. I understand there are ways to avoid detection, but this piece is intended to inform, not quibble about the exceptions. I will mention, though, that magical wards can make seeing the target tougher, as with standard barriers such as walls. Natural earth is nearly impossible—entities in astral space can't even pass through it.

B. Concentration: To hold onto spells that are sustained, casters need to concentrate. Signs of intense concentration can be a clue to magical activity. Many spells don't have this issue, but almost all of the stealthy and mentally manipulative ones do.

C. Magic is physically taxing: Whether it's a tiny spell to move a box or a large one cast while riding in a crashing plane with a caged lion in an effort to stay invisible, spells have a cost to them. Signs of exhaustion are a key clue to look for when seeking the source of spellcraft.

🔹 Once the spell is cast and in place, detecting it is outside the capabilities of mundanes without manatech. There are a few small exceptions, and I guess this is the place to put those.

Extremely powerful spells draw a lot of mana across the threshold—enough so that they affect the physical plane just by their very existence. A chummer named Dozer wanted to show off and whipped up an invisibility spell that, as he put it, "channeled so much mana that even a dragon wouldn't see him." Don't worry, I already pointed out the whole dual-natured thing. The point was, he really did drag through some serious mana. The problem is the spell left a trail of warped space all around him as it bled mana from the astral. Sure, my eyes got fooled in terms of seeing him, but I hit him with random objects several times because I could hit the center of the wavy rift that had formed. There's a fine line in magic as to where you cast; often, if you use enough mana to fuel your spell, you start to overbleed mana from the astral.

🔹 Haze

🔹 That's the whole essay. Not terribly long, but with enough info to wet your lips and use as a general primer for this next open-air session. Awakened members, please help with constructive comments. Explain your magic, what casting or summoning looks like, or just give us some insight from a school of magic you know.

🔹 Glitch

🔹 Let me start out this little dog-and-pony show so that we of the rarefied nature and heightened talent can tell all the shlubs, mundos, and groggies just how to see real magic. Oh wait, how fraggin' stupid is that?! Hit the streets and figure it out. You get burned by someone throwing fire and you don't see a napalm tank, it's magic! Suddenly find yourself doing things you wouldn't normally do for a pudgy guy with a pendant fetish (and I don't mean the magical kind), it's magic! Seriously, I'll be elsewhere. This is a waste of all our time.

🔹 Five Card

🔹 Dissenting opinions are allowed. But as a point of education, JackPoint is still all about spreading info to others in the shadow community. Not everyone has this rare skill, so we help others understand them. Plus, the more people understand that magic is not what they see in the trids, the faster "Geek the mage!" becomes a piece of history and we stop culling an aspect of our metahumanity purely out of fear and jealousy.

🔹 Glitch

🔹 There are many reasons why I, and others like me, do not spend our time tempting fate with acts of exciting daredevilry. The gift of Seeing is one of the least common among all the Talented. The hard truth is that too many fear knowing. They fear seeing their final day and living in dread. I know my day. I have known the day of many of my fellows. I have changed both. That is magic.

Time is fluid. We see a path, not the path. We can redirect, but great wisdom is needed, for we know well that we could be the architects of our own divination.

How does it look? I sit, I meditate. Others have told me the world around me fills with a haze, but I do not see that. I see the next day, the next week, the next year, the next millennium. The power surrounding me warps the lodge where I work. It twists the items of my tradition and leaves behind reminders of my visions.

The few parlor tricks I can manage are taught through my tradition. The trappings of the shaman are mine, but not the shamans of the NAN. Runes, stones, and crystals that are focused with Gaelic chants pull power across the Veil.

How was that for cryptic to freak out the mundanes checking this out? We aren't all freaks. I really do use all those things, but don't think of it like I'm some old-world anachronism who can't live in the modern day. My commlink is top of the line, and I'm up on most of the latest innovations in magic. Especially in divination. Listen to the guy who wrote the above, and perhaps listen a little to Five Card. Learn from everything. Look for the magic, or the tech masquerading as magic.

🔹 Arete

🔹 Well, that was more dickish than usual, Arete. What gives?
🔹 Slamm-0!

🔹 In need of a little entertainment as I get older. Amusing myself is often my only course of action.
🔹 Arete

🔹 I learned much of what I know in a formal setting. But I learned far more on the streets. Magic is not static. The UMT is no different than my own learnings, and the appearance of magic isn't going to change by any great degree just because you learned it a different way. Honestly, the blogger's term manableed and the relationship between the power of one's channelings and the level of skill with which they perform their arcane acts are the best gauges for identifying magic in use.

Reckless or unskilled magicians (along with all other aspects of the Awakened) produce blatant phenomena when they channel mana. Yes, there may be a difference in the color of the lights or smoke, and one may flare flames while the other crackles with lightning, and a third becomes swirled in darkness, but fundamentally, they're the same.

Channel mana without control, and mana makes itself known regardless of your desires for stealth or subtlety.
- Axis Mundi

- Fire-Bringer provides my gift, and his essence infuses all of my powers. From the smallest trickle of mana to the purifying fires, everything brings over a little of Fire-Bringer's essence. A small aura of flame around my hands as I heal; the flash of fire around my head as I seek out enemies; the fire that cascades across the targets and then seeps into their bodies when I make them faster; all of my spells have an element of fire.

    I've been told by many others that this isn't necessary, that it's my beliefs that make it happen. My counter-argument is that it is also my beliefs that make the magic happen, so how could I have one without the other? I know others learn a way to practice magic that is ferreted from formulae and books, but my magic is granted to me by Fire-Bringer. The ire of Fire-Bringer means I lose my connection.

Others will argue that there is no external punishment; instead, I'm punishing and limiting myself when the connection is lost. Their beliefs are theirs, mine are mine, and the power of Fire-Bringer is hard to disbelieve when I call fire from the sky.

My power is pure and comes from a place on the metaplanes they do not touch with their formulae. The taint that their spells and spirits leave behind on our plane is evidence enough that their magic is a sad theft of the gifts provided by the entities we shamans call totems.
- Ecotope

- I love you Eco, but I'm not touching this with a ten-meter stick. Let's boil this down to a useful insight: If you see someone wreathed in flame, it might be magic.
- Slamm-0!

- The sad truth is that most magic, you will never see coming. My spells can be cast with a minimal of physical effort, and as long as I control the flow of the mana I am using and avoid letting it slip from my control, no one sees my spells. I use a mental script based on formulae from proprietary research from my days at MCT that I've expanded with my own research. I don't create a haze, smoke, fire, electrical energy, or any other blatant sign that something arcane is going on.

Neither does MCT, for that matter. Keep that in mind. They train their mages to avoid that. They teach that magic is simply a science to be understood and then manipulated with formulae by those who have access to its power.

My lesson here is that you simply need to accept magic as being there and part of what is going on in our world. You don't seek to understand how pulling the trigger makes the gun work—you just know that guns are bad news, and there's a good chance you may run into one someday. If you see someone who has a gun who isn't using it, or who is holding it in a way that makes it look like a decoration, you may have spotted the mage, or the decker, or the face. Or a street sammie who loves to quickdraw, so they don't keep the weapon in hand.

Believe in magic. That's my advice.

> Ethernaut

> Wires make most sammies as fast as the bullets flying at them. Teach them to spot the signs, and most mages won't get halfway through two finger-gestures and the slightest flicker of something before they put two in the chest and one in the head. When you work at bullet speeds, magic mutterings just don't keep pace.
> Jimmy No

> Ethernaut makes a good point. Some mages don't learn with flash, and they're good enough to keep the manableed to a minimum. Recognizing the style of dress or the outfitting for a mage can be just as good as identifying the magic itself.
> Mihoshi Oni

> Seeing magic with mundane eyes is simply a matter of opening yourself up to the details. Magic will always change the physical world with its presence. The chill in the air, the slight shimmer of heatwaves, a subtle scent of lavender, the tinkling of bells, a taste of copper. All have been physical effects of my casting.

Even the complex methods of magic that a certain painted elf taught me, which are designed to be harder to detect, still create secondary signs that can be sensed by mundanes. Mana has that effect on the physical plane. It wants to do more. It wants to change everything it touches.

When it comes to spotting magic, the secret is, sweat the small stuff.
> Frosty

> I'm a big fan of trying to get people to know not just when magic is being used on them, but also when magic is being used on someone else. There are plenty of signs I've seen (besides the really strange behaviors). This mostly pertains to spells that manipulate minds and emotions, because if the glowing forcefield around someone who's protected by an armor spell isn't enough to tell you there's magic on them, you have a deeper need for insight than I can currently fill.

One big tell I've come across are the signs of an internal debate being made external. You've got to be able to read body language for this, but an internal tension while doing things that really shouldn't cause such issues is a good clue that magic is involved. Sure, it could be from some other force getting someone to act against their will, but with magic the fight to regain control appears as jerky movements, sweating, shifting eyes, or stiff motions. It's only a few signs, but it can start clueing you in to trouble.

Another sign is the eyes. I mentioned the shifting eyes above when someone is fighting the arcana-induced impulses, but there are three other eye conditions that indicate magic in use: the glow, the haze, and the bleeding. The glow is a faint glow within the pupil of the eye or a radiance to the iris. The cause is similar to some of the earlier discussions on manableed. Here the power being used to muddle, control, or manipulate the mind comes through as a glow within the eyes. Extremely powerful spells can make the entire eyeball glow. The haze is a deadening of the eye, similar to the way people describe mages perceiving the astral plane. Their eyes just kind of gloss over and become glassy and empty. The bleeding sounds terrible, but the reality is less sinister—and easy to mistake for more natural events. The eyes become bloodshot (sometimes to the extreme, but that's rare) as with the glowing eyeballs. As a result of the individual trying to fight off the mental manipulations, they overstrain the blood vessels in their eyes, making them burst. There are plenty of other things in the world that cause bloodshot eyes, so don't presume everyone with bloodshot eyes is under the influence of magic, but use it as a stepping stone to look for other indicators in their behavior.
> Haze

> My tricks and trappings aren't like anyone else's on JP, so I'll give you the lowdown on more traditionally Eastern styles of magic and what it looks like. Thanks to years of pre-Awakening traditions and a culture that never truly stopped believing in the mystical, the Wujen tradition has quite a bit of flash and flare within our traditional practices.

The casting of spells, summoning of spirits, and enchanting of foci are accompanied by glowing eyes, electrical discharges, glowing patterns etched in the air, and auras of energy.

The physical trappings of Wujen talents are many. Traditional casting styles are taught to all Wujen that involve the use of focusing crystals and traditional fans. The use of specific body positioning and movements in order to gather and focus mana into the forms we know can be beautiful and deadly at the same time. Most of the forms are based off the movements of hand-to-hand combat, and the remainder come from traditional dances. A rare few are neither martial nor graceful, but rather they channel energies for powerful spells, spirits, and enchantments (though those who have witnessed such things are unlikely to recall what they saw, because most of the forms leave them without life or remaining wits). Along with movement, Wujen wrap themselves in the traditional trappings of their art and the culture it is built from.

The most common is the fan. Often enchanted as a focus for power, some are weapons or even complex multi-faceted foci merged in a single form. Traditional weapons come next, though rarely used in their intended form. Instead, they flash and flutter in a way that frequently draws attention from the power being drawn. Watch for the magic behind the flashy sword work. You could be prepping a parry when suddenly you're slammed by a bolt of lightning.

Basically, Wujen is just as flashy, sometimes even more so, than trid magic, but its flash gives it power.

- Jimmy No

- Loud, flashy, and full of howling and growling. At least that's what I like most people to believe. It's also what a lot of pups think is the way to go. Howl to Wolf for power, and that makes you a better shaman. I howl every once in a while—sometimes in pain, sometimes in pleasure, and sometimes to give myself a little more connection to Wolf—but I don't do it in the middle of a run. I'm old and wise, though. If you are looking for a young shaman, look for the animal behaviors. Wolf and Dog shamans often howl or growl, even as a social behavior. Followers of Cat can't sit still, constantly keeping their distance until suddenly they're on top of you.

Those are social behaviors, though. How do you spot their magic? It's ritualistic and often tied to some native or local tradition that they've taken as their own. It's also full of manableed, as everyone keeps calling it. They don't control the mana coming over, and the excess is shaped by their style into some physical manifestation. The howling you hear, sometimes it's not the shaman's voice, but rather the mana bleeding over.

The shamanic mask is the best example. Doesn't happen to all of us, but many take the visage of their totem as an honor. I am among those, but I know how to be subtle with it. But I know that even my techniques can be spotted by the careful.

No matter how much control we exert, magic is a living power. It wants to be revealed. Don't think too much on it. There are always signs. I can't see myself, but I've been told that even when I'm being subtle, my eyes flicker between colors, my aura appears for a moment, my voice ascends to vibrato, my fingernails turn black and claw-like, or my hair waves in the wind with no helping breeze. Little things that stick out, but aren't necessarily flashy or completely other-worldly.

Be on the lookout for the subtle.

- Lyran

- Magic is both within and beyond the senses of the untouched. It flows around them, and yet they are as much a part of the mana as any conjurer or adept. Linking the power between realms and shaping the flow may be beyond most, but feeling its touch is not.

We can see the magic by opening our mind to its presence. The subconscious will notice. Our minds will see the change. We are only blinded by our own sight. Open eyes with a closed mind will see little.

- Man-of-Many-Names

- There's easy stuff to tell for adepts, and also harder stuff. Since the mana is being focused inward, it's often tough to tell when the channeling occurs because it's infusing muscles or shifting bones around inside the body, hidden from view. The giveaway is usually when you see their actions and reactions are supermetahuman. The problem is many people don't understand what that means. Prior to the Awakening, the fastest and strongest humans could perform feats without magic that today even some trained adepts can't manage. Strongman Paul Anderson lifted almost three tons without the aid of magic. Usain Bolt could run almost forty-five kilometers per hour without magic. Can these feats be beaten now? Yes, but not easily.

To tell when magic's going into a physical feat, you have to see more than just the act. You have to really look at the individual. Paul Anderson and Usain Bolt are unique physical specimens, and though the media portrays almost all adepts with models and body builders, it's not what the majority of us look like. I'm lean and lithe, but I'm not ripped in the way Ursk Bane is in Hammer Fists. Keep an eye out for the average Joe doing above-average things.

I know Ma'Fan is going to want to talk too, so I'll leave the over-the-top and externally focused stuff for her to talk about.

- Mika

- As much as Mika likes the dig he thinks he just got, I was actually planning on talking about the ways to spot an adept through the term introduced earlier, manableed, because I wasn't sure he had a strong enough gift to ever experience it.

The two most common sources for the powers of an adept becoming apparent to the mundane are pushing too much mana and losing concentration, sometimes at the same moment. Though the energy is channeled inward, it still passes from astral to physical to adept. Some learn to gather it outside and move it in, while others keep the channeling internal. There is no right or wrong. The former is easier to detect as adepts use kata, hand sign, or scripts to shape the power before letting it cascade over or into their body. The same movements of body or mind can also be used by internalists without the external energy becoming visible.

The appearance of the adept's energy isn't standardized. Adepts have yet to get fully roped into the UMT mindset, but many adept schools and training facilities are creating a standard style that lacks individuality but increases the efficiency of learning. It is also creating a standard style for the identification of their powers. They teach the same katas and focusing movements, as well as the same meditations in order to enhance and develop new abilities.

The utilization of certain gifts among adepts can result in small flashes of energy as eruptions of light or sound. Returning a thrown object in a flash leaves a trail of images. The whip crack has been a staple of the killing hands power for almost a decade. Speed and power enhancements create energy flares that wreath the adept in energy, sometimes in the form of flames, lights, smoky energy, or trails.
* Ma'fan

* Oh, I forgot to mention something I know much more about than Mika: the benefits of connection to a totem. Cat smiles on everything I do. As with many others who gain guidance from an otherworldly power, it infuses and flavors my gifts—with a touch of feline charm, in my case. Wolf's adepts are beastly; Wise Warrior infuses discipline; Owl seeks wisdom and wise followers; Bear's people grow strong and powerful.

And the shamanic mask falls over its adept followers just as it does casters and summoners.
* Ma'fan

* Anybody hear from 'Hawk lately? I expected a post but haven't seen him log on in a bit. Anything?
* Bull

* Magic is not ours to hide. The loa want magic to be seen. Or they don't. It's not a choice I make, but I know my magic has flash and flare far more often than not. Even the weakest of efforts shows the presence and gifts of the loa. The most common is the smoke wreathing my hands and the scent of burning incense.

I know others of my tradition who gain the pallor of death or a ragged wildness to their hair. Some have smoking breath, eyes, or ears. The white eyes are also common, as well as pointy teeth. All of these are illusory but still obvious changes that can identify the use of magic.
* Ferris

* Everything I do is otherworldly! Every spell I cast comes with a whole lot of extra flash and flare. Smoke, light flashes, fire, shifting colors, arcs of electricity—and that's just how I light a cigarette. When I came into magic, it was the most wondrous thing in existence, and I built my spells, and style, around making it so flashy no one could possibly miss what was going on. Now, how long am I meant for the shadows? No clue. Maybe I'll get noticed and get my own trid, maybe I'll get noticed and be the next victim of the "geek the mage first" mentality, but for now, I got no choice but to work on the periphery and use every trick I've got. That means being flashy.
* Havoc

THE WILL OF THE MANASPHERE
POSTED BY: FROSTY

The discussions about spotting magic and all the talk of what it looks like for different folks made me think about how often those expectations are twisted or shifted—not by the beliefs of the user, but by the alterations to the mana field of the astral plane itself. What we commonly refer to as a background count does not just provide a challenge to utilizing magic under its influence but also shifts the appearance of magic within it. I pulled from my own experiences and the experiences of many of my contemporaries, as well as readings from older sources, to come up with some of the explanations and examples I present here.

We have spoken on how our magic works when it works under the control of our will, but let me review how it works when our will isn't nearly enough to control its shaping. Those times when mana simply wants to *be*, not to be controlled.

First, I'll point out that any changes to the local manasphere can change how mana works and the appearance it takes on. Whether these changes are an increase or decrease of the local mana pool, a change in the aspect of the local mana toward a specific flavor or style of magic, an area of disjointed astral/physical connection known as an alchera, the rippling changes of the mana storms, or even the variations injected into local magic through various spells or metamagical techniques, it will shift one or more elements of the efforts put forth by mana users when connecting to the power in a region of altered mana. These effects run the gamut of changes, and being ready for these shifts could save a runner's life. Being prepared could save that second of shock that could cost your life in a dangerous situation.

Mana ebbs are places where the local mana is diminished, meaning there is less to draw on to fuel powers and spells. For spirits summoned in these spots, it's like operating in thin air. Everything they do is a struggle. It all takes more effort, or their effects are diminished within the ebb. Spirits are going to be unhappy when summoned or tasked to operate in an ebb. If you don't care about the spirit, no biggie, but if you try to maintain a decent reputation within the spirit realm, you'll want to ask less or offer more for their assistance. They also, really, really, really, hate being asked to materialize in a major ebb. The ones I've spoken to equate it to being forced to sprint at the top of Everest. They also tend to feel physically diminished and appear as if they are ragged or falling to pieces while they're present on the physical plane.

Adepts almost instantly feel the effects of an ebb as it limits the amount of mana they have access to—and therefore the abilities they can utilize—on a continuous basis. Most adepts also appear tired and a bit worn down after only a short stay in an ebb. Their powers often lack the gusto they have in areas of normal mana. Besides their own appearance of wear, their powers can manifest in strange ways. While the ability to kill with a touch may lead to a flash of light, a crack of thunder, or possibly no visuals at all, within the ebb the light turns to weak lightning that cascades over the target when struck, the thunder instead rings like a gong, or a normally plain strike gains a visual accent that shows power traveling through the adept and into their opponent. The ebb makes the powers used even more obvious as the local mana sometimes has to borrow from natural forces to complete the desired effect.

Spellcasters suffer the most drastic alterations to their expectations. Their tried-and-true formulae, gifts of their totem that have been accessed a hundred times, or the powers loaned them by their loa are shifted and twisted by the diminished mana of the ebb. Their methods are practiced and true, so the spells still try to draw the same power. But the diminished mana has to give somehow. Casters that have their effects fizzle and come out weaker are the luckiest. These fizzled effects are reflected on the physical plane as spells initiate but appear to struggle for coherence, blurring at the edges or appearing to dissipate as they travel or progress.

Diminished effect is an expectation when mana is not as abundant or accessible, but there are other, far worse results of the weakened areas of the astral plane. Casters who are forced to complete their magic but must push and struggle to get the desired effect increase the strain put on their bodies and minds. Being trapped in the process of trying to complete an incantation is distressing and has resulted in many a magician being worn to unconsciousness. Trapping magicians in the spellcasting process can also prolong that process. Spells that usually take no more than an instant to cast could take seconds, or even minutes in some cases, for the process to come to fruition. And there is no cancelling the process. The mana of the ebb begins the flow and refuses to stop. The largest problem with this is the ever-changing nature of events. Preparing to cast a lightning bolt at a foe who is far more quickly dispatched by your samurai associate risks bringing additional unwanted attention.

One of the effects on spellcasting, and magic use in general within an ebb, is the occasional need for mana to draw additional energy from its surroundings in order to complete a magical effort. This effect applies to adepts, casters, summoners, and enchanters (though enchanters rarely perform their processes in an ebb) with varying levels of disgust, disdain, fear, or concern depending on the individual. I personally find these effects quite unpleasant. As those who understand the precepts of blood magic know well, mana can be pulled from the life force of an individual. Mana is, in essence, the life force of all things on the planet, from the lowliest bacteria to the greatest of the world's beasts. Sentience provides additional power but isn't necessary as those magickers of the last century learned with the sacrifice of goats and chickens. In an ebb, the mana will be pulled from surrounding plants or small animals, creating rings of withering or death around a caster. Disturbing to say the least. The effort is in no way controlled and can occur as a circle, a series of radiant lines, or even as a cracked lightning-like pattern shooting out for hundreds of meters.

I know ebbs aren't always about diminished mana but are sometimes intentional changes to the "flavor" of the local mana. I'll discuss that later, as the effects there are specific to that kind of ebb, and they also occur as part of the spike in that style over the area. The only other interesting effect I care to discuss about ebbs is the darkness. While it may sound foreboding, the effect I refer to is as simple as a darkness that surrounds the caster as mana steals energy from the physical plane in the form of light. It's not the usual, as light and mana show no other connection in areas of normal mana; this is just a random occurrence I've seen. The shadows don't diminish the view of the caster and instead create a stark contrast of unnaturalness from surrounding shadows and darkness, so this is not a technique to utilize for stealth.

On to those places where mana flows like the waters of the Amazon: mana spikes. In these rare spots, trying to control the flow of mana can be like trying to hold onto a fire hose all by yourself or trying to do your best Hoover Dam impression, trying to hold back the flow of the Colorado all by your lonesome. With excess power comes overflow and spillage that makes using magic in these areas a difficult feat to control, a tiresome effort to manage, and a herculean labor to hide (if you're trying).

Adepts flash and flare with power even from minor bits of exertion that taps their magic. Rippling energy cascades over their body, light erupts from their eyes and with their strikes, secondary physical effects occur with greater frequency, and the rush of easy power often fills them with a sense of invulnerability that the extra mana doesn't provide them. I have seen very few adepts who do not suddenly resemble over-the-top trid characters while functioning within a mana spike. The few I have seen put forth massive efforts to focus their abilities and limit themselves from touching the excess of mana. It's not something most adepts even have to learn, as they rarely channel more power than they can handle.

Spirits that are summoned in a spike are willful, and anyone who has failed to keep their name clean in the eyes of the spirit world would be better off never asking for favors or seeking to order even a bound spirit to do their bidding. The additional mana is like a combat drug for the spirits and disobedience, even to a friendly summoner, is common, sometimes to the point of breaking the bonds that hold them and using the fuel they are surrounded by to place the shackles on their masters. When they materialize they almost always appear bigger than expected and have crisper looks, even when pulling material from an imperfect physical setting.

Spells have every effect you would expect in a place where you are drawing on an overabundance of power. Spells flare with excess energy as mana pours through the connection created between the astral and physical planes. The flares take a lot of forms. I can't cover them all here, but expect the normal light and sound bursts with everything, even those spells you use to hide yourself. The manasphere doesn't care, and if you can't control the flow because the pressure of ambient mana is too great, then you should not try to connect in the first place. In intense concentrations, the spells create ripples of overflowing energy that cascade out from the caster. The energy could just appear as a little wave of bent light or it could carry an actual arcane effect with it. I've seen random items suffer changes in physical state, appearance, and material. I've seen sparks of fire and lightning that are not as harmless as those in an ebb. The excess power wants to be something on our plane, and without a sentience guiding it, the mana wills what the mana wills. Now, these huge effects aren't always going to be the case. Sometimes the effect is localized with changes to the physical space around the caster. The colors of their clothes may change, water may suddenly erupt around them, a small cloud may form over their head and begin pouring rain and lightning, static may spark off them with every step, or their clothes or hair may start on fire or start smoking. I've seen all of these.

Excess mana sneaking in may also create secondary spell effects that were not part of the original spell. A fireball that also causes some petrification. Invisibility that also creates a field of darkness. Light that also burns. Healing that comes with lightning. A spell intended to detect enemies that also detects rodents. A wave of acid that brings with it invisibility. Sometimes the second effect can be helpful, but it's at the whim of the mana. The best method I've seen of playing this game for a caster's benefit is throwing several spells at once and pulling through the mana and shaping the overflow. It's brutally taxing, but at least it comes with more of a guarantee that you won't be providing your enemies with armor while you're trying to detect them.

Now let me quickly talk about both ebbs and spikes in terms of mana being shifted to a specific aspect. The mana is there; it just has a certain twist to it, making it easier or harder to touch based on one's training and beliefs. The same side effects can occur in these places, but while one side is feeling the overflow, the other is forcing every bit of mana they can pull to light a spark. The thing is, these changes can often force a caster to alter their style in order to get anything going. Hermetics howling or growling to make spells work in a shaman's domain. Shamans being forced to pull and shape the mana they draw into patterns that are very unshamanic. Both needing to take on the behaviors of a voodoo patron in order to make things work in a houngan's realm.

As aspecting an area is independent of the natural ebb or spike, such spots could be extremely difficult and unpredictable for those trying to perform magic when the area is aspected away from them. If the overall mana level is low in such a place, you may strain too hard in the effort to get anything to use. When there is excess mana, the lack of connection to an area's aspect may result in magic slipping from your control and manifesting in ways you didn't plan.

In the same vein, we can talk about mana storms where the ebb and spike of mana can shift positions on a whim, vary between two points, or dilate in an instant. These changes make using magic inside a mana storm chaotic at its best and deadly or crippling at most times. They also offer a fate worse than death for those who dare try their hand at magic. There are fewer things in the world as dangerous as using magic in a mana storm. I would go so far as making a deal with dragon to avoid it.

Adepts are in constant danger of fading and blossoming in power. One moment unable to channel enough mana to break a board, the next uncontrollably leaping fifty meters in the air. And then falling those fifty meters. One never knows what the mana within the storm will do from instant to instant. Not using any powers is the best choice, but I know some adepts infuse themselves with power rather than activate things. The power is just there most of the time and takes almost as much concentration and effort to stuff down as it would to harness. In a mana storm, the effort is worth it.

The discussion about spirits in one of these spots is easy, because there's just one thing to know: Don't do it unless you are an ass or have a death wish. They are going to fight you, be driven mad by the mana fluctuations, or more likely, both. For spirits, a mana storm is like living inside a picture painted by the child of M.C. Escher and Salvador Dali—emphasis on the child.

Spells are a mixed bag. Of course, there are relatively harmless effects like a spell simply going off target. Sometimes hitting nothing, other times switching to another aura in the area, and occasionally circling back to whack the caster. Yes, that counts as "harmless" in terms of a mana storm. Changes to the physical nature or appearance of spells should be expected, alongside bonus effects like sudden rain or snow of a variety of colors, powerful gusts of wind, gaps opening in the earth, spontaneous windows to the astral, and honestly, just about any weird and random drek you can think of. Mana storms make magic even more mercurial than Mercurial, and that's saying something.

A horror I have seen and used as a warning about mana storms is what I refer to as a "casting lock." Sadly, I've seen it twice, and neither time did the caster last more than a few hours once it occurred. A casting lock is a forced state of continuous casting or mana channeling. One of my lost compatriots tried to use the flow of mana to cast small, inconsequential spells over and over. The strain of the process started small, but it grew more and more wearisome as the minutes rolled by. At least he lasted longer than the acquaintance who just left themselves open and didn't try to bleed off the magic. They burned out in less than a minute as the mana pouring through him was too much. It took an hour before he fell to the strain.

If mana storms are the chaos of magical variability, alchera are the stoic calm with the predictable change to local mana flows. Kind of. As places of great local mana with enough of its own identity to change the physical world, these spots force mana to match their local paradigm. Shadows of the past force casters and adepts to use anachronistic styles or be unable to touch the local magic. Adepts often adapt quickly. Magicians are so trained and ingrained in their own systems, it can take minutes, days, or weeks to get adjusted, if they ever manage it.

Even when they do, their magic is rarely the same in appearance and often varies in function as well. Invisibility spells that don't bend light but rather give the caster the appearance of a peasant that no one pays attention to; elemental effects that shift because fire and lightning have a holy significance; spells that limit the final form of earth-shaping spells because the local architecture and geology are an integral part of the alchera.

Elements that don't match are sometimes stopped, sometimes changed, and sometimes allowed to play out with the user forced to deal with the social ramifications in places where the alchera has a local indigenous population.

In the end, magic and mana are only predictable and within our control when we have complex systems to manage and shape it. Without that, mana is an unpredictable force with unlimited potential for both order and chaos.

MAGIC MASTERY

There is always a next step. Any mage who thinks they have reached the pinnacle of what magic can do need only look at a great dragon, or an annoying face-painted immortal elf, and see just how much there is to learn. Unfortunately for most metahumans, they don't have long enough lifespans to gain the full range of mastery as those who have sprawled their education over centuries. Some spellcasters and adepts have realized that ascending to the ranks of greatness may require focus, choosing an area in which to concentrate their talents so that they may emerge as true masters of a particular type of magic.

The Magical Mastery options presented here give mages a chance to find their particular calling, selecting an area where they can excel and make themselves into a true legend of magic. Most of the options here are qualities that work in a fashion similar to regular qualities, though the following rules govern their use:

- Unless otherwise specified, all of the mastery qualities in this section require a Magic rating. Most also require characters to be a Magician, Adept, Aspected Magician, or Mystic Adept.
- Characters may purchase mastery qualities that don't require initiation during character creation, but they must also purchase all of the requirements for their Mastery qualities before leaving character creation.
- The cost for mastery qualities is always the same, even after character generation; they don't experience the same Karma cost increase that other qualities do.

ALCHEMICAL ARMORER

Though metaphysicists have been trying to develop genuine, spell-shooting "magic bullets" for a few decades now, progress has never gotten very far. Enchanting firearms doesn't increase their ranged accuracy or allow them to shoot spells, and the limitations of alchemical triggers and the fragile nature of preparations (see p. 305, *SR5*) have prevented even the most limited production of enchanted ammunition. In most instances, magic bullets are just bullets that have been made into alchemical preparations of combat spells that are subsequently fired out of a gun barrel. These are just standard alchemy preparations that must be activated with the normal triggers. This is universally recognized as a poor design for several reasons: Primarily, they are hard to aim, and activating a combat spell inside of a firearm will often damage the user or the weapon itself. Until recently, it's simply been more effective to have a trained operator fire their weapon normally rather than bring alchemy into the equation.

While dozens of corporate R&D teams wasted decades of research and billions of nuyen trying to develop bullets that could deliver alchemy spells, a pair of neo-anarchist rebels in Yucatan figured out how to use alchemy to better deliver bullets. Aztlan patrols first encountered Sara Blanco and Esteban Carrillo leading a ragged group of about three dozen rebels among the ruins of Chichen Itza back in 2064. While the rebels nearly doubled the number of soldiers in the Aztlan patrol, intelligence reports had suggested that the rebels in that area were armed only with basic firearms—mainly bolt-action or lever-action rifles and revolvers. A skirmish between the two groups quickly broke out. Surprisingly, after a few hours of exchanging gunfire, the Aztlan patrol was forced to completely withdraw from the area. When questioned by military officials during their debriefing, members of the patrol team made wild claims about the rebels having lever-action rifles that could fire silently and pierce the armor plating of their armored personnel carriers.

In an attempt to back up their story, the sergeant in command of the patrol presented the projectile portion of a bullet used by smaller hunting rifles as evidence. The sergeant claimed that, after the first hour of fighting, this bullet had passed through the side of his APC and then pierced the helmet of his second-in-command; killing her instantly. The projectile showed no signs of ballistic markings and completely lacked deformation from any kind of impact. Aztlan military officials were still skeptical about these "magic bullets" and ultimately decided to bury the story after a larger force returned to Chichen Itza to reclaim the ruins, but failed to verify the presence of the Blanco and Carrillo or their group of rebel fighters.

- Some qualities have more than one requirement. Some qualities also have alternative requirements that can be met instead. Qualities with more than one requirement will list the requirements separated by the word "and," while alternative requirements will be listed after the word "or."
- Mastery qualities count toward the maximum amount of Karma a character may spend on positive qualities at character generation.
- A character may exchange spells they receive from their selection on the Magic/Resonance priority chart for 5 Karma to spend on mastery qualities, but any Karma that is leftover from purchasing these qualities cannot be spent on other things or kept after character generation.
- Mastery qualities that require a skill specialization may be purchased without the specialization if the character possesses the required skill at a level that is two ranks higher than the listed requirement.
- Mastery qualities that have a magical tradition listed next to them have all of their skill requirements lowered by 2 ranks for individuals of this particular tradition. This includes the skill ranks that may be required to gain the next level of a mastery quality.

ADEPT HEALER

10 KARMA

Minimum Requirements: Adept Power: Empathic Healing (p. 171, *Street Grimoire*)

An adept with this quality heals significantly more damage per hit when transferring damage from another person with the Empathic Healing power. Additionally, they suffer a slightly lower cost to their own health. When using the Empathic Healing power, each net hit removes 3 boxes of damage from the wounded character and inflicts 2 boxes of damage on the adept.

ALCHEMICAL ARMORER

15 KARMA

Minimum Requirements: Alchemy 4, Armorer 4, and advanced alchemy metamagic

This quality gives the character a spell that allows her to alter the ballistic properties of bullets by making them target and lynchpin of preparations. The cost of the Alter Ballistics spell (see p. 51) is factored into the cost of this quality, and the character does not need to spend any extra Karma to learn the spell.

ALCHEMICAL BOMB MAKER

10 KARMA

Minimum Requirements:
Alchemy 4 (with Combat Spell specialization) and advanced alchemy metamagic

A character with this quality can increase the radius or base DV of alchemical preparations that have their range listed as LOS(A). For every 2DV increase in damage or 10m increase in radius (rounded up), the Drain Value is increased by 1. A character with this quality may also reduce the drain from one type trigger of her choice by one, down to a minimum of zero.

ANIMAL FAMILIAR

5 KARMA

Minimum Requirements: Animal Handling 5

Using this quality can make a non-Awakened animal follow the same rules as an animal bonded via Attune Animal, though this bond cannot be broken except by death (type and cost of animal allowed is up to the gamemaster). If a familiar dies, the quality must be purchased again if the character wants a familiar. Characters may only have one familiar at a time. The character and animal share a limited Sense Link (p. 198, *Street Grimoire*). They are connected emotionally and the character can issue commands mentally to the animal, but no other senses are shared. If the familiar is within (character's Magic x 50) meters of the character, the character knows where the familiar is. Adepts with a familiar can reduce the Karma cost of the Way of the Beast by 3.

APT PUPIL
5 KARMA

Minimum Requirements: Arcana 6 and Knowledge: Magical Theory 4

All that studying has finally paid off. All of the magical training times for a character with this quality are reduced by 25 percent.

ARCANE BODYGUARD
20 KARMA

Minimum Requirements: Counterspelling 4

A character with this quality has double the amount of spell defense dice, but they may never use more than (spell defense dice / 3) dice on herself, even when they have no one around to protect. The quality also doubles the number of people a character can protect with their spell defense dice at any one time.

ARCANE IMPROVISER [CHAOS]
5 KARMA

Minimum Requirements: Spellcasting 6, Counterspelling 6, Arcana 7 (with Spell Design specialization), and 4 spells from each category

A character with this quality can spend a point of Edge to cast any spell they have not previously paid Karma to learn. Characters may only cast this spell once per week with a Complex Action, but it is always considered **Reckless Spellcasting** (p. 281, *SR5*) when calculating drain DV.

ARCHIVIST
10 KARMA

Minimum Requirements: Arcana 5 and two Academic Knowledge skills related to magical studies at rank 4 or higher

Studying is no substitute for practice when it comes to learning many of the finer points of most magical skills, but there is something to be said for the value of dedication to one's studies. The archivist has spent many hours in dusty libraries and hidden collections of scrolls and tomes, studying knowledge few have ever seen. Their mind has become a living catalog of arcane knowledge, and their skills benefit from this knowledge.

Knowledge is power. A character with this quality has extensively studied the inner workings of magic, which grants them the ability to manipulate mana at a higher level than they'd normally be able to. For every two Academic knowledge skills related to magical studies that the character possesses at rank 4 or higher, their Magic attribute is considered to be one level higher for the purposes of determining whether the Drain Value from a magical action will be **Physical** or **Stun**.

ASTRAL BOUNCER
10 KARMA

Minimum Requirements: Assensing skill 4 (with Aura Reading specialization)

A character with this quality has astral sight that is so keen that they've developed new ways of sizing up everyone they meet. Along with the normal results, every two net hits on an Assensing skill test can also be used to reveal one of the following about a living being: all positive qualities, all negative qualities, physical attribute ratings, mental attribute ratings, initiate grade, an initiate power, an adept power, or Edge rating.

ASTRAL INFILTRATOR
15 KARMA

Minimum Requirements: Astral Combat 5 (with Astral Barriers specialization), Initiate Grade 1

Any astral barrier that a character with this quality successfully passes through has its Force lowered by their Initiate Grade. If passing through the barrier lowers the Force to zero, the barrier is disrupted, and the mage who set it up is alerted. A character with this quality can instead choose to leave a barrier at Force 1 if they would normally disrupt the barrier by passing through it. A single character can only reduce the Force of a barrier once, but multiple characters with this quality can combine their efforts to weaken or remove an astral barrier.

BAREHANDED ADEPT [BUDDHISM]

10 KARMA

Minimum Requirements: Must be an Adept and have Unarmed Combat 6

This quality allows an adept to cast a number of touch spells equal to their (Magic attribute / 2); a new touch spell is granted as the character's Magic attribute rises high enough after acquiring this quality. An adept with this quality does not actually have to use their hands to cast a spell, but their bare skin must make contact with the target of the spell (or the target's clothing). A barehanded adept uses their Unarmed Combat skill in place of the Spellcasting skill and must still make the normal unarmed attack required to target a touch spell. Drain is double what it normally would be and is resisted with Body + Willpower. The maximum Force of any spell cast with this ability is (Magic / 3), rounded up.

BLOOD NECROMANCER

15 KARMA

Minimum Requirements: Blood Magic, Spellcasting 6 (with Health specialization)

When a creature dies, it takes a short period of time for their essence to fade as their individual organs and cells begin to fail and die. Characters with this quality can use these minuscule traces of life to revive and stabilize characters who have filled their overflow damage within a number of minutes equal to their (Essence – 1, rounded up). For every minute that the character was dead before being revived, they lose one point of Essence. If the loss would reduce the character's Essence to zero, that character cannot be revived. Metahumans who have returned from the dead and the mage who revived them must immediately make a Composure (4) test to avoid acquiring long-term mental, physical, or spiritual ailments. Critters with the Sapience power make a Composure (2) test, while critters without the Sapience power only make a Composure (1) test to resist permanent adverse effects. If a metahuman or critter fails to beat the Composure threshold, they must take a number of negative qualities equal to (threshold

POTENTIAL NEGATIVE QUALITIES AFTER REVIVAL

ROLL	NEGATIVE QUALITY
2	Amnesia (Neural Deletion)
3	Astral Beacon
4	Deaf
5	Insomnia (15 Karma)
6	Allergy (Sunlight, Moderate)
7	Compulsive (12 Karma)
8	Loss of Confidence
9	Weak Immune System
10	Infirm (15 Karma)
11	Infirm (10 Karma)
12	Compulsive (8 Karma)

– hits) from the table listed below. These negative qualities can be purposefully chosen, or they can be rolled for randomly at the discretion of the gamemaster.

CHAIN BREAKER [SHAMAN]

10 KARMA (ASPECTED MAGE: 5 KARMA)

Minimum Requirements: See description

A character with this quality refuses to bind spirits and takes umbrage with any magician who does. A chain breaker is known to the astral world as an ally, which means that spirits are more willing to forgive them at first, but less forgiving if they develop a bad Astral Reputation. Characters with this quality double the amount of Spirit Index required to reach their first point of Astral Reputation, but require only 10 Spirit Index to gain subsequent points of Astral Reputation. As a reward for their devotion, a character with this quality may choose two additional spirit types to summon in addition to the spirit types allowed by their tradition. The character must forfeit the use of the Binding skill as an active skill, but they may still use any previously acquired ranks as a Knowledge skill. Additionally, the character must succeed in a Composure (2) test to avoid verbally or physically lashing out at any nearby mage currently binding a spirit, including teammates.

If the Astral Reputation of a chain breaker ever reaches 3 or higher, the character loses the ability to summon the extra two spirit types, and this quality is considered a negative quality until it is paid off with Karma (at twice the listed price) or the character can adequately atone for their transgressions by performing the Atonement ritual (p. 123, *Street Grimoire*).

CHAKRA INTERRUPTER

10 KARMA

Minimum Requirements: Nerve Strike adept power and Assensing 4 (with Aura Reading specialization) OR Unarmed Combat 6 (with Martial Art specialization), Dim Mak Technique, and Assensing 4 (with Aura Reading specialization)

When striking nerves, arteries, and pressure points, the character doesn't just disable limbs; they block the ability to control and channel mana. The attacker must have previously assensed the target and gotten at least 2 net hits to use this ability. Along with the normal effects of Nerve Strike or called shots to an arm or leg, a character with this quality may temporarily reduce the Magic attribute of a target by 1 for every two net hits on her melee attack. The defending character's Magic attribute is reduced for a number of Combat Turns equal to the melee skill rank of the attacking character. Using this ability without the Nerve Strike power requires a Called Shot (Specific Location) targeting either an arm or a leg.

CHARLATAN

10 KARMA

Minimum Requirements: Palming 3 (with Prestidigitation specialization) and Assensing 5 OR Performance 3 (with Magic specialization) and Assensing 5

Charlatans are able to use prestidigitation and stage magic to hinder any attempts to notice or identify their magic or magical items for what they really are. When a character with this quality is per-

CHARLATAN

The ability to make someone miss what's happening right under their nose is a valuable one. The charlatan has learned to use "parlor tricks" to hide their real magic from other Awakened beings. Performance magic, or mundane magic, has seen a steep decline in popularity since the beginning of the Sixth World; audiences just aren't as impressed with staged illusions in an era where a simple Matrix search will reveal the secrets to most magic tricks and there are people with the ability to summon spirits and create real fireballs out of thin air. Real magicians were eager to relegate performance magic and sleight-of-hand to derision-laced footnotes in modern thaumaturgy textbooks, allowing them to move on in pursuit of higher knowledge.

Even though old-school magic may have fallen by the wayside a bit, there are still plenty of mundane and Awakened practitioners in the Sixth World. This is because one of the underlying principles behind stage or street magic—exploiting flaws in memory and sensory perception—has a variety of potential uses beyond the realm of entertainment. Researchers have been working with mundane magicians for decades to piece together the gaps between reality and our mental perception of it. Meanwhile, the corps and governments of this world have been waving their right hand in our faces while picking our pockets with their left for longer than any of us can remember.

Ironically, performance magic still had a few tricks left to teach modern magicians who were willing to look at it seriously. Researchers at the Dunkelzahn Institute of Magical Research have recently published a paper that details several experiments wherein magicians were asked to identify magical items used or spells cast as part of a mundane magic performance. The initial findings suggested a slight decrease in the Assensing skill ability of participating magicians, but as the experiment progressed researchers noticed that their test subjects were getting progressively worse at spotting magic. During the six-week experiment, their performing magicians had apparently learned how to fine-tune their performance so as to better fool the audience. They claimed that combining some of the more obvious "tells" of casting a spell with sleight-of-hand allowed them not only to hide the verbal and somatic elements of their Spellcasting skill, but also to temporarily blend their magical signature into the natural background count. As long as they concentrated on the performance, they were able to extend this effect to anything connected to their aura, as long as they used it in the performance or kept it near them.

Charlatans are clever and charismatic tricksters by nature, but not all tricksters are necessarily malevolent. Often all it takes is a wave of the hand to distract an opponent long enough to avoid violence altogether, and the charlatan is a master at navigating tense situations. Whether surprising someone at a social gathering by pulling a coin out of their ear or sawing an assistant in half in front of a large audience, charlatans know that the key to any good magic trick is controlling what their audience perceives. As the renowned stage magician and DIMR professor Dr. Cara Busara writes at the end of her most recent study, "You can't see what you aren't looking for."

forming a mundane illusion, they add their Performance (Magic) or Palming (Prestidigitation) skill rank to their Spellcasting rank for the purposes of determining the Perception test threshold to notice them casting a spell (see **Perceiving Magic**, p. 280, SR5). Anyone watching their performance suffers a dice pool penalty to Assensing tests targeting the performer, their spells, or their magical equipment. The dice pool penalty to Assensing tests is equal to the Performance or Palming skill of the performer. This dice pool penalty applies for the entire duration of the performance and an additional number of minutes equal to the performing character's Charisma. This quality is not a true replacement for the Masking and Extended Masking metamagics and will not hinder attempts to assense the character outside of when they are performing mundane illusions, but the negative dice pool modifier to Assensing Tests can be combined with the use of those metamagics.

CHOSEN FOLLOWER
10 KARMA

Minimum Requirements: Mentor Spirit quality

Characters with this quality have earned the right to receive magical instruction from their mentor spirits by showing ceaseless devotion to their ideals. The wisdom bestowed by a mentor spirit is granted instantaneously as a potent vision delivered via the shared connection between the character and their mentor. This instruction can only be received once every three months during an equinox or a solstice event, and each type of instruction can only be received once per year. A character with this quality may ask their mentor spirit to aid them in one of the following ways:

- Learn two spells or rituals.
- Improve a magical active skill from rank 1 to rank 3.
- Reduce the training time for improving a magical active skill, skill group, or specialization by fifty percent.
- Reduce the training time for improving their Magic attribute by fifty percent.
- Improve an Academic knowledge skill related to Magic from rank 1 to rank 4.
- Ignore glitches or reduce critical glitches during Step 5 (Craft the Focus, p. 307, SR5) when crafting a single focus.
- Ignore glitches or reduce critical glitches during Step 7 (Seal the Ritual, p. 296, SR5) when performing a single ritual.
- Reduce the threshold for the Arcana + Logic Extended Test to create an ally spirit formula to (Force x 3); see p. 201, Street Grimoire.

CLOSE COMBAT MAGE
5 KARMA PER LEVEL

Minimum Requirements: Spellcasting 4 (per level of quality) and spell shaping metamagic

When this mastery quality is purchased, the character may choose one benefit per level from the list below. Each benefit may only be chosen once.

- The total dice pool penalty for using the Spell Shaping metamagic is reduced by 2, down to a minimum of zero.
- Spell radius can be increased or decreased by two meters per –1 dice pool penalty to the Spellcasting test instead of 1 meter.
- Spherical areas unaffected by the spell can be up to three meters in radius.

DARK ALLY (SPECIFIC SPIRIT)
10 KARMA

Minimum Requirements: Binding 7, Ritual Spellcasting 9

Magicians are capable of binding a specific spirit after using a Calling ritual (p. 126, Street Grimoire). This spirit is limited to a specific kind of spirit (for example, a boggle) rather than a spirit type (for example, fae). A bound spirit is subject to the limit on the number of bound spirits, and it can provide services related to manipulation spells. Spirit gains the Restless quality when binding is attempted. Force of the spirit cannot exceed the Magic rating of the magician.

DEATH DEALER
15 KARMA PER LEVEL (MAXIMUM 3)

Minimum Requirements: Spellcasting 4 (with Combat Spells specialization) or Critical Strike adept power

All Combat spells cast by a character with this quality have their DV increased by 1 per level of this quality. However, channeling even more destructive forces wreaks havoc on the character's system. The drain code for any affected Combat spells is increased by +1 per level. Adepts with this quality add an additional +1 DV to any attacks made with active skills affected by the Critical Strike power, but they may only purchase the first level of this quality.

DEDICATED CONJURER

10 KARMA
(ASPECTED MAGE: 5 KARMA)

Minimum Requirements: See description

Characters must completely forfeit use of the Spellcasting skill as an active skill and the ability to cast spells, but they may still use any previously acquired ranks in the Spellcasting skill as a Knowledge skill. In exchange, the dedicated conjurer can choose a new type of spirit to summon and bind for every two full ranks they have in their Summoning skill. These spirit types can be summoned in addition to the spirit types normally allowed by their tradition, and they do not replace any of the other types of spirits a character with this quality can summon. When using the Conjuring skill group, characters with this quality add 1 to their Magic rating when determining whether drain they must resist is Physical or Stun damage. Aspected mages who are able to learn skills in the Conjuring skill group automatically meet the requirements for this quality.

DEDICATED SPELLSLINGER

10 KARMA
(ASPECTED MAGE: 5 KARMA)

Minimum Requirements: See description

Characters with this quality completely forfeit use of the Summoning and Binding skills as active skills, but they may still use any previously acquired ranks in those skills as Knowledge skills. In exchange, characters gain a new spell for free every time they raise their Spellcasting skill, and the Karma cost of learning new spells is reduced by 1. The character also receives a free spell for every rank they possess in the Spellcasting skill at the time of purchasing this quality, including character generation. Specializations count as one rank in a skill for the purposes of the free spells offered by this quality, but the selected spell must be compatible with the specialization. Aspected mages who are able to learn skills in the Sorcery skill group automatically meet the requirements for this quality.

DUAL-NATURED DEFENDER

5 KARMA

Minimum Requirements:
Dual Natured quality and Astral Combat 3

Characters with this quality have learned that the Sixth World is not the kindest place to dual-natured creatures, and it's forced them to learn how to defend themselves against a variety of astral threats. A character with this quality may stop astrally perceiving with a Free Action to avoid astral barriers or threats. The amount of concentration required to disconnect from the astral causes a –2 dice pool penalty to all actions the critter makes when they are not astrally perceiving. A dual-natured critter cannot use any of its critter powers (except Sapience) while in this state, and shapeshifters are stuck in whatever physical form they are currently in. A dual-natured critter cannot stop astrally perceiving for more minutes than its Magic attribute in a twenty-four-hour period before it must reconnect with the astral. For every minute past the allotted time that a critter does not perceive the astral, it permanently loses one point of Magic. If a character with this quality is knocked unconscious, they automatically reconnect with the astral. This quality does not hide the fact that a critter is Awakened when the critter is assensed, but it inflicts a –2 penalty on any attempts to astrally perceive the critter.

DURABLE PREPARATIONS

5 KARMA

Minimum Requirements: Alchemy 6

The character's intimate knowledge of the materials and skills used in alchemy gives them insight to reinforce the magical bonds of the preparation. Increase the time before the preparation starts to lose potency to (potency x 3) hours, instead of potency x 2.

ELEMENTAL MASTER [WUXING]

20 KARMA

Minimum Requirements: 5 spells related to a specific natural element (air, earth, fire, or water), or Conjuring 4 (with specialization in conjuring spirits of air, earth, fire, or water)

The elemental master has chosen a natural element (air, earth, fire, or water) on which to focus, and developed an intense connection to that element. A character with this quality reduces all incoming damage from their chosen element by half, and they are immune to any secondary effects it might normally cause (see **Elemental Damage**, p. 170, *SR5*). Because incoming damage is halved before rolling for damage resistance, this quality protects both the character and their worn equipment from elemental damage.

FLESH SCULPTER

10 KARMA PER LEVEL (MAXIMUM 3)

Minimum Requirements: Spellcasting 4 (with Manipulation Spells specialization), Zoology 5, and Spell: Shapechange or (Critter) Form

A character with this quality is able to turn themselves and others into a larger range of animal forms with the Shapechange or (Critter) Form spells. For each level of this quality, a Flesh Sculpter can transform a voluntary subject into an animal form with a base body that is two points greater or lower than normally allowed by these spells.

HEALER

10 KARMA

Minimum Requirements: Spellcasting 4 (with Health specialization) and First Aid 3

You decided a long time ago that no one dies on your watch. Characters with this quality become so in tune with the auras of the sick and injured during their training that they establish a much stronger empathic link when healing them magically, even if their patient has lowered Essence. The character can use net hits from Spellcasting skill tests to reduce the time it takes for a health spell to become permanent by 2 Combat Turns per net hit instead of 1. Additionally, dice pool penalties to casting health spells on characters with lowered Essence are halved (round down).

ILLUSIONIST

10 KARMA PER LEVEL (MAXIMUM 3)

Minimum Requirements:
Spellcasting 4 (with Illusion specialization)

Each level of this quality allows a character to sustain a single Illusion spell without taking a penalty. The character must choose

ANIMAL FORMS AND FLYING

Critters with the ability to fly do so by using the Flight active skill. They learn this by spending their formative years learning this critical skill or dying in the attempt. Normally, the Flight skill is only possessed by critters, which means that a mage/adept in an animal form would default on any skill checks that involve flying. Gamemasters who feel that this level of realism doesn't suit their game may use one of the following alternatives or come up with their own.

- Allow characters to learn Flight active skill by spending Karma as normal. Remember that adepts with the totem form metamagic must succeed in an Arcana + Magic [Mental] Test to shift forms. This could potentially make training take longer or result in an adept becoming an animal permanently.

- Allow characters to use any of the Athletics group skills or the Pilot Aircraft skill in place of the Flight skill and apply a –1 dice pool penalty to all skill checks that involve flying.

- Allow characters to use the average rating (rounded up) of their Athletics skill group in place of the flight skill. If a character has not broken up the Athletics skill group, the average will be equal to the rating of the skill group.

- Allow mage characters to the use half the (Force) of their spell (rounded up) in place of the Flight skill; adepts should be allowed to use their Initiate grade.

which type of spell they can sustain (Physical or Mana) when purchasing a level of this quality. The character cannot benefit from this quality if they sustain spells with a Force that exceeds their Magic rating.

ITEMS OF POWER

25 KARMA

Minimum Requirements: Artificing 6

The Magic attribute of a character with this quality is increased by 3 for the purposes of determining the total rating of foci the character can have before risking focus addiction.

MAGE HUNTER

15 KARMA

Minimum Requirements: Spellcasting 4 (with Combat Spells specialization); see description

Each level of this quality allows a character to reduce a Counterspelling dice pool aimed against

them by 2 in exchange for adding 1 to the drain of a Combat spell they are casting. Prerequisites increase if characters want additional levels—for level 2, Spellcasting rank must be 7; for level 3, must be 9.

MISSILE DEFLECTOR

10 KARMA

Minimum Requirements: Adept Power: Missile Parry (1) and Adept Power: Counterstrike

Adepts with this quality may use the Counterstrike adept power as an interrupt action to immediately throw an object that they have successfully caught using the Missile Parry power. The adept can target anyone or any area within their normal throwing range.

MYSTIC FOREMAN

10 KARMA

Minimum Requirements: Spellcasting 4 (with Manipulation Spells specialization), Industrial Engineering 4, and Chemistry 4

Shape [Material] spells cast by a character with this quality apply the Force of their spell as a negative dice pool modifier to the target material during the Object Resistance test. Additionally, their Shape [Material] spells now reduce the Structure ratings of reinforced materials by (Force x 2) points per combat turn instead of (Force) points per combat turn.

MYSTIC PITCHER

10 KARMA

Minimum Requirements: Fling spell, Spellcasting 4 (with Manipulation Spells specialization)

A character with this quality can use the Fling spell to hurl objects more accurately at selected targets or over long distances. This quality allows you to shift the range modifiers for attacks with the Fling spell down by one category cumulative with any qualities or vision enhancements that also reduce range modifiers. Alternatively, you may choose to use aerodynamic grenade ranges instead of reducing a range modifier. Additionally, this quality reduces the dice pool penalty for all called shots using the Fling spell by 1; this is compatible with any other qualities that reduce the dice pool penalties for called shots.

PACIFIST ADEPT
5 KARMA

Minimum Requirements: Pacifist quality (10 or 15 Karma), Cool Resolve adept power, Notoriety less than 2

Adepts with this quality have dedicated years of training to using the powers granted by their qi to further their pursuit of peaceful conflict resolution. This quality offers special benefits for each level of the Pacifist quality that the adept possesses, but also requires a deeper dedication to their vow of non-violence.

- **10 Karma:** Any attacks that would cause Physical damage made by anyone, or at anyone, within a number of meters equal the adept's Magic Rating has its associated limit reduced by 2. This includes attacks made by anything that lacks an Essence attribute, but not attacks against them. After all, you can't really kill something if it's not (debatably) alive. The character also receives an additional +1 to their dice pool and limit for any opposed social skill checks or Knowledge skill checks they make to avoid using violence. Any attacks against the Pacifist Adept or made by the Pacifist reduce the number of 1s needed to glitch by one.
- **15 Karma:** Any attempts to cause harm (Physical or Stun damage) performed by anyone, or at any living being, within a number of meters equal the adept's (Magic Rating x 2) have their limit reduced by 4. This includes attacks made by anything that lacks an Essence attribute, but not attacks against them. The character also receives an additional +3 to their dice pool and limit for any opposed social skill checks or Knowledge skill checks they make to avoid using violence. Any attacks against the Pacifist Adept or made by the Pacifist reduce the number of 1s needed to glitch by three.

POTION MAKER
15 KARMA

Minimum Requirements: Alchemy 4 and Chemistry 4

The Potion Maker doesn't take any extra drain from the basic lynchpin triggers when creating alchemical preparations if the lynchpin is a liquid. The lynchpin must have some component in it that pertains to the nature of the spell (a Fireball spell could use gasoline, a Manipulate Earth spell could use a handful of dirt, a Heal spell could have ground aspirin tablets, etc.). If a spell contains more than one elemental component, both elements must be represented in the lynchpin. The entire volume of the liquid must either be consumed by or poured over the target before the preparation can be triggered in any way other than with a timer trigger. Advanced lynchpin triggers still add drain as normal.

PRACTICED ALCHEMIST [ISLAMIC]
5 KARMA

Minimum Requirements: Alchemy 6

Each alchemical preparation created by a character with this quality lasts twice as long before the potency begins to diminish and receives a dice pool bonus equal to (1 + Initiate grade) whenever it is triggered.

PUPPET MASTER [BLACK MAGIC]
10 KARMA PER LEVEL (MAXIMUM 3)

Minimum Requirements: Psychology 5 and Spellcasting 4 (Manipulation spells)

This quality allows a character to sustain one Mental Manipulation spell per level of the quality without taking a penalty. The character cannot benefit from this quality if they sustain spells with a Force that exceeds their Magic rating.

RECKLESS SPELL MASTER
10 KARMA PER LEVEL (MAXIMUM 6)

Minimum Requirements: Spellcasting 6

Once per day per level of this quality, a character may choose not to increase the drain value for casting a spell as a Simple Action (see **Reckless Spellcasting**, p. 281, *SR5*). The caster must get a full eight hours of uninterrupted rest before they may cast spells without increasing the drain value again.

RENAISSANCE RITUALIST [CHAOS]

8 KARMA

Minimum Requirements: Arcana 4, Knowledge: Magical Traditions 5, and Ritual Spellcasting 4

When characters with this quality are leading a ritual, a number of participants equal to their Magic + Initiate Grade may observe different traditions without penalty.

REVENANT ADEPT

5 KARMA

Minimum Requirements:

Adept Power: Rapid Healing adept power

An adept with this quality may use the Regeneration power up to four times a year. When activated, the power functions until all injuries are healed. The adept must then wait until the next equinox/solstice event (or thirty days, whichever is longer) before they may use the Regeneration power again.

SHOCK MAGE

15 KARMA

Minimum Requirements: Spellcasting 6, at least one electricity-based skill

When a character with this quality successfully inflicts damage with a Combat spell, after rolling their Damage Resistance test, the initiative scores of their targets are reduced by an amount equal to the caster's (net hits / 2), rounded up. Any Combat spells with secondary effects that reduce initiative are compatible with this quality, and the effects stack.

SKINWALKER [SIOUX]

5 KARMA PER LEVEL (MAXIMUM 3)

Minimum Requirements: Spellcasting 4 (with a Manipulation Spells specialization), Zoology 2, and the (Critter) Form spell

A character with this quality is able to take on a larger range of animal forms with the (Critter) Form spell. For each level of this quality, a Skinwalker can assume an animal form with a base Body Rating that is 6 points greater or lower than her own, as long as they possess the pelt or skin of that animal. This only applies when the Skinwalker casts the spell on themselves, not on others.

SPECTRAL WARDEN [HERMETIC]

15 KARMA

Minimum Requirements: See description

A character with this quality always chooses to summon a spirit as part of a binding, which allows them to summon a more potent spirit than would previously be possible. Spirits the character summons during a binding ritual have one optional power for every 2 full points of Force instead of every 3. The character must forfeit the use of the Summoning skill as an Active Skill, but they may still use any previously acquired ranks as a Knowledge skill. The character may also use their Binding skill in place of the Ritual Spellcasting skill to perform rituals with the Minion keyword; the Binding skill is used in place of the Summoning skill when the character tries to pacify a bound spirit (see **Bad Feelings with Bound Spirits**, p. 301, *SR5*).

Characters with this quality are often known in the spirit world as slavers or, at the very least, incredibly ill-mannered. Because the character's tendency to bind is already known, their Spirit Index does not accrue any faster, but the spirits are more demanding of them when they try to atone. The amount of karma they must spend to buy off their Astral Reputation when performing the Atonement ritual (p. 123, *Street Grimoire*) is doubled.

SPELL JAMMER

20 KARMA

Minimum Requirements: Counterspelling 6

Characters with this quality may spend a Complex Action to make a Counterspelling + Magic [Astral] v. Spellcasting + Magic [Astral] Opposed Test against a number of characters, within line of sight, equal to their Magic / 2. Any net hits on this test are inflicted as a negative dice pool modifier to any Spellcasting Tests made by the afflicted targets for (net hits) Combat Turns.

SPIRIT HUNTER

20 KARMA PER LEVEL (MAXIMUM 3)

Minimum Requirements: Banishing 4 or Astral Combat 4 (Spirits) or Killing Hands adept power; see description

A character with this quality has the ability to prevent spirits from using their powers for a short period of time. Any time a character with this quality successfully uses the Banishing skill to remove a favor that a spirit owes, damages a spirit in astral combat, or damages a spirit with the Killing Hands power, that spirit cannot use any of its powers for two Combat Turns per level of the quality. Characters may purchase another level of this quality at skill rank 8 and skill rank 12. Adepts with the Killing Hands power may receive the higher levels of this quality if they raise their Astral Combat skill to skill rank 6 and then skill rank 8.

SPIRITUAL LODGE
5 KARMA

Minimum Requirements:
Ritual Spellcasting 6, Artisan 3

The magician can create a magical lodge through meditation without the need for materials. For every hour that the magician meditates, the lodge increases by 1 in Force, with a radius of Force in meters. A group of magicians of the same tradition with this quality can quickly build a foundation for ritual magic, as they can increase the Force of the lodge by 1 per hour per magician. Maximum Force of the Lodge is two times the highest magician's Magic Rating. The lodge activates when the magician stops meditating. This lodge lasts until the next sunset or sunrise. This lodge has no physical presence, save for a sense of calmness within.

SPIRITUAL PILGRIM [BUDDHISM]
5 KARMA

Minimum Requirements: Assensing 4 and Academic Knowledge: Magical Theory 3

A character with this quality has learned to take on the energy of new places rather than fight it instinctively. They acclimate to one point of background count every three days instead of every ten days.

SPRAWL TAMER
10 KARMA

Minimum Requirements: Animal Handling 6

The Sprawl Tamer is a magical beast master of the urban jungle. The number of tricks (p.184, *Howling Shadows*) a critter is capable of learning is increased to twice the critter's Logic. Domesticated critters (p.186, *Howling Shadows*) that a

Sprawl Tamer trains have the number of tricks they can learn increased to triple their Logic. Additionally, the Sprawl Tamer is always opposed by the critter's Willpower x 2 when asserting dominance, regardless of the type of critter. Lastly, the threshold for training any type of critter is reduced by 1.

STALWART ALLY

15 KARMA

Minimum Requirements: Ally spirit and Binding 4

A character with this quality has an ally spirit that has been with them for a long time. Their connection with this spirit is particularly deep and has extra benefits. Once per day, a character with this quality or their ally spirit may give a point of Edge to the other member of the pair; this can only be done by one of them per day, not both of them. This point of Edge lasts until sunrise or sunset, whichever comes first. Additionally, either the spirit or the conjurer may spend a Complex Action to add their Force or Magic attribute as a dice pool bonus to a single Drain Resistance test that the other member of the pair will make within the same Combat Turn.

TABOO TRANSFORMER [WICCA]

15 KARMA

Minimum Requirements: Spellcasting 4 (with Manipulation Spells specialization), Zoology 5, and the Shapechange or (Critter) Form spell

A character with this quality can use the Shapechange or (Critter) Form spells on involuntary targets. The spellcaster must succeed in a Spellcasting + Magic [Force] vs. Body (+ Counterspelling) Opposed Test. The spell's Force must also equal or exceed the subject's Body attribute. Subtract 1 from the resulting critter's base attribute ratings for every hit the caster generates, down to a minimum of 1. The mental attributes of the target remain unchanged.

VEXCRAFT

7 KARMA

Minimum Requirements: Suppress Focus (LOS): Disenchanting 6, Grounding Focus (LOS): Disenchanting 10

SUPPRESS FOCUS (LOS)

Suppress Focus is a more powerful version of Deactivate Focus that disrupts the focus for a number of Combat Turns, depending on the outcome (and net hits) of the Disenchanting + Magic [Astral] v. target's Force + owner's Magic Test. Suppression lasts for (net hits) Combat Turns.

GROUNDING FOCUS (LOS)

The magician uses the interface with a construct to overheat the focus with magic so that it damages its owner with jolts of arcane energy. The test is a Disenchanting + Magic [Astral] v. target's Force + owner's Magic Opposed Test. If the arcane hacker succeeds, the focus' owner receives Stun damage equal to the focus Force + any net hits that were achieved by the attacker. The target does not resist the damage. This can also be applied to fetishes (treat the Force of a fetish as being zero). If successful, the fetish is destroyed. In either test, spending a point of Edge by the magician can turn the damage from Stun to Physical.

WORSHIP LEADER

5 KARMA

Minimum Requirements: Leadership 4, Ritual Spellcasting 5

The worship leader is able to make use of mundane participants in Ritual Spellcasting tests as long as they believe in her tradition. For every (60/Charisma) mundane participants who are willing to participate in the ritual, the leader receives a +1 bonus to their dice pool and to the limit of the ritual. The maximum bonus that a leader can receive from mundane participants is equal to their Ritual Spellcasting skill rank.

FOCUSED AWAKENED

Some Awakened choose to focus their talents in a particular area, gaining skills in one area of expertise at the expense of others. Other Awakened are trying to make the best of their limited abilities. Here are some different ways Awakened individuals focus their abilities.

THE ELEMENTALIST

The Elementalist emphasizes their magic toward one of the four elements (earth, air, fire, water). This focus is not only with spells, but of spirits too. Such a strong devotion does cost parts of the Awakened's capability in other areas.

- Cannot take any skills from the Enchanting skill group.
- Cannot astrally project.
- Must choose one of the four elements (earth, air, fire, water).
- Can only cast spells of the category specified by the element in their tradition.
- Can only summon spirits of the chosen element in the fashion of their tradition.
- Receive +2 dice in Banishing/Binding skill tests spirits of the element they've chosen.
- Get –2 dice in Banishing/Binding skill tests for spirits not of the element they've chosen.

THE HEDGE WITCH/WIZARD

Hedge wizardry contains those who for some reason have an unusual focus with regard to Spellcasting. They have a talent for one spell category that inexplicably causes teir aptitude for other spell categories to atrophy. While they are often lumped together with aspected magicians like Sorcerers, they are still talented in Alchemy for the same spell category.

- Cannot take the Conjuring skill group.
- Cannot astrally project.
- Choose a spell category (Combat, Health, Detection, Illusion, Manipulation); hedge wizards can only learn/cast spells/create preparations of that category. Rituals can be done only if they relate to spells of the chosen category.
- Reduce drain in the casting of spells and preparations of the chosen category by 2.
- Hedge wizards get –2 dice for Dispelling/Disenchanting spells and preparations of other spell categories.

THE NULL WIZARD

The null wizard is an odd manifestation of magic. These Awakened, if you call them that, cannot actually create anything magical. They are, however, talented in disrupting or redirecting magic.

How some individuals have Awakened this way is a mystery, though one theory suggests that the metahuman condition as a whole subconsciously perceives magical threats, and some manifest this awareness as null wizards.

- Cannot use any of the following skills: Alchemy, Artificing, Binding, Ritual Spellcasting, or Spellcasting.
- Cannot astrally project.
- Gains Reflection metamagic for free (p.151, *Street Grimoire*).
- Gains Spell Resistance quality for free.

THE SEER

The seer is theorized to be the earliest manifestation of the rise of magic, with the exception of "spike babies." It's also one of the hardest to prove, as the people involved do not manifest magical talent. Seers, as a category, also include dreamwalkers—those that can astrally project. Those who believe this theory have theorized that authors like H.P Lovecraft and L. Frank Baum were aspected magicians whose inspiration came from the astral planes.

- Cannot take any magical skill group.
- Astral Perception is a Complex Action instead of a Simple Action.
- Gains psychometry metamagic for free (p. 145, *Street Grimoire*).
- Gains sensing metamagic for free (p. 158, *Street Grimoire*).

NEW METAMAGICS

PARADIGM SHIFT

Perhaps the single most interesting technique yet discovered, paradigm shift allows a magician to set aside their old tradition and choose a new one. Once chosen, this new tradition defines their use of magic, and they lose all access to their old tradition. When the magician initiates again, they may choose paradigm shift as the new metamagic if they wish to change again.

PARADIGM SHIFT: INSECT SHAMAN

Leaving their old tradition behind, the magician now follows the insect shaman tradition. This differs from a normal paradigm shift in two ways. The first is that the magician may never take another

paradigm shift to leave this tradition. The second is that the insect patron gifts the magician with Karma equal to what it cost to initiate and take this technique. That's so kind! You'd think that there'd be something in the fine print about paying the queen back with something else down the line, but maybe the queen assumed the candidate would be aware.

PARADIGM SHIFT: TOXIC

This is less something you learn, more something you become. Any magician may turn toxic once given a good enough reason, or having been exposed to enough corrupted energy. On the downside, there is no known way for a toxic mage to leave this tradition behind and take a new paradigm. On the positive side, the act of going toxic gifts the magician with Karma equal to what it cost to initiate and take this technique. All it cost was their sanity ...

SPIRIT EXPANSION: UMT

Requirement: Must be able to summon at least five types of spirit

One of the defining moments in Universal Magic Theory was when a group of shamans in Prague were able to call forth an elemental, previously the exclusive domain of hermetic magicians. It took some time to perfect the technique, but it has since been expanded. Each time that this technique is taken, the magician learns to summon one new type of spirit, chosen from air, earth, fire, water, beasts, man, guardian, guidance, plant, or task. As the new spirit is from outside the magician's tradition, they do not slot into a spellcasting area, but may otherwise serve as normal for a spirit of their kind.

SPIRIT EXPANSION: SHEDIM

Requirement: Must be able to summon at least one spirit. Must negotiate with a master shedim who knows the metamagic.

With the closing of the DeeCee portal, the pathway for more shedim spirits to enter our world was lost. This meant that each one destroyed or banished was one less that would ever exist here. Realizing that extinction was the final result, several master shedim in Europe gathered together and crafted a technique not unlike that of insect shamans, allowing them to teach a metahuman to

summon their kind. In exchange for serving a new master, the shedim would be allowed entry into this plane of existence and, like any spirit, would have a small chance of slipping free. These master shedim have been quietly teaching this technique in hopes of saving their kind. Most magicians who have seen it call it "necromancy," conflating it with previously discovered necromantic traditions, an error that the shedim have seen no reason to correct. A shedim summoner may also summon a master shedim as a great form ritual.

IMPROVED ASTRAL FORM

A magician draws energy from their body to create the astral form, leaving their physical frame in a sleep-like state in the process. Those who take this technique have learned to draw more energy, putting their frame in a deeper slumber in exchange for more time away from it. This technique allows the magician to add their initiate level to the duration that they may remain projected. If this technique is used, the deep slumber means that it takes one minute for a magician's body to wake up after the astral form rejoins it.

ASTRALNAUT

Requirement: Must know improved astral form

By truly mastering the act of drawing energy from the physical frame, an astralnaut can drain so much that their body enters a coma, their physical processes slowing to a crawl. This allows the magician to greatly expand the duration of their astral jaunts, including metaplanar explorations. When using this technique, the magician's allowed time in an astral form is measured in days, not hours. Due to the coma-like state, it requires twenty-four hours for the magician's body to wake up once the astral form has rejoined it.

STRUCTURED SPELLCASTING

This metamagic seeks to take the risk (and some reward) out of spellcasting by making it more tame and controlled. A mage with this metamagic may not use reckless spellcasting. Another effect of this metamagic is that in no case whatsoever may the mage ignore the limit on Spellcasting tests, even by using reagents or Edge. For giving up this freedom, the drain the mage suffers for casting spells is reduced by 1 (but always at least 1).

TAROT SUMMONING

Only usable by mages of the tarot tradition

This metamagic may be taken up to five times. At the first level of Tarot Summoning, mages choose one suit of the tarot: blades, coins, batons, or cups. The mage can only summon spirits from this suit using tarot summoning (see **Tarot Summoning** sidebar, p. 93). If a card is drawn that is not of a suit chosen by the mage, no spirit is summoned (or a spirit is summoned but refuses to obey the mage, gamemaster's discretion). Tarot mages may remove suits from their deck that they are unable to summon, but only entire suits, rather than individual cards of some suits

For each additional time tarot summoning is chosen, the mage may select another suit that they are able to summon. When a tarot mage takes the fifth and final level of Tarot Summoning, they are then able to summon the Major Arcana.

RECKLESS NECRO CONJURING

Unlike normal reckless conjuring (p. 192, *Street Grimoire*), reckless necro conjuring allows a necro mage to summon a spirit without a Necro Summoning ritual. When reckless necro conjuring is used, a necro mage summons a necro spirit in the same way a normal mage would summon a spirit, except the host needed for the spirit (see **Necro Summoning Ritual**, p. 52) is still required. Only one necro spirit can be summoned at a time in this fashion, and the mage must resist drain like a normal mage does when summoning a spirit, except the drain value is now equal to two times the hits (not net hits) on the spirit's defense test, with a minimum drain value of 4. This metamagic only applies to summoning necro spirits.

NOBLE SACRIFICE

Superficially similar to blood magic, the noble sacrifice metamagic is actually its opposite. The Awakened individual with noble sacrifice is convinced of the inherent goodness of risking harm to one's self for the benefit of others. As such, when they are suffering on behalf of others, they become much more powerful than they would be otherwise.

This metamagic requires the mage to take a Free Action to activate. Once activated, the mage designates a metahuman individual or individuals within X meters of themselves (where X is Magic Rating). When any of these individuals take damage, it applies instead to the magician, who may resist it normally, as if the damage was happening directly to them (before the designated individual(s) do their own resistance rolls). Their own stats, skills, and attributes are used to resist the damage. Every three boxes of Physical or Stun damage suffered by the magician in this way generate one Protection Magic Point that must be used before the end of the next Combat Turn.

Protection Magic Points generated by noble sacrifice can be used in any of the following ways, in any combination:

- Increase the Force of a non-offensive spell or ritual being cast by one per point; this can exceed twice the caster's Magic Rating.
- Reduce the amount of drain a Health spell inflicts by one per point, to a minimum of 0.
- Increase the Force of a summoned spirit by one per point.

Additionally, if the magician has not attacked an enemy this round, they receive +4 dice to Spellcasting, Counterspelling, and Ritual Spellcasting tests using Protection Magic Points.

HARMONIOUS DEFENSE

A character with harmonious defense has learned the ability to use their connection to magic to shield themselves and others from hostile magic. When the adept declares that they will use harmonious defense (a Free Action), they receive a dice pool equal to their Willpower + Magic + initiate grade, which can be used in the same fashion as spell defense dice from the Counterspelling skill. Note that whenever an adept uses harmonious defense, they automatically begin perceiving astrally.

HARMONIOUS REFLECTION

Harmonious reflection is the adept version of the reflection metamagic. Instead of using the Counterspelling Skill, however, the adept focuses their own magic and discipline to counter offensive magic.

If an adept using harmonious defense sees that they or those they're protecting with spell defense are being targeted by a spell, they can use an Interrupt Action to protect the group instead. With each reflection, the adept uses up 1 die from the harmonious defense dice pool. If no more harmonious defense dice remain, then harmonious defense cannot be used. Using harmonious reflection is described below.

HARMONIOUS REFLECTION

INTERRUPT ACTION
(–5 INITIATIVE SCORE)
Prerequisite: Harmonious Defense,
Way of Unified Mana (Hapsum-Do)

With this action, the adept can use Willpower + Magic [Astral] versus the caster's Spellcasting test. If the reflecting adept scores more hits than the spellcaster, the spell is redirected back at the caster at half the spell's Force, and the original target takes no damage. The reflecting adept suffers drain as if they had used a Reckless Spellcasting action to cast it (increasing the customary drain by 3). This reflected spell only affects the caster, regardless of whether it was an area-effect spell or not. Treat the net hits in reflecting as Spellcasting hits, as if the adept were a magician and had actually cast it. This would add to any net hits from the original Spellcasting test. If the adept does not get more hits than the caster, then the spell hits as if the magician didn't attempt to defend against it. If the adept instead takes –8 to their initiative score and uses 1 Edge, then the spell is reflected back at the caster at full strength, rather than half.

EXPANDED ASPECTS

While the three standard aspected magicians (conjurer, sorcerer, and enchanter) are well known, they shouldn't be thought of as the be-all end-all of options. Three of these "lost" aspects follow, plus a brief note of the Aware, the least magically active of all.

ASPECTED AWAKENED ABILITIES

TYPE	CONJURING	SPELLCASTING	POWERS	ENCHANTING	PROJECTION	PERCEPTION
Full Magician	X	X	—	X	X	X
Mystic Adept	X	X	X	—	—	X
Adept	—	—	X	—	—	†
Apprentice	*	*	—	—	—	X
Enchanter	—	—	—	X	—	X
Explorer	—	—	—	—	X	X
Aware	—	—	—	—	—	X

† Physical adepts do not gain astral perception by default, but they may take it as an adept power.

* Apprentices may cast spells from only one category of spell and may summon only one category of spirits.

THE APPRENTICE

(PURCHASED AS A NORMAL ASPECTED MAGICIAN)

Once known as shamanic adepts, dating back to when they were first discovered in 2011, the rise of the Universal Magic Theory, and the spread of mentors beyond shamanic circles, led to a renaming that continues to be debated in academic circles. More interesting is that there are some apprentices who have never had a mentor, instead following a tradition that doesn't invoke them, such as psionicist. Regardless of the philosophical side, the thaumaturgical side of this aspect is quite well known. Apprentices may cast a single category of spells (Combat, Health, etc.), summon a single type of spirit (air, beast, etc.) appropriate to their tradition, and have astral perception. This puts them in a middle ground between conjurers and sorcerers, with the vast majority matching their access to the bonuses provided by a mentor. Thus, someone who can summon water spirits is well-served following the Sea, while one who casts healing spells is helped by following Bear. An apprentice is not required to take the Mentor Spirit quality, but most do all the same.

THE ENCHANTER (OPTIONAL)

(PRIORITY C: MAGIC 5, ONE RATING 4 MAGICAL SKILL GROUP)

Familiar to most magicians as "just talismongers," enchanters are, in fact, one type of aspected magician, just one that tends to avoid the dangerous life of a shadowrunner in order to shine as a sort of a support network for other magicians. In addition to talismongers, some find work as alchemists, others as artisans and craftsmen whose work contains a magical quality, and still others undertake a dangerous life of questing after reagents, training themselves as dangerous combatants who also happen to have a magical trick in their back pocket. In particular, several people who hunt paracritters, up to and including dragon slayers, are often enchanters behind all the bristling weaponry. Enchanters cannot cast spells, summon spirits, or astrally project, but they have a Magic Rating and may use skills from the Enchanting skill group and related abilities such as searching for reagents. They may also use astral perception. This quality may be selected in place of the normal aspected enchanter for this priority level at the discretion of the gamemaster.

THE EXPLORER

(PRIORITY C, MAGIC 5, TWO RATING 6 MAGICAL SKILLS)

Perhaps the most overlooked mages of all, explorers possess the rare ability of astral projection, as well as astral perception. The bravest of them serve as trailblazers, testing the limits of the metaplanes, but many simply serve as astral protectors, selling their services to guard areas or provide personal astral protection. Most consider the astral plane to be a fun place to explore as a hobby, but they focus more on their mundane life. While the explorer has neither spirits at their beck

MENTOR TABLE

MENTOR	SPELLS	HERMETIC	SHAMAN
Bear	Health	Man	Earth
Cat	Illusion	Water	Air
Dog	Detection	Air	Water
Dragonslayer	Combat	Fire	Beasts
Eagle	Detection	Air	Air
Fire-Bringer	Manipulation	Fire	Ma
Mountain	Health	Earth	Earth
Rat	Manipulation	Earth	Beasts
Raven	Manipulation	Air	Ma
Sea	Detection	Water	Water
Seducer	Illusion	Fire	Man
Shark	Combat	Water	Beasts
Snake	Detection	Man	Water
Thunderbird	Combat	Air	Air
Wise Warrior	Combat	Fire	Man
Wolf	Combat	Earth	Beasts
Berserker	Combat	Fire	Beasts
Chaos	Illusion	Water	Air
Peacemaker	Detection	Air	Water
Oracle	Detection	Fire	Water
Adversary	Manipulation	Man	Man
Alligator	Combat	Man	Water
Bat	Detection	Air	Air
Monkey	Manipulation	Man	Man
Boar	Combat	Earth	Beasts
Giraffe	Detection	Air	Earth
Dolphin	Health	Water	Water
Whale	Detection	Water	Water
Horse	Health	Air	Earth
Raccoon	Manipulation	Earth	Beasts
Spider	Illusion	Man	Air

and call nor the power of spellcasting, their vast experience in the astral realm often leaves them extremely dangerous, doubly so when facing the more typical mage who has never developed their own skills in astral combat.

THE AWARE

(PRIORITY D; MAGIC 3, ONE RATING 4 MAGICAL SKILL)

While most "sparks" have so little magic that they're not worth consideration, one type, the aware, are. The aware have astral perception as their lone magical ability, a truly minor ability that nonetheless sets them higher than the truly mundane. The aware have been known for ages as readers of auras, palms, or other forms of psychometry, but simply being able to see magical activity is power enough to serve them as researchers, observing the magic used by others and taking note. The largest place for them, by far, is in the world of security, serving in personal security details to ensure no magic is used to influence negotiations, to keep an eye out for spiritual intrusion, or to direct security details against enchanted intruders. Several have found a place as musicians as well, as being able to read the emotional state of a crowd and adjusting their performance to it is a significant asset.

NEW SPELLS

BRANCH

MANIPULATION SPELL (PHYSICAL)
Type: P	**Range:** LOS
Duration: S	**Drain:** F – 2

VINES

MANIPULATION SPELL (PHYSICAL, AREA)
Type: P	**Range:** LOS (A)
Duration: S	**Drain:** F – 1

THORN

MANIPULATION SPELL (PHYSICAL)
Type: P	**Range:** LOS
Duration: S	**Drain:** F

ROSEBUSH

MANIPULATION SPELL (PHYSICAL, AREA)
Type: P	**Range:** LOS (A)
Duration: S	**Drain:** F + 2

These spells are used by the spellcaster to conjure plant life and bind the target with branches or vines that spring from the ground. Every net hit reduces the target's Agility by 1. If Agility is reduced to 0, the target is constricted by the plants and unable to move or use their limbs. Bound targets may still defend and dodge against attacks, but they suffer a dice-pool modifier equal to the caster's net hits. A bound target may attempt to break free of the plants by making an Opposed Test, pitting Strength + Body against the spell's Force x 2.

Branch and Thorn work on single targets, while Vines and Thornbush are area spells.

Thorn and Rosebush have the additional effect of damaging the target. At the end of every Combat Turn, including the one in which the target was bound, these spells inflict damage equal to the net hits of the spell, with an AP of -(spell's Force).

GROWTH

MANIPULATION SPELL (PHYSICAL)
Type: P	**Range:** LOS
Duration: S	**Drain:** F + 3

The growth spell causes the target's physical attributes to grow (and if the caster desires, the target grows larger as well). For every three net hits (minimum 1), the target's Body, Agility, Reflex, and Strength temporarily increases by 1 for as long as the spell is maintained. If the caster desires the target to grow physically larger as well, the target grows half a meter for every three nets hits.

LASH

COMBAT SPELL (INDIRECT)
Type: P	**Range:** LOS	**Damage:** P
Duration: I	**Drain:** F	

SLASH

COMBAT SPELL (INDIRECT, AREA)
Type: P	**Range:** LOS (A)	**Damage:** P
Duration: I	**Drain:** F + 3	

Depending on the mage's tradition, Lash can manifest as a whip, a tentacle, a vine, or even a stream of water. No matter the form, however, Lash stretches across the divide between caster and target, striking them with incredible force. For every two boxes of unresisted physical damage this spell does, the target also takes one box of stun damage. Lash affects a single target, while Slash affects an area.

CLAW

COMBAT SPELL (INDIRECT)
Type: P **Range:** LOS **Damage:** P
Duration: I **Drain:** F

BARRAGE

COMBAT SPELL (INDIRECT, AREA)
Type: P **Range:** LOS (A) **Damage:** P
Duration: I **Drain:** F + 3

The Claw and Barrage spells manifest sharp shards of mana resembling claws (or talons, nails, spikes, etc.) that tear into the target, rending armor and flesh alike. The damage value for this spell is reduced by 2, but the AP rating is increased by 4.

MULTIPLY FOOD

HEALTH SPELL (ESSENCE)
Type: P **Range:** T
Duration: Permanent **Drain:** F - 2

Multiply Food allows the spellcaster to effectively make copies of any food that she or he is touching. This food is not created from mana, but rather, the space around the food is altered to magically speed up and duplicate the natural processes which produced it. For each hit on the spellcasting test, whatever food is touched by the caster is multiplied by ten. That is, one soyburger becomes ten soyburgers, two loafs of bread becomes twenty, and so on. Food that has been duplicated in this manner cannot be duplicated again.

COMET

**COMBAT SPELL
(INDIRECT, AREA, ELEMENTAL)**
Type: P **Range:** LOS (A) **Damage:** P
Duration: I **Drain:** F

Comet creates a flaming ball of earth that appears above the targets and slams into them with

a violent explosion. The melting earth acts as both fire damage and acid damage (p. 170, *SR5*). Only the associated effects, not the damage itself, may be mitigated by fire or acid resistance.

GRAVITY

MANIPULATION SPELL (PHYSICAL)
Type: P **Range:** LOS
Duration: S **Drain:** F + 1

GRAVITY WELL

**MANIPULATION SPELL
(PHYSICAL, AREA)**
Type: P **Range:** LOS (A)
Duration: S **Drain:** F + 3

Gravity spells alter the fundamental forces of the universe around the targets, magically applying gravitational force to them like that of far more massive objects. Every net hit results in a dice pool modifier of –1 for all actions connected to Physical attributes the target takes, including Initiative rolls. If the penalty to the target's dice pool is greater than their Strength attribute, the gravity is too strong and they are unable to move. Bound targets may still defend and dodge against attacks, but they suffer a dice-pool modifier equal to the caster's net hits. Targets of Gravity spells may make a Strength + Body Test with a threshold of the caster's net hits to break free, but they only can make this test after being held motionless for a Combat Turn. Even if they succeed in this test, the dice-pool modifier remains. Gravity affects a single target, while Gravity Well affects an area (including the caster and allies, if applicable).

EVIL EYE

DIRECT COMBAT
Type: M **Range:** LOS
Duration: I **Drain:** F - 3

Legends of the evil eye usually take the form of a curse upon a person, causing them misfortune. In this case, the Evil Eye is a mental attack causing the opponent indecision. Net hits from this attack reduce an opponent's initiative score. The opponent feels the attack with psychosomatic dread (hairs on the back of the neck standing up, fear in the pit of their stomach, etc.). Each net hit on the Spellcasting test decreases the target's initiative score by 1.

ALTER BALLISTICS

MANIPULATION SPELL, PHYSICAL

Type: P   **Range:** T
Duration: I   **Drain:** (F−2)

The Alter Ballistics spell is a spell unique to the Alchemical Armorer that allows them to alter the ballistic properties of bullets or add helpful effects like noise reduction. This spell only works as an alchemical preparation that uses a bullet as the lynchpin. Bullets used as a lynchpin may only be fired by Single Shot weapons. The preparation must be activated before it is fired or the lynchpin will be destroyed by firing the bullet. When using a command trigger, a character may choose to activate a single preparation normally (with a Simple Action) or any number of bullets (including all of them) at a time with a Complex Action. When activated, the preparation lasts for a number of minutes equal to the Force of the preparation. When crafting the lynchpin, the character must specify and make a record of the effects they would like the bullet to have, in order, from most desired to least desired. When the preparation is activated, each net hit will add the listed properties to the bullet in the specified order until net hits or the list of chosen effects is exhausted.

LIST OF EFFECTS

1. Double weapon range (changing all categories of range modifiers).

2. -4 dice pool modifier to Perception tests to notice gunfire.

3. +1 Accuracy.

4. *Deformation Resistance:* -2 AP, -1 DV. Deformation-resistant bullets do not deform when fired or upon impact, which inflicts a -4 dice pool penalty to any Armorer tests to identify the weapon that fired the bullet. Cannot be used with hollow-point ammunition.

5. *Increased Deformation:* +2 AP, +1 DV. Cannot be used with APDS.

6. Astral signature fade time reduced by 50 percent.

7. *Impact Dispersion:* Reduces the Physical limit of a character by 2 when comparing it to the DV to determine knockdown.

8. *Frangible:* Treat any barrier the ammo hits as if its Armor were twice normal.

NEW RITUALS

FOREST TRANSFORMATION (ANCHORED)

Like the Shapeshifting spell, this ritual changes the type of non-Awakened tree growing in a location. The area affected is Force x 100 meters. The type of tree that it can be changed into is any other non-Awakened tree known to the leader. This ritual was used to transform the pine woods of Ireland to the diverse forests of Tír na nÓg. When the ritual ends, the trees have changed permanently. The number of hits from the ritual determines the number of trees within the area that are transformed. The transformation is permanent, though if the climate doesn't agree with the tree, it will die over time.

Ritual takes (Force) hours to complete.

NECRO SUMMONING
(MINION) RITUAL

This ritual is similar to homunculus and corpse cadavre, but instead fills the dead or inanimate objects with spirits from the Dominion of the Black. Necro Summoning changes the nature of the thing inhabited, including fire, earth, or plants.

Unlike a corpse cadavre, a dead body (metahuman or otherwise) retains no knowledge of its former life, nor any of its skills. It is just a shell for inhabitation, raw material to use on our plane. Use the Force of the spirit for any skill ratings the spirit has. A necromantic spirit will last for a number of days equal to net hits on the Sealing test times the sum of the participants' Magic ratings. Net hits cannot be used to raise more necro spirits. Once the number of days is over, the necro spirit exits the form it was using; if the form was corporeal, it becomes a shapeless mass. Necro mages may summon a number of necro spirits equal to their (Magic Rating - 6, minimum 1). Each spirit that is under the control of the necro mage reduces the effective Magic Rating of the mage by 1. So if a necro mage has Magic 8, but has two spirits summoned, they will only be able to use magic as if they had a Magic Rating of 6 until the spirits spend out their time. They cannot be voluntarily dismissed.

The stats for necro spirits are below. In order to use necro summoning, an appropriate vessel must be available—an animal carcass, metahuman corpse, dead tree, or sufficient quantity of ashes or dust.

NECRO SPIRITS

CARCASS SPIRIT
(REQUIRES DEAD ANIMAL CARCASS)

B	A	R	S	W	L	I	C	EDG	ESS	M
F+3	F	F	F+2	F	F	F	F–1	F / 2	F	F

Physical Initiative	(F x 2) + 2D6
Astral Initiative	(F x 2) + 3D6
Skills	Assensing, Astral Combat, Perception, Unarmed Combat
Powers	Animal Control, Astral Form, Deathly Aura, Enhanced Senses: Hearing, Enhanced Senses: Low-Light Vision, Enhanced Senses: Smell, Fear, Immunity to Normal Weapons, Immunity to Pathogens, Immunity to Toxins, Movement, Possession, Sapience
Optional Powers	Concealment, Confusion, Guard, Natural Weapon, Noxious Breath, Paralyzing Touch, Search, Venom

CORPSE SPIRIT

(REQUIRES CORPSE OF METAHUMAN)

B	A	R	S	W	L	I	C	EDG	ESS	M
F+2	F−1	F+2	F−2	F	F	F+1	F−1	F/2	F	F

Physical Initiative	((F x 2) + 2) + 2D6
Astral Initiative	(F x 2) + 3D6
Skills	Assensing, Astral Combat, Perception, Unarmed Combat
Powers	Accident, Astral Form, Concealment, Confusion, Deathly Aura, Enhanced Senses (Low-Light, Thermographic Vision), Guard, Immunity to Normal Weapons, Immunity to Pathogens, Immunity to Toxins, Influence, Possession, Sapience, Search
Optional Powers	Concealment, Confusion, Fear, Guard, Movement, Noxious Breath, Paralyzing Touch, Psychokinesis, Search

ROT SPIRIT

(REQUIRES DEAD PLANT, TREE, ETC.)

B	A	R	S	W	L	I	C	EDG	ESS	M
F+3	F−2	F	F+1	F	F−1	F	F−1	F/2	F	F

Physical Initiative	(F x 2) + 2D6
Astral Initiative	(F x 2) + 3D6
Skills	Assensing, Astral Combat, Counterspelling, Exotic Ranged Weapon, Perception, Unarmed Combat
Powers	Astral Form, Concealment, Confusion, Deathly Aura, Engulf, Fear, Guard, Immunity to Normal Weapons, Immunity to Pathogens, Immunity to Toxins, Magical Guard, Possession, Sapience, Silence
Optional Powers	Accident, Confusion, Movement, Noxious Breath, Paralyzing Touch, Search

PALEFIRE SPIRIT

(REQUIRES LARGE AMOUNT OF ASHES FROM A DEAD FIRE)

B	A	R	S	W	L	I	C	EDG	ESS	M
F+2	F+1	F+3	F−2	F	F	F+1	F−1	F/2	F	F

Physical Initiative	((F x 2) + 3) + 2D6
Astral Initiative	(F x 2) + 3D6
Skills	Assensing, Astral Combat, Exotic Ranged Weapon, Flight, Perception, Unarmed Combat
Powers	Accident, Astral Form, Confusion, Elemental Attack, Deathly Aura, Engulf, Immunity to Normal Weapons, Immunity to Pathogens, Immunity to Toxins, Possession, Sapience
Optional Powers	Fear, Guard, Noxious Breath, Paralyzing Touch, Search

DETRITUS SPIRIT

(REQUIRES LARGE AMOUNT OF DUST OR LIFELESS EARTH)

B	A	R	S	W	L	I	C	EDG	ESS	M
F+5	F−3	F−1	F+4	F	F−1	F	F−1	F/2	F	F

Physical Initiative	((F x 2) − 1) + 2D6
Astral Initiative	(F x 2) + 3D6
Skills	Assensing, Astral Combat, Exotic Ranged Weapon, Perception, Unarmed Combat
Powers	Astral Form, Binding, Deathly Aura, Guard, Immunity to Normal Weapons, Immunity to Pathogens, Immunity to Toxins, Possession, Sapience, Search
Optional Powers	Elemental Attack, Engulf, Fear, Paralyzing Touch, Search

TEA & SYMPATHY

The sounds of their bickering could be heard through the thick, real oak doors of the Taoist temple. Even from across its expanse. Even to human ears. But the thing that smiled to himself had not been human for a very, very long time.

The vast creak and clatter of metal fittings announced the arrival of his students, even if one of them thought he was the teacher. Red dropped his voluminous hood, shaking off the ash-tainted rain, while the younger one, EB, closed a clear plastic umbrella with LED lining its outer rim. She seemed about to say something to him before she paused, turning to take in the vast chamber, a long stretch flanked by great pillars, hung with silks and censers that made the air heavy with scented smoke. The shadows in the ceiling and between the pillars gave the impression of a great, unknown space overhead, so that the warm abyss might be as big as a cathedral. Across the room, three great statues, each taller than a troll, sat on golden thrones. And standing between two of them, lighting fresh coals with a flame at the end of one long, black talon, the Incense Master of the Yellow Lotus Triad, Su Cheng.

EB hesitated before she followed Red, trying to match his casual stride. She wasn't used to feeling humbled by a place. The smoke, the hangings, even the way the red carpet muffled her boot steps—the whole of the place seemed to swallow her, making her feel minute. More than that, from the moment she had crossed the threshold, she felt the aspect of the place. It was as

sudden as stepping out of a crisp, cool night and into a sauna. Even through the thick blanket of mana, she could feel the vast power of the figure before her, contained only barely by his masking. She wondered if even mundanes could feel it when they entered this place. Would it inspire awe? Would they call it faith?

Blinking the sting from her eyes, she approached the lone figure in the temple. Just ahead of her, Red bowed low and spoke. It was as though the smoke absorbed the sound.

"Good evening, Great Master."

The Incense Master turned, a broad, open smile greeting them. His eyes cast a sickly yellow glow in the hanging fog, and his canines were already extended. Among some Infected circles she had run with, that was either a sign of trust or dominance. Given his status, and seeing his power, she hoped for the former.

"Richard! And you bring your young friend." Su Cheng's voice creaked like an old tenement on the verge of collapse, words feigning false surprise and false frailty. He turned to them, folding his hands together under the great volume of his heavy silken robes.

"I appreciate you taking the time."

The elder vampire dismissed Red's words with a wave, descending the steps to stand closer than EB liked. He extended a talon under her chin, lifting it to look into her eyes. His hands, his smile, his words were like knives, and she knew instinctively that he spilled blood with all three. His grin deepened, and she felt defiance rise in her like sickness. She jerked free, scowling

BY KEVIN CZARNECKI

at him. He cackled, the light in his eyes dimming, and he turned and walked to a side room. With a casual pass of his hand, the pressure seemed to diminish, and she drew a long, quiet breath before following.

Past a lacquered door, a hallway lined with chambers on either side, a glance through their curtains showing an esoteric collection of knicknacks: a tea set and pillows behind one, a suit of mil-spec armor standing on display behind another. And then the hallway opened to a sprawling, empty space. The floor was soft underneath, like at a gym or dojo, the walls clear of ornamentation or clutter. Only a single row of pillars bordered the space on all sides. Here, the pressure was all but gone, no more present than the lingering incense on her clothes.

Su Cheng turned, suddenly, his yellowed smile hideously wide.

He's just one of us, she reminded herself. *He's just old. I can take care of myself. I know what he is.*

She almost reminded herself that Red would never let the elder vampire hurt her, but just the beginning of the thought frustrated her. Fear wasn't her style.

"But ignorance is?"

She looked at the amber-eyed monster.

"Does listening to this stupid lesson mean I have to deal with having you in my mind?"

Su Cheng's expression softened, and he lowered his gaze modestly. "I am sorry. Your thoughts are simply so loud. Can you blame the neighbor when your voice carries so far?"

She blinked. "You can't just read minds. We don't do that. You have to want to. You have to cast a spell."

"It is not a spell, simply your aura."

"I can see auras, too, you know. I don't see how you could make out something I don't."

Red, looking at the floor, grinned. "Precisely why I brought you here."

Su Cheng held a single finger before Red, silencing him, his eyes never leaving EB's. He studied her for a moment before turning away.

"Richard tells me you paint, yes?"

She glanced at Red. The chatty vampire was quieter than she'd ever seen him.

"Yeah."

"And he tells me you do not fully comprehend the idea of traditions?"

She scoffed. "I 'comprehend' them just fine. I—"

A single finger again, held where she could see it. Her mouth stopped before she chose to start speaking, but she felt no spell.

"Forgive me, I misspoke." He turned, and his expression was calm, moderate. He exuded contemplation. "You do not respect the differences in perspective. Rick only mentioned magic. I inferred that it encompassed much more."

He laughed, warm and affable, and waved a hand. Through the ether and astral, energy coiled into color, otherworldly mass into shape, and Su Cheng stood next to EB, waving his hands much like people did with manual VR. The colors separated into three blobs, like floating paint: yellow, red, blue.

"What do you see?"

She glanced at Red. He only stood there with his hands in his jeans pockets, smiling and nodding for her to answer.

"I see the three primary colors."

"Indeed! Three colors that no other color could mix to make, yet which can be combined to create any other color in the spectrum of regular human vision." As he spoke, his hands wove patterns lazily, and the globes split as though in zero-g, each breaking into dozens of smaller bubbles of different sizes, mixing and matching until the dozens represented varying shades like a watercolor palette.

He continued. "You see the way colors can be combined. You see the root of new things that will be from the components of what are. Some cannot see that."

...

"So?"

He smirked. "Perhaps we try this ..."

He wove his hands again, and the colors split wildly, recomposing themselves into new shapes, until the blues had taken on the form of the coat of a young girl, the shades of water behind her, the deep of her eyes. The yellows into hats and hair, the reds into hats and blossoms.

"Do you know this work?"

EB didn't hesitate. "Two Sisters, Renoir, 1881." She said it without any attitude. She didn't notice Red blink in surprise.

"Good," Su Cheng said, weaving his hands again until the colors had melted and reformed into a great image of a soup can.

"It's from 1962. Andy Warhol."

Again the colors shifted.

"Girl with a Pearl Earring, Vermeer." A note of impatience had crept into her tone.

"What do they make you feel?"

She scoffed. "What is this, a visit to a shrink? Or just an art appreciation society? Who cares what I think of it?"

Su Cheng had moved behind the displays, and he now walked through them, the illusions warping and disappearing around him like colorful smoke. His eyes were no longer friendly. She cringed involuntarily but held her ground.

"Because, young one, I read the colors of your aura like you might read the swirls of paint, and I knew everything about you from the moment you arrived based on nothing more than that."

EB met his eyes. "So you've got a lot of practice reading auras. Great. Guess I'll work on that."

The slightest growl escaped his lips, and she paled.

"Listen, girl. Listen."

He turned away, and the colors bled back into the air. Again, the Renoir.

"What do you see?"

She blinked, stammered. "I—I see two girls sitting by a lake." "No. What do *you* see?"

"I see the dilution of color and the scatter of details in the flowers and trees around the lake. I see the diffused borders around the subjects. Abstracts. The less you focus on it, the clearer it is."

"Mmmm. Richard?"

Red looked up, startled. "What?"

"What do you see?"

"Um ... Isn't this for—"

"What do you *see*?" Su Cheng's tone brooked no argument.

Red took a deep breath, hissing it out as he squinted at the image, thinking.

"The blue of the coat and the red of the hat. You can make out the textures of the coat from the shades of blue. They're subtle, but they work really well. All the boldest colors surround the older girl's face, which is right at the center. It draws the focus there."

"Good." The color melted like dyes in water. Su Cheng clasped his hands within the sleeves of his robe, shifting his gaze between them. "EB. What is the difference between the way you saw it, and how Richard sees it?"

She glanced at Red, uncertain. "I see the whole picture."

"What? I see the whole thing. I just focus on the points that draw the eye."

She grimaced. "I'm *not* saying you aren't seeing the whole thing. What I *am* saying is that you didn't even mention the rest of it. You went right to the center, right to the bold stuff." "You didn't describe the girls at all. It's called Two Sisters, right?"

"You have to take in the whole picture!" Red was gesturing now. "But there's a point to the picture, the dressing is just ..."

Su Cheng cut them off with a gesture, his spell dousing their argument. Even then, it took them a second to stop mouthing their quarrels before they even noticed. They looked at him, glowering. The elder vampire lowered his claw, and the effect vanished.

"You are both correct. You are both seeing things through your own lens, your own perspective. That does not invalidate what you see. But if you listened to each other instead of proving your point, you would learn more about each other. And you would understand how the other thinks. You would see how to work with them ... or defeat them."

They sat on soft pillows in a chamber of burning orange silks and black, thick-lacquered wood, subtle inlays of lotuses worked everywhere in fine gold leaf. Su Cheng poured thick, alchemically treated blood into three cups. It streamed as smooth and hot as if from a fresh wound.

"A tradition is simply a paradigm. It is the way you interpret magic."

EB licked a spiced crimson drop from her lips. "Yeah, I know that. I'm not saying one tradition is better than another."

"Of course. But do you recognize the value of traditions aside from your own?"

Her eyes flicked upward in thought. "I guess? I mean, hermetics tend to think of things in a logical way, right? But shamans tend to be better with spirits."

Su Cheng nodded, savoring the scent of the hot blood from his cup. "Quite often. Not always, of course. What is your tradition?"

"Asatru."

"Ah, Norse! Do you follow a god?"

"Loki," Red said with a grin. EB narrowed her eyes at him.

"I suspected as much."

"How?" EB asked. "My aura?"

"By how you saw the painting."

"How could you do that?"

He smiled as he looked up from his sip. "A follower of Yggdrasil would have focused on the plants entirely, Odin on the girls as people. Balder would have noted the smile, Frigg their beauty, and so on. Loki is a god of chaos and margins, blurred lines."

"But wait," Red said, setting down his cup. "You could just as easily have said the smile is mischievous, or Frigg might see that smile as romantic."

"And who would worship a tree?" EB arched a brow, smirking.

Su Cheng traced a claw along one of the golden lotus leaves, scratching a small coil of gold before it. "Some find guidance from all kinds of sources. British Druids often feel the call of a guiding spirit that takes the form of trees or stars." He ignored Red's statement entirely.

"That seems kind of silly."

"Any more ridiculous than obeying the edicts of a god said to bring about the end of the world?"

EB gritted her teeth to hold back a snarl.

"Of course, Universal Magic Theory says that mentor archetypes are more like Jungian—"

"You hold to a god who called to you," Su Cheng said, ignoring Red's words. Red pursed his lips.

"So my god is real?"

"Your god is your god. You believe it is real. Does the belief make the god, or does the god inspire the belief? Is magic proof of its existence, or is your tradition simply your way of understanding a universe that is too big to fit into a little human brain?"

"You talk about it like it's an operating system."

"For a computer? Yes, very much like that. Ones and zeros become icons and sounds and games and dating apps." EB grinned as Su Cheng returned to his drink. It was cute to imagine this old man, older than even his aged form suggested, playing AR games or skimming a dating app. Then again, she used them to hunt sometimes, too.

Red nodded. "That's the same thing UMT tries to do. Find the underlying—"

"Of course," Su Cheng interrupted again, "some will argue over which faith is true and which is not. Some psychics, for example, believe they are the only ones who are right, and all ideas of mentor spirits, religion, or even sorcery itself, are mental crutches used by weaker minds bound to superstition."

EB scoffed. "I'd like to see them say that to a vampire. Or a troll, for that matter. How far up your own ass can you be?"

The elder shrugged. "We must all have our beliefs, and some beliefs only exist to attack others."

Red grimaced. "Well, that's not necessarily—"

"Young lady, you might find the writings of—"

"Why do you keep interrupting me?"

Su Cheng did not spare him a glance. "—Schwartzkopf quite enlightening. *27 Facets,* in particular, suggests there is far more to Universal Magic Theory than a reductionist-"

"Why are you ignoring me?"

Finally, Su Cheng turned his gaze to Red. EB looked over to see Red's eyes blazing, his fangs ever so slightly extended. Su Cheng looked back to EB and gestured at the enraged man.

"Tell me what you see, EB."

"Um ..."

Red's crimson stare flicked to her before he closed them, took a deep, calming breath, and exhaled, opening his now normal, blue eyes. She continued.

"You kept ignoring him or interrupting him."

"Yes. Do you know what his tradition is?"

"Black magic, right?"

Red sighed, and Su Cheng chuckled. "In the '60s it was called Black Magic. Now, Black Magic has become something a bit different, while Richard's tradition is more a schism."

"So we call it Dark Magic. Which is just as melodramatic. Which is the point."

"Right," she said.

"So, EB, how does Dark Magic work?"

"I... honestly don't know. I never asked."

Su Cheng looked at Red, who hesitated, unsure if he would be interrupted, before explaining.

"We use a combination of ecstatic will to power and exacting ritual forms that focus on ..." Red's eyes went wide, and he looked pained as he continued, "... impressing our desires onto the magical world."

"What?" EB looked confused. "What is it?"

Su Cheng smiled at her. "His tradition is based around his ego. The tradition fits the personality of the person, and Richard despises being ignored. He hates not being taken seriously."

"Yeah, I knew that. How does that help me?"

The elder looked back to her, his hands folded on the table.

"When you know how someone thinks, you know how to manipulate them. It took no more than a minor annoyance to drive Richard to shouting. His tradition demands recognition. So does he. He uses up a tactic completely, then moves to the next, more and more frustrated when something doesn't work the first time. He attacks in a straight line, direct and clear. You? I expect you revel in confusion and disorder. Disguises, distractions, chaos and seduction."

EB leaned back, impressed. "Whoa."

"Tradition is more than a paradigm of magic. It is a way of thought, a path that reflects the one who walks it."

They walked to the door together, Red trailing behind EB and Su Cheng. It seemed the Incense Master had taken a shine to the girl. As long as she didn't start hanging around him (and his syndicate) more often, it shouldn't be a problem. Still, he had to worry about the connection he had made.

More than that, he wondered at his own predictability. At his rising to the bait. Was he really so easily manipulated? If he were someone else, looking from the outside in, would he like who he saw?

The door opened, and EB hesitated before stepping out into the fog following the rains.

"I never did ask ... what is your tradition?"

Su Cheng smiled. "I follow the path of Wuxing. I study the bindings and connections of *qi,* the force of the five elements and life, itself." He leaned close and whispered, "I see the margins, too."

They chuckled, and she bowed low before skipping out into the rain-slick sheen of a Seattle Chinatown. "C'mon, Red! Let's find some dinner. I'll let you talk all night without interrupting."

TRADITIONS

POSTED BY: AXIS MUNDI

When magic returned to the world, it was chaos. Not many knew what they were doing, and they were often surprised when they were able to do even the most basic magic. Strangely, some of those not surprised were Daniel Howling Coyote and the coalition of tribes who helped him perform the Great Ghost Dance in 2017. There isn't any way Howling Coyote could have come up with that ritual by himself. In fact, we know he didn't. That ritual had been a part of his tradition since well before the Awakening, and was likely created in the Fourth World, around ten thousand years ago. Howling Coyote's commitment to the tradition of his people changed our world forever.

> ● Many would say for the better.
> ● Old Crow

> ● Not everyone, trust me. And I don't just mean the powers that be.
> ● Frosty

But even early on, as we all know, there was another side to magic. Howling Coyote and his Native American Nations followed a shamanic path, but there were soon others who discovered magic through what came to be called the hermetic tradition. Rather than follow totems and "feel" the magic inside them, hermetics understood magic to be more properly manipulated by formulae and logic. By the mid-twenty-first century, however, more than a few traditions beyond shamanism and hermeticism manifested, both old and new.

> ● One of the earliest manifestations beyond hermeticism and shamanism was Christian Theurgy, although the disagreement about it was fierce among the church hierarchy. Thankfully, the church universal wasn't, and still isn't, all that unified.
> ● Fianchetto

Many of these alternate traditions are as ancient, if not more ancient, than shamanism. They were forgotten, but they live again. The younger ones are particularly fascinating, for reasons I'll get to in a moment. The point is, there continue to be a growing number of traditions that the finite number of mages on Earth are practicing.

By the 2060s, the universities of Prague and Erfurt were making their research on Unified Magic Theory known. The theory itself was not new to Prague or Erfurt, but they were essentially the first to systematically study it, popularize the name, and experiment with it. Unified Magic Theory, or UMT, in a nutshell states that all magic stems from one source, and that all traditions of magic are simply different paths to that truth. The antecedents to this now-quite-popular theory are Ehran The Scribe's *The New Magic: Life After 2001*, numerous discussions of magic on Dunkelzahn's *Wyrm Talks*, the great dragon Schwarzkopf's lectures and classes at Charles University in Prague, as well as practice within the so-called Chaos magic tradition.

Not all roads lead to UMT being truth, however. Before I upload my two nuyen's worth on traditions, I wanted to poke a bit at the now-accepted wisdom of Unified Magic Theory.

First, and perhaps most relevant to what follows, is the fact that most mages are now trained in a post-UMT paradigm. That is, they know of the theory even if they are trained in another. The possibilities that UMT promises, along with the Matrix, ever-increasing globalization, and the idea that most knowledge is easily obtainable, all point toward a future where traditions, as such, become less and less relevant (or necessary, or desirable) than they had been. But when we look around, that is not what is happening. The number of mages isn't growing, percentage wise, but the number of traditions is. There are more traditions in practice now than there were before

UMT began to become the default position of scholarly mages. I'll share a thought about why this might be later.

Second—and more research needs to be done here—but if UMT was truly what we have been told it is, then surely the great dragons of the world would have access to all forms of magic, since they have such a strong connection to mana and have been alive so long as to have dabbled, if not mastered, all of its forms. And yet once again, we see that this is not the case. It is a well-known fact that the great dragon (and former president of the UCAS) Dunkelzahn could not access divining magic, which explains his reliance on, and frequent visits to, the Seer's Guild. I don't want to get myself in trouble, but Lofwyr also seems to share this reliance. If a great dragon can't learn something but a human can, UMT has no answer for that. Given that Lung and other greats seem to be able to divine just fine, it seems that even among dragons, magic isn't just one big free-for-all.

- Do mortal legs ever get tired?
- Orange Queen

- From what?
- Glitch

- Jumping to conclusions?
- Orange Queen

Third, Dunkelzahn himself seemed to argue, if not against UMT, at least in favor of something UMT simply dismisses: faith. Some of you will remember the upload on Aztlan decades ago that caused such a stir. This was before JackPoint, but among the shadow community, it was a big deal. Somehow, the sysop got a text conversation between Dunkelzahn (Big D on the Matrix) and a few others we are familiar with, such as The Laughing Man. In this upload, Big D admits that he, and his dragon and elf counterparts, "have striven to weaken the hold of faith on the human heart for generations, so that when magic returned they might be more open to it and embrace it more quickly. I believe we have made a terrible mistake." The mistake, he went on to say, was to weaken faith, as it reduced everything to sterile formulae without ultimate meaning. We all know the Big D was a remarkable dragon, but to admit on one hand that the foundations for UMT were draconic and elven manipulation, while also admitting that the baby tossed out with the bathwater was actually important? That makes me even more leery of UMT than I was.

- How did you get that file? Many, *many* people tried to have that convo scrubbed off the Matrix. When Crash 2.0 hit, most assumed any remaining copies had been lost.
- Frosty

- A new friend of mine hooked me up.
- Axis Mundi

- Care to share who?
- Frosty.

- Hey Axis, I'd be interested in that name as we...

- **NEXT 30 REPLIES DELETED**

- Take the inquiries to PM.
- Bull

- Sorry, all. Not right now. But know they are a reputable and trustworthy primary source.
- Axis Mundi

Lastly, and this point is controversial, there was a hushed conversation not meant to be heard by mortal ears, but a small group of runners heard it anyway. Lugh Surehand, former prince of Tir Tairngire, spoke not long ago to a certain Sean Laverty, himself a well-respected and long-lived elf. In this conversation, they spoke of the Fourth World and the changes that have occurred since. It was a rather maudlin, wistful affair, but one bit stood out to me. Laverty mentioned something in a language I didn't grok, but the context clued me into that they were speaking of beings revered by ancient people in the way that some today worship gods. They spoke of how dragons knew about these beings as well. If, during a time of higher magic, elves and dragons followed or revered beings higher than themselves, who then empowered followers with magic ability, that is a paradigm shift. Unified Magic Theory doesn't come close to explaining that kind of thing. Were these beings gods? Mentor spirits? Metaplanar beings? Do they still live?

The point of all this is that there are some traditions for which UMT is a clear evolution: Hermeticism, Chaos Magic, Wicca, Black Magic, Druidism, and others—perhaps Wuxing and Psionics, perhaps more. Within these traditions, borrowing and building from other traditions seems intuitive, even right. But there are others, traditions that point beyond the user to someone or something else, in which this crossover doesn't quite fit. Perhaps the ability to become invisible might be common to shamans and hermetics, but what if the source is not the same? What if the intuitive and charismatic traditions are tapping into something greater than themselves or greater even than magic itself? It simply doesn't follow that the ability to perform the same actions (whether fireballs, healings, or clairvoyance) means that the magic used is essentially the same. Just like the ability to punch through a wall doesn't mean that adepts and street samurai are the same.

Who knows? Maybe I'm wrong. Most Jack-Pointers seem convinced I am. But I think that the higher the mana gets, the more traditions we will see. And maybe we'll even find out which traditions are worth more than others. But until then, I'll go with what the opposition party at Prague and Erfurt said. While the weight of scholars and dragons pushed toward UMT, there were others studying the same phenomenon who concluded that the best way forward wasn't to combine all traditions into a new, super tradition, but instead to value pluralism and what diversity and a variety of many practices can teach us about magic and ourselves.

◉ **NEXT 457 REPLIES DELETED**

◉ Geez, Axis. Way to stir the pot. Safe to say not everyone shares your beliefs.
◉ Bull

◉ My beliefs don't require them to.
◉ Axis Mundi

Okay. Enough waxing philosophical. There are some new traditions making waves around the globe, and a few traditions that have been discussed previously but have finer points that bear further elucidation. Here they are.

TRADITION UPDATES

BLACK MAGIC (UPDATE)

DESCRIPTION (P. 44, STREET GRIMOIRE)

Many people perceive practitioners of Black Magic as evil and as destructive as Toxic or Bug Spirit followers, and the media haven't helped change that view with their representation of magical practitioners of this tradition. Technically this tradition is a more selfish style of magic, generally used for personal gain. Like everything in the shadows, it boils down to morality and price. So you can have the magician whose use of black magic involves nothing more than leveraging magic to live the good life, or the corporate executive whose use of black magic brings down his enemies as he climbs toward more power.

RELATED MENTOR SPIRITS

Common choices for Black Magic have been the Moon (p. 98) and the Dark King (p. 98), but in the end practitioners can focus on any mentor spirit that will play into their self-interests.

IDEALS

Black Magic values the self above all else. The self it values is not the spirit-quest, walkabout, find-yourself-type self, but the unfettered selfishness that comes from viewing yourself as the center of your own universe. Nothing is more important than you and what you can get, grab, steal, manipulate, and own. Black Magic isn't evil, per se, in that it doesn't have any grand plan to destroy the universe or corrupt the youth, but if you consider selfishness to be evil, well, that's what it is.

Power, and keeping as much of it to yourself as possible, is what drives Black Magic practitioners.

SORCERY

The practice of magic is always for personal gain. Spells are chosen based on what the mage needs to further their own goals and influence others. This means that more often practitioners pick Manipulation and Health spells over Combat. Ritual spellcasting is used, but often with a team of one due to the fact there can only be one leader chosen when performing a ritual. There can be rare occurrences of teams, but then you have to question what is the motivation of the others besides survival.

CONJURING

Black Magic conjuring has long been associated with so-called "demonic forces." This perception has influenced the appearance of conjured spirits, giving them a more frightening visage. For traditional Black Magic magicians, this is sometimes more than skin deep; bent to the will of the Magician, the spirits can have surprising abilities.

ENCHANTING

Alchemy and the creation of preparations are acceptable but are directed more toward psychological manipulation than direct combat. Items of healing are rare, given that the magician is often trying to stay out of harm's way—and to not heal any harm they or their minions might inflict on others.

TRADITIONAL BLACK MAGE RULES

Traditional practitioners of Black Magic follow strict rules:

- Selfish Magic: Beneficial health spells specifically can only be cast on self instead of others. Cannot cast ritual health spells. Health preparations cannot be created with alchemy. The practitioner gains +2 dice to spellcasting or the ritual spellcasting of spells that the they cast on themselves.
- Receive Animal Familiar quality for free.
- Receive Dark Ally quality for free. Spirit is a boggle (p. 117, *Howling Shadows*).
- Personal Demons: Spirits summoned automatically gain one of the following:
  - Fear power (automatic instead of optional).
  - Flight skill equal to Force.
  - Natural Weaponry (DV = Strength + 2).

BLACK MAGIC

Combat: Fire
Detection: Water
Health: Earth
Illusion: Air
Manipulation: Man
Drain: Willpower + Charisma

PREFERRED SPELLS
Chaotic World, Control Actions, Control Thoughts, Death Touch, Opium Den

---

NOTABLE TEACHERS

Traditionally, practitioners of Black Magic don't like to share what they know, and they especially don't like to advertise it if they do. A notable exception is **Juliette Burma**. She's based out of Manhattan, and a few years ago she put up a post on the Matrix saying she was looking for students. While most Black Mages are wary of those who advertise their commitment to the Black Arts, Juliette seems to have gathered quite a cadre of fairly competent mages. That is either very stupid for her or very dangerous for Manhattan.

THE BUDDHIST TRADITION (UPDATED)

DESCRIPTION (P. 43, STREET GRIMOIRE)

For Buddhists in the Sixth World, magic springs from personal self-development and spiritual enlightenment. The Buddhist magical tradition mainly stems from one sect of Buddhism—Vajrayana or Tantric Buddhism, generally—as the other sects do not teach specific techniques related to sorcery and summoning and instead see magic as another part of reality that must be overcome to find enlightenment (Nirvana). Many magicians who follow the Wuxing or Shinto tradition also consider themselves followers of Buddhism. Buddhists can be called yogis (or yoginis), though this is a general term for practitioners of Southeast Asian religions including Hinduism, Buddhism, and Jainism. Traditionalists prefer the title Bodhisattva. While Vajrayana Buddhism originated in Tibet (which is now magically sealed off from the rest of the world), it can be found in communities throughout Asia, from India to Japan, and into North America, especially the West Coast.

RELATED MENTOR SPIRITS

Buddhists do not have any particular mentor spirits that are common to their practice, but neither do they discriminate against them. Buddhists have shown a wide diversity in mentor spirits when, and if, they follow one.

IDEALS

The teachings of Buddhism, common to all Buddhists, include the "four noble truths": 1) existence is suffering (dukhka); 2) the causes of suffering are craving and attachment (trishna); 3) the end of suffering can be found and is called Nirvana; and 4) the path to Nirvana is the eightfold path: right views, right resolve, right speech, right action, right livelihood, right effort, right mindfulness, and right concentration. Buddhism teaches that reality is most correctly understood as process and relation instead of entity or substance.

SORCERY

The weaving of mana into spells is performed through the proper chanting of mantras and the state of mind that activity creates. The pattern of motion can be included as a way to focus. Some see it as a way of changing reality. Buddhist ritual spellcasting techniques are called mantras. It is a method of mind and body meditation incorporating qi-like channeling of mana energies.

CONJURING

Spirits summoned by a Buddhist are believed to be enlightened divinities that have decided to remain on earth out of compassion for those who still strive to attain Nirvana.

ENCHANTING

Bodhisattvas believe that material tools prevent progress on the spiritual path, therefore the creation and use of preparations, reagents, and foci are discouraged. Non-traditionalists allow exceptions as part of their progress to enlightenment. Reeds, lotus flowers, chalk, and other natural plants and earth materials can be used as reagents. Beads or religious items may be used as fetishes.

BUDDHISM

Combat: Air
Detection: Guidance
Health: Earth
Illusion: Fire
Manipulation: Water
Drain: Willpower + Intuition

PREFERRED SPELLS
Hibernate, Mask, Resist Pain, Silence, Spatial Sense

TRADITIONALIST BUDDHIST RULES

Traditional practitioners of Buddhism adhere to the following rules:

- Cannot use the Enchanting skill group.
- Cannot use reagents or fetishes.
- Gain Barehanded Adept for free (magicians resist drain normally).
- Gain Spiritual Pilgrim for free.
- Gain Spiritual Lodge for free.
- Bodhisattvas must take an ordeal when initiating, as there is no knowledge won without sacrifice.

NOTABLE TEACHERS

In Bellingham, in the Salish-Shidhe, there is a Buddhist teacher called **Jeremy Blue Sky**. You can find him at the shrine he built in Sedro-Woolley. He doesn't suffer any distractions, so don't go see him unless you have a good amount of time to devote to his tutelage. Blue Sky is a full member of the tribe and participates fully in its doings, but he doesn't seem to have an agenda for his Buddhist devotion besides reaching Nirvana and teaching others to find the same.

CHRISTIAN THEURGIST TRADTITION (UPDATED)

DESCRIPTION (P. 44, STREET GRIMOIRE)

Christian Theurgists, in their perspective, are those gifted by God with the ability to wield the natural energies of magic and devote their skills to the service of the congregation of the faith. While the public version of Christian Theurgy didn't officially get sanction by Pope John XXV until 2024, secretive orders kept mystical practices alive since first century Gnosticism. A few of these orders are listed below.

ORDER OF ST. SYLVESTER

Also known as Sylvestrines, this is an order of mostly Awakened metahumans that investigates magical phenomena for the Church. This order is also publicly known for promoting magical awareness and beneficial magic such as the healing arts and exorcisms. A few of the order are not Awakened but have done much research into Awakened subjects such as parazoology and parabotany. The Order started in 1841 as an honorary title for those who exceed in their duties in various arts, but then was reformed in 1905 with their present agenda of investigating magical phenomena. The Knights and Dames of St. Sylvester only became publicly known in 2025 after an official sanction from the Pope.

NEW KNIGHTS TEMPLAR

The Knights Templar were originally accused of practicing dark magic and were almost completely destroyed in 1307. While publicly disbanded in 1312, the Knights were reestablished in 1910 after hearing the visions of Dame Grace, a young Sylvestrine. New Knights Templars are Awakened followers supported by the Vatican and are actively involved in the affairs of the church. They are sworn to protect the world against the dark forces, though some have taken to interpreting the visions as protecting the Church. This has caused some factions to have alternate goals, leading to conflicts. With the exception of Westphalian Theurgists, the NKT are the most confrontational of the orders.

VIGILIA EVANGELICA

This is not an order, but rather a secret clerical organization with a motivation to safeguard the world from magic too dangerous to be known. It was created in 1274 by Pope Gregory X following the death of Thomas Aquinas. Since that time they have hidden libraries and collections of magical artifacts deemed too dangerous to mankind. There are, as far as observers of the order can tell, four of these Aquine Vaults to secure the largest and most dangerous collections. Vigilia Evangelists also work behind the scenes, supporting other orders with intel and magical supplies. The order includes more than just Awakened individuals, there are also deckers who scour the Matrix for magical works and rituals, hoping to isolate or remove the most dangerous ones.

WESTPHALIAN THEURGISTS

Rooted in Germany, the Westphalian Theurgists are the most restrictive and aggressive of these orders. In 2014, when Imago Dei reversed previous church stances on metahumans, this group split from the rest of the church. They believe in restrictive rules of magic; only Christian Theurgy is acceptable, and all others are heresy and must be destroyed.

ORTHODOX EXARCHS

When bug outbreaks were discovered in Eastern Europe, the Orthodox Exarchs gathered the strength of the Awakened from their churches and proved decisive against the invading spirits. They had the advantage of early preparation—after the Awakening, they were on the leading edge (at least as far as church members went) in diving into magical research. Members of the order originally consisted of Church members who were friendly to mysticism, so their mental adjustments to the Awakening were not exceptionally difficult. They are the oddest of groups in the Sixth World—individuals focused on fighting evil and not bringing any reward, or even attention, to themselves. Sure, there are power struggles sometimes—that's part of having power—but for the most part, the Exarchs do their research, learn their secrets, then use what they've learned to keep magic from being abused. Simple, but also quite rare.

RELATED MENTOR SPIRITS

Aside from Sacred Text, there usually is no mentor/totem to directly guide Theurgists on their journey, but some will choose a patron saint and adjust their life to follow the virtues of that saint.

IDEALS

The ideals of Christian Theurgists are far more varied than might be initially thought. While all practitioners would swear that they follow the teachings of Jesus Christ, the church, or some particular saint (not necessarily in that order), what that looks like in practice can vary greatly. Due to the prominence of Christianity in the West for over 1,500 years, many branches have developed, which means it is not uncommon to find Christian Theurgists who are pacifist, militant, accepting, judgmental, giving, hoarding, and every position in-between. One could spend years untangling how Christian theology snaked off in so many different and often opposing directions, but examining how the doctrine became what it is is perhaps less important than acknowledging that this variety exists.

SORCERY

Pope John XXV has said that Awakened abilities are not, by nature, evil. Rather, like any other human abilities, they may be used for good or evil. The use of spellcasting is an approved practice by a majority of churches. Ritual spellcasting is questionable due to its possible ties to paganism.

CONJURING

Pope John XXV also goes on to say that spirits are living manifestations, which means conjuring is not in itself evil. Since it touches on so many questions of faith and morality, however, summoning spirits is generally frowned upon, especially when attempts to bind them are involved. Traditional Theurgists are forbidden to summon or bind spirits except under permission from Rome, which only comes in unique circumstances. The banishing skill is allowable, relating to the role of banishment of evil spirits, including modern examples of insect and toxic spirits.

ENCHANTING

Theurgists frown on the use of the whole enchanting skill group as it ties to witchcraft and paganism—many witches in media are associated with wands and amulets. The use of reagents is permissible, unless you attempt to make them.

CHRISTIAN THEURGY

Combat: Fire
Detection: Water
Health: Air
Illusion: Earth
Manipulation: Guidance
Drain: Willpower + Charisma

PREFERRED SPELLS
Detect Life, Heal, Increase Inherent Limits, Influence, Lightning Bolt

TRADITIONAL THEURGIST RULES

Traditional Theurgists follow strict rules for their practice of magic:
- Cannot use the Enchanting skill group (Vigilia Evangelica does not follow this limit).
- Gains the Exorcism metamagic for free.
- Cannot use the Binding skill.
- Summoning can be done, but only through special dispensation by those of higher authority. A geas prevents the Theurgist from summoning without it.
- Cannot practice magic on the Sabbath (geas).

VIGILIA EVANGELICA HAS ADDITIONAL RESTRICTIONS:
- Practice a Vow of Silence (geas), though the written word is acceptable.
- Swear an oath of secrecy to not reveal any of the knowledge learned in the vaults.
- Gain the Pacifist quality (in exchange for the ability to use the Enchanting skill group).

WESTPHALIAN THEURGIST ADDITIONAL REQUIREMENTS:
- Can only learn Combat and Health spells.
- Can use the Disenchanting skill.
- Gain +2 dice pool modifier for Banishing skill tests.
- Gain Vexcraft for free (note: skill requirement must be filled to use secondary ability).

NOTABLE TEACHERS

Father Pietro Rinaldi, a Catholic priest of the Order of St. Sylvester, has been in and around the shadows for decades. Now an old man, he finds purpose in teaching others what he knows of Theurgy and magical theory in general. Rinaldi isn't a full mage—in fact, he can't cast spells—but he has shown himself to be a capable teacher, and many well-known pupils of his have risen quite far in the Order. Seekers, even non-faithful ones, will find Father Rinaldi a willing professor. When he is not in Rome, he can be found at one of the various monasteries he frequents in Seattle.

If you are looking for a less traditional mentor, you can head to Bavaria and knock on the door of a Westphalian monastery. Archbishop Timothy Stemple spends his time there, away from the extravagant trappings that normally accompany an archbishop. He demands strict adherence and utter servitude, but he is kind-hearted and willing to teach. He doesn't back down on his beliefs, though, so if you are a shaman or some smart-ass hermetic, be prepared for lectures about the scriptures and your heathen lifestyle.

- ❥ Any truth to the rumors that Bishop Stemple is Unseelie?
- ❥ Chainmaker

- ❥ He certainly has an extreme hate-on for the Tírs. But Westphalians are pretty rigid. I can't see how the two mix.
- ❥ Axis Mundi

- ❥ They don't mix. As Bishop Stemple himself would say, you can't serve two masters. Stemple's as religious as they come. But he ain't Westphalian.
- ❥ Rose Red

THE DRUIDIC TRADITION (UPDATED)

DESCRIPTION (P. 45, STREET GRIMOIRE)

Druidism is a religion and magic system originally practiced in parts of Celtic Europe. Druids were an important part of Celtic society, notably in worship, divination, and judicial procedure. They were charged with the custody of the mystical bond between the sacred spirit of the land and its people. Prior to 2040, most knowledge of Druidism was lost to antiquity, and what accounted for modern Druidism and Neo-Druidism was based on interpretation from archeology and Greek and Roman records. It wasn't until the Song of Bodhmall and the Voice of Cathbad were heard by Sixth-World druids as they journeyed to the spirit world that druidism was finally understood. So from Neo-druidism, Modern Druidism, Bardic

Mysticism, and other druidic groups came three branches to use this new knowledge of their ancient heritage.

CELTIC DRUIDS

Celtic druids are by far the most common and have revived ancient Celtic culture wholesale. Their practices are a conglomeration of everything that has been discovered so far relating to druids. This knowledge is for the most part passed as an oral tradition to the next generation, though like other practitioners of magic, the *Digital Grimoire* was an appealing item for them to understand magic. Celtic druids include Welsh and Scottish druids. They make themselves unique with subtle differences in their practices as well as the spirits they follow.

SACRED CIRCLE

A sacred circle is a unique version of a lodge that certain traditionalists can build. The cost of construction is (Force x 1,500) nuyen, and it takes twice the normal time to set up. The size is (Force) meters in diameter. Once constructed, it can't be disassembled and moved. The owner would have to destroy it (no recycled materials), then start over. Once built, it can be used like a lodge, but it also holds special power for the Awakened. If the magician is within (Magic x 10) kilometers of their sacred circle, they may draw upon that power. The magician can reduce the force of the lodge by 1 and add +2 dice to a single magical skill test. This can be done every combat turn until the Force of the sacred circle is reduced to 0. As long as the Force of the circle is above zero, it is replenished by 1 per day, up to its initial Force. It can be completely restored in a day if the magician spends (500 x [original Force-current Force]) nuyen in ritual materials.

DRUIDIC TRADITION

Combat: Beast
Detection: Water
Health: Plant
Illusion: Air
Manipulation: Earth
Drain: Willpower + Charisma

PREFERRED SPELLS

Camouflage, Control Pack, Invisibility, Resist Pain, Stunball

WILD DRUIDS

Wild druids follow a deeply primeval, totemic tradition, much like shamans. They prefer to believe that some of their magical practices existed prior to any Celtic influences, distinguishing themselves from Celtic and English druids. They only worship natural/animalistic mentor spirits. They are more hermits in habit, shunning modern society and technology and living off the grid with nature. A subset of wild druids includes those who've blended bardish mysticism into their practice. The bards are nomadic and live off the land, but unlike the rest of these druids they don't avoid modern society. Bards also have some artistic talent in music or song, passing down their traditions through it. They are much like the street shamans you can find in most North American sprawls.

ENGLISH DRUIDS

English druids borrow the esoteric correspondences, potent symbology, and trappings of Druidism. In the opposite direction of wild druids, the English druid encompasses more of the Celtic mysticisms than the natural magic. For this reason, "English druid" is something of a misnomer, though it is true that this specific orientation originated in England. They believe what they summon are aspects of a greater spirit of the land, so their attitude toward such spirits is more like hermetic mages.

Four annual festivals hold immense ritual significance to all branches of Druidism: Imbolc, Beltane, Lugnasad, and Samhain. Druidic circles (magic groups) reserve great rituals and initiation rites for these sacred dates. Druids create magical lodges called sacred circles to practice their magic. These are monolithic stone circles where they practice magic. "Modern" druids, or those that followed the Neo-druidic movement, scale down their lodges into rooms with zen rock gardens or a central water feature—a token gesture to their unity with all things of nature. Traditional druids invest more into their stone circles, with great stone structures grounded into the earth. For traditional druids, this becomes the main magical lodge and the only location for learning. This does not prevent them from establishing temporary circles for rituals. Older druid sites such as Stonehenge are built on mana lines to enhance the druid's magic. The Druidic Tradition is widespread in the British Isles, Tír na nÓg, France and parts of central Europe

RELATED MENTOR SPIRITS

Druids tend to favor those mentor spirits connected with the land in which they find themselves. Nature spirits (and thus, most animal totems) are natural fits within the Druidic paradigm. Some Druids, notably the so-called "English Druids," also find mentors who are not so typical— they have been known to follow a broad variety of mentors.

IDEALS

Druidism is largely free of dogma and fixed beliefs. There is no "sacred text" or equivalent in Druidism, but despite this, there are a number of ideas and beliefs that most Druids have in common.

Nature is an important locus of their reverence, and whatever beliefs that individuals hold about the universe, all Druids sense nature as sacred. This doesn't mean all Druids are above manipulating nature, but they believe their power is rooted in it. This power could be nature's universal scope, or a particular piece of land sacred to a single Druid.

SORCERY

Druids practice spellcasting normally.

CONJURING

Druids practice Conjuring as normal.

ENCHANTING

While the harvesting of reagents is acceptable to Druids, Alchemy is not practiced.

TRADITIONAL DRUID RULES

Traditionalist (optional)
- Cannot use the Binding skill.
- Reduce the opposing Force of ritual spellcasting by 2 when summoning the Wild Hunt.
- When engaged in ritual spellcasting, reduce Drain by 1 for each Druid participating.
- Gain the Mentor Spirit quality for free.
- Cannot use the Enchanting skill group.
- Substitute Arcana for Alchemy when harvesting reagents (p. 17, *SR5*).
- Sacred Circle: A traditionalist can't build lodges, so instead they build Sacred Circles. The Druid form of a sacred circle is a circle of standing stones.

WILD DRUIDS (OPTIONAL)

- Wild druids reduce the opposing Force of ritual spellcasting by 2 when calling the Green Man (p. 123, *Howling Shadows*).
- Substitute Arcana for Alchemy for harvesting reagents (p. 17, *SR5*).

ENGLISH DRUIDS (OPTIONAL)

- English Druids reduce the opposing Force of ritual spellcasting by 2 when calling the Heart of the City (p. 123, *Howling Shadows*).

NOTABLE TEACHERS

In Scotland's highlands, there is a Fomorian known as **Dodman Daniel**. Daniel walks the ley lines, cleansing and aligning them as he passes. He has only one trusted acolyte, a young man named Angus, but often finds himself teaching ancient Celtic Druidism to those who wish to learn. Be advised—he doesn't teach the highest secrets he knows except to Angus and a few other acolytes over the years, but if you want to cut your teeth and learn from one of the best teachers around, Dodman Daniel is your best bet. Also, the scenery isn't half bad.

- Depending on your loyalties, you may want to be a bit more choosey about who you learn from. The Dodman isn't all he appears. Back in the '50s "Dodman Daniel" was known as Unseelie Dan, a revolutionary/terrorist who caused trouble in Tír na nÓg. Not sure why he's gone the route of "holy man," but I doubt he has left his loyalties behind.
- Thorn

THE NORSE TRADITION (UPDATED)

DESCRIPTION (P. 4, SHADOW SPELLS)

Norse magicians believe the Old Gods once again watch over Midgard. Ásatru, the old faith of the Norse, has seen a popular comeback, and with it the revival of its visceral and pagan magic. Even with the association to the apocalyptic actions of the extremist Ásatru cult known as Winternight, growth of this tradition has been steady. While the origins were in the time of the Vikings, modern Ásatru began in 1972, organizing and legalizing their specific practices and traditions. This contributed to a smoother transition into the Sixth World. Both Awakened and mundane Ásatru gather for great ceremonies known as blots and sumbles. These are traditionally held on Midsummer's or Midwinter's Day and the spring or autumn equinoxes. Common elements of these rituals include liberal drinking and the sacrifice of a game animal for consumption (for urban Ásatru practitioners, real meat sausages can be used).

Awakened practitioners of the Norse magic and Ásatru are called Godi, though non-religious Awakened could be called vitka (sorceress) or heiðr (cunning woman). Many Awakened followers of the Norse tradition specialize in a specific magical skill group. **Godi** are mostly spell weavers, priests practicing sorcery through prayers to the Norse pantheon. They are given respect by other followers of Ásatru. Unlike other traditions, it's a part-time religious position, with a Godi holding another profitable job for support. They use a more hierarchal structure than other Ásatru adherents. **Runemasters** have delved into futhark runes (the written language of the Norse) and have been able to incorporate their work into more persistent magic as they carve the words into stone. **Seidmen** focus their attention on gaining access to the nine realms and communicating with the creatures found within. Some of these Awaken and then focus their efforts on mastering all nine realms.

Of particular note are berserkers or bear sarks who adopt totemic animal mentors (such as Bear or Stag); most are adepts, though mystic adepts or magicians are not unknown. Bear sarks only manifest shamanic masks when in frenzies, and their abilities closely parallel those of their mentors.

RELATED MENTOR SPIRITS

Norse mages typically have individual members of the Norse pantheon as mentor spirits. Odin may be represented in a way similar to the Wise Warrior totem, Thor has similarities to Dragonslayer and Berserker, Freya and Goddess are similar, and Loki, of course, has much in common with the trickster totems such as Coyote and Raven. Berserkers and sarks often claim particular animal totems related to Germanic homelands, such as Bear, Raven, Wolf, and Stag.

IDEALS

While possibly disappointing to those who wish to pillage and plunder as part of their belief system, the Norse paradigm is much more complex than simple berserkers and warriors. Courage, truth, honor, fidelity, discipline, hospitality, industriousness, self-reliance, and perseverance are their core values. While each individual values these in various amounts, the Norse tradition finds common purpose with many of the Sixth World's current values. The trope of the noble barbarian surely exists for some, but for others, it is the ancient family- and honor-based system that fits best with them.

SORCERY

Spellweaving, as it's called, is common among the Awakened of the Norse tradition. It involves the use of futhark runes and prayers to one of many gods in the pantheon.

CONJURING

Norse magicians believe they deal with the denizens of the other Realms of the World Tree. Those who can cross to Midgard are the fire giants of Muspelheim (fire spirits), the wild fae of Alfheim (plant spirits), the dwarfs of Nidavellir (earth spirits), the storm spirits of Thrudheim (air spirits), and the Valkyrie (guardian spirits). While traditional Godi acknowledge them, they do not summon them. Their interaction is more akin to prayers to the gods. It is the Seidman and Vitka who would bring and deal with denizens from the nine realms in Midgard (Earth). Many of the spirits summoned from the Realms of the World Tree dislike metahumans or the process of being brought to Midgard. They require tributes before they perform services for the Awakened.

ENCHANTING

Enchanting is also common among the Norse magicians. Many stories and sagas tell of magical weapons for the heroes to wield, and every hero has given their weapon a name. This practice has been modernized with the additional knowledge of alchemy and runemasters' use of futhark runes in the creation of preparations.

NORSE MAGICIAN RULES

GODI/RUNEMASTER
- Cannot use the Conjuring skill group.
- Reduce opposing Force of ritual spellcasting by 2 when Imbuing (p. 133, *Street Grimoire*) or Attuning items (p. 124, *Street Grimoire*).
- Can Attune normal items as per an adept.
- Durable Preparations: Increase the preparation's potency by x3 instead of x2. Double the time it takes to lose potency.

NORSE TRADITION

Combat: Guardian
Detection: Earth
Health: Plant
Illusion: Air
Manipulation: Fire
Drain: Willpower + Charisma

PREFERRED SPELLS
Death Touch, Eyes of the Pack, Insulate, Personal Warmth, Shape Ice, Shatter

---

CUNNING WOMAN
- Treat as an aspected magician (p. 69, *SR5*) with a Sorcery focus and an inclination toward Health spells.

SEIDMAN
- Cannot use the Sorcery skill group.
- Gains Dedicated Conjurer quality for free.

BERSERKERS (ADEPT ONLY)

FREE ADEPT POWER
Berserker Temper: When you take Physical damage in combat—or if someone under your care is badly injured—make a Charisma + Willpower Test (wound modifiers apply). You go berserk for 3 Combat Turns minus 1 turn per hit, so 3 or more hits averts the berserk temper entirely. If your totem also has this disadvantage, then any turns they might impose stack with the results of your test those additional turns (for example, if a Berserker chooses Bear, then they can possibly go berserk for as long as 6 turns). Berserk power bonus does not apply while raging with Berserker Temper. When Berserk, you go after characters without regard for your own safety.

NOTABLE TEACHERS

Alva Hansen is a second-generation Ásatru shaman, focusing on seiðr magic. While outside of the mainstream of Norse magic, her tantric, shaking, ritual-sex-based magic is gaining quite a following, mostly for the obvious reasons. She has written numerous books about seiðr, which have become bestsellers, especially in the UCAS, perhaps more for their illustrations than their content. Regardless, Alva tends to teach more women than men, as seiðr developed a reputation as a "womanly" art. However, Hansen is willing to teach any willing students to practice magic as she commands, no questions asked.

ISLAM (UPDATED)

DESCRIPTION (P. 46, STREET GRIMOIRE)

What started off as a small fringe group has turned into a much larger movement within the Islamic world. The Islamic Renaissance Movement, along with broader globalization and long-suffering examples from Sufism, have been cracking the door open further for Awakened Muslims to practice magic in ever-broadening ways. Studies in Licit Qur'anic Magic and alchemy have become even more popular since Ibrahim Kamel became the caliph of the Arabian Caliphate. Joseph Chamseddine, the caliph's childhood friend and spiritual mentor, has had a profound impact on the caliph's encouragement of the burgeoning Islamic Reformation. Not all within the Caliphate welcome this change, however, so it is still a good idea for Islamic mages to be discreet when practicing their abilities.

ISLAMIC ALCHEMISTS

Most in the Alchemist branch of Islamic magic do not consider themselves mages at all. Rather, they view alchemy as just another form of science. Experimentation, formulas, rigorous notes—all of these things are important to the Islamic Alchemist, who either view mana as another element to be dissected, or simply refuse to acknowledge mana at all. Islamic Alchemy is the exception to the rule against magic in the Islamic world. Nearly all forms of Islam accept Alchemists in their ranks, as Islam has a rich history with alchemy going back to the Middle Ages.

LICIT QUR'ANIC MAGIC

There is another branch of Islamic Magic that has always been present, but until the recent changes in the Caliphate, has not been mainstream. Thanks to the teachings of Joseph Chamseddine, Islamic mysticism is on the rise. What makes Licit Qur'anic Magic different from Islamic magic in general is the razor-sharp focus on what is permissible (licit) and what is not permissible (illicit). For many in the Licit Qur'anic tradition, the Qur'an is the only sure-fire way to know if magic is permissible. The logic is that in Islam, the Qur'an is given by Allah, and therefore always permissible. So any "magic" or power that flows from use of the Qur'an or its contents is always permissible. Use of amulets with Qur'anic verses is typical among LQM practitioners, guaranteeing spells remain under control and giving the caster peace of mind.

ROLE-PLAYING AN ISLAMIC MAGE

Given the deep persecution that the Awakened suffered under the Arabian Caliphate, it is no surprise that mages still do not feel comfortable in their own skin there. Outside of the Caliphate, things are different. Acceptance and belonging, whether it is in shadowrunning teams or groups like the Islamic Renaissance Movement, have allowed space for the tradition to grow. There will always be those, within the Islamic world and without, whose prejudice will not allow them to see an Islamic mage as anything but a threat. So a little paranoia might be helpful.

RELATED MENTOR SPIRITS

Islamic mages do not take mentor spirits, due to a deep mistrust of spirits in general, and an avoidance of anything that could be interpreted as idolatrous. The one exception is the Holy Text.

IDEALS

It is, of course, a mistake to attempt to generalize the ideals of hundreds of millions of people. But most Islamic mages seem to cling fairly tightly to the Five Pillars at very least. Most, but not all. The declaration of faith that "There is no deity worthy of worship except God (Allah), and Muhammad is the Messenger" is common to all Islamic mages. Islamic mages are also bound to daily prayer five times per day, giving 2.5 percent of earnings to charity, feasting on Ramadan, and the Hajj Pilgrimage to the Kaaba in Mecca. The strictness of the adherence varies from mage to mage, however.

SORCERY

Islamic mages practice spellcasting normally. As a general principle, Islamic mages discourage casting spells recklessly or at too high a Force, as this can lead to a loss of control. Further, ritual spellcasting is discouraged.

CONJURING

All branches of Islamic mages discourage use of Summoning. Banishing is permitted, although it is still considered dangerous. There are examples, however, of advanced initiates in Islamic magic who summon and bind djinn, but unless permission is given from religious authorities, this is forbidden. Angels, or Guardian Spirits, have been summoned (never bound) to give aid to Islamic mages who call for them, although this practice is not widely accepted.

ENCHANTING

Islamic mages practice skills in the Enchanting skill group normally.

ISLAMIC MAGICIAN RULES

ISLAMIC ALCHEMIST
- Cannot practice spellcasting or ritual spellcasting, but may use counterspelling normally.
- When **Islamic Alchemists** initiate, they must choose the following four metamagics, in the following order, before choosing any others: Fixation, Quickening, Advanced Alchemy, Anchoring.
- For each level of initiation, the Alchemist may reroll one die on tests using the Enchanting skill group.
- May not use the Conjuring skill group unless an initiate of grade 5 or higher.

LICIT QUR'ANIC MAGE
- Must always cast spells through fetishes (amulets, scrolls, texts) based on or containing Qur'anic verses.
- Ritual spellcasting is not permitted without permission from the proper religious authority.
- Must take the centering metamagic when they initiate for the first time.
- When second grade of initiation is reached, must take the structured spellcasting metamagic.
- Summoning is not permitted unless the mage is an initiate of grade 7 or higher and only with permission from religious authority.

DJINN

In the Islamic tradition, spirits are called djinn. These creatures are not angels in a religious sense, but other creatures that were created. To most westerners and Aetherpedia, there is only one type of spirit, which is djinn (or genie), but in truth there are actually five types of djinn, acting as spirit tribes similar to the fae of Europe. The five tribes of djinn are Marid, Ifrit, Shaitan, Jinn, and Jann. These djinn come from a metaplane they call Ginnistan. Ginnistan is hot and arid. A great glass city, Schadou Kiam, rests

between two vast deserts. Schadou Kiam is the seat of power where all the tribes meet. It is sometimes called the invisible city, as the shimmering heat and transparent towers brings the illusion of invisibility. To the left is Badiat-Goldare, a desert of black volcanic sand and sulfur odors. It is the desert of monsters, where dark and demonic creatures, along with some banished spirits, survive. To the right is Badiat-Tealgim, a desert of white silicon sand that sings when the wind blows. It is the desert of Peris, where the more benevolent spirits dwell. It wasn't always like this. Many lifetimes ago, a great Jinn prophet had a vision of a vast crescent rift and war that would engulf all of his people. He saw that the djinn would all perish if they did not choose a side. When the five tribes had to choose to support man or support the demons, the Jinn, Jann and Marid chose to support humans. The Ifrit and Shaitan chose demons. When the djinn made their choice, their metaplane physically transformed with the formation of the two deserts.

At the end of the Great Rending, when the demons were locked away, the Ifrit and Shaitan pleaded not to be locked away as well. The Marid, oldest of the djinn tribes, believed they should not suffer the fate of demons. The other djinn agreed and took them back, hoping they will be redeemed. This is why a sufi can summon all five tribes. Because of Marid, Jinn, and Jann's choice to side with metahumanity, they often appear in the humanoid form. Ifrit and Shaitan's choice, however, transformed their visage to something more frightening.

- There's a grey area even with the IRM—namely, why summon an Ifrit or Shaitan, who chose demons over metahumanity? How can their actions ever be trustworthy?
- Crescent Moon

Marid are the eldest, and some say the most powerful, of the Djinn. They can be proud and arrogant. The Marid tribe appears often as fireless smoke or large blue humanoids. This appearance is what is most commonly described by legends and a generic description of djinn in general due to the frequency with which Marid is summoned. This also is why there are fewer Marid than of the other tribes.

Note that each type of djinn prefers to be called by their name or tribe but they will answer to the term "djinn." Calling any of them that is probably the safest bet if you're not certain what tribe they represent.

For many in the Islamic world, djinn are considered demons who often trick humans into doing bad things. There are exceptions as portrayed by stories, in particular 1,001 Arabian Nights. Most often summoned djinn appear in metahuman form with eyes that sparkle with fire. They can also have blended animalistic features of desert creatures (scorpion tail, lion head, etc.). Ifrit commonly take on inhuman features of a bat, while a Shaitan bristles with thorns/horns. Free djinn, or those who are found in the desert, can appear as animals (like a white camel) or natural weather phenomena (like a dust storm). More dangerous and powerful free spirits are not confined to such simple forms, taking shapes like sand sculpted into a camel, a giant scorpion, or even a fire-breathing camel spider.

As the djinn grow in power, the spirit's skin tone actually changes. The younger, weaker ones are shades of green; then they change to blue, then red, while the most powerful are black. This can be seen in their metahuman form more than any other shape. The djinn's aura is also tinted by this unusual color pattern

- There are also yellow djinn, but they are rare. No one knows where their color falls on the power scale.
- Crescent Moon

Some djinn have a vulnerability to metal, such as copper or iron. It is believed that with this knowledge, King Solomon was first able to trap djinn. Various arcane pursuits used legends of genies in bottles to find ways to not only summon or bind spirits but keep them imprisoned. The myths speak of another aspect of djinn that has been known to pop up in reality—they sometimes offer wishes, though mostly what happens is a djinn offering illusions, which helps build their reputation as deceivers. In modern study, djinn are perceived as carrying strong resentment when bound to a magician, citing Solomon as the original cause of their angst.

⊙ Wasn't there an old flatvid with a crazy blonde genie in a bottle?

⊙ Slamm-0!

⊙ That, and stuff from further back, like the aforementioned 1,001 Arabian Nights. The book has a collection of stories of djinn and how they can grant wishes and put magicians on flying carpets and the like. That last one is especially interesting. Literal magicians are still working on an efficient flying carpet, though some say stories of flying carpets should be taken as metaphors for astral travel.

⊙ Crescent Moon

DJINN RULES

For those who would like to play one of the rare Islamic mages who dare to summon djinn, the spirit types used are slightly different. For this alternate tradition of Islam, use the following chart for summoning djinn.

Jinn: Beasts
Jann: Earth
Shaitan: Air
Marid: Water
Ifrit: Fire
Drain: Willpower + Logic

ADDITIONAL SPIRIT FEATURES

A djinn may take a severe allergy to one metal (copper, iron, silver, or gold) in order to gain an additional optional power. Note that the metal must be of reagent quality in origin to affect a djinn. This selection can only be done once. Alternatively, a djinn can substitute an existing severe allergy for one to metal; this does not result in them gaining an additional optional power.

All djinn have an inherent will to resist bonding and are considered to have the Restless quality (p. 199, Street Grimoire).

All djinn have the optional power Innate Spell (Trid Phantasm).

The skin tone of a humanoid-shaped djinn changes depending on its force. This cannot be hidden except through masking or illusion. An Arcana + Logic (2) [Mental] Test can estimate the power of a djinn based on its appearance.

FORCE	COLOR
1–2	Green
3–5	Blue
6–9	Red
10+	Black

While all summoned spirits technically don't have to tell the whole truth, Ifrit and Shaitan can lie if it suits their purpose like being set free from doing tasks. A magician must Judge Intentions (p. 152, SR5) to know if their summoned spirit is telling the truth. The spirit is still compelled to perform tasks as they interpret the commands.

NOTABLE TEACHERS

Within the Arabian Caliphate, there is no more influential teacher-sheikh than **Joseph Chamseddine.** Chamseddine is the childhood friend and spiritual mentor of Caliph Ibrahim Kamel. As a Sufi mystic, his ideas are not always in line with majority views, but Joseph presents himself as a bridge builder rather than a dogmatist. The protection afforded to him by the caliph allows him the freedom to teach Sufism, though Medina still does not seem ready for a Sufism-friendly university. If you are serious about learning from Chamseddine, try getting in touch with his mother, Hilal, who runs a restaurant in Qana, Lebanon.

⊙ Don't get the wrong impression. Chamseddine doesn't dictate policy or belief to the caliph. Far from it. They don't see eye to eye on many things. However, there is a deep respect between the two men, which has softened the new caliph's posture toward those who are different. That posture only extends so far, however. The caliph still seems to hold on to much of the xenophobia of his predecessors. The West has many hurdles to overcome in relationship with the Caliphate.

⊙ Am-mut

⊙ I hear Johnny Spinrad's been doing just fine in his "relationships" within the Caliphate. He's as Western as they come.

⊙ Clockwork

- Yeah. He's doin' alright. But believe me, there are many, many within the leadership of the Caliphate who oppose Spinrad's upcoming marriage to Gabrielle Al Thani, daughter of Qatar's Emir, Jassim bin Joaan Al Thani. However, money has long driven the decisions of ambitious men. And if they can hold their nose long enough, they will be the ones dictating relational terms to the world, not the reverse.
- 2XL

For those wishing to gain the best instruction in Islamic Alchemy, head to Constantinople's Grand Bazaar and look for Uday "Azoth" Antar. Azoth used to work for the Iraqi president back before Iraq was absorbed into the Caliphate. Once he fled, he headed for the Bazaar and has set up quite a nice life for himself running an odd shop there. Azoth sells Qur'anic talismans (non-magical), reagents, licit spell formulas, halal and kosher ingredients, but if he likes you, or if you pay him a lot, he can teach you a great deal about alchemy.

- Azoth is well-respected, and feared, in Istanbul. He can do wonders for those he likes, and for those he doesn't, life becomes ... challenging.
- Goat Foot

Sulaiman Istihkara is a teacher of Licit Qur'anic Magic at Brite Divinity School in Fort Worth, Texas. Yes, it is ironic that the only place he felt safe enough to practice and develop his theories was at a liberal divinity school, but since the Awakening, many divinity schools opened up their study programs to multiple religions. Istihkara, as his name implies in Arabic, is a master of "cutting of the Qur'an" in order to gain wisdom. He is easy to find, and you can sign up for his classes with no real trouble, assuming you have a fake SIN.

SHAMANISM (UPDATED)

(P. 279, SR5)

All shamans share one belief in common: Magic is not something to be dissected and formulated; it is something that is felt and honored. Excepting the toxic variety, shamans tend to seek balance between the natural and spiritual worlds. Even those shamans who live in urban areas, so-called street shamans, have learned to find harmony with the city's ecosystem. While the world around them sees nature and life as resources to be exploited, shamans see the world and its spirits as allies.

TRADITIONALIST SHAMAN

While many shamanic mages embrace the Unified Magic Theory to some extent and have benefited from its application, there are many shamans who resent the implication that magic can be tidied up and placed in neat boxes. These shamans follow older paths and keep strict boundaries around their practices, as they feel it is truer to the spirits and helps maintain an ancient harmony. These Traditionalists always have mentor spirits, only summon spirits native to the local environment, and never bind spirits.

ANCESTOR SHAMAN

The practice of venerating ancestors is as ancient as human civilization. While most shamans revere the Earth and its spirits, Ancestor Shamans primarily interact with the spirits of those who once lived. Ancestor Shamans do not bind spirits, have a deep concern for their honor/shame reputation in the spirit world, and often have an easier time initiating due to communion with the dead who share their tradition.

RELATED MENTOR SPIRITS

Most of shamanism resists the urge to call their totems by the designation of "mentor spirits." This has not stopped others who subscribe to Unified Magic Theory from doing so. Most shamans choose animal-based totems. Ancestor Shamans do not choose animal totems, however, as most prefer the Wise Warrior, representing an ancestor with particular resonance to the shaman.

ROLE-PLAYING A SHAMAN

Shamans are different from other traditions in that they actually care. They may not care about individuals per se, but they do care. This concern for the Earth in general, or a particular place or group of spirits, causes them to act, or not act, in ways others may not understand. This misunderstanding can be a great source of tension (drama) within a group. Don't move for others against your principles. Plant yourself, and make others go around you.

IDEALS

Shamans are not one-size-fits-all when it comes to ideals. A Wolf shaman from the Sioux Nation is going to have a much different set of values than a Sea shaman from Lagos. Yet these two will always agree that spirits are to be respected (at least certain spirits) and there are some things in the universe greater than them to which they owe their power. What form this reverence takes will always depend on the individual.

SORCERY

Shamans practice spellcasting normally.

CONJURING

Shamans practice conjuration normally.

ENCHANTING

Shamans practice enchanting normally.

ALTERNATE SHAMANIC PATH RULES

TRADITIONALIST SHAMANS

- Must take the Mentor Spirit quality.
- Gains Code of Honor: Harmony with Nature, the Shaman's Code, for free.
- Gains an additional +1 when casting spells related to their mentor spirit or related to the local environment (ex. Traditionalist Shaman Kokii gains +1 to cast her Fireball close to a volcano, while the Traditionalist Shark Shaman Mako gains an additional +1 to Combat spells as the Shark mentor spirit already gives a bonus to combat spells).
- May only summon spirits native to local environments (water spirits near sources of water, spirits of man in inhabited places, etc.).
- May not bind spirits.
- At initiate grade 3, gains the Spirit Affinity quality for free.
- At initiate grade 5, gains +2 dice pool bonus to summon a spirit type of the shaman's choice.

ANCESTOR SHAMANS

- Receive +2 dice pool bonus when summoning spirits of man.
- Suffer –2 dice pool penalty when summoning all other types of spirits.
- May not bind spirits of man.

SHAMANIC TRADITION

Combat: Beasts
Detection: Water
Health: Earth
Illusion: Air
Manipulation: Man
Drain: Willpower + Charisma

PREFERRED SPELLS
None

- At initiate grade 2, may channel spirits of man as if they had the channeling metamagic.

NOTABLE TEACHERS

There is no shortage of shamans willing to teach what they know. But if you are stuck, head to **Derek Branch-Breaker** in the Cascade Mountains. He lives there in a semi-friendly alliance with the Cascade Orks, which means if you need to find him, you'll be going through unfriendly territory if you don't have tusks or horns. Rumor is that he ran afoul of city planners in Seattle who seized his land. He fought back—and lost some loved ones in the process. After that, he's been training other shamans nonstop. Some say he is training an army; others think he is just following his totem Bear and trying to heal old wounds. Either way, he'll teach you if he thinks you're worth it.

> ◉ Branch-Breaker is indeed training an army, but not one recognizable as such.
> ◉ Man-of-Many-Names

If you are looking for someone to teach you Ancestor Shamanism, head to Ordos City in Mongolia and find **Gansükh Khünbish** at the Shrine of Genghis Khan. Be warned: Khünbish (always Khünbish—Gansükh is his father's name) is not friendly. In fact, he can be downright hostile. So read up on Mongolian culture before you even think about reaching out to him. He doesn't use modern tech often and never replies to correspondence, so if you want a teacher who is the best of the best, you're going to have to go ask him yourself. He values fighting, so expect a brawl when you get there.

NEW TRADITIONS

COSMIC

Since the first human (or metahuman, if you like) appeared, the stars have been a source of fascination and wonder. For some mages, simply pondering the heavens was not enough. For these Awakened, the cosmos is the source of life and the most powerful agent in all reality. The harmony of the celestial bodies, their perfect orbits, and their predictable nature pleases Cosmic Mages, and they aspire for their magic to be similarly perfect and predictable.

Cosmic Mages point to ancient worship of heavenly bodies in Babylon, Egypt, and Rome as the basis for their belief, although their forebears tapped into power they didn't understand. While Cosmic Mages are the first to admit their knowledge is limited as well, they believe that their ex-

panded understanding of the universe and its nature gives them further insight through which to channel their magic.

The fundamental forces behind the universe, the planets, the stars, and even dark matter have replaced ancient anthropomorphic symbolism, but honor for the sun, moon, and stars has resurged, often in corporate settings, as a non-threatening tradition for corporate mages to participate in. Cosmic magic is not idealistic, but skews more deterministic. While Cosmic Mages believe in individual will, they assert that everything happens as a result of the cause-and-effect process begun by the creation of the universe itself.

RELATED MENTOR SPIRITS

Cosmic Mages exclusively follow the Sun, Moon, or Star mentor spirits.

ROLE-PLAYING A COSMIC MAGE

Cosmic Mages are rarely one-dimensional. While they value the universe as the ultimate source of life, time, and power, there is no consensus about how those beliefs should affect one's life. Cosmic Mages tend to be scientific and rather detached about the world, but at the same time they encourage every individual to create their own meaning within the universe's vast space.

COSMIC MAGES

Combat: Earth
Detection: Guidance
Health: Water
Illusion: Air
Manipulation: Fire
Drain: Willpower + Logic

PREFERRED SPELLS

Analyze Magic, Analyze Truth, Comet, Detect, Gravity, Shape, Sunbeam

IDEALS

Beyond recognizing the universe as the ultimate source of power, Cosmic Mages have few unchallenged ideals. They value science and exploration and have little patience for other traditions, which they consider fairy tales.

SORCERY

Cosmic Mages practice spellcasting normally.

CONJURING

Cosmic Mages practice conjuring normally.

ENCHANTING

Cosmic Mages practice enchanting normally.

COSMIC MAGE RULES

- At initiate grade 1, choose a spell from Preferred Spells list. Receive a +1 dice pool bonus on Spellcasting tests to cast this spell.
- At initiate grade 3, choose a spell from Preferred Spells list (different from spell chosen at earlier initiate grades). Receive a +1 dice pool bonus on Spellcasting tests to cast this spell.
- At initiate grade 5, choose a spell from Preferred Spells ist (different from spell chosen at earlier initiate grades). Receive a +1 dice pool bonus on Spellcasting tests to cast this spell.

NOTABLE TEACHERS

Busiko Demba, in the Empire of Zambia, instructs all who come to him in the Cosmic Magic tradition. He claims his teaching stretches back millennia, and he says he weathered hot and cold persecution during the Fifth World. Now, he teaches more traditional Cosmic Magic, focused on older, anthropomorphic paradigms but infused with modern science and understanding. A thoughtful teacher, he is also a mage of no small skill who will train those who are willing to give him five years of service.

- Demba seems to know more about magic than he should. The way he speaks, you would think that he has been around for thousands of years. But he's a human, so there's no way. But for a man who looks forty or fifty, he sure has the wisdom of someone much older.
- Lyran

Luca Brilhart at Stockholm University is another option for those who prefer a more academic approach to Cosmic Magic. Once a professor of Roman studies, Luca discovered the foundations of ancient Roman Sun worship fit with his nascent magical abilities. Once he applied his rigorous methodology to that ancient practice, his treatise on Cosmic Magic was born. He is making an ardent attempt to gain popularity both for his books and his tradition, so he offers scholarships and personal lessons to those willing to learn.

DRACONIC

When magic returned to the world, it was chaotic. Not many people knew what they were doing, and they were often surprised when they were able to do even the most basic magic that the Awakened take for granted today. But there were some who knew exactly what they were doing, since they have been doing it since well before the beginning of the Awakening: Dragons. When dragons awakened from their slumber, they had access to terrible and wonderful power, manipulating mana as if they were born to it. They may indeed be born to it, but it is closer to the truth that dragons have had multiple millennia to develop a tradition that is elegant, efficient, and exclusive to themselves.

Strictly speaking, however, dragons are not the only ones who are able to use this paradigm. Often, dragons teach their drake servants how to spellcast, summon, or use adept powers in a way that even the most learned scholar of the Sixth World cannot grasp. The leading theory is that the draconic brain is simply wired differently than (and, dragons would add, superior to) metahumanity, and thus non-dragons cannot grasp the concepts required for Draconic magic. There are a few exceptions to this, mainly rumored among Seelie Court elves, but it has never been witnessed to anyone's satisfaction. Other theories suggest that in some ways, despite their ancient traditions and long lives with which to master them, dragons are actually at the disadvantage. Draconic scorn of faith is legendary, but what if that were a weakness, rather than a strength? What if dragons are forced to rely only on their own resources rather than being able to tap into higher mysteries and beings that metahumanity has often stumbled upon?

- ❂ This brings up an interesting point that I have been trying to research. Many Awakened metahumans have had encounters with various totems or mentor spirits. These beings grant power and guidance to the mages who follow them. I know that some doubt the existence of mentor spirits, as their existence cannot be proven by conventional means, but the abilities they grant are hard to argue with. Which brings me to my hypothesis: I don't think dragons can interact with totems or "gods." There may be some sort of mental block preventing them from doing so, almost like they are deficient in a spiritual way. My research is ongoing, but that is where it is leading.
- ❂ Old Crow

- ❂ That is simply not true. Dragons know of these totem spirits. We simply have nothing to gain by worshiping them or allying with them.
- ❂ Orange Queen

- ❂ No disrespect, your worship, but it is unsurprising for your kind to disagree on this point. No one likes to feel inferior.
- ❂ Old Crow

Regardless, the Draconic tradition has some points of similarity with various other traditions, but it also transcends them in some ways. For example,

ROLE-PLAYING A DRACONIC MAGE

Drake mages rely on older dragon tutors to teach them new aspects of their tradition. Learning new spells and initiating requires the drake to embrace the tension between learning from another and self-determination. Older dragons may pass on some information, but it will always be up to the drake to figure out how to apply the lessons learned and will the improvements to happen.

Further, while drakes are using the same tradition as their Draconic masters, drakes are never taught how the tradition works. They are only allowed to access its power through their relationship with their tutor. The Draconic tutor acts as a contact for role-playing purposes, but they will never divulge any relevant information to the PC, only act as a conduit and tutor for the Draconic tradition.

with regard to summoning, the Draconic tradition teaches its initiates to summon only those spirits that can materialize. But it seems that older Dragons can cross this line, allowing Dragons to summon spirits that can't materialize, but instead use inhabitation or possession. Overall, Draconic magic is incredibly robust and breaks many "rules" of traditional magic, and in that way, their magic reflects their own nature as much as metahuman traditions reflect them. Thankfully, drakes who use this tradition are not initiated into the Draconic tradition proper, but are allowed to "channel" magic through their Draconic tutor. As a result, every drake who uses Draconic magic has a tutor they pay homage to—or serve, to put it bluntly—and without a tutor, the drake's magic no longer works properly, reverting to hermetic magic until another tutor is found.

RESTRICTIONS

Only characters with the Drake quality may choose this tradition.

RELATED MENTOR SPIRITS

Followers of the Draconic tradition cannot take the Mentor Spirit quality. Likewise, those with the Mentor Spirit quality cannot learn Draconic magic unless they remove the quality.

IDEALS

Draconic spellcasting is inherently self-focused. Dragons have learned over millennia to trust only in themselves, and it shows where their magic is concerned. Draconic spellcasters cannot join magical groups, and they must initiate alone. They may help others in rituals, initiation, etc., but they will never benefit from the help of other mages.

SORCERY

Due to the radical self-reliance dragons practice, those following the Draconic tradition do not need ritual materials or magical lodges.

CONJURING

Due to the special relationship that dragons have to magic, all restrictions based on spirit types are removed. Draconic practitioners can summon any type of spirit (other than spirits that use inhabitation or possession rather than materialization), and spirits can aid or assist the mage in any task, regardless of type.

ENCHANTING

While the greater and more ancient of their kin look down upon foci and fetishes, drakes can use Enchanting as normal.

INITIATION

Continuing on with the theme of Draconic self-dependence, drakes are expected to forge their own paths and initiate on their own once they are strong and learned enough to do so.

NOTABLE TEACHERS

There are no true teachers of Draconic magic, at least that metahumans have access to. Dragons only teach the true tradition to each other, and the diluted version that drakes are taught cannot be learned by other metahumans.

ELDER GOD MAGIC

Many traditions, including the ancient Greeks, Germanic tribes, and Near-Eastern peoples, spoke in hushed tones about the gods that came before the ones they worship. Titans, Old Ones, primordial entities—whatever term you use, these Elder Gods represent the forces of chaos and power that existed before time began to have meaning.

Known in various regions as Ba'al, Nergal, Dagon, Yam, Ktulu, Moloch, Ashtoreth, Kronus, or in-

finite other names, these gods are altogether alien to metahumanity. Their goals, if any, are completely unfathomable, and the ends they desire are equally obtuse. What is known is that they desire followers and have granted power and guidance to those who have sufficient will to resist the madness that comes from interacting with them.

Most religions consider their own pantheons (or gods) to be mostly benevolent, having some overarching good that can be accomplished if their will is done. The Elder Gods, on the other hand, do not pretend to share any sort of benign goodwill for the universe. They simply are. They have innate power. They hunger.

Thankfully, the risks of following these beings seem too great for most mages. But for the few who choose to pursue this path, the lack of boundaries and secret knowledge they gain is worth the madness and the slight chance of being devoured and dissolving into nothingness.

RELATED MENTOR SPIRITS

Those who dabble in this forbidden tradition often profess to learning from mentor spirits that resemble Adversary, Arcana, Dark King, or Tohu Wa-Bohu.

* Honestly? Tohu Wa-Bohu is a mentor spirit? That makes no sense. How can something defined by being without function or form be anyone's mentor?
* Mr. Bonds

* I don't even know what that is. Since when were you a mage? How do you know what this is?
* Slamm-0!

* Because once upon a time, a rabbi made me memorize large chunks of Torah, that's why.
* Mr. Bonds

DRACONIC TRADITION

Combat: Any
Detection: Any
Health: Any
Illusion: Any
Manipulation: Any
Drain: Willpower + Magic

PREFERRED SPELLS
None. Or all. Depends on your perspective.

- To answer your question, if one can bear the looking, there is much that can be learned from the void.
- Man-of-Many-Names

- Nothing good, I bet.
- Mr. Bonds

IDEALS

These mages, often deridingly called cultists, have few ideals to speak of. If they value anything, it is truth, no matter how ugly and harsh, and perhaps an exaggerated sense of their own importance to their masters' plans. In a perfect world, these horrifying deities are simply manifestations of their believers' passions rather than beings of corporeal fact. If they actually exist, though, their true purposes are as mercurial as the names these cultists use to refer to them. Almost by definition, metahuman logic is insufficient to understand their actions.

SORCERY

Elder God mages practice spellcasting normally.

CONJURING

Elder God mages practice conjuring as normal.

ENCHANTING

Elder God mages practice enchanting normally.

ELDER GOD MAGE RULES

- Receive a –2 dice pool penalty on all Drain tests.
- Gain a +3 dice pool bonus when casting Illusion spells.
- At initiate grade 1, must choose the corruption metamagic.
- At initiate grade 3, gains the taint metamagic in addition to a metamagic of their choice.

NOTABLE TEACHERS

There are no known teachers of this tradition. Many current practitioners claim to be trained by **Titus Sloven**, but since Sloven threw himself into the maw of an Awakened kraken, many of his students have gone into hiding to escape the persecution that usually follows these cultists. Rumor persists that Sloven survives, but no

ROLE-PLAYING AN ELDER GOD MAGE

This can be a tricky tradition to role-play, especially at a table with diverse characters. In some ways, it would be easier to determine beforehand what the character's motivation for shadowrunning is before they begin playing. If they have a long-term goal, perhaps they view teaming up as a means to an end. Alternatively, they may be touched by a bit of madness and even they don't know why they do what they do. Whispering to yourself, hearing strange voices, paranoia even beyond what is typical for shadowrunners, and certain self-and-team-defeating behavior can make this tradition come alive. It is important to remember that ultimately, these are not necessarily evil characters, but even if they are, their evil should rarely be turned on other players, as there are plenty of other targets in the Sixth World, and teammates can be valuable pawns to accomplish the will of your lord. Basically, find a way to play that works with, instead of against, the goals of the other characters—while possibly making their lives more interesting along the way.

ELDER GOD TRADITION

Combat: Task
Detection: Guardian
Health: Earth
Illusion: Fire
Manipulation: Water
Drain: Willpower + Intuition

PREFERRED SPELLS

Agony, Bugs, Chaos, Confusion, Foreboding, Phantasm, Mob Mind

concrete evidence has appeared to support this claim.

- For the record, that was not an Awakened kraken Sloven threw himself into.
- Elijah

- Okay, Mr. Mysterioso, what was it?
- Slamm-0!

- Well?
- Slamm-0!

- I hate it when he does that.
- Slamm-0!

GREEN MAGIC

On the surface, Green Magic seems to have much in common with eco-shamanism or nature-based Druidic traditions. But dig a little deeper and, common interests aside, they are startlingly different. This "newer" tradition was not created as much as rediscovered by Tzuri Group archeologists investigating one of two cities found resting underwater in the Gulf of Khambhat off India's northwestern coast. Tzuri found that plant worship was common 10,000 years ago and led by "Priests of Green."

> ◎ Didn't the Tzuri Group discover two sunken cities on that expedition?
> ◎ Elijah
>
> ◎ Yes, they did. Check out the next entry for what they discovered at the other.
> ◎ Axis Mundi

Green mages view their magic as coming from an elemental power beyond our world that connects all plant life together in one metaplanar eco-system called the Domain of Green. Green mages don't necessarily focus on balance and harmony with nature or honoring all spirits equally. Rather, they give primacy to plant life and only pursue goals that aim to increase the growth and spread of plant life.

In return, the Green mage gains tremendous power in the domain of plants. According to archeological evidence, this focus often placed the more dogmatic Priests of Green in conflict with the more aggressive Red Mages.

RELATED MENTOR SPIRITS

Many Green mages have found the Green Man (Tree/Viridios) mentor spirit calling to them, or they are called by another spirit with a similar purpose.

IDEALS

Green mages hold respect for plant life above everything else. In their mind, life on Earth, and everywhere else in the universe, not only started with plant life, but is sustained by it. The idea that metahumanity, animal life in general, or any other sapient life holds more value than the world's plant life is abhorrent to them. As long as Green survives, the rest of life will find a way also.

ROLE-PLAYING A GREEN MAGE

Green mages are not the same as eco-shamans. Green mages may respect the earth and seek balance, but they are first and foremost dedicated to the plant kingdom. How this plays out in individual games could include anything from radical, plants-rights activism to providing a reasoned voice of representation for the Domain of Green.

GREEN MAGES

Combat: Plant
Detection: Earth or Plant
Health: Water or Plant
Illusion: Air or Plant
Manipulation: Fire (Sun)
Drain: Willpower + Charisma

PREFERRED SPELLS

Branch, Growth, Heal, Lash, Opium Den, Rosebush, Slash, Stink, Sunbeam, Thorn, Vine

SORCERY

Green mages practice spellcasting normally.

CONJURING

Green mages practice conjuring normally.

ENCHANTING

Green mages practice enchanting normally.

GREEN MAGE RULES

- Cannot summon beast spirits or spirits of man.
- Gain +2 dice pool bonus to summon plant spirits.
- At initiate grade 1, must choose the cleansing metamagic.

NOTABLE TEACHERS

One of the friendliest people I've ever met is **Holland Hara**. The irony is that Hara isn't a person at all. Hara is a great form plant spirit who became free through circumstances lost to time. Explorers found Holland meditating at the bottom of the Gulf of Khambhat, sustaining an entire eco-system of underwater plant life, which he claims to have been doing somehow for over four thousand years. Once discovered, the explorers offered to help Hara transplant seeds of these plants to various locations, and he agreed to teach them Green Magic. Once he learned of new technologies that he could use to help plant life, as well as repair the damage that industry had done to the eco-system, Holland Hara has been on a mission to restore balance to the world, winning one heart at a time.

- So, does this tradition only conjure plants and use magic that is green? That seems rather limiting.
- Mika

- That is definitely not the case. A Green mage I know by the name of Krenger could cast other types of spells. While they didn't necessarily all look like plants, they were from domains that we normally associate with plants and their nurture. For example, his Flamethrower-like spell was a beam of sunlight. His Healing manifested as water. Whenever he was using a Detection spell, he stuck his hands in the ground. That kinda stuff. What he never did, though, was bother with domains like beasts or man.
- Ethernaut

MISSIONISTS

Since the Awakening, the Christian churches of the world (Catholic, Protestant, Orthodox, and beyond) have argued about what the reappearance of magic means for their faith. In the early part of the twenty-first century, there was a massive divide, even within denominations, between those who accepted magic as another aspect of God's creation and those who despised magic as anathema. Eventually, many within the Christian tradition began practicing magic in Neoplatonic or theurgist paradigms.

Much of Christian theological history focused on the vast chasm between the body, considered corruptible and "bad," and the spirit, considered pure and "good." This value was shared by Neoplatonists, who, along with Gnostics, believed that mysticism held the secret to spiritual power. This Neoplatonism had a strong influence on the Christian faith, but not all Christian traditions followed this path.

The so-called "Missionist" tradition (coined by Rev. Belle Robinson) began more or less by accident in Detroit, Michigan. Since Detroit had become an Ares company town, those without a connection

ROLE-PLAYING A MISSIONIST MAGE

Missionist mages can function most efficiently as healers within a group. Violence is not something they ever enjoy, and when they fight or kill, it will always be "punching up"—that is, they will only do so to those they consider oppressors, never to the oppressed, and even then they will do so reluctantly.

MISSIONIST TRADITION

Combat: Man
Detection: Air
Health: Water
Illusion: Fire
Manipulation: Earth
Drain: Willpower + Charisma

PREFERRED SPELLS

Alleviate, Armor, Cure Disease, Deflection, Forced Defense, Heal, Knockout, Multiply Food, Stunball, Stunbolt

to the megacorp were often left destitute. Many of Detroit's churches had signed the accord of 2023, committing to non-engagement in debates about magic while continuing their focus on serving the poor, the outcast, and marginalized. In 2044, the coalition spontaneously performed a ritual that fed all of Detroit's homeless population for a day. The next week, at a similar meeting, many were healed of various diseases. Rev. Robinson from St. Giles Presbyterian Church soon founded a divinity school dedicated to studying this phenomenon. 2075 saw the first graduating class of Remnant Divinity School and the first official practitioners of Missionist Magic, which focused not on obscure texts or mystic power, but on the healing of people, nations, and the planet.

- Uh, look. No offense, but these cross-hippies seem utterly useless as shadowrunners. I mean, I guess they don't need to be runners, but … yawn.
- Turbo Bunny

- You're missing the point. They aren't included here just because they might be threats or potential members of a team (although I can think of a few times one would come in handy). But knowing one could save your life if you happen to be shot up, stranded, and need to lei low. They'll help, even if you got nothing in trade. There's your incentive to know something about 'em. Too bad there aren't many around.
- Bull

RELATED MENTOR SPIRITS

The only mentor spirits common to Missionist Mages are Peacemaker and Holy Text.

IDEALS

Missionist mages exist to heal broken things. They are not necessarily dogmatic in their beliefs, although they can be. They tend to be the first to de-escalate situations of violence, but they are not universally opposed to using violence to reach their goals. Many Missionists find themselves at similar purposes with anarchist movements, as they see corporations as the largest oppressors of the poor. They pursue healing and aid while giving preferential treatment to the poor and marginalized, as they see this as their mission. Most consider spirits to be another aspect of their God's creation, and as such, will not bind them.

SORCERY

Missionist mages practice spellcasting normally.

CONJURING

Missionist mages practice conjuring as normal but cannot bind spirits.

ENCHANTING

Missionist mages practice enchanting normally.

MISSIONIST MAGE RULES

- Gain +2 dice pool bonus when casting Health spells.
- Suffer –2 dice pool penalty when casting Combat spells.
- At initiate grade 1, must choose the shielding metamagic.
- At initiate grade 3, must take the noble sacrifice metamagic.

NOTABLE TEACHERS

Although **Reverend Belle Robinson** is the "founder" of the Missionist tradition, she is the first to correct you and say that the tradition began long ago by someone better than her. Further, while she still holds a ceremonial position at Remnant Divinity School, she spends most of her time in Detroit, working among the down-and-out.

> Robinson seems like the real deal. There isn't much light that is legit in the shadows, but Rev. Belle doesn't over-promise, and she helps wherever she can. Unfortunately for her, that is why her tradition is so small. There isn't a lot of money, power, or fame in suffering on behalf of others. Still, while I pursue the finer things in life, people like Robinson keep me from having to spend too much of my nuyen on hospital bills and food when I'm in town.
> Kane

> I am not sure if that was complimentary or condescending. Knowing you, it's both.
> /dev/grrl

> Come on. Haven't we all learned our lesson? There is no such thing as an altruistic organization or group. These people just haven't showed their true colors yet. Universal Brotherhood, anyone?
> Black Knight

> Sorry, bud. I just can't work myself up about these folks. They are too insignificant.
> Kane

Now, if one wishes to learn Missionist magic, **Rev. Baily Warner** is the one to speak with. He is the current president of Remnant Divinity. If you want to learn, he'll encourage you to enroll in the school and learn alongside the other students.

However, if you want to learn in a less-formal setting, from those with boots on the ground, check out **Sister Francisca Tancredi** in Bogota. She is part of the Catholic resistance in Aztlan, preferring to fight with healing magic and food rather than with guns. She was not formally trained but practices a non-formal version she developed among the warzone's most needy.

> Sister Tancredi helped Aufheben often in the resistance to Aztlan. She stood against the Azzies, which he liked, so he overlooked her Catholic side because she patched up his grunts and fed his sympathizers. His biggest beef with her was that she refused to take up arms. She always said that she had a bigger battle to fight.
> Old Crow

NECRO MAGIC

Not to be confused with Black Magic, Necro Magic is described by its practitioners as welling up from a force they call the Domain of the Black. The power wielded by these mages is a force of decay and destruction, but practitioners insist that their tradition is not toxic, despite what they call superficial similarities.

Dr. Jennifer Stinson, who has claimed the title "High Priestess of Black," famously demonstrated the power of Necro Magic in 2075 when she performed a ritual ending the burgeoning VITAS-4 outbreak in Milan. While there were some casualties among the poorest citizens, the rest of the city was so grateful that it hailed Stinson as a savior.

The current incarnation of the Necro Magic tradition began in earnest following the return of the Tzuri Group from a metaplanar archeological expedition in 2064. For a decade, practice of Necro Magic remained secretive and restricted to those within the Tzuri Group which took part in the expedition. When Dr. Stinson saved Milan, however, many interested parties began to seek her out for instruction.

Stinson cites the magic of the Green and Red when discussing how Necro Magic is not unnatural or evil, but simply another facet of life in the universe. Necro mages claim that while their power can seem only destructive, it is actually peaceful in the same way that arms manufacturers actually seek peace and safety when they create weapons. Stinson vows that her tradition only uses Necro Magic for the greater good, and thus far, everything she has shown the outside world has been consistent with that claim.

- Anyone else thinking it is what she hasn't shown the outside world that is going to bite us in the hoop?
- Netcat

- Come on, 'Cat. You of all people should know better than to condemn what you don't understand.
- Butch

- No, Netcat is right to be scared. Stinson has skeletons in her closet. Actual skeletons. And she speaks with them nightly after her grisly blood rituals.
- Plan 9

- Are you even trying to differentiate between real and make-believe anymore?
- Snopes

Stinson and the Tzuri Group are adamant that their beliefs are not new or novel. They claim that, according to discoveries they made on their journey, their magic has been practiced on Earth and elsewhere for more than ten thousand years. Necro Magic, they claim, is the basis for much of the magic practiced in many existing traditions.

ROLE-PLAYING A NECRO MAGE

Necro mages will always be looked upon with suspicion. Even in areas like parts of Tsimshian and Yakut, where Necro Magic is accepted, the average person will still more than likely fear a Necro mage because of their power and morbid nature. It is up to the player to decide how evil a Necro mage really is. Is Necro Magic really malevolent, while trying to masquerade as a simple force of nature? Are mages in the thrall of a force much darker and more heinous than they let on? Or perhaps they really seek the good of all through one of nature's more hated but necessary forces?

NECRO MAGIC

Combat: Corpse (Man)
Detection: Carcass (Beast)
Health: Rot (Plant)
Illusion: Detritus (Earth)
Manipulation: Palefire (Fire)
Drain: Willpower + Logic

PREFERRED SPELLS

Death Replay, Death Touch, Manabolt, Manaball, One Less, Slaughter, Slay, Shattershield, Rot, Death Mark (ritual), Necro Summoning (ritual), Whisper of Bones (ritual)

RELATED MENTOR SPIRITS

Many Necro mages follow the mentor spirit Death or Dark King, if they follow a mentor at all.

IDEALS

The Necro Magic tradition teaches that death is not only an inevitable aspect of life, but also one that ultimately leads to peace. Necro mages tend to value quiet and stillness, as they believe the universe was at its most peaceful before there was life. Most consider their fascination with the dead to be unhealthy, but Necro mages counter that most religions in the Sixth World also value communion with the dead, albeit in a way that Necro mages believe is sanitized, delayed, and distorted.

SORCERY

Necro Mages practice spellcasting normally.

CONJURING

Necro Magic is a possession tradition. It cannot summon as normal, but uses the Necro Summoning Ritual instead.

ENCHANTING

Necro mages practice enchanting normally.

NECRO MAGE RULES

- Must take Ritual Spellcasting.
- At character creation, must choose one (and only one) Necro Summoning ritual.
- Cannot summon normal spirits, but are restricted to Corpse, Carcass, Rot, Detritus, or Palefire spirits.
- At initiate grade 1, learn one additional Necro Summoning ritual.
- At initiate grade 2, learn one additional Necro Summoning ritual.
- At initiate grade 3, learn one additional Necro Summoning ritual.
- At initiate grade 4, gain an additional +2 dice pool bonus to summoning rituals.
- At initiate grade 5, learn one additional Necro Summoning ritual.
- At initiate grade 6, may take the reckless Necro Summoning metamagic (in place of normal metamagic).

NOTABLE TEACHERS

Dr. Jennifer Stinson is the premier teacher of Necro Magic. The chairperson of the Tzuri Group, she fills most of her days running Tzuri's corporate HQ in Mumbai. Almost all current Necro mages trace their tutelage back to her. Since the reveal of Necro Magic to the world in '75, however, she has not taken on any pupils, at least that we know of. That isn't to say that she isn't trying to grow her craft.

Dr. Henry Hwang, Dr. Stinson's associate (and fellow metaplanar archeologist) has taken on more students in the last five years. Hwang runs the Tzuri Group's Korean operations out of Pyongyang, and his Necro School (professing "Peace and Power Through Acceptance") is actively taking new recruits, as well as scanning East Asia for potentially Awakened individuals.

A former associate of Stinson and Hwang, **Dr.**

Jesse Hodges, apparently broke ties with the Tzuri group and has taken on at least two pupils that we know of. His current location is unknown, and according to one of his students, he is rather reclusive. If you can find "Hermit" Hodges, he may teach you, but it may not be the same formal education you would get from the "official" Tzuri teachers.

- I can't post it here, but if anyone wants to know why Hodges broke with Tzuri, I have the goods. It'll cost you 4,000 nuyen for the info, though. So keep that in mind before you ask.
- Haze

- It's no secret. Hodges was touched in the head. He had a breakdown and was fired. No conspiracy.
- Snopes

- Oh yeah? Tell me about his breakdown. Anything specific?
- Haze

- No? I didn't think s... Heh. Thanks for the 4,000, Snopesy. Check your inbox.
- Haze

OLYMPIANISM

The legends of the classical gods and goddesses of ancient Greece are still as prevalent in public education today as they were last century. And the fascination with the ancient Greeks doesn't end there. Books, trids, architecture, philosophy, and even the form of government in some countries still reflect a never-ending fascination with all things Hellenistic. And that is without even mentioning how Ares Macrotechnology keeps that culture alive in many less obvious ways.

So it should come as no surprise that since the Awakening, many have retread ancient texts and rediscovered ancient forms of worship and devotion to these classical gods. This restored worship is called Olympianism, after Mount Olympus, where the gods had their home. Olympians point to the mysterious veil around the summit of Mount Olympus that appeared some years ago as evidence that their faith is correctly placed.

Olympianists are a robust and diverse group, accepting all metatypes and abilities, as they believe all life was made by the gods. Greek spirits are commonplace in Olympian lore, from household gods and ancestor spirits to fairy-like spirits of air, water, earth, and fire. The Olympians take great care to not offend spirits if possible.

Olympianist priests generally venerate all of the Greek Pantheon, but once initiated, they specialize in service to one particular deity. The most common devotion goes to Zeus, of course, then Aphrodite, then Hera, followed by Ares and Hades. Even though these gods receive more praise, strong followings of Neptune, Apollo, and Artemis exist, as do smaller devotions to almost every other god within the pantheon (including a small sect of powerful mages bound to Hecate).

Gregorios Argyris leads the renewed Olympianist temple in Athens. With visual aid given by a stable alchera, the Parthenon was magically restored to its former glory and now serves as the epicenter of the new and swiftly growing faith.

> ⊘ The renewed Parthenon is something to behold. It really isn't a wonder why so many are flocking to hear Gregorios speak and learn of the old ways.
> ⊘ Arete

RELATED MENTOR SPIRITS

While some Olympianists are committed to serving the entire pantheon, most eventually choose a patron deity. Those wishing to follow a particular deity can find existing mentor spirits that represent ideals their patron encourages. While not a deity, Oracle also fits well within the Olympianist paradigm.

IDEALS

The Olympianists don't always value the same things that the ancient Greeks did. Specifically, most Olympianists favor Athens and their democratic ideals rather than Spartan cruelty or Epicurean hedonism. While each god has their own focus, the pantheon as a whole and the Olympianists value learning, philosophy, martial prowess, and order.

SORCERY

Olympianists practice spellcasting normally.

CONJURING

Olympianists practice conjuring normally.

ENCHANTING

Olympianists practice enchanting normally.

NOTABLE TEACHERS

Gregorios Argyris and his democratic ekklesia (or principal assembly) lead the Hellenistic revival

---

ROLE-PLAYING AN OLYMPIANIST

The Greek pantheon should be fairly familiar. As such, the diversity of the gods provides an equally diverse way of playing an Olympian mage. Play up the superiority that such an ancient culture might command, or alternatively, humbly seek to spread the wisdom of ancient Greece to the masses.

OLYMPIANISM

Combat: Guardian
Detection: Air
Health: Earth
Illusion: Water
Manipulation: Fire
Drain: Willpower + Logic

PREFERRED SPELLS
Clairvoyance, Intoxication, Lightning Bolt, Napalm, Shapechange

---

in Greece. Gregorios may lead the movement, but he is hardly the most powerful member. In fact, the so-called **New Argonauts** are the highest-profile teachers of Olympianist magic.

The New Argonauts—**Hercules**, **Orpheus**, and **Atalanta**—form the leadership of the Olympianist Academy of Magic. While the academy is committed to training all seekers in the philosophy and use of Olympianist magic, they also handpick the best recruits to join the New Argonauts as mercenaries for hire. The New Argonauts travel where the Oracle leads them, and their prowess has gained them a herculean reputation in the shadows.

> ⊘ These guys are serious risers, quickly moving to elite levels. There are not many mercs I'd rather have at my back than these guys. Honorable and damn efficient in a scrap.
> ⊘ Hard Exit

PATH OF PARIAH
(FOR THE AWAKENED WHO HATE MAGIC)

Those who adhere to the Path of Pariah, appropriately called Pariahs, are radically different from every other mage in the Sixth World. That is because no other tradition of magic hates magic. But the Pariahs do. They see it as their mission to destroy magic in all of its forms, and they have a radical distaste for what they consider to be the corruption of the world since the Awakening.

Although this may seem contrary to their beliefs, Pariahs do in fact use magic. They view their gift as a curse: the curse of being able to fight magic with magic. As such, their art often seems more like magical defense to the casual observer.

Since Pariahs are often seen helping those who also hate the Awakened and other metahumans who have appeared since the Sixth World began, they are often mistaken for a tradition of hate. There is some truth to that, but their hate is not for any particular group or person, but for magic itself.

> ◉ Actually, there is a lot of truth to it. They don't just hate magic. They hate everyone who uses it. Yeah, they are super warm and fluffy to mundanes, I bet, but once they find out you sling, they turn cold and murderous. These fraggers are kin to a self-loathing troll joining Humanis and pounding other gobs.
> ◉ Thorn

> ◉ Not all of them are hateful like that. But I must say that too many are, so the point stands.
> ◉ Winterhawk

RELATED MENTOR SPIRITS

Pariahs loathe the idea of being helped or influenced by spirits, so they never have mentors.

IDEALS

Pariahs only have one over-arching commonality, and that is their desire for a world without magic. The most influential teachers of the Path of Pariah preach that if the world will give up its fascination with mana and strange things beyond our world, that false world, the astral plane, will lose its power and eventually fade away. Pariahs are the evangelists for this view, and they are sent as sheep among wolves, protecting humanity from itself.

SORCERY

Pariahs cannot use any skill in the Sorcery group except for Counterspelling.

ROLE-PLAYING A PARIAH

Role-playing a Pariah can be as varied an experience as the player desires. On one hand, the Pariah could be someone who hates all aspects of the Awakening, including elves, dwarves, trolls, orks, and all other magical creatures, in addition to magic. On the other side of the coin, a Pariah could see all of these creatures and people, including mages, as being afflicted by magic and thus worthy of pity. That means they never turn their anger on them directly, but only use their abilities to stop magic from doing what they consider to be damage.

PATH OF PARIAH

Combat: —
Detection: —
Health: —
Illusion: —
Manipulation: —
Drain: —

PREFERRED SPELLS
None

CONJURING

Pariahs cannot use any skill in the Conjuring group except for Banishing.

ENCHANTING

Pariahs cannot use any skill in the Enchanting group except for Disenchanting.

PARIAH RULES

- Cannot use Spellcasting, Ritual Spellcasting, Alchemy, Artificing, Summoning, or Binding.
- Gain +2 dice pool bonus to Counterspelling, Banishing, and Disenchanting tests.
- At initiate grade 1, must choose the shielding metamagic.
- At initiate grade 2, must take the opposition metamagic.
- At initiate grade 3, gains an additional +2 to Disenchanting tests.
- At initiate grade 4, gains an additional +2 to Counterspelling tests.
- At initiate grade 5, gains an additional +2 to Banishing tests.

NOTABLE TEACHERS

Brother Thomas Nesmith is a radical anti-magic preacher from north of Seattle. He has formed a small community in Salish-Shidhe land. They tolerate his community because they pay taxes and don't cause much trouble—at least, not that is obvious. Brother Nesmith does all his trouble-making subtly. There have been rumors of Pariah "justice," dealt out to unwitting mages who happen into their community, but no bodies or other confirmation have been seen. If you are not Awakened, or non-human, you will find Brother Nesmith a welcoming and humble teacher. If you are Awakened, steer very clear.

> ◙ Brother Nesmith is the creepiest fragger I've ever met. And I have met some doozies. Of course, they were pleasant as punch to me, because I'm mundane, but to hear these guys blessing the food and bringing the happy one moment and the next talk about stabbing the Awakened … It's just damn unsettling.
> ◙ Sunshine

Not all Pariahs are as nasty as Brother Nesmith, though. **Captain Digger Kelph** leads Lone Star Dallas' anti-magic task force. She isn't meta-racist and doesn't take pleasure in her job. She does, however, have a deep distrust of magic. She sees magic (and spirits) as sicknesses to help other overcome. As such, she cares deeply about those she is dispatched to help. Unfortunately for her, she rarely gets to help in the way she wants. Rather, she spends all of her time dealing with rogue mages, and more often than not, having to put them down. She teaches her trade freely, but with a sort of sadness that comes from seeing too much of the Sixth World's underside.

PLANAR MAGIC

After Dr. Daniel Gordon began publishing his work on metaplanar mapping and travel, interest in the so-called metaplanes peaked and has not slowed since. Gordon's final and most secretive work, descriptions of myriad metaplanes themselves, from first-hand knowledge, is still not published, and in fact was only made known narrowly here on JackPoint. For those interested, see Magister's upload called *Aetherology*.

But even without all the facts (or guesswork as the case may be) contained in Gordon's work, a rather new religion has emerged since the metaplanes made their way into the common parlance of magicians. I call it a religion because it checks all the boxes of traditional religion. But in some ways, it bears more resemblance to traditions of magic, which justifies its inclusion here.

The short version is this: Rather than the worship of traditional gods and ideals typically depicted on Earth, the discovery of other realms beyond our own has led certain mages to seek out quantifiable sources of power rather than invisible, untouchable deities. As such, these "Planar mages" first study the metaplanes and their effects on our world, then travel to these planes to form pacts with extra-planar entities, exchanging their souls (or less-fantastic prizes) for enhanced magical abilities.

The contacted entities act as mentor spirits for these mages, and although they are clearly not omnipotent beings, they are given reverence bordering on worship. Not all Planar mages give unwavering devotion to their patron, but whether they share common purpose or are compelled to obey, Planar mages end up serving the goals of the metaplaner entity on earth. Finally, it should be said that the Planar Research Society of Magic (PRiSM) is non-partisan and does not judge between planar entities. That is, while some within the society are bound to extraplanar entities that are benevolent, others are clearly bound to selfish or far more vile spirits. While PRiSM has strict conduct for meetings and interactions between members, it is the sharing of information and best practices that draws them together, not any common goals.

> ◙ I don't see anything here that doesn't scream danger. I am in awe of the stupidity of some people.
> ◙ Ethernaut
>
> ◙ That sounds like a bit of either jealousy or ignorance. How much personal experience do you have with the metaplanars?
> ◙ Red
>
> ◙ It is neither. I speak from experience, not with these fools, but with the metaplanar entities they are making pacts with. I don't see anything good coming from this.
> ◙ Ethernaut
>
> ◙ With respect, Ethernaut, the metaplanes and their entities are not good or evil, but both and neither. But if power is what they seek, this tradition will certainly give it to them. It is the cost I would worry about.
> ◙ Man-of-Many-Names

RELATED MENTOR SPIRITS

A Planar mage always has a patron entity that acts as their mentor spirit.

IDEALS

Planar mages share no ideal other than the metaplanes hold answers that Earth does not. They believe life and magic began on these metaplanes and do not accept the theory that Earth and life on it affect the metaplanes. They rather think Earth and our universe is just expressions of the greater mana-system that existed before time in the astral beyond.

SORCERY

Planar Mages practice spellcasting normally.

CONJURING

Planar Mages practice conjuring normally.

ENCHANTING

Planar Mages practice enchanting normally.

PLANAR MAGE RULES

- Must learn the Spirit Pact ritual before initiating.
- After reaching initiate grade 1, each additional initiation requires the mage to first travel to a previously unvisited metaplane.
- In order to become initiate grade 3, a Planar mage must make a Spirit Pact with a Metaplanar entity or spirit (the exact nature of the pact is decided between PC and GM).
- At initiate grade 4, and each grade after, may switch current spirit type associate with tasks (Combat, Detection, Health, Illusion, Manipulation) with a spirit or entity encountered in metaplanes.

NOTABLE TEACHERS

Learning Planar Magic is not difficult, if one is prepared to face the dangers of the metaplanes. The **Planar Research Society of Magic**, or PRiSM, as it is called, accepts all comers. They refer to themselves as "travelers" and gladly share what they know in return for whatever knowledge the initiate brings back with them from their own travels. A Planar Mage called **Taxidot** is currently the chairperson of PRiSM, although there is no strict

ROLE-PLAYING A PLANAR MAGE

There is no set way a Planar mage behaves. The only thing to keep in mind is that Planar mages are obsessed/convinced by the idea that the metaplanes are a truer, more pure expression of mana than what Earth can offer. As such, they believe the entities found there are more true as well. The spirit pact that the mage shares with the entity acts as a filter for the mage's perception of the word and should affect their behavior accordingly. A malevolent spirit, therefore, should constantly tempt the mage toward violence or abhorrent behavior, while a harmonious entity might act as an angel on the shoulder of a runner.

PLANAR MAGES

Combat: Guardian
Detection: Guidance
Health: Water
Illusion: Air
Manipulation: Task
Drain: Willpower + Logic

PREFERRED SPELLS

Agony, Chaotic World, Convert Blood To Ichor, Euphoria, Ghoulish Strength, Inflict Disease

hierarchy within the group. But Taxidot is currently the curator of the PRiSM library, so contacting it would be a good first step.

- I can't speak to their magic ability, but their databases are incredible. They have more collected about various metaplanes than anywhere else I've seen. They let me browse a bit when I gave them some information regarding a spirit quest I took last year. Of course, most of their stuff is small-time: little demi-planes, elemental stuff, etc. But once in a while, you'll come across a gem. Taxidot is a strange little thing, though. Nice enough, but a pretty odd duck.
- Red

RED MAGIC

Practitioners of Red Magic believe that all animal life across the universe (and beyond) is connected through a force the call the Domain of Red. While not ultimately related to Green Magic, the ancient practice of Red Magic was discovered around the same time, in the second of the two sunken cities explored by the Tzuri Group.

Of course, many Red mages believe that there are those who have been tapping into Red Magic since the Awakening began, even if they didn't know they were doing it. In particular, Bali Rand-hawa, a Red mage, teaches that all those who shapeshift from animal to metahuman or reverse, are using magic from the Domain of Red to do so. Likewise, those adepts who follow the Beast's way are considered kin by Red mages.

The exact relationship between Red Magic and Green Magic is unclear, although they were rediscovered in close proximity to each other, both by the Tzuri Group, who have not been heard from in over a decade.

- Tzuri knows more than they are revealing about these traditions. It is what they do not know that may be the doom of many.
- Man-of-Many-Names

RELATED MENTOR SPIRITS

Any animal mentor spirit fits in well within the paradigm of Red Magic.

IDEALS

Red mages do not see intelligence as a sign of importance. Rather, they see each branch of the animal kingdom as having its own evolutionary paths, which have overlapped in the past and will continue to intertwine in the future. In the minds of Red mages, it is the blood that gives the power. They may or may not respect plant life, but every animal has value, even if it is for food, and they have a high aversion to wasting blood, which includes using it for dark magic.

SORCERY

Red Mages practice spellcasting normally.

CONJURING

Red Mages practice conjuring normally.

ENCHANTING

Red Mages practice enchanting normally.

RED MAGE RULES

- Cannot summon Plant spirits.
- Gain +2 to summon Beast Spirits.
- At initiate grade 2, may learn the Attune Animal ritual as if they were an adept.
- At initiate grade 4, gains the Totem Form (Animal) ability.

ROLE-PLAYING A RED MAGE

Red mages are not barbaric, nor are they mindless. They tend to be animalistic, however. What that means to each individual Red mage is up to the player. What they have in common is a deep respect for animal life in all of its forms. This applies to metahumanity as well, but many Red mages blame metahumanity in general for the poor treatment of the world's animal life and thus may be more willing to deal out vengeance to those they see as responsible.

RED MAGIC

Combat: Beast
Detection: Air or Beast
Health: Water or Beast
Illusion: Earth or Beast
Manipulation: Man
Drain: Willpower + Intuition

PREFERRED SPELLS

Animal Sense, Barrage, Calm Animal, Calm Pack, Claw, Control Animal, Control Pack, Critter Form, Shapechange, Translate

NOTABLE TEACHERS

I can't recommend anyone seeking out **"Battle-Dog" Ramone**, as I've never heard of anyone being able to stand him for very long, and he has an incredible tendency to caustically offend even the most easygoing of seekers. Having said that, he is the most knowledgeable Red mage on the planet. More often than not, he trains pupils for a year or so until they get the basics down, and then they quit, seeking other means of communing with the Domain of the Red. After leaving Battle-Dog, Reds tend to join the Redwork, a network of Red mages who count being taught by Ramone as a badge of honor. But if you are a glutton for punishment, head to New York City.

- I hate that Ramone. He is a grade-A drekhole. Some of his "students" are real pros, but this guy is impossible to work with.
- Picador

THE ROMANI TRADITION

Romani spiritualism has been strongly influenced by the mysticism of the ancient Vedic culture from which the Romani people emerged nearly a millennium ago. Almost all Roma magic is shamanic and related to nature. Except for a few basic, general precepts, the Roma subscribe to no consistent world view; many Roma have Catholic or Orthodox Christian leanings, others have an Islamic bent, and a growing number seek to explore their people's Indian roots. Most Roma fetishes are nature-oriented, though they also use tarot cards to forecast the future. The city of Berlin is home to the Roma's most important institution, the Zentralrat (Central Council). The Roma maintain loose but friendly connections to the Weise; nationalistic schools of magic such as the Runenthing treat them with open hostility. With the significant exceptions of Erfurt and Berlin universities, academia's magicians tend to ignore the Roma.

RELATED MENTOR SPIRITS

Almost all Romani tribes see the Great Mother as the most important power. By whatever name the different tribes choose to call her, she is the idol of most Roma magicians. The Dragonslayer and the Wild Huntsman are the next most common. Totems related to birds, horses, or water are also common among many Romani mages.

IDEALS

Romani mages typically disdain organized religion. Alternatively, they often adopt the dominant religion where they live, describing themselves as "many stars scattered in the sight of God." They live by a complex set of rules that govern cleanliness, purity, respect, honor, and justice. These rules are called "Rromano." Rromano means acting with dignity and respect as a Roma person, as part of the worldview known as "Rromanipé."

SORCERY

There is a connection to spiritual and bodily cleanliness and the flow of magic for practitioners of the Romani tradition. Such purification rituals are done at the beginning of the day prior to using magic, otherwise bad karma can befall the caster. This also puts the use of healing magic out of the hands of the traditionalist because of the contact with the unclean body/bodily fluids.

CONJURING

While the Romani can conjure spirits, what is summoned depends on the other religious influences on the tribe.

ENCHANTING

Romani mages use Enchanting as normal.

ROMANI MAGE RULES

Traditionalist Romani practice magic with the following rules:

- Cannot stay in the same place for more than a week.
- Cannot own a permanent residence that is not readily mobile.
- Romani must bathe daily for bodily and spiritual cleansing before practicing magic. (Cannot practice magic if they have not bathed in the previous twenty-four hours.)
- Cannot cast Health spells or preparations.
- Gain one 5 Karma Mastery quality.

NOTABLE TEACHERS

Vadoma Shaw is the founder of the Linked Chain, a network of Awakened Romani individuals. She is part diva, part Matrix icon, part performer, part teacher, and all parts intense. I know it is cliché, but she literally ran away from home and joined a Romani circus. She studied magic and circus skills while performing on the streets of various western European cities. She doesn't teach often, but she is regarded as the best (or at least most well-known) practitioner of Romani magic.

ROMANI TRADITION

Combat: Fire
Detection: Air
Health: Plant
Illusion: Water
Manipulation: Earth
Drain: Willpower + Willpower

PREFERRED SPELLS

Clairaudience, Clairvoyance, Deflection, Detect Spells, Fashion, Inflict Disease, Light

TAROT

The recent revelations regarding the so-called Sixth World Tarot stirred up quite a bit of discussion and controversy among the Awakened community. See the recent JackPoint upload *Book of the Lost* for more details, most of which I don't wish to unpack here. However, something I did want to comment on was the resurgence of Tarot magic as a tradition, not simply some sort of add-on to another magical worldview. Even before the Awakening, practitioners of tarot had extensive networks used to compare notes, share best practices, and otherwise gain support.

In more recent years, one particular network, the **Arcane Tarot Guild**, began to shed light on far less mundane topics. Spotty reports came in from tarot practitioners within the guild that spirits were randomly manifesting during routine client readings. At first, these reports were few and far between, but as the influence of the Sixth World Tarot has grown, instances have been much more frequent. The guild quickly pieced together the circumstances and practices common to each of these events, and these common elements formed the basis of the Tarot tradition. In truth, the Tarot tradition is quite old, with various cultures grasping only pieces left over from widespread use in ancient times.

In essence, Tarot is a Divination and Manifestation tradition. Depending on the skill of the practitioner, spirits can aid not just in prophetic readings, but also in any tasks where the mage wishes to receive assistance.

Finding a group or a mentor to teach the Tarot tradition is not difficult. The difficulty lies in finding someone who is truly in tune with the Arcana and not just a huckster who happens to be awakened trying to earn a buck from you. The Arcane Tarot Guild is a good place to start, but as with all things related to the Tarot, there is no one group that has every answer. Another good place to start is the Oracle Society, an alliance of interested academics pursuing any and all knowledge of the Sixth World Tarot. They aren't as into practice as the Guild, but there is at least some overlap in the groups.

Lower-level initiates of the Tarot tradition would do well to remember that just because they have devoted themselves to the Arcana, the Arcana are not nearly as devoted to them in return. The full extent to which the Tarot reflects or guides history and life in the Sixth World has yet to be determined, but it is certain that the cards, and the associated spirits, do not serve practitioners in the same way as spirits in other traditions. The Tarot serves as a sort of matrix or lens through which the mage interacts with the astral realm. This protects the summoner to some extent, but it also allows much more freedom on the part of the spirits to act as they see fit.

While the Tarot gives access to potential power, spirits whose power is too great in relation to the initiate's grade may simply refuse to answer at all, or may deliberately choose to ignore the wishes of the mage.

- So, chip-truth. This mage I know decides that the Tarot tradition is his speed. He's always been into it, and so he gives it a whirl. Unfortunately for him, his training wasn't complete. He's going up against Ares CorpSec and draws the King of Batons. Fire spirit appears and torches the Ares guys, his runner team, and the rest of the building with him in it. Swear to Ghost.
- Old Crow

RELATED MENTOR SPIRITS

Many initiates of the Tarot tradition say that they were led there by the spirit of Oracle (or a similar mentor, such as Teacher or Mystic). The focus on Divination often leads a Tarot mage to seek a mentor spirit with a like purpose.

IDEALS

Many Tarot mages are accused of being detached from the world. In many cases, their readings and outlooks seem like cold acceptance or unfeeling determinism. And yet, this is not quite true. Tarot mages describe themselves not as

ROLE-PLAYING A TAROT MAGE

Role playing a Tarot mage can be quite fun. On one hand, there is an element of chance involved, which can make using Tarot summoning in combat rather interesting. On the other hand, a mage committed to the Tarot can play up being mysterious and enigmatic, blaming any strange reaction to circumstances as "this is just what I have seen in the cards …" As often as the mage can reference the Tarot or offer odd bits of wisdom or advice to other players or NPCs, the better! Further, being able to use the Sixth World Tarot deck as a prop and role-playing tool in-game allows one more level of immersion.

unfeeling, but struggling to understand the universe through the Arcana, which they believe has true insight on the past, present, and future. What seems like determinism to the uninitiated is instead a way of practicing patience. There is no use for the Tarot mage to jump to conclusions or act rashly when a new reading or experience could alter a previous interpretation. As a result, Tarot mages might seem resigned, even while their personalities are often passionate, but in reality, they are simply waiting for more truth to be revealed.

SORCERY

Tarot mages practice skills in the Sorcery skill group normally.

CONJURING

Tarot mages can use the Conjuring skill group as normal, but once they reach a second level of initiation, they are able to perform a special form of Summoning called Tarot Summoning.

When a mage summons a spirit using the Tarot, normal Summoning rules do not apply. Instead, the mage declares they are Tarot Summoning, and then shuffles the deck and draws a card (a Complex Action). The mage must resist Stun Drain equal to the Force of the spirit indicated by the card (use Force 10 for Major Arcana). If the mage remains conscious, the corresponding spirit is summoned for one task only, and it may be commanded by the mage immediately with a Free Action. If the requirement for the card has not been met, no spirit is summoned.

TAROT SUMMONING

Use the following chart to see what kind of spirit is summoned when a card is drawn.

The different suits of the Arcana correspond to different spirit types—the Suit of Blades aligns with air, Coins with earth, Batons with fire, and Cups with water. When a card from any of these suits is drawn, the summoned spirit matches the corresponding type. The number on the card will be the Force of the spirit summoned. Aces count as 1. This means that if the Tarot mage declares they are using Tarot Summoning, then draws the Five of Batons card, a Force 5 fire spirit will be summoned, and the mage may immediately give the spirit a command.

The exceptions to this are the face cards (King, Queen, Knight, and Page) and the Major Arcana (cards that do not correspond to Blades, Coins, Batons, or Cups). When a face card is drawn, the spirit summoned will still be of the type corresponding to the suit drawn, but with the following differences:

- Spirits summoned by Page cards will always be Force 9 and will immediately use their Guard power on the summoner's entire team. If summoned outside of combat, the spirit continues to guard the summoner and allies until either dawn or dusk arrives, or until it prevents an accident or glitch. The spirit then returns home.

- Spirits summoned by Knight cards will always be Force 10 and will immediately materialize and use one elemental attack power against an enemy. If summoned outside of combat, the spirit returns to its home.

- Spirits summoned by Queen cards will always be Force 11 and will immediately materialize and use Magical Guard on the summoner and allies until the end of combat. If summoned outside of combat, the spirit instead offers a single use of its Divining ability. It then returns home.

- Spirits summoned by King cards will always be Force 12 and will immediately materialize and use the Engulf power on whoever the spirit deems the largest threat to the summoner (gamemaster discretion). The spirit will remain until the enemy is subdued and combat is over. If summoned outside of combat, the spirit instead offers a single use of its Divining ability. It then returns home.

Whenever a card from the Major Arcana is drawn, an unknown spirit grants the following effect (treat as a Mentor Spirit advantage/disadvantage). If in combat, the effect lasts until combat ends. If summoned outside of combat, the effect lasts five minutes.

- **The Bastard:** All enemies gain +2 to dice rolls against summoner.
- **The Matrix:** Summoner and allies gain +2 dice on Matrix-related tests.
- **The High Priestess:** Summoner gains +2 dice to Conjuring skill group.
- **Aes Sidhe Banrigh:** Summoner may immediately draw 2 more cards, summoning or applying both.
- **The Chief Executive:** Summoner may make an immediate Intimidation test against an enemy with a +4 dice pool bonus.
- **The Higher Power:** Summoner gains 1 free point of Edge until the end of combat.
- **The Avatars:** Summoner gains +2 to attack rolls and +2 to Spellcasting tests.
- **The Ride:** Summoner gains an immediate +2D6 to their initiative score (max 5D6).
- **Discipline:** Summoner gains +2 to all limits.
- **The Hermit:** Summoner gains +4 to all dice rolls, everyone else within 5 meters suffers –2 to all dice rolls.
- **The Wheel of Fortune:** Roll 1D6. On a 1, 3, or 5, the summoner gains +3 to all rolls. On a 2, 4, or 6, summoner experiences a –3 penalty on all rolls.
- **The Vigilante:** A Force 12 spirit of man is summoned and may immediately be given one command.
- **The Hanged Man:** Summoner receives a –3 dice pool penalty to all defense rolls.
- **...404...:** The Edge value of the summoner is reduced to 1 until the end of combat.
- **Threshold:** Summoner may immediately choose a card from the minor arcana and summon that spirit.
- **The Dragon:** A nearby dragon is alerted to your presence on the astral plane. (Gamemaster chooses what this means for the summoner.)
- **The Tower:** Summoner gains +4 to armor and ignores wound penalties.
- **The Comet:** Summoner gains +4 to Spellcasting rolls.
- **The Shadows:** Summoner gains +4 to defense rolls.
- **The Eclipse:** Enemies are at –4 to hit summoner.
- **Karma:** Summoner immediately gains a temporary point of Edge. After combat is over, summoner loses 1 Karma.
- **The Awakened World:** Summoner and allies gain +3 to Conjuring, Enchanting, and Sorcery rolls.

ENCHANTING

Tarot mages practice skills in the Enchanting skill group normally.

NOTABLE FEATURE

Tarot mages rely on Tarot decks for their access to magic. Truthfully speaking, it is the symbolism on the deck that is important, so in a pinch, a Tarot mage could get by using scraps of paper with scribbles on them, as long as the mage has had time to bond with the deck.

TAROT MAGE RULES

- Initiates of the Tarot Tradition must take Divination for their first metamagic.
- At the second grade of initiation, Tarot mages may take the Tarot Summoning metamagic.

NOTABLE TEACHERS

Karmen Na'ib is the current head of the Arcane Tarot Guild. While she rarely accepts new students, many of her pupils teach newer initiates on her behalf. The Arcane Tarot Guild is not particularly hierarchical, so there is not much harm in joining the guild and beginning to network with other Tarot mages.

Alternatively, **Jasper Dejong** is a Tarot mage who broke off from the Arcane Tarot Guild in its earliest incarnations. He has the reputation of being harsh and often using the Arcana for personal gain, yet he eagerly accepts new students.

Professor Stuart Bronswick is a member of the Oracle Society who actually practices the Tarot as well as studies it academically. He operates out of Elemental Hall as part of the University of Chicago's Magical Studies program and works closely with the Astral Space Preservation Society there. He's a busy guy, but if he thinks you can help him research the Tarot, he'll teach you what he knows in exchange for field research.

- ⊗ Be careful. "Field research" essentially means that Bronswick sends you out on some crazy-ass magical road trip where you get kidnapped and sent to a different world where you get your ass kicked, your gear stolen, and your hospital stay assured.
- ⊗ Borderline

- ⊗ Speaking from experience, hon?
- ⊗ Frosty

TAROT TRADITION

Combat: Air
Detection: Fire
Health: Water
Illusion: Man
Manipulation: Earth
Drain: Willpower + Logic

PREFERRED SPELLS
Clairaudience, Clairvoyance, Combat Sense, Thought Recognition

- ⊗ I needed the money.
- ⊗ Borderline

- ⊗ Don't we all.
- ⊗ Bull

MENTOR SPIRITS

POSTED BY: AXIS MUNDI

Along with the new traditions, I have been paying attention to some mentor spirits that are also new to me. Some of these—well, they aren't necessarily new, but the way they are being followed is. See the bit below on globalization for more details. I'm always interested in more info regarding totems or mentor spirits, as I am working toward a theory about how they fit into our discussion about UMT, so when you hear of any, send the info my way.

DOVE

The mentor spirit Dove is a messenger of peace and a mediator for harmony. Often, those who are found following Dove care so deeply that they are willing to endure harm for the safety of others. Doves seek to remain aware and in touch with the environment around her. She is in tune with her environment, and she prides herself on remaining aware in all circumstances. Encouraging purity and integrity, followers of Dove often have difficulty remaining true to their highest ideals, but Dove also represents gentleness and forgiveness, allowing those on her path to dust themselves off and try again.

ADVANTAGES

All: +2 dice pool modifier for Negotiation tests.
Magician: +1 dice pool modifier for casting Health spells, +1 dice pool modifier to summon air spirits.
Adept: Gain 1 free level of Enhanced Perception.

DISADVANTAGES

Dove discourages combat whenever possible. As such, those who follow Dove are at –2 dice pool modifier to cast Combat spells or when using lethal force.

Similar Archetypes: Peace

PLANAR ENTITY

Taking Planar Entity as a mentor spirit is only available to Planar mages. The Planar mage must choose (with gamemaster permission) a free spirit or extraplanar entity to serve as a mentor spirit. The gamemaster determines what advantages the spirit brings to the pact with the player, but they should be complementary to the spirit's influence. For example, a free fire spirit may grant +2 when casting fire-based spells, whereas a she-dim may grant immunity to aging.

ADVANTAGES

All: Determined by spirit type and gamemaster approval.
Magician: Determined by spirit type and gamemaster approval.
Adept: Determined by spirit type and gamemaster approval.

DISADVANTAGES

Taking on an extraplanar entity into one's soul is not without its drawbacks. Much of their mental ability is taken up keeping themselves from losing their identity as a result of their shared existence. Mages suffer a –2 dice pool penalty when making tests involving Willpower.

Similar Archetypes: None.

ARCANA

Arcana is not a traditional mentor spirit as such, but an interaction that its followers describe as an intimacy with the Tarot. Followers of the Arcana place their decisions and fates in the hands of the cards, as they believe that their destiny can be found there, along with great power. While the traditional mentor relationship isn't present, the influence of the Arcana is felt in more tangible ways. Those under the sway of Arcana are not just seers or fortune tellers, but believers in the will of magic itself. Of course, the will of the Tarot is always open to interpretation, and so adherents are not monolithic in their belief or practice. For its part, while Arcana might not speak with words, the cards are always present for guidance.

ADVANTAGES

All: Once per day, when making a decision or test influenced by a Tarot reading/card, may re-roll misses as if they had used Edge.
Magician: +1 dice pool modifier for casting Detection spells, an additional +2 dice pool modifier to cast Clairvoyance spells.
Adept: Gain 2 free levels of Danger Sense.

DISADVANTAGES

Followers of the Arcana must use Tarot decks or individual cards as foci and fetishes, or else take –2 when attempting to use them.

The Tarot Arcana plays such a major part in the lives of its adherents that when a follower of Arcana becomes a grade 1 initiate, they must choose centering or adept centering for their first benefit, with the cards of Tarot being the focus of their centering.

Similar Archetypes: Gambler, Lady Luck

HOLY TEXT

Throughout history, the faithful of myriad faiths have claimed that their particular sacred scriptures spoke to them. For some, this guidance may come in the form of the words themselves, but for others, it is a more mystical experience where the text comes alive. Those who follow these texts have a solitary commitment to the values and insights they glean from them, and as such, there is nothing in this world that can shake their confidence or commitment to them. While the texts are all different, the discipline used in reading, understanding, and practicing their words is common.

ADVANTAGES

All: Gain +4 ranks of (Choose Holy Text) Knowledge Skill.

Magician: +2 dice pool modifier when casting Health spells or using the Banishing skill (choose one).

Adept: Gain 1 free level of Empathic Healing or Mystic Armor (choose one).

DISADVANTAGES

Having a Holy Text means that some actions will be considered illicit or counter to the teachings of the text. When a follower of a Holy Text wishes to take an action that is contrary to the teaching of the text (whatever that text is), they must pass a Charisma + Willpower (4) Test to take the action.

Similar Archetypes: Vedas, Dhammapada, Torah, Bible, Qur'an, Book of Mormon

DEATH

Every belief system deals with Death. Either they worship it as a god, or their god fights against it. But it is present. Those who take Death on as a mentor spirit are not necessarily evil (although there are those), but they would suggest they see the world for what it truly is. Temporary. Those who follow Death are not bothered by the final destination of the living, but rather they celebrate it and spend their time alive preparing for the inevitable. Along with the fixation on the un-living comes a knowledge of and fascination with those subjects that are traditionally taboo in most societies: undead, necromancy, corpses, and disease. These aren't the focus of death followers, but they are well-versed in them, as they have all been touched by their master's cold embrace.

ADVANTAGES

All: +4 ranks of the Knowledge Skill Anatomy, Disease, Infected, or Undead (choose one).

Magician: +2 dice pool modifier when casting the spells Death Touch, Manaball, Manabolt, One Less, Slaughter, Slay.

Adept: Gain 1 free level of Killing Hands or Plague Cloud (choose one).

DISADVANTAGES

While followers of Death understand more than many how the body works, they are loathe to heal it, as they see the process of death and dying as the most sacred of events. In order for a follower of Death to attempt to help someone who is dying or injured, they must first pass a Charisma + Willpower (3) Test.

Similar Archetypes: Hades, Osiris, Hel, Dis Pater, Grim Reaper, Mannanan, Sheol

WAR

Some have said war is hell. Others have said war is all there is. One thing is certain, however. War is inevitable. Since the first time one tribe fought another, there has been war, and there always will be. That is why gods of war have always been present in every pantheon. That is why the world's nations and megacorporations still pay homage to War through military industrial complexes, R&D departments, troop deployments, flag-waving civil religion, and honoring the military above all else, regardless of right or wrong. The Worship of War is alive and well, and as War's followers know, there is always more that can be taught to those willing to listen and act. War can't be considered "good," but not truly evil either. War is inherently selfish, using violence as a means to get what one wants, although sometimes what one wants is violence for its own sake. Either suits War just fine.

ADVANTAGES

All: After character creation, may purchase combat skills at rank 3 or higher for 1 less Karma.

Magician: +2 dice pool modifier when casting Combat spells, preparations, and rituals.

Adept: Gain 1 free level of Critical Strike.

DISADVANTAGES

There is a distinct difference between noble combat, fighting when one has to, and winning at all costs. War is about the latter. As a result, those who follow War fear losing more than they fear anything or anyone else. If it looks as if they are going to lose a battle, those with the War mentor must pass a Charisma + Willpower (4) Test, or else use all means necessary—including the lives, nuyen, and honor of their teammates—to overcome their adversary.

Similar Archetypes: Ares, Mixcoatl, Chi You, Woden, Indra, Mars

TOHU WA-BOHU

In the beginning, there was only chaos. A vast, swirling morass of emptiness without form or function. Sources vary about what comes next, (the Big Bang, YHWH, Marduk, aliens) but Tohu Wa-Bohu is the name given to the nameless IT that preceded the more-or-less ordered universe we have now. Tohu Wa-Bohu is no devil, demiurge, or force of evil. Neither is it a trickster, prankster, or simple force of chaos out to mix things up. Rather, it is the primal force of entropy that seeks to break down all life, all structure, all elements back into the chaotic dark from whence the universe emerged. Followers of Tohu Wa-Bohu do not seek to rule the world, nor do they seek to correct it. They seek its end. Whether they want it now, or after they have had their fun, is up for debate, as followers of Tohu Wa-Bohu live to see every form of order brought low and for everything reasonable to be tossed into disarray.

ADVANTAGES

All: +2 dice pool modifier for Intimidation or Demolitions tests (choose one).

Magician: Gain the Witness My Hate quality for free.

Adept: Gain the Adept Accident power for free (p. 190, *Hard Targets*).

DISADVANTAGES

Followers of Tohu Wa-Bohu can be difficult to work with, as they don't like goals, which seem to them like building instead of tearing down. Followers gain the Driven quality, in which the focus is the opportunity to destroy something meaningful. Further, they find it hard to work in groups given their destructive nature. They can never benefit from teamwork or leadership bonuses.

Similar Archetypes: Tiamat, Yam, Abyss

GREEN MAN

The Green Man mentor spirit, not to be confused with the green man extraplanar spirit, is a totem of the natural life and death cycles of plants. Green Man is that life-giving and nurturing aspect of nature, and the embodiment of it. While most consider vegetation to be passive, there is rather a wild element to the growth and death gathered together in plant life. While other, more particular totems like Oak and Great Mother are also nature spirits, Green Man is solely focused on plant life in all of its diversity and breadth.

ADVANTAGES

All: +2 dice pool modifier for Negotiation Tests.
Magician: +2 dice pool modifier to summon Plant Spirits.
Adept: Gain 2 free levels of Rooting (p. 23, *Shadow Spells*).

DISADVANTAGES

Followers of the Green Man value Earth's flora above almost anything else. As such, they will not stand idly by while plant life is wantonly destroyed. That isn't to say that every follower must avenge every broken branch, but when significant damage is being done to vegetation, they must pass a Charisma + Willpower (3) Test or use all means possible to stop the destruction.

Similar Archetypes: Tree, Viridios

SUN

Sun is the life giver of the world. Sun loves to shine on and give warmth to everyone. On the other hand, it does not trust those who do their deeds where Sun cannot see them. Similar to fire, the Sun can be a force for life through heat, light, and life, but can also be a force for great destruction if not respected. Those who follow Sun value honor, honesty, and integrity. As a result, shadowrunners who follow Sun are a rare sort indeed, often falling into groups of like-minded individuals. Sun is among the most likely mentors to strip powers away from wayward shamans, so those who follow it should be on their guard against giving offense.

ADVANTAGES

All: +2 dice pool modifier for Perception tests when outside during the day.

Magician: +2 dice pool modifier when casting Sun- or Fire-based spells.
Adept: Gain 3 free levels of Temperature Tolerance (only to heat, not cold).

DISADVANTAGES

Followers of Sun must pass a Charisma + Willpower (4) Test in order to purposefully deceive others.

Similar Archetypes: Apollo, Ra, Doumu, Sol, Aryaman

DARK KING

Most know him as the keeper of the dead with a kingdom in the underworld. Followers of the Dark King know him as the keeper of many secrets, as "taking it to the grave" doesn't apply to him. Followers are business suits who deal with secrets. Some are simple blackmailers or insider traders; others are more mystical, looking to negotiate with spirits for more esoteric knowledge. Unfortunately for some, the cost is at times no object.

ADVANTAGES

All: +2 dice to Intimidation tests.
Magician: +2 dice to Contractual Rituals.
Adept: Gain Spirit Ram for free.

DISADVANTAGES

The odd connection followers have to the Dark King makes pain and dying much more significant. It's as if the Dark King wants his followers to join his court soon and tell him of their collected secrets. Followers receive a –1 dice pool penalty when resisting physical damage.

MOON

Moon is changeable and secretive. She sees much from her high vantage point and keeps many secrets hidden from prying eyes under the veil of night. Moon is also a transformer, ever changing and unknowable. Followers of Moon are not aggressive, taking the subtler approach with any mission. They prefer to keep a low profile and act through subterfuge.

ADVANTAGES

All: +2 dice to Negotiation tests.

Magician: +2 dice for Illusion and transformation-focused Manipulation spells, preparations, and spell rituals.

Adept: Gain 3 levels of Stillness for free.

DISADVANTAGES

Followers of Moon must make a Charisma + Willpower (4) Test in order to engage in direct confrontation; failure means they cannot make any action considered as such. Negotiation is not considered confrontation (Moon loves discussion), but arguments fall into that category.

OAK

Followers of Oak are stalwart and silent. They listen to the world around them and calculate their next action. A follower may be slow to act, but when they make their move, they do it with conviction. He protects others, shielding small plants and moss from the elements. Strong shields, buildings, and ships are made from Oak. Followers protect anyone they have agreed to defend steadfastly, even unto death.

ADVANTAGES

All: +1 to Damage Resistance tests.

Magician: +2 dice pool bonus when summoning plant or air spirits (choose 1 when selecting this mentor spirit).

Adept: Gain 2 levels of Stillness for free.

DISADVANTAGES

Must have a natural (meaning unaugmented) Body and Strength of 4 or greater to select this mentor spirit

STAG

Stag is noble and swift, a spirit of life and death. Stag represents the timeless cycle of birth, death, and rebirth that encompasses all living things. Followers of the Stag live life to the fullest and do not forget slights to their dignity. Vengeance in the form of duels or single combat is quite common.

ADVANTAGES

All: +2 to Blades tests.

Magician: +2 to summoning earth spirits.

Adept: Gain +2 levels of Light Body for free.

DISADVANTAGES

Followers of the Stag demand respect, especially to those they give it to. Once disrespected, they must succeed in a Charisma + Willpower (3) Test, or they will deman satisfaction against the slight.

GREAT MOTHER

The Great Mother is the embodiment of life-giving nature, giving her bounty freely to all who need it. Those who mistake her generosity for weakness are asking for trouble. Like any mother, she fights to the death to protect her children. Followers of the Great Mother are healers, both of the body and the spirit; they cannot refuse aid to anyone who needs it. Strict followers have a very stringent moral code. They must fight against the forces of corruption, whether environmental, social, political, or magical.

ADVANTAGES

All: When not in an urban area, gain +1 to any skill test with skills in the Outdoors skill group.

Magician: +2 for health spells, preparations, and spell rituals.

Adept: Gain Empathic Healing for free.

DISADVANTAGES

Treat any background count due to pollution or twisted element as twice the actual rating.

GLOBALIZATION AND MENTORS

One of the fastest growing fields of study at magical universities is the comparative study of indigenous spirits. After the initial shock of the Awakening, much ink has been spilled observing how spirits from one region differ from their counterparts in other countries or cultures. One type of spirit in particular has been more difficult to observe, however. Mentor spirits have proven challenging to compare as they are not directly observable, but subsequent interviews with followers of these spirits have yielded surprising results.

One example is the mentor spirit Raven. Present in nearly all cultures (and having followers in most of them), Raven nonetheless presents itself differently in each of these cultures. The differences between followers of Raven in the Pacific Northwest compared to those in Northern Europe, for example, have been extensively noted. As such, the scholarly consensus has been that the totem Raven in one place is not the same spirit as Raven in another. The totem Spider is another such example. What is recently being studied, however, is how these totem manifestations are similar to each other. This line of inquiry has led a few researchers to hypothesize that these totems are not actually different entities, but the same entity condescending to interact with their followers in ways that they expect. Thus, when the followers of Raven from different cultures began corresponding, they concluded the actual spirit Raven (if there is such a thing) must be something more than the individual expressions in each culture. See discussion on Raven (alt) in the recent *Book of The Lost* upload for an example. Expect to see more of these alternate or "globalized" mentor spirits as the study of these spirits continues.

SPIDER (ALT)

Spider is one of the more feared and despised totems in the Sixth World. The threat posed by insect spirits is never far from the world's consciousness, and most metahumans still group spiders together with insects (although they are arachnids, scientifically speaking). But the fear of spiders goes deeper than that. Metahumanity has an almost biological fear or spiders, and for good evolutionary reasons, but that isn't all Spider is. As many cultures know, Spider is not just one thing.

Also known as Anansi, Iktomi, or Grandfather Spider, this totem has adapted quite well to the Sixth World. In regions across the globe, Spider presents as a trickster, schemer, and hunter. Followers of Spider embody all of these traits and see Spider not as a boogeyman, but as a wise and powerful patron.

ADVANTAGES

All: +2 dice pool modifier for tests using the Stealth skill group.

Magician: +2 dice pool modifier when casting Manipulation spells, preparations, and rituals.

Adept: Gain 2 free levels of Spirit Claw (although in this case, it manifests as a fang).

DISADVANTAGES

Spider followers, like their mentor, become anxious when events happen beyond their control. As such, they go to great lengths to limit the randomness of their encounters. When not following a plan or a plan doesn't go according to plan, followers of Spider must pass a Charisma + Willpower (4) Test or suffer –2 to all rolls until a new plan is established.

Similar Archetypes: Grandfather Spider, Anansi, Iktomi

WOLF (ALT)

While Wolf can often be a positive totem in Native American cultures, for most of the world and its mythologies, wolves have been nothing but trouble. Whether among the Germanic peoples, Indic, Finnic, Christian, Islamic, or Middle-Eastern, or in folk and fairy tales, wolves are often the hunter and enemy of the civilized world. That is not to say they're evil, but certainly hostile and predatory on those too weak to defend themselves.

ADVANTAGES

All: +1 dice pool modifier for tests using the Sneaking, Perception, Survival, and Tracking skills.

Magician: +1 dice pool modifier when casting Combat spells, preparations, and rituals.

Adept: Gain 2 free levels of Danger Sense.

DISADVANTAGES

Wolf is not honorable. Wolf is a survivor and preys on the weak. Whenever a follower of Wolf sees an opportunity to survive by attacking or sacrificing the weak, they must pass a Charisma + Willpower (4) Test or attempt to seize the opportunity. This does not apply to those the Wolf considers friends or family.

Similar Archetypes: Hyena, Vulture

RAT (ALT)

Contrary to the way that Westerners understand rats to be dirty, disease-ridden filth that exist within the cracks of society, Chinese culture has a much more positive understanding of the totem Rat. As the first animal of the Chinese zodiac, Rat occupies a place of prominence, with none of the negatives typically associated with dirty rodents. Rather, rats are seen as bringing vitality and intelligence. Rat encourages creative problem-solving and alertness to potential threats. A life of following Rat can lead to tremendous fortune.

ADVANTAGES

All: +1 dice pool modifier for tests using the Perception and Sneaking skills.

Magician: +1 dice pool modifier when casting Health spells, preparations, and rituals.

Adept: Gain 1 free level of Analytics.

DISADVANTAGES

Rat is a loner by nature. As such, it is sometimes hard to trust others. Combined with Rat's intolerance for incompetence, this could lead to problems in a team environment. Followers of Rat cannot receive aid or aid others with a Teamwork test unless they trust the individuals they are teaming with. Further, if they do trust the individuals, but that trust is broken through incompetence or betrayal, they must pass a Charisma + Willpower (4) Test to be able to use teamwork with that individual each time in the future.

MAGICAL ODDITIES

POSTED BY: AXIS MUNDI

No matter how much we learn about magic, there is always that which lies outside of the fences we try to place around the arcane arts. Below are a few of those odd bits that don't fit into any of our existing paradigms, but I can't deny that they exist.

HYBRID TRADITIONS

I remember once I met a guy who was raised in a strong Protestant family, and he practiced the faith quite strongly. In his twenties, he escaped corp life through a series of misadventures and ended up in the shadows. Once he displayed that he was touched with magic, a hermetic mage—Sally Tsung, I believe—tried to give him training in the arts, but couldn't figure why he was such a slow learner. Given time, Dog appeared to this guy, who was now calling himself Twist, and revealed that he belonged to the shamanic tradition. Now, nothing in Twist's past or family history suggested that he should would be a shaman, let alone have an animistic totem, which is why Twist resisted the gift so strongly. Given time, however, without giving up on his Protestant faith, he merged the two. Still believed in God, in the tradition of his Protestant upbringing, but also accepted the tutelage of Dog. Ended up doing some pretty fantastical stuff, too, if the rumors are true.

Point being, for lack of a better phrase, Twist had to find his own truth. Over time, I've seen quite a few of these tradition-bending mages. They remain rare, and they struggle to find adequate training, but they are just as effective as others, regardless of the secrets of their power.

HYBRID TRADITIONS

A player wishing to follow a Hybrid Tradition may merge two traditions together to create something different. In order to create a Hybrid Tradition, choose two existing traditions and replace one or all of the Ideals, Related Mentor Spirits, or Preferred Spells from one tradition with the same categories from the other. For example, a hermetic-shaman may have been raised in the Native American Nations, valuing the land and harmony with nature and follow Coyote, but instead of "feeling" magic, they may instead take a scientific and formulaic approach to mana. They take the ideals and mentor spirit from a shamanic tradition and use the rest of the hermetic tradition paradigm. No other parts of the traditions may be swapped (unless the gamemaster gives permission).

AWAKENED MARTIAL ARTS

I didn't really know where else to put this, but once I saw it for myself, I had to share. Hapsum-Do, or the Way of Unified Mana, is the first truly Awakened martial art. There have been others who have combined elements of magic into existing martial traditions, but this is the first art available only to the Awakened. Trust me, once you see it in action, it is hard to forget.

WAY OF UNIFIED MANA (HAPSUM-DO)

Bearing similarities to Aikido and Jujutsu, the Way of Unified Mana seeks to use the power of its opponent against them. While other martial arts are limited to physics and anatomy as they strike opponents with their own force, the Way of Unified Mana goes a step further, using the enemy's own essence against them, and their magic as well, if available. Practitioners must be Awakened to use this technique, but they use as little of their own mana as possible during a fight, preferring to defeat opponents with their own force. Only officially taught by Grandmaster "Barghest" Knorr, it

NEW MARTIAL ARTS TECHNIQUES

NEW MARTIAL ARTS TECHNIQUES

MANA CHOKE

This technique is a variant of normal Constrictor's Crush, except instead of doing damage to the target by restricting air or blood flow, the user interferes with the flow of mana to the target instead. Similar to disrupting ley lines, the user inflicts drain on the target equal to physical or stun damage the attack would have done. This technique only works on Awakened foes.

MANA STRIKE

Many threats in the Sixth World are resistant, or immune altogether, to mundane attacks. This technique functions as a normal unarmed attack, except that the martial artist channels mana through the strike. As a result, the attack functions as magical for the purposes of fighting enemies resistant or immune to normal weapons.

has been gaining favor among adepts as the Barghest's renown grows. Unfortunately, the grandmaster is itinerant and never stays in one place very long. He has taken on students recently from Neo-Tokyo, Seoul, and the DWF sprawl of all places, and shows no signs of slowing down his instruction despite rumors that he is over eighty years old.

- I knew Knorr's mentor, Grand Master Duvall. Duvall wasn't Awakened, but when he saw Knorr was, he adapted his training and guided Knorr into developing the art. But you are right, Axis, that was a long, long time ago. There's no way Knorr is human.
- Red

- Well, he isn't an elf or a dwarf, either. Perhaps some form of magical longevity?
- Axis Mundi

- Why do they call him Barghest?
- Borderline

- Because he kicks ass, he's scary as hell, and it sounds cool.
- Red

Available Techniques: Called Shot (Disarm), Mana Choke, Counterstrike, Yielding Force (Counter Strike, Throw), Mana Strike

New Metamagics available: Once initiated, practitioners gain access to the Harmonious Defense and Harmonious Reflection metamagics (see p. 46).

Prerequisites: 15 Karma cost, must be an adept or mystic adept

MAGICAL DEMOGRAPHICS

POSTED BY: WINTERHAWK

Thanks to Axis for the post regarding traditions. However, without a discussion about magical demographics, the discussion is incomplete. Understanding how rare magicians are, and what sort of magical practitioners they might be, is in many ways more important than knowing what form of magic that they follow. A fireball from a shaman or hermetic will cook you the same, but knowing that the security mage armed with one can't do anything about spirits? Now, you have a tactic.

Magical Talent is found in about one percent of the population, as is often reported, but that's something of an illusionary number as about half of those people don't know they have any Talent, or it's so minor (I can turn blue into a lighter shade of blue!) as to be effectively useless. The worst of these cases are those semi-aware of the astral, who hear and see just enough to go mad, never able to gain enough to hear what the whispers say. Or perhaps they learn that the things they see out of the corner of their eye are real but can be dealt with. Young suicides are tragic, and the importance of avoiding them can help mages find each other, making secondary families—which, in turn, is something corporate headhunters value when they can find them.

- Suicide rates jumped five-fold during the run-up to Halley's Comet and remained high until it left Earth's general area. A boost in magic while it was around is blamed for this, as many more people than usual developed minor magic.
- Butch

So, there's seven mages in a thousand, right? Wrong! Six out of seven of those with enough magic to count are aspected, not full mages. These are your sorcerers, your conjurers, your travelers ... they're not as powerful in general, but with only one area to focus on, you'd be surprised by what kinds of tricks they can roll out. This puts the number of full mages at around one in one thousand. That means that there are about a thousand mages per million people in any metropolitan area, but this ratio is skewed by demand; more mages are found in cities than in rural areas, as corporations actively recruit them with high pay and prestige.

> ◉ As of January 1, 2079, Seattle has 1,414 registered full mages, but 8,849 aspected. There clearly are SINless mages who would bulk up those numbers.
> ◉ Icarus

◉ Six-figure salaries plus perks are a given for full mages. There simply aren't enough good mages to go around, let alone ones who also have a knack for, say, deep-delving into the astral or who care to learn complex molecular biology instead of enjoying sex, drugs, and rock and roll. Management is quite forgiving of mage quirks and eccentricities due to this.
◉ Winterhawk

◉ If corporate life is so good, why do so many run the streets?
◉ Riot

◉ Coyote and time clocks don't mix.
◉ Man-of-Many-Names

◉ Tradition pushes people in odd directions; some can't handle the pressure, others are natural rebels, some have a core of civic justice, and so on and so forth. Many shadowrunners could have a great life working for The Man if they so choose.
◉ Kia

- All it costs is your soul.
- Chainmaker

- Honestly, most shadowrunning teams don't even have magical support, while most of those who do have adepts of some kind. Full mages are as rare as hen's teeth out here. If you're lucky enough to have one, your team is elite by default.
- Stone

- Hoist one for Sally Tsung.
- Bull

Since everyone wants magical support for their department, but there aren't enough full mages, it means that many roles are filled by aspected individuals instead. Security teams tend to have sorcerers who can drop battlefield spells, but who can't do astral recon. Conjurers keep spirits on patrol or work on wards, but they can't generate the spark of a fireball. Travelers, or astral adepts, are the most overlooked, focusing on research and exploration for the most part, but some focus on astral combat and are absolutely brutal in that field. We all know spellcasters and banishers, but how many of you know an astral combat expert? Physical adepts are also frequently trained for security teams, but sometimes they develop into social adepts or other, more unusual, paths. These roles don't have the pay or clout of the full mage, but you'd better believe that they still get a good rate of pay.

- For the most part, this level of mage brings in around 60K a year. Keep that in mind when it comes to bribery.
- Hard Exit

Which brings me to a final consideration. You about never hear of them, but those marginally Talented that I talked about before? There's a category in that group called the Aware that number about one in a thousand, making them as common as all other Talented combined. These guys have trained themselves to perceive the astral. That's it? Yeah, that's it, but there are a *ton* of them, and the sheer volume means that you can find them in all walks of life. Many talismongers are probably Aware, for instance, and there are always a few in security details and police stations who keep an eye out for magical influence or spiritual shenanigans. A Mr. Johnson of any heft will have one of his people Aware and watching for magical touches during the meeting, such as mind con-

trol spells, spirit tails, or social adepts doing their thing. Needless to say, this doesn't go over well. You can also trip over them in day-to day-life, from bartenders with "a good feeling about people" to a data-pusher who reads auras to that one mechanic who talks to machines and seems to have a knack with your car that nobody else does.

- These guys are working schlubs, pulling around 2K a month, with their sight being a little more valuable than the ability to speak Aztlaner Spanish, but not much. Those with the right mindset go into magical research, serving as eyes on experiments and pushing the boundaries of magical theory. They can't cast, but they can observe and suggest tweaks to make something new.
- Had Exit

- Some turn to music, adjusting their tune to the emotional flow of the crowd. Pisses me off, just how sad they can make me.
- Kat-o'-Nine-Tales

TRADITIONAL DEMOGRAPHICS

Traditions are somewhat trickier to track than Talent. With magic, it's something of a switch, either on or off. Traditions are largely split between the hermetic and shamanic, but there's a large swath of other, some of which are completely unique to themselves. As a rough rule of thumb, forty percent of all mages are hermetic, forty percent shaman, and twenty percent other, but those numbers vary by nation, culture, and so on, by a large degree. The Ute had a ratio of eighty-eight percent shaman before the nation collapsed, for instance, while the UCAS leans sixty-four percent hermetic. This lends weight to the Unified Magic Theory's core thought that magic is magic and that practitioner views define how it's used, but there are always corner cases that fly in the face of it, which is why it's never become the Law of Unified Magic.

- And I'll go ahead and direct *that* debate to the dedicated discussion area, not here, thanks.
- Glitch

- I'll skirt that somewhat by noting that the first days of magic saw an explosion of shamans in the Native American population, but the high numbers were something of an illusion. Daniel Coyote's band attracted spirits, and as we mentioned, most magicians are aspected, not full. Those early pioneers had few spell formulae, but the conjurers were born into the middle of a feast. This was helped by the "shamanic adepts" that we'll talk about later. Between conjurers, physical adepts, and apprentices, the Ghost Dance movement saw a rate of Talented five times greater than you'd have expected. This was an insurmountable edge in the early days of the Sixth World.

- Elijah

- The UCAS military has worked on assorted counter-magical protocols ever since.
- Stone

- Due to raw population figures, the strongest magical power in North America is, weirdly, the CAS, followed by the UCAS, then the PCC. The great unknown is the Great Ghost Dance. Until the UCAS understand it, they simply can't risk open warfare with the NAN, despite having a general advantage in magical power in today's world.
- Icarus

- I'm very curious where you obtained those numbers.
- Winterhawk

- I assure you that they're accurate.
- Icarus

- I know that, but you shouldn't. We need to talk.
- Winterhawk

- My private consultation fees remain posted in the hiring hall.
- Icarus

- They are right to fear the power of the Great Ghost Dance.
- Man-of-Many-Names

- That's direct enough to keep me worried.
- Sunshine

THE MAKE-UP OF MAGIC

In order to help with visualization, here's a small chart about commonality of magicians.

FOR EVERY 10,000 PEOPLE:
- There are ten full mages, most commonly a hermetic or shaman, or a physical mage.
- There are forty aspected magicians
- There are one hundred "Sparks" who are technically magical.
- There are 9,850 non-magical (or mundane) people.

OF THOSE FORTY ASPECTED MAGICIANS:
- There are eight conjurers.
- There are eight physical adepts.
- There are eight sorcerers.
- There are four apprentices.
- There are four enchanters.
- There are four explorers.

OF THOSE ONE HUNDRED "SPARKS"
- There are twenty who are Aware.

BLOOD MAGIC

- I don't like this post. Not one bit.

  It wasn't too long ago that rumors started about blood magic making an appearance on the streets. More and more, you'd see a dagger to a bleeding arm and a bunch of barrens hoods turning into literal splatterpunks. Things like that make you wonder if we haven't hit the epilogue as a species. But if Cap ever taught me anything, it's that we've been through worse, we'll get through worse, and we never say die. Still, blood magic, prolific and street level … that's enough to make anyone want to lock up with some deep bottles and a lot of ammo.

  It was hard figuring out who to talk to for this. Blood magic means Aztlan, right? So Glitch reached out to Pyramid Watcher. But Red has experience hunting blood mages, and he understands blood in ways most of us never will. And Ethernaut had some notes, as did Lyran, and then Frosty. Next thing I know, I'm getting a call from Netcat, of all people. Says she reached out to the only person she knew could tell her anything.

  So here it is: the best info we can get from a bunch of professionals who have run afoul of it, fought it, studied it, and in a couple cases, embraced it.
- Bull

WORDS FROM THE CONTRIBUTORS

NETCAT

- I managed to contact an … old friend. He's still kinda touched, so I didn't bring him on to talk. Just posting what he had to say. And he knows this stuff, in the academic sense.
- Netcat

- Who? Oh, shit … no, not him.
- Slamm-0!

- Honey, he trusts me. We need what he knows, so let's trust him.
- Netcat

- **USER:** IRE HAS BEEN GIVEN PROBATIONARY ACCESS

- This is a bad idea.
- Slamm-0!

RED

- I've dug up a runner who is learning the new stuff, a bounty hunter who specializes in blood mages, a friend with some insights into the corps involved in them, and one friend who prefers I don't share any details about her. I can't vouch for their ethics, but I can confirm they all have experience pertaining to the subject at hand.
- Red

- **USERS:** FEATHER-DANCER, EB, BLOODHOUND, SILK HAVE BEEN GIVEN PROBATIONARY ACCESS

FROSTY

- I've drawn on an unusual contact. I suggest you trust whatever they say and don't talk to them. Just listen.
- Frosty

- **USER:** WORDSMYTH HAS BEEN GIVEN PROBATIONARY ACCESS

GLITCH

- It's kinda obvious: I called up Pyramid Watcher for some details on Aztlan, everyone's favorite home of blood-everything. Blood magic, blood sports, blood money …

- **USER:** PYRAMID WATCHER HAS BEEN GIVEN PROBATIONARY ACCESS

THE PULSE OF MAGIC

POSTED BY: IRE
Let's start with the basics.

WHAT IT IS

Blood magic is ...

Hotly contested. At present, it is considered illegal in most first-world countries and megacorporations, with Aztechnology being the notable exception. Bounties are attractive, and all known blood mage criminals are automatically considered armed and dangerous. Most organizations will pay on delivery, dead or alive.

Dangerous. There is no way to cast blood magic without causing harm to someone, and the caster risks psychological or magical addiction to the practice.

WHAT IT ISN'T

Blood magic is not ...

Human sacrifice. Not always. Until quite recently, the practice was considered exclusively the domain of madmen and among the darkest of magics. It has never demanded death, but it only worked most efficiently through an unwilling victim's pain and harm.

Easy power. Its initial appeal is the ability to shift drain to others, but the toll it takes on the mind and soul of the user is not to be underestimated. The addiction turns the means into the ends.

HOW IT WORKS

THEORY

Magic that inherently requires harm is inherently scary, even if the person being harmed is the caster. A lot of religions had a hard time accepting the existence of magic, and then a harder time excusing it, until religious leaders and authorities came out with their own various takes on how magic could be responsibly handled within the limits of their faith's morality. Imago Dei, for example, excused Catholic magic that could be used to heal almost out of hand, compared to the loopholes and qualifiers required of other kinds of spells.

- If you think that's complicated, you should see the doctrinal calisthenics Muslims must engage in.
- Goat Foot

There is an underlying psychological reason that blood magic is so instinctively offensive: namely, blood. As obvious as it may seem, blood has enormous connotations on a visceral level. The sight of it invokes an immediate emotional response in all but the most inured or alien minds. Blood means harm: when enough is spilled, people die. Blood also means life: there is no metahuman birth that does not involve blood. Blood is family. Blood is revenge. Blood is bond and bread and legacy and passion. The idea of blood as a sacred medium likely evolves from this reaction, seen in everything from Christian stigmata and transubstantiation to Aztec blood rites to Wiccan binding rituals to the Great Ghost Dance itself. Sacrificial foci are even called athame, after the ritual blades Wiccans wield.

- Actually, I've wondered about that. Wicca is usually a very peaceful religion. How the hell did one of the most reviled foci come to be named after an innocuous tool from a faith that preaches three to one retribution on all wrongdoing?
- Red

- I've been thinking the same thing for years. It's even worse than you think, though: Many traditions and covens of Wicca don't allow for the athame to be used for physical

cutting. It's not a tool for material-plane work. You use an entirely different knife to cut up roots or trim candle wicks. Been that way since at least the 1950s, and possibly (even probably) much farther back. You wouldn't believe how many misunderstandings it has engendered over the decades. We really need to put it to bed and come up with another name for them.
o Lyran

o Blood focus? No ... I mean sacrificial focus is too long and obvious. It's gotta sound scary. Aetherpedia says "sanguine" means blood, that could be cool, but, oh, it also means "being positive in a negative situation," so ... Oh! Death focus! Oh! Band name! Called it!
o Whippet

o **WHIPPET HAS BEEN DISCONNECTED**

o Thank you.
o Frosty

o NP
o Bull

o ... Obsidian focus?
o Glasswalker

o You know, this banhammer is a lot lighter when I swing it ...
o Bull

o Point taken.
o Glasswalker

It is possible that this same psychological import lends blood its power, and not the blood itself. This theory is popular among proponents of Universal Magic Theory, who claim that the passions of the mage are far more important than the traditions and philosophies they follow or the nature of the rituals they perform. A mage who does not have any feelings regarding blood would not draw any more power from it than they might a cup of caffeine-free soymilk. There is some merit to this, but only insofar as any magic is possible to cast in an emotional vacuum. Magic is willpower, and willpower often entails emotion. Several reports submitted by law-enforcement magical-crimes departments have noted that serial killers who perform blood magic are often elevated from a seemingly emotionless state into one of ecstasy. 2047's Azroth the God killings in LA make for an excellent example.

o That was in the Awakenings upload on the old Shadowland server. I remember reading that file ... damn, in 2057. I'm old.
o Bull

o I still have a copy of that datafile. Let's see ... shit. Wow. His magic worked, and he thought he was becoming a god, but he didn't even know he was Awakened.
o Lyran

o Data search turns up a reference to it in a thesis paper on UMT at Universitas Carolina Pragensis. My agent is giving me the cliffnotes version now. Basically says that if a human with sufficient conviction can manifest power by calling on a made-up god, then it invalidates all traditions as ... this is really wordy. "Paradigm crutches?" "Psychomanasomatic operating systems?" Oh, for fuck's sake, this little shit got an A! I'm gonna trace him down and kick his ass.
o Pistons

o That's weird. Some guy called Kazuo commented on that post, said the killer didn't create his own tradition.
o Lyran

o Wait, Kazuo? Oh, no. No no no no. Lyran, can you send me that file?
o DangerSensei

o It's from '57...
o Lyran

o NOW, LYRAN!
o DangerSensei

o Okay, okay, geez, sent.
o Lyran

o **DANGERSENSEI HAS DISCONNECTED**

o What do you think that was all about?
o Chainmaker

It is certainly true that cold, stored blood is not particularly effective, nor is dried, dead blood, but both have their potential use in rituals. The most efficacious blood you could find, however, is from a still-living host, the most powerful being the lifeblood drawn in a killing blow. From this, we can establish a theory: that the power of blood magic draws not on the psychodrama of blood, but an actual, measurable property of the sacrificial victim's life force. Similar parallels can be drawn especially with Type-1 Infected, but also will-o-the-wisps, shedim, free spirits, and other Awakened entities that feed on what might be considered the "souls" of their victims.

- Hardly a theory. It's been pretty well established that sacrificial metamagic techniques just use blood as a medium to get at the soul, same as vampires.
- Axis Mundi

- It's not as cut-and-dried as that. There are documented cases of the spirits of people who have been used as sacrifices being conjured. Of course, they do seem tainted by the experience, twisted by the pain they endured and possibly continue to experience. Most conjurings collapse as they continue to shift the background mana to match their ordeal.
- Winterhawk

- I'll be honest, I get really uncomfortable with the vampire comparison. There are a number of theories about what vampires really feed on. The one I favor suggests that we feed on some magical quantity that is a sort of bonding element between the body and the soul. Considering the way overly augmented victims aren't able to offer as much, it makes sense. Still, I can see why the connection is made.
- Red

- It never bothered me much. I mean, pick a black enough soul and you're just saving them toll money on the road to Hell.
- EB

- Whatever helps you sleep through the day.
- Sticks

- Not gonna lie. What she said? Kinda hot.
- Clockwork

HISTORY

First, we begin with the old.

Sacrificial techniques have existed through all recorded history. The methodology of Aztlan practitioners is, without a doubt, the most infamous, harkening back to at least pre-colonial Mesoamerica, when the Aztec empire was at the height of its power. While there is no way to verify its efficacy in pre-Awakening times, the practice is believed to have been carried forward to the Awakening, if only by smaller cults and traditionalists, when its power became evident again. I can only assume this translated to temporal and political power, considering

what was an underground cult practice for centuries has become a major state religion for Aztlan.

- I can vouch for working blood magic in the Fifth World. I truly wish I couldn't.
- Red

- Care to expand on that?
- Jimmy No

- On a personal level, I'll only say I was a secondary victim. On an academic one, blood magic could provide a temporary background count that allowed potential Awakened humans and otherwise dormant vampires (and, I presume, other magical creatures) to exercise a measure of power greater than the whispers and intuitions normally experienced by individuals or families who, in a more mana-rich environment, would express magical talent.
- Red

- Very good. There were a number of such beings who maintained their power that way through the Fifth Age. Most succumbed in time, but some potent few were able to survive the millennia until the next Age of Magic. The more adept of them chose instead to internalize their power and simply endure quietly, while the leviathans preferred to sleep, half of this world and half of another, as is their custom.
- Wordsmyth

- How would y– RESPONSE BLOCKED
- Lyran

- I can sense someth– RESPONSE BLOCKED
- Arete

- Thanks, Bull.
- Frosty

Modern practice is often derived from a form of extreme exercise of one's tradition; there are no known traditions that insist on the practice of sacrificial techniques, aside from isolated aberrations that might as well be considered novel, if twisted, forms of chaos magic. Sacrifice is a primal concept that resonates particularly well in the hyper-capitalistic mindset of the twenty-first century, in that the first and most important element is the overriding desire for power at any cost.

- You are discounting those who are raised in a culture that treats the practice with reverence and respect. If you grow up around twisted behavior, it becomes normal to you.
- Pyramid Watcher

- Yeah, just look at Slamm-0!.
- Netcat

- I'd say you'll pay for that, but you married me, and that's punishment enough.
- Slamm-0!

Sacrificial metamagical techniques, up until recently, have been the domain of the wicked, the desperate, and the mad. It could not be learned "safely" except by tutelage from someone who had already been instructed in its use. The only alternative would be to learn it from an astral quest to some dark dimension where such knowledge resides, or from a spirit, possibly from those same metaplanes. Both routes, as far as I know, are more than human sanity can bear, and no one has returned with their mind intact for the power they have gained.

- You could debate the sanity of anyone who actually seeks this kind of knowledge out.
- Glasswalker

- I have to believe you can come back from that. If only for Serrin's sake.
- Netcat

- There is no healing from a wound to the soul. Only learning to live with the scars.
- Man-of-Many-Names

The most recent developments, however, see a kind of diversity coming to blood magic. A degree of finesse heretofore unseen. There is some speculation regarding its genesis: the current popular theory suggests that, as the mana level gradually rises, more and more power, as well as the detail and shape and subtlety of that power, will manifest in the world and practitioners of magic in particular. If so, blood magic is catching up to other disciplines that have seen remarkable development in recent years, such as alchemy.

- If so, such phenomena as Halley's Comet generating mana spikes and revealing new expressions are not aberrations or mutations, but previews of the shape of things to come.
- Axis Mundi

- Alas, while true, it is not quite accurate in this context. True, this age has seen more violent upheavals and exceptions than any that has come before it, and the manasphere of

the Sixth Age is akin to a sleeper too-soon awakened and still getting its proper bearings, but the scale of time at work is measured in centuries and millennia. By present calendars, there are at least two millennia before magic once again reaches its apex. Taken at that scale, the world is not only too-soon Awakened, but violently startled.

This is not a product of the evolution of magic, but your understanding of it.
- Wordsmyth

- Oh, so you're sayi- RESPONSE BLOCKED
- Lyran

- Fine, fine …
- Lyran

THE BENEFITS

Blood magic is powerful. Those who engage in it can, at great expense, explore past the boundaries experienced by metahumans, leaping forward into the realm of effects normally available only to the most accomplished of mages, or such immortal beings as dragons. Through its practice, some groups have pressed past the known limits of magical development, performing acts which have shaped the world and all history to come after.

The most obvious of these moments actually harkens back to the Awakening. The Great Ghost Dance might well be considered a massive sacrificial ritual. Participants engaged by the thousands in such acts of ritual exhaustion and self-destruction on a national scale that they were able to harness the power of storms and volcanoes, and consequently jump-started the process of Awakening and goblinization as a side-effect.

- Very astute! The Awakening was predicted to occur very differently, with a far more gradual, easy transition. Some races arrived more violently than was necessary, while others have failed to arrive at all, or continue to sleep in human form. But with an act of dangerous, advanced sorcery far ahead of its time, humanity hurled themselves into the next Age with blind abandon. Perhaps not wise, and certainly the act of understandably desperate people, but still, only time will tell what price must be paid for an Age of Magic ushered in with grand blood sacrifice.
- Wordsmyth

THE RISKS

The appeal of blood magic is obvious: vast power without consequence. Sacrifice is akin to utilizing a focus, except there is no need to invest your-

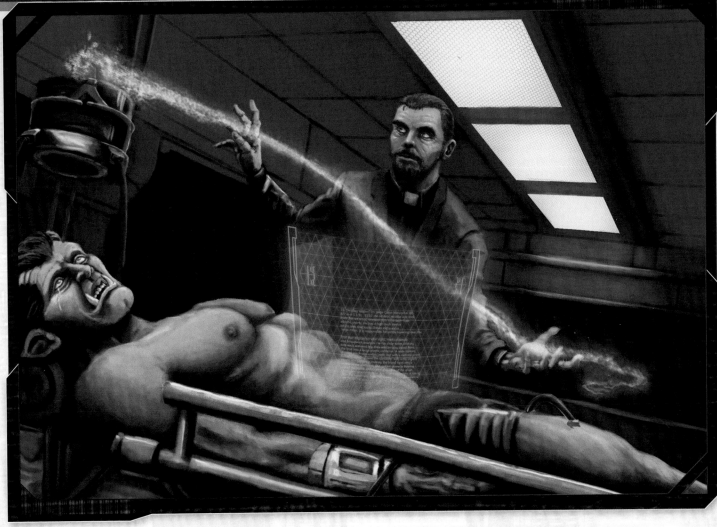

self into binding with it. It is relatively cheap, not too technical or difficult once you understand its techniques, and can offer extraordinary results beyond what you could achieve on your own. Its applications in ritual and even real-time melee combat are astounding. Given the hostile nature of battle, profiting off of one's enemies is a very easy justification to make for some mages. This mercenary outlook allows the temptations of blood magic a way in. A tremendous advantage at someone else's expense. Some even like to think of it as "stealing magic."

- ◉ You'd be amazed how many mundanes try it, thinking it'll give them a way to harness magic. Scary how deep their envy runs.
- ◉ Axis Mundi

- ◉ The Aleph Society has turned it into an art.
- ◉ Bloodhound

The ease is, perhaps, why it is so simple to initially ignore the most insidious peril of blood magic: how good it feels. Many mages will describe the shocking sense of "oneness" or how it feels "right" when they use magic, even when drain takes its toll. Blood magic is like a drug, a quick and easy path without pain to achieve goals. That, of itself, would lead to psychological addiction. But the magic is powerful, and the taste of another metahuman's life energy is seductive. Perhaps it is an as-yet unknown quality of this strain of magic, but blood mages almost always abuse this power, casting bigger and more dangerous spells, hooked on the rush of casting without the consequences of drain. Or perhaps the nature of the magic itself is too intoxicating for any mage to long endure. Regardless, blood magic is habit-forming.

Once the habit sets in, the mind begins to change. Again, the chicken-and-egg dilemma holds true as academics wonder if the power is inherently mutative, or simply having such power is likely to lead anyone to these ends, blood magic or no. The point is, those who have become addicted see distinct personality changes. In some cases, witnesses and associates have noted major differences in taste, judgement, and temperament. Practitioners tend to display patterns of antisocial behavior and become irritable, easily provoked, quick to anger. They are likely to see metahumans in the worst possible light, as though looking for an excuse to hurt or kill them. This, I believe, is a kind of enabling mechanism for the addiction. Another common expression of psychological damage is a rapidly developing sense of paranoia. Given the empowering sensation of blood magic, it would stand to reason that as the practitioner's ego begins to grow, he starts to see other metahumans as jealous of his power, (understandably) fearful of him, or perhaps simply keen to claim one of the generous bounties available for his capture. It comes as little surprise, then, that megalomania is another frequent manifestation, as the blood mage begins to see himself as above his fellow metahumans. People are less sapient creatures with free will and inherent value and rights, and more resources to be drawn on by those with the power and will to do so.

- I was going to make a joke that the derangements a blood mage develops sound like megacorporate talent scout wish lists, but ...
- Cosmo

- ... you realized it wasn't a joke?
- Sunshine

- Sounds like some of the psychological imbalances metahumans often develop after traumatic or extensive augmentation. I've seen street sams with Superhuman Syndrome, augmentation addiction, dissociative disorder, and worse. You cope with a subconscious fear of being less metahuman by devaluing metahumanity in general, resulting in antisocial habits and overconfidence in your abilities.
- Butch

- It's far from unheard of in normal mages, too. When you can shape the world with your will, it's not that hard to develop a god complex. That's one of the best reasons for traditions. Mentor spirits, in particular, provide a kind of ceiling, so the mage doesn't develop delusions of apotheosis.
- Axis Mundi

- Very good. But don't mistake a step on the path with its destination.
- Wordsmyth

- Remember when Man-of-Many-Names was the only cryptic one we had to deal with?
- Snopes

- I must be slipping.
- Icarus

And, of course, there is the aforementioned bounty. Blood magic is highly illegal, culturally taboo, and teams of elite hunters make entire careers specializing in neutralizing blood mages. Outside of Aztlan, a blood mage's paranoia is well warranted, as their very auras are stained with their deeds. Even the unAwakened may feel a creeping sense of dread in the presence of a blood mage, and any mage can quickly identify the dark practices. Many of those blood hunters are more than happy to spare a few thousand nuyen for quality intelligence of blood mage sightings, so there is always the fear that the wrong person will see the mage and sell them out. Blood mages are outcasts of their own making, forever on the edges of society, or ready to bolt at a moment's notice.

- This is why most blood mages who survive for a while learn flux metamagic. Of course, their intimacy with material links means they've got a whole store of tricks to throw hunters off the scent.
- Bloodhound

CONCLUSION

I am unwilling to share what I know of the practical application of blood magic. It has cost me too much and has never brought anything but pain to anyone I have ever known. My circumstances are irrelevant. My sins will never wash clean, the stain of blood something I will never escape. Whatever new paths the practice of blood magic takes, I will not be the one walking them.

- That's where I come in.
- EB

THE NEW SHIT

POSTED BY: EB

Hello, JackPoint! Looks like I finally managed to get Red to introduce me to all of you. Took long enough. All I had to do was learn a new style of magic so intensely objectionable that he had no choice but to let me explain it myself. Easy enough, right?

- Keep it up and it'll be the last time.
- Red

- You know you can't get enough of me.
- EB

SO WHAT IS IT?

For starts, it's not strapping someone down to the table and sticking a knife in their heart. I mean, I can infer the method to do that. Sort of like how you could plan to throw a rager by multiplying the elements that go into throwing a regular party. Which is actually a nice segue into what it really is!

It's bite-sized blood magic.

- This girl can't be for real.
- Glasswalker

- She's actually dialing it back for us.
- Red

Until now, the folks who worked with sacrificial magic tended to think in very grandiose terms. Like, picture a corp brat who only knows how to spend nuyen in denominations of a hundred or more. The kid only thinks in terms of big money (well, big for someone living in the barrens, anyway). His hookers are either top-shelf or by the dozen. His dinners are designer, and so are his threads. If he ever went into a Seattle's Choice and got a cup of kaf, he'd give a hundo and wouldn't wait for the change. He would never even think to look.

So here we've got these dudes at the top of AZT, stabbing fuckers in the chest and tearing out their hearts to the adoring cheers of tens of thousands, deflecting big bad dragon spells and bringing rain to the crops and ushering polluted prosperity on the whole of their wholly owned subsidiar—ahem, nation of Mexic—ahem, Aztlan. If those guys know anything about microeconomics, I'd be shocked. That's what this is. Microeconomics of blood. Drops instead of rivers. And if anyone can compare blood and money, it's me.

- Huh?
- Kat-o'-Nine-Tales

- Doing a little digging, our girl here is Infected, and Daddy Dearest makes his fortune running legal defense for the mob.
- Pistons

- For fuck's sake, aren't there enough of you bloodsuckers around here?
- Clockwork

- The vampire or the lawyer?
- Cosmo

- I dunno. I kinda dig her vibe.
- Kat-o'-Nine-Tales

In the past, people were painting in very, very broad, bloody strokes. Kill a human, get power. Slice 'em up, get power. Hell, slice on yourself and get power (though honestly I never fully understood that one. I mean, drain is drain, right?). Meanwhile, you've got all these normal traditions that incorporate elements of sacrifice into their rites and rituals. Like, normal, non-Petro Voodoo doesn't consider it evil to hypnotize and snap a chicken's neck when they're calling on a loa, right? Druids will sacrifice a dove or something, use its blood to paint their faces, some shit like that. I've got no love for the New Druidic Movement. Norse Ásatru like me might consume blood and mead. Or just blood, that works pretty well. I met a Wiccan once who used her menstrual blood as a sacrament, and I once fought with a Sylvestrine whose palms bled when he called on his saints.

Blood magic was always everyday. We just never made the connection.

So what happens when you pull out the big, mean magic concepts and start looking at blood in a positive way? Blood magic is all about power, yeah, but is power evil? I say no. People are evil. People are corrupted by power. But power, itself, is as neutral as the sea and the storm and the acid rain. So how do you mitigate the evil of power?

Word on the street says one of the first people who figured this out was a blood mage down in Tenochtitlan with a kid. Kid gets sick, and she draws on her own life-force to push past her own limits to heal him. The crazy thing? She didn't feel the same rush she normally did. No heady high, no godlike power waiting to be unleashed on the foolish mortals. Just a mother who would give her life if it meant saving her kid. That's what parents do, right? They make sacrifices. This one just did it with a big obsidian knife. And she survived, and discovered a new path.

I'd love to say I know more about her particular case, but this is one of those "A guy I know has a cousin who talked to a guy at the airport she swore was telling the truth" kind of scenarios. I've heard a few others: some Catholic priest reenacts a crucifixion on himself and gives freely of the power he gains, never accepting reward and objecting to praise. Or the barrens shaman who was sacrificing devil rats to his totem when he saw the connection and somehow figured it out on his own. They all sound pretty unlikely to me, but that's rumors for you. The fact is, blood magic is hitting the streets, and I'm gonna tell you how to keep it from ruining your life.

SELF-SACRIFICE

Understanding, moderation, intention.

Keep chanting it. They say the road to Hell is paved in good intentions, and now it looks like the same road leads back out, too.

> ◈ Slippery slope is slippery.
> ◈ Turbo Bunny

> ◈ Blood makes for a slick path.
> ◈ Man-of-Many-Names

The first thing to remember is that too much of anything is bad for you, no matter how much you like it. Actually, no, things you like are especially dangerous, because you like them. They are subtle. You'll just gorge yourself until you burst or burn out. Doesn't matter if it's cigs or BTLs or burritos or whatever. You can die from drinking too much water, did you know that? I can't, but you certainly can. And you're mostly made of water!

That's what's so dangerous about addictive things. The whole point, really. It changes you so you want more of it. Sure, willpower can carry you along, but you do enough and willpower can actually get turned toward getting more. A clever mind works out new justifications. Really charming people create an audience that approves of what they are doing. Addiction makes you complicit in your own self-destruction.

> ◈ Damn.
> ◈ Turbo Bunny

But that's the thing: The worst addictions take place in the mind. And yeah, any mage worth their

salt is going to have a pretty strong will. But, the bigger you are, the harder you fall. That's what makes blood mages who give in so damn dangerous. And when you use blood magic, it's very tempting to give in, because it feels really, really good. You don't have to hold back anymore. You feel free. You feel powerful and free and strong, and you don't want to stop feeling that way ever.

> ◈ So you're saying you aren't addicted to it?
> ◈ Arete

> ◈ Well, in my case, one addiction is so good I didn't go in for another. I have, how shall I put it, a drinking problem.
> ◈ EB

> ◈ Ha ha.
> ◈ Red

So, let's treat blood magic as a tool and not as a toy. A very dangerous tool, like a lathe or a hydraulic press or a monofilament whip. Yeah, it's cool, but you shouldn't be playing with it, or you'll slice something off. You check yourself, establish routines, meditations, centerings. You sort of disassociate yourself from the sensations and get caught up in the ritual, instead. Sorta like when a guy starts doing math problems in bed. It keeps you from giving in, keeps you focused on the task at hand.

Then comes moderation. A friend of mine who drinks once told me, "I'm not afraid I'll have a beer, I'm afraid I'll have twenty." That's addiction. A guy I know has a glass of red wine every night with his pasta. Says it's for his heart (which I swear is cyber, anyway, but I digress). This guy isn't going to have a panic if he doesn't have his glass of wine. Another example: I knew a runner who had some nasty strains after a run. I goofed the healing spell and he had to patch up the old-fashioned way. He had to take some opioids to deal with the pain and relax his back so it would heal. He really enjoyed those pills, but when the bottle ran out, he didn't go get more, just rested and mended. I asked if he wanted more, and he said, "Yeah. But they're for my back, not for me. My back doesn't need 'em, anymore, so I'm not taking more." Yeah, it'd be easy to get those pills on the street, and pretty cheap, too, but he knows they are a tool, not a vacation.

Rick is looking at me like I'm crazy, because he knows I love my vices. I mean really, *love* 'em. But when it comes to blood magic, it's too dangerous to be a vice worth pursuing. I've seen the people who fell into it and let it consume them. They sacrifice themselves to feed the need. Nothing's worth that.

So that brings me to the most important part, and the part that makes this weird little mystery work: intention. You have to know exactly what you are using it for and, I shit you not, it has to be as benevolent as possible. See, that's the one thing about the myths that you hear the most. It's sacrifice, but it's not greedy. It can't be done for you, and it can't be done in rage. Blood magic is all about getting more, but if the sacrifices are made for someone else, the feeling is totally different. Instead of your whole soul filling up with stolen energy, you sort of feel it pass by you. Like a subway train going past you instead of riding on the roof. And you have to really care, too. You have to want to save someone's life, without calculating what they owe you. You have to want to give of yourself so badly that you would bleed, you would hurt, you would die to save them.

I mean, you can bleed some devil rats, too, but that's not going to be all that powerful. That's almost more utilitarian, just getting some blood to make certain spells and rituals work at all. And it's not powerful enough to have any real kick to the magic, anyway. So unless you're summoning a blood spirit (which is about the dumbest thing you can do, sugar), you probably aren't going to be carrying around a bandolier of squirming rats for gutting.

GREED PAYS, BUT CAUTION STAYS

So let's talk about the big kick of bad blood magic: human sacrifice. I know you're thinking about some damsel tied to the altar in a gothic setting, and oddly enough, you're not wrong, but human sacrifice is possible in lots of other settings. Maybe it's a blade through the heart in the heat of battle, or slashing someone's throat when you sneak up behind them. Sacrifice happens in a moment, with spilled blood and wicked words. It's what makes blood mages and adepts so damn tough. Every time they make you bleed, they get a little stronger. It's also why so many of them get so good with their blades. The damage has to be done with a close, physical connection. Your auras have to touch, so they can bleed your power out of you.

* Again, sounds a lot like Infected feeding.
* Kia

* Oh, it totally is. Don't listen to Rick.
* EB

But here's that big difference: An unwilling victim, for whatever reason, generates more power. I honestly don't know why this is. I have a theory that it's all about the resonance of the energy taken. Fear, pain, even hate are passionate, vibrant emotions of the moment. A lot like when I'm feeding—I can't do a deep feed unless they are feeling a strong stirring of passion, whether it's lust or fear or whatever. You get an unwilling subject, and you get a lot more energy than if you were using a willing one. That's one of the reasons human sacrifice isn't performed on anesthetized or unconscious subjects. They wouldn't feel anything, and that's worth the same for an old-school blood mage as a willing participant, or even themselves, because they know it's coming, they believe in it, and that just doesn't have the same zingy pop that fear and shock inspire. In short, the mean, cruel, heartless blood magic is a big, easy boom, but it's really addictive.

* Links up pretty well with what Ire was saying about how people perceive blood.
* Dr. Spin

So, if you want a sacrifice that works effectively, but doesn't tempt you into cackling crazy psycho mode, what's the secret? Easy. Be selfless as hell.

* You've got to be kidding me.
* Clockwork

* Is it really so offensive to you to find out that ethics might actually have tactical merit?
* Pistons

* Touchy-feely blood magic. I think I'm going to be sick.
* Clockwork

* Feel free to log off. I'm all the more interested now that you're tuning out.
* Pistons

Aztlan has been bandying their heart-ripping blood rituals for so long that the popular picture of sacrificial magic involves a victim. You can watch it live on their trid channels, priests in big headdresses slowly cutting into some death-row convict, screaming through a gag while a crowd cheers and chants prayers and corporate anthems. But sacrifice doesn't have to be on someone else, and it doesn't have to be motivated by greed. It can be selfless, even downright heroic.

- If you've ever seen a barrens bum give a shivering child their coat in winter, or their last pouch of soy paste to a starving friend, you know exactly what she's talking about.
- Red

- I'm only here because someone was willing to take a bullet for me. They survived, but it was close. I wouldn't have made it.
- Picador

When you slice on yourself for power, you pay the price. When you are willing to bleed for a friend, without any thought to your own profit, without any notion of calling on them later? That's noble. That's selfless. That's potent stuff. Loyalty. Friendship. Love. Actual, real self-sacrifice calls on something just as primal in the blood as fear and pain. And just as powerful.

- Well, that rules most runners out.
- Hard Exit

- Most people in general.
- Dr. Spin

- Hey, I've seen some real moments of heroism in the shadows. Don't be so cynical.
- Sunshine

- Seriously? No, really, seriously?
- Clockwork

- You have no idea what it is like to love someone, do you? To look at a woman and know you would die for her? To hold your child in your arms and realize that he's your life, now? Fuck ... I actually feel sorry for you.
- Slamm-0!

- God ... honey ...
- Netcat

- Ugh. This ... I'm out of here.
- Clockwork

- CLOCKWORK HAS LOGGED OFF

BLOOD, SWEAT, AND MURDER

So, now you're kinda turned off, right? I mean, when corpsec is bearing down and you need to start dropping them, what good is all this sacrifice stuff if it's just going to weaken you?

A fine old vampire once told me, "There's nothing so human as self-defense." Ain't it the truth?

It's pretty primal, the instinct to fight in our defense. When your back is to the wall, when you're cornered, that's when we fight the fiercest. Rats can tear through cats if they feel like there is no way other than fighting. So you might think the instinct to kill is pretty human, under those circumstances, right?

Sure. You're right. It is. It's also an addictive sensation. The ability to deal death is power. Bullies, thrill-kill go-gangers, serial murderers, corpers, they all get off on it. There's a rush. You can end problems with a bullet or a blade, and they stay gone and dead. You inspire fear, and in the dark, it feels a lot like respect. Everyone likes respect. Everyone likes safety. Everyone likes power.

I just described how a gun affects you. Add in blood magic, ripping life force out of your foe to power your own prowess. Try to imagine the battle-fever on you, jazzed on adrenaline and instinct, and now you're becoming *more* powerful at your enemy's expense. That survival instinct? It gets a predator's edge. The mix in your head says, "If I kill more, I'll be more powerful, and I'll be safe." And it's probably right. It's so right that it brands itself right across your heart. You'll never forget how good it feels to kill and be safe. Some part of you will always be itching for that sense of control over your own destiny. Your reflex changes from "Assess" to "Kill," and you're not fighting it, because your subconscious is already justifying it. You dream of the kill. You live for the kill. The kill makes you feel alive.

- So, you're saying that blood magic makes you a serial killer?
- Thorn

- I've seen more than one runner go down this path. You can always tell a new kid when they get off on body counts.
- Hard Exit

- I seem to recall you've been willing to put an enemy down without too much hesitation.
- Thorn

- I don't kill for sport or pleasure. I don't kill at all, if I can find another solution. But if it comes down to me or some guy who wants to put me in the ground, brother, they are going down.
- Hard Exit

- It doesn't haunt you?
- Goat Foot

- Of course it does. I hope it always does. When you stop feeling your conscience altogether, you know you've gone too far.
- Hard Exit

- Seriously, what's this "conscience" everyone keeps bringing up?
- Kane

- Don't let him fool you—Kane and his sense of morality, warped as it is, are at least on estranged-but-speaking terms.
- /dev/grrl

- It sends me a birthday card every other year.
- Kane

Fact is, though, blood magic is a beast in combat. As long as you don't mind getting close and personal, every wound, every kill gives you a huge boost to blast the next guy. You can daisy-chain along from one mook to the next, lickety-split.

- I've seen what Aztechnology Bloodpanthers are capable of when they are unleashed in this way. Every time they score a kill, they channel the power into an augment spell, becoming faster, then more armored, then more precise. By the end, they're flying through the enemy like a monoblade through overripe melons.
- Pyramid Watcher

- Wait, what the hell is a Bloodpanther?
- 2XL

- Aztechnology Special Forces. They're all vampires, devoted to the corporation and followers of the Path of the Sun. You never want to meet them.
- Picador

- Fuck.
- Hard Exit

So, how do you use it without becoming a junkie for your own juice?

Iron fucking willpower.

Blood magic is playing with fire. It's like the street sam who jacks over-hyped skillwires to get the edge. Yeah, she's kicking lots of ass, but you know she's on her way to getting addicted. How long before she's plugging in all the time? How long before those instincts she's got grafted in her skull go off at the wrong time? Her girlfriend mouths off at the wrong time and out come the razors. By the time she realizes what's happening, there's blood everywhere, and the screaming has stopped. You can bet plenty of blood mages have fallen off that edge. And you're so hooked, you can't stop. You literally cannot stop. You will kill, and kill, and kill again, weeping or laughing the whole way. And nothing will stop you except a bullet to the head.

- And with the bounty? Plenty of people willing to pull the trigger.
- Johnny No

- Shit, knowing they are suffering or psycho just makes it easier.
- Sticks

- As if you ever needed any incentive. Or excuse.
- Red

But then, there are some people who are just hard to hook. You know the guys. The ones who can drink six pots of *hurlg* a night and then go a year without a drop, no problem. The ones who jack BTLs and, aside from fried synapses, never feel the itch. Others have the opposite—addictive personalities are screwed if they try this stuff. Any good head shrinker can figure out if you fit the profile. Then again, if you're going to start doing blood magic, you should probably get your head examined, anyway.

- Don't you use blood magic, though?
- Glasswalker

- Sure, but I'm not claiming a sound psyche. I dunno how any of you do.
- EB

Still, even the mightiest teetotaler can end up a lush. It happens. It's not just a rush of pleasure and power; there's sexy black magic running through your veins. It's like focus addiction. But magic obeys emotions and patterns. That's where all that selflessness comes in. Yes, I am repeating myself, because this is the crux of the whole shebang: blood magic done on yourself or a willing donor, with a heart full of sacrifice of the self and love of the other, doesn't carry the rush. You still get the stain of blood on you, but it doesn't feel as sinister. It's hard to explain. But the only blood magic that isn't going to risk getting its hooks in your head and your heart is the kind that gives freely and never expects anything back.

I bet religious sects love that. The blood of a martyr has healing properties?
> Goat Foot

I'll bet cults love it, too. Bloodhound mentioned the Aleph Society.
> Johnny No

So, you get the stains on your soul, marking you for a bounty, and it would only work on a very few people you care enough about to bleed for unconditionally? How many runners are actually going to find a use for this?
> Lyran

Hey, now, there's lots of kinds of "love," you know. It's not like this only works on family you actually like and the poor slot you are banging who you actually have feelings for. Sometimes you make a real friend, someone who you want to keep around. The kind of chummer who is a sentimental investment, not a nuyen one.
> EB

In other words, the kind of term you'd take a bullet for. Rare, but it happens. And when it does, I'll bet a mage will be glad they've got the power.
> Arete

It'd have to be some kind of friend if you'd learn this stuff just to keep them safe.
> Lyran

PAINTING IN SCARLET

Of course, there is one more path, much less passionate, that I haven't mentioned yet: oaths. I bet at least some of you remember Thunder Tyee, all those "blood brother" moments when he would slash his palm, a friend would do the same, and they clasped hands?

Yeah, it's like that. Except it's more than bro hugs and symbolism. It's blood and brotherhood, risk and reward.

The ritual is easy enough. You find someone you trust, and you both open veins and swap blood. You speak the words of oath and loyalty and all that jazz, and you create a connection between the two of you. A blood bond.

Isn't there a way to do it that's less stabby and more hygienic?
> Beaker

I guess you could do it with an IV, but then you've got blood typing to worry about. Just get some prets, take a salt tablet, and spray some antiseptic on it.
> Butch

What's the salt for?
> Sounder

Oh, for fuck's sake …
> Butch

So, bad news first. The bond astrally links you to the blood mage. You can now be used to track them down with the usual ritual tricks, meaning you are now a means for bounty hunters to get their big payday. And you better believe there'll be some money for you, too. The bond leaves a smaller stain on you, harder to detect but easy to see for someone who is looking for it specifically.

The good news? The bond astrally links you to the blood mage. Yes, I said it again, because that's one hell of an asset. You can find each other over any distance as though you had a link anywhere. You'll always have a feeling for where one another are if you get separated, assuming they don't enter an area too heavily warded.

If they trust you, and you know the right metamagics, you can even cut on yourself and have them take the damage, juicing up the spell for you like a sacrifice without having to die. And you get the full power as though it was taken with fear and pain. Just make sure they know why their skin is splitting and the blood is going up in red flame.

You can bet some magic circles will start using this for more powerful ritual casting.
> Arete

I hear rumors of new uses for the oath developing, new kinds of runes and pledges that work like a geas. I don't know any of these, myself, but it's like signing a contract with blood or swearing a sacred vow. You get some benefit from the oath when you are acting in accordance with the promise you made. You hear other stuff, too, like breaking the oath, or failing to act within the allotted time frame, and you suffer for it. Or reinforcing rituals that buffer you from the addictive element. Or not needing line of sight to cast on people you are bonded with. The rumors keep mentioning "pattern magic," but I'll be damned if I know what the hell that means.
> Jimmy No

- Interesting. You should listen to those rumors. There may be something well worth your time at the end, if you survive.
- Feather-Dancer

- The price for those answers may be more than you're willing to pay.
- Wordsmyth

RIDING THE TIDE

So that's blood magic. It's powerful and wicked and damn useful. But—and you know this refrain—everything has a price. Blood magic is running the bleeding edge, literally, and it gives you the advantage. Just know what you're getting into, because when it comes to paying up when the debt comes due, nothing, nothing is more dangerous—or precious—than blood.

CRIMSON CRYSTALS

POSTED BY: BLOODHOUND

- I've got Bloodhound here as a little bit of a courtesy. He does work as a bounty hunter specializing in blood mages, and I thought it would be useful to hear what he has to say about fighting them, but he had something a little juicier to share.
- Red

- I take being called blunt, cold, and methodical as a compliment, so I am just going to lay out what I have discovered. It's big and I don't like any of it one bit. Y'all make of it what you will.
- Bloodhound

There are all manner of injuries and maladies that can happen to a person. The wonders of modern medtech make it possible to replace what is lost, including cyberlimbs, biotech organs, or even cloned replacement parts. Awakened individuals in need of such care have tough choices to make though. Cyberware and bioware replacements are easy to find but require losing a bit of that magical power they have been fighting for years to master. Cloned parts are possible but are beyond the reach of most street docs. In most cases, you have to be willing to trust a corp clinic with your genetic samples and cough up a lot of nuyen to make yourself whole again without taking a hit to your magic. Considering quite a few corps have what you might call "aggressive hiring practices" when

it comes to talented magicians, many are loath to take the risk.

Some Awakened individuals who have suffered great injuries such as lost limbs or permanently damaged organs are on rare occasion approached by unidentified individuals. These individuals offer them another option. They offer the Awakened person the answer to all their prayers—magically active crystals which will bond to them and grow faceted, crystalline replacements to the lost limb or organ without diminishing their magical abilities. On rare occasions these crystals can be found on the magical black market. All attempts to trace the source of these crystals have met at a dead end. Interrogation of individuals who have acquired these crystals reveal they can never remember details surrounding the source. Subjects show signs of powerful magical memory manipulation. It is currently unknown where these crystals come from or how they are made. It has been speculated that they are created by a newly developed branch of blood magic, or they are machinations of the Black Lodge, or a rediscovered technique from a lost age, or they are gifts bestowed by spirits for an unknown reason.

Prior to bonding, the crystals are transparent. Upon bonding, the crystals turn blood red and become opaque. During bonding, the blood crystal grows and takes the shape of any missing or severely damaged limb or organ. Existing damaged tissue appears to be absorbed and supplanted by the crystal, replacing the whole limb or organ in a matter of minutes. In the case of replaced limbs, the musculature appears hard and faceted while retaining the warmth, mobility, and tactile sensitivity of natural flesh and blood. If the individual the crystal is bonded to dies, the crystal turns black, becomes extremely brittle, and loses all of its magical properties. Once a crystal has bonded to an individual it cannot be removed and bonded to someone else.

The few known attempts that have been made to use these blood crystals on non-Awakened individuals have proven disastrous. The crystals grow over a period of several days, replacing more and more tissue until the individual becomes an inert crystal statue. This has led to speculation that the blood crystal feeds off of the magical energy of an Awakened individual, and when bonded to a mundane individual feeds off their life essence instead. This theory is strengthened by that fact that blood crystals will not bond to any individual with an active HMHVV infection, presumably because the virus interrupts the bonding process.

- Y'know, for just one moment, I got kinda excited at the thought of getting magic like this.
- Sounder

- I'm not surprised it won't bond with infected. HMHVV is a greedy sonofabitch.
- Doc Fangs

- It's also possible that they represent incompatible magical elements.
- Lyran

- Elements?
- Elijah

- It's about half-theoretical, but certain types of magic simply aren't compatible with one another. You see the most evidence of this in conflicting background aspecting, but plenty of manatech labs are trying to unlock the specific components that obstruct each other to find ways around that. Not unlike dissecting the DNA of a living organism to find which components trigger which expressions.
- The Smiling Bandit

- And here I thought you meant spells that don't mix. I saw some joker wizganger claim he had designed a spell that shot fire and ice at the same time. When I told him to put up or shut up, he swaggered over and shouted something like, "Icy Hot!" like he's in an anime, and he gets covered in boiling water.
- Riot

- Let's stay on topic, folks.
- Glitch

- Absolutely. But, Riot? Can you get me that boiling water spell, please?
- Ethernaut

- I've heard about some wiz-gangs turning blood magic into a kind of rite of passage. The stain on the soul commits you to the gang so you can't just up and leave their protection, and it proves you're a badass. Of course, most of these jokers are prime material for blood hunters. At their low level, it's a pretty sweet payday and a decent way to cut your teeth.
- Hard Exit

- Yeah. And weed out the wannabes.
- Sticks

There are benefits and downsides to bonding a blood crystal. During bonding, the crystal reduces an individual's essence much in the same way cyberware would. The crystal, though, seems to replace this essence with its own energy, providing a sort of augmented essence. This prevents any reduction in an Awakened subject's magic and does not impair magical abilities in any way. However, if the blood crystal is removed, the augmented essence supplied by the crystal is removed as well, and the individual suffers the effects of essence loss as normal. During bonding, the blood crystal will grow and take the shape of any missing or severely damaged limb or organ.

Additional abilities are often attributed to blood crystals, although they seem to be highly dependent on the individual and the body part replaced. Little is known about the long-term effects of the use of a blood crystal, as this is a relatively new phenomenon. Very few live subjects have been studied, and the results of studies that were performed are secrets closely guarded by the parties involved. I have acquired what information I can on the subject, but the picture is frustratingly incomplete at this point. Several corporations and magical groups have outstanding bounties for anyone bonded to a blood crystal, most notably the blood mages of Aztlan. That there is something apparently related to blood magic that Aztlan allegedly doesn't know about troubles me greatly. Because of these bounties, most crystal bearers have gone into hiding. We know the most about those with crystal limbs, as they are harder to keep concealed. Several have exhibited limited ability to shape their limbs, growing claws or shaping their entire forearm into a blade at will. We don't know too much about internal crystal augments, as there are no outward signs of their bond. There are rumors of a man who had severe lung damage from exposure to some sort of toxic gas which was cured by implantation of blood crystal that then allowed him to breathe underwater. Another rumor hints at a woman who was dying of cirrhosis of the liver, but when the organ was replaced with a blood crystal, she received great endurance and resistance to toxic substances.

- That, and she'll never enjoy a drink again.
- Beaker

- About the same for a bioware toxin filter. Saves your life, so I wouldn't complain.
- Butch

- There are degrees of survival, doc. And survival ain't always livin'.
- XXL

- Damn, man. That was like a street-level version of Man-of-Many-Names.
- Whippet

- ... thank you?
- XXL

- Where is our resident Man-of-Many-Cryptic-Statements, anyway? This sounds like his kind of thing to pretend he knows everything about.
- Slamm-0!

- Listening.
- Man-of-Many-Names

- That is the scariest thing I've ever heard him say.
- Slamm-0!

- Anybody met anyone with one of these?
- Hard Exit

- Just once. Awfully rare. The guy … I don't know. It was like he had a real stick up his ass. Which was weird, considering I looked him up because the word on the street was that he was a guy who knew how to have a good time and paint the town.
- Traveler Jones

RIVERS OF POWER

- So, where is blood magic happening? Who has the lore and is putting it to use? We called on specialists to post what they know, but this one is open forum. Throw in what you know, and try to stay on topic.
- Glitch

AZTLAN (AZTECHNOLOGY)

- Aztechnology is the number-one producer of consumer goods in the world. The top corp in magical research. It effectively owns a whole nation. It's the biggest corp in North America, and might just be biggest in the world, depending on who you ask. Statistically, you've likely eaten something made by one of AZT's subsidiaries today. But the first thing people like us think of when they see the logo and the pyramids is blood. While consumers love them and find them cuddly, we've

NOTES ON BLOOD CRYSTALS

What may at first seem a blessing can turn into a curse. A number of disturbing side effects appear to plague those bearing blood crystals. They reportedly may experience dramatic changes in behavior, becoming more strict in their ethical principles, feeling compelled to perform certain actions, or possibly hearing voices giving them orders. The ethical realignment is most common in those with internal organs replaced, compulsions are most common in those with limbs replaced, and hearing voices is most common in those with a spine replacement, though any can be experienced at times no matter what is replaced. The more supplemental abilities that are learned and the more Essence that is lost to blood crystal implantation, the stronger the effects. Greater effects are possible, though blood crystals are a new phenomenon, so the full range of effects they might display has not yet been seen.

heard the tales of them slicing the still-beating hearts out of convicts. They aren't terribly open about it, but we know it's part of their corporate culture. From the bloodsport fighting pits to the tlachtli ball courts to metamagical R&D to special forces, Aztechnology has no qualms about using sacrifice to power the prosperity of country or corporate interests (which are, of course, the same thing).

The Path of the Sun holds sacrifice in high regard, and as the state religion of Aztlan, shrines to Tezcatlipoca show up in plenty of homes, possibly with some blood stains, depending on the level of devotion of the owner. Public executions are on the trid and cheered by thousands, and while the blood magic part of the ritual is not discussed, those in the know can see what is happening. Strike teams in Bogota were said to have worn blood like warpaint, POWs sacrificed, and if you can believe it, worse than that.

It's only rumor, but seeing as that's the stock and trade of the shadows, they say there is an elite cabal at the top of the priesthood—or possibly it's just an individual, depending on who you ask—called the Smoking Mirror. This cult is the stuff of conspiracy-theory nightmares: They've got members on the board of directors, they worship a living god, and they use their power to win wars at the cost of souls. Some people even say the Blue-227 weapon was a result of their magic. The one thing everyone agrees on is that they must be old-school blood magic. With the Big A's long history of covering up nefarious deeds, it's impossible to discount anything, no matter how outlandish the accusation.

- Pyramid Watcher

- It's not unusual to see a normalized attitude about sacrifice in everyday life in Aztlan. Animals are pretty normal at temples, for example. People just don't even think about it. Makes me think they're jaded. One trip to a pit fight is all the proof you'll ever need.
- Traveler Jones

- The reports of blood magic in Bogota are true. Many of the soldiers going up against Aztlan troops were advised not to be taken alive. Awakened Amazonian troops were terrified of their souls being used to fuel the enemy war effort.
- Picador

- Some gods are real. Others are nothing more than smoke and mirrors.
- Man-of-Many-Names

- Please tell me that wasn't a pun …
- Snopes

- Godhood is a matter of perspective. To the ant, the descending boot is a god.
- Feather-Dancer

- Better not be the ant, then, huh?
- Hard Exit

ORDO MAXIMUS

- Ordo. Oh, Ordo, you beautiful monsters, I paid for my vacation house in Hawai'i with nothing but bounty money from taking out your initiates. When it comes to European blood magic, I say look no further than these bastards. Rumors abound of their inner circle being composed of nosferatu and other intelligent infected, or cybermancy, or demon worship, but I can definitely confirm that a whole passel of them are down-and-dirty old-school blood mages. While I have yet to run across any vampires, and certainly no cyberzombies, a few of their goons have turned out to be high on Renfield, and plenty more besides made lots of threats about my soul being torn out to feed their masters' unholy appetites. That's me paraphrasing, by the way; they really love their purple prose.

  Aside from those rumors, the facts about the Ordo Maximus are that they are a magic club for old money blue bloods. They aren't all Awakened, but anyone who wants to do more with their membership than get private invitations to the secret rooms (in elite clubs to smoke cigars wrapped with print money, one assumes) has to have the gift. That's when you become an initiate, and the real fun begins. Everything I can tell says they count as a big magic group, and while their mundane members can help with grand rituals and serious power brokering, the initiates are playing big leagues with the promise of forbidden lore. I'm no mage myself, but I employ them regularly. I had one of them do a mind probe on a captured initiate, and there were visions of pale old men holding books that practically smelled of power. Really ancient stuff. Bad stuff. (And then some kind of failsafe kicked in, and my mage got brain-scrambled. She knew the risks, but she gets all her food intravenously now.) The Ordo likes to say they maintain and protect very old collections of the finest magical texts in the world for their own protection, and they command enough influence to keep megacorps from just buying them out. Evidently some of that ancient lore includes slitting wrists for power.

  The problem with hunting Ordo bloods is that you run into money. Yeah. Just plain old money, and everything it can buy. Rumor has it they actually buy people through slave-trafficking markets, which means they can snatch up all kinds of SINless for a power boost. They dash into luxury hotels with lots of cameras and security and witnesses and grin at you, knowing you're the outsider. But if you can corner one outside of their gilded cages, they fight like hellions. I guess they feel like they have more to lose than other people. They'll use every dirty trick in the book, and they have ancient tomes full of instructions for dirty tricks that the rest of the world has forgotten. They feel little restraint, because they think the world belongs to them, and they have the money to buy lawyers, judges—hell, they can buy the law. They do seem to have a fetish for control over others, so expect blood-puppet effects. They like the pain and the screams of those who would dare to defy them. Makes it a lot more satisfying when they piss their designer pants after a taser dart hits them. Then you just have to turn them in and hope their legion of lawyers aren't at the Draco Foundation before you are.
- Bloodhound

NAN

- It's not a secret, but most people don't think about the first major (and arguably most powerful) magical act of the Sixth World being one of mass sacrifice. The Great Ghost Dance was an ecstatic, selfless ritual, where participants often whipped themselves into a frenzy until they died, their essence joining what might constitute the largest magical ritual in known history. Exact numbers are hard to track down, but thousands likely gave their lives to the ritual, giving the NAN the power to fight off the USA, Canada, and any other comers with the raw power of hurricanes and volcanoes, as well as jump-starting the Awakening.

  Even today, there are those alive who can recall the terror of those times. Whether you believe their cause was righteous or not, the show of power the nascent NAN displayed has never been repeated. Still, the NAN retain a reputation for those who would cross them: They can, and will, lay down their lives to harness the power of the living world to take and defend what is theirs. Whether the realization that it is a form of blood magic makes that threat any scarier is a moot point.

◉ Lyran

◉ The world was not meant to Awaken quite so suddenly. As was observed earlier, blood magic has a particular utility in that it can generate mana spikes in locations. The Great Ghost Dance represents the same principle on a world-shifting level. Such trauma was akin to a shot of stims into a sleeping person. They awaken, disoriented, conscious but raw and confused. So it is with this Awakening. It may be some time, if ever, before the world has its chance to regain its clarity and perspective. Already much of what was seems irretrievably lost.

◉ Wordsmyth

◉ You've got to wonder if the manasphere has somehow been permanently colored by that. Like, if the whole Awakened world, being jump-started by blood magic, somehow aspected the world to be more conducive to blood magic. Or even just gave us all an unconscious inclination toward violence and pain.

◉ Ethernaut

◉ Wait, you're suggesting that if the Great Ghost Dance hadn't happened, not only would magic and other Awakened stuff have taken longer to show up, but we'd all be less violent, and the world would be a nicer place? C'mon.

◉ Jimmy No

◉ All places, all things in this world, bear the echo of that which touches them. The Dance was a scream to the heavens. Its echo rings still.

◉ Man-of-Many-Names

◉ In a world filled with dragons and magic and artificial intelligence, the concept of what is strange seems to lose meaning. Or perhaps that is simply a matter of perspective. Most, if not all of you, grew up in this world. Some few of us remember when much of what is now our reality was nothing more than flights of fancy.

◉ Red

WICCA

◉ Wiccanism is a fairly complicated religion. Much like how Christianity is split into numerous denominations and dogmas, so too is Wicca. The concept of sacrifice is not unknown, and bloodletting acts as a component (often optional) in several rituals, particularly if it is a higher-level or more complex enchantment. Blood is symbolic in this regard, representing an investment of the self

into an endeavor, and so isn't necessarily a matter of physical harm or even true blood magic. It's just a proof of commitment. If your friendly neo-pagan is mixing some of their own blood into warding materials, for example, it's probably of a higher density or complexity than simple chalk and sage smudging.

The famous karmic rule of Wicca is that all your deeds are revisited on you threefold, so the idea of sacrificing someone else is particularly horrifying when your belief structure teaches that you will endure thrice the pain and loss of your own victim. Wiccans ted to be particularly sensitive about being misunderstood as blood mages. Some will cite their history of being burned at the stake (which many carry like a chip on their shoulder), others will point out that an essential tool of their craft, the athame, had its name misappropriated to describe soul-draining foci. Despite a faith that preaches healing and harmony, the classic image of the witch practicing their dark craft continues to hound the modern Wiccan, and likely will for some time more.

Of course, that doesn't mean the occasional fallen practitioner won't try to utilize sacrificial metamagic techniques. Some consider it a way of subverting the Threefold Law, making someone else take the weight of their sin all at once. Others consider themselves agents of a greater karmic cycle, or they subscribe to a darker view of the Horned God and the Goddess, anointing themselves with glyphs painted in stolen blood and offering up the sacrifice as proof of their devotion, shifting the crime into a form of service for their higher power, at least in their own mind. Given the vast disparity between the core tenets of the faith and these justifications, they are the rare exception, and any traditional follower of Wicca will offer their support in bringing down such hideous practices.

◉ Doc Fangs

◉ You're a Wiccan, Doc?
◉ Lyran

◉ Following the Great Mother in my own way, I share some of the same methods and beliefs. You of all people should know: ask five mages of the same tradition about their beliefs, you'll get at least seven different answers.

◉ Doc Fangs

THEURGY

◉ Christianity is a religion of blood, no matter how you slice it. The blood of the Savior, the Eucharist, transubstantiation, sacramental wine, you name it. Leviticus 17:11, Hebrews 9:22, Genesis 9:4, the list goes on and on. Believe me, there are some Infected who take Christianity very, *very* literally. But for the practicing theurgist, blood can be a spontaneous manifestation of casting. While many priests

BLOOD MAGE BOUNTIES

At present, the Draco Foundation offers bounties on live blood mages based on their power and infamy, primarily focusing on a Most Wanted list of particularly dangerous criminals. In game terms, this may be determined by their Notoriety and the Magic attribute.

Minor blood mages may fetch a price of five thousand to ten thousand nuyen from the Draco Foundation, who usually prefer them alive, or from local law enforcement, who may pay on the lower end of the scale but accept dead ones readily.

Powerful blood mages, with a Magic rating from 10 to 15, may be worth anywhere from seventy-five thousand to three hundred thousand. The price is almost always for the mage being brought in alive, and is usually offered by the Draco Foundation or another megacorporation interested in the mage's capture.

The blood mage will likely be wanted alive if their Notoriety is 10 or below. Above that, they are often accepted dead, as they have proven to be too dangerous to be taken alive.

These are bounties that are generally considered to be the most risky around, and they carry a significant amount of prestige. The majority of the Most Wanted have been responsible for the deaths of multiple teams of shadowrunners and should represent an enormous challenge to your players. You may consider giving them a point of Street Cred for the accomplishment if word gets out, or Public Awareness if it makes headlines.

In all cases, verification of the bounty's use of blood magic is required to collect the reward. This may take the form of eyewitness accounts, reliable footage (perhaps from a third party), or magical forensics.

See pp. 25-28, *Hazard Pay*, for some of the most notorious blood mage bounties.

and lay casters are known to manifest "shamanic masks" in the spirit of their patron saint, some powerful castings have occasionally expressed stigmata, bleeding from the palms, feet, ribs, or pin pricks around the crown of the head, much like the wounds of Christ. It's not a big jump from there to blood magic.

I mean, let's face it: from the right point of view, Jesus sacrificed himself, and that resulted in some damn big mojo. In the same spirit, a theurgist might practice self-flagellation, lashings, use of a cilice, or even crucifixion, deriving advanced power from the practice. If that's not blood magic, I really don't know what is.
- Hannibelle

- I've heard some congregations in Italy and Spain use a form of blood alchemy in their transubstantiation, achieving a much more "true" practice of the Eucharist. I didn't try it.
- Traveler Jones

- I strongly suspect the Templars use blood magic, both on themselves and on "lambs," victims sacrificed in the name of their holy causes and conspiracies. You don't really hear about Sylvestrines doing it, but then, I suspect plenty of them have no idea who is really pulling the strings of their organization.
- Elijah

DIMR

- The Draco Foundation, acting on behalf of the Dunklezahn Institute of Magical Research, is a primary mover and shaker in opposition to blood magic practices. Dunklezahn's Will stipulated a standing bounty for any blood mages captured and turned in alive, paying out to the tune of a cool million nuyen per head. These days, the money from the will seems to have run low, or perhaps the sheer number of blood mages has grown too much for the funds to be enough to maintain the bounty. Personally, I have a hard time believing Dunklezahn didn't plan for it. He seems to have planned for everything. But trying to understand the complexity of a draconic plot is one hell of a way to spend your life accomplishing nothing.

  The big question for a lot of people has been, "What is the DIMR doing with these live captures?" It's the "live" part that arouses suspicion. Rumors abound about the possible uses the Institute may have for living specimens, from interrogation to rehabilitation to brainwashing to dissection. There is, of course, no evidence of any of those, though the question remains. In the meantime, bounty hunters continue to stalk and capture these miscreants, and as long as the Foundation keeps paying, the world remains a little safer.
- Silk

- More and more, we're recognizing that dragons know how to use blood magic. It's not much of a stretch to think that the Foundation wants to see what innovations humans may have come up with, or even gauge our relative power level. Or maybe there are certain spells that require more mages, or even a sacrifice of those who have sacrificed others. This is all conjecture, of course.
- Arete

- I have it on good authority that at least one of their captures was later seen in the field carrying out directives on behalf of the Foundation. Given the rumors of Ares using brainwashed bug shamans to hunt bugs, it's not too

far of a stretch to think they might be turning blood mages against their own kind.
◉ Plan 9

◉ "Good authority?" Care to cite your sources?
◉ Snopes

◉ Well?
◉ Snopes

◉ I thought not.
◉ Snopes

◉ For most of my life, I have been considered something of a conspiracy theorist. Nothing so sensational as Plan 9, but more, I have believed in the possibility of extraordinary implications in this extraordinary world. The more jaded among us still resist ideas they choose to label as "outlandish," amusingly enough while parsing through articles in a shared consensual digital hallucination and talking to their friends, who belong to metahuman subspecies which were considered no more than fiction and myth a mere century ago.

There are people alive, today, who remember the world before any of this. They remember when only humans walked the world. A world before the Matrix, before the megacorps, before magic and dragons and SINs. Had you told them what would happen in their lifetime, what they would live to see, they would have called you crazy, and been right to do so.

How are we still clinging to this outmoded sense of the mundane when we are surrounded with what was so recently implausible? How can we possess the ignorance and hubris that makes such doubt possible?

Today, I learned that there are degrees of sacrificial magic. That a sacrifice can be noble, even selfless, or made in love.

I also listened to mysterious people speak with the sanction of people I trust and respect, talking about previous ages as though they were there. People who offered tantalizing pieces of the truth in an environment where they were shielded from all questions. And if there is one thing I have learned about piecemeal knowledge, it is that those who offer it are trying to lead you somewhere.

I'm not making accusations, nor am I resentful. Quite the opposite. Frosty, Red, I appreciate you bringing the guests you did, and I respect their need to be cryptic. I have never been more motivated to find the truth than I am now.
◉ Elijah

◉ Fascinating discoveries. Far-Scholar would have been proud.
◉ Mameleu

◉ This is nothing we didn't already know.
◉ Script-Diver

◉ It is not what we know, but what they know that matters. It will make all the difference in the days to come.
◉ Orange Queen

◉ Who the hell are they?
◉ Glitch

◉ Expectedly unexpected guests. Oops, guess that includes me, too!
◉ The Laughing Man

◉ Jane ...
◉ Wordsmyth

◉ Bull, shut down the board! Now!
◉ Frosty

◉ **CONNECTION TERMINATED**

BLOOD IN, BLOOD OUT

Want to dive deeper into blood magic? Here's how.

BLOOD SPELLS

All spells with the Blood descriptor require use of at least 1 Blood Magic Point generated by the Sacrifice metamagic to cast. The spells themselves do not expend the Blood Magic Point, a point *must* be used to either increase the Force of the spell, increase the caster's Magic Rating for purposes of determining if the spell is Stun or Physical, or reduce the amount of Drain inflicted by the spell (per the Sacrifice rules, p. 90, *Street Grimoire*).

COMBAT

BOIL BLOOD

(Blood, Direct, Elemental)
Type: P **Range:** LOS
Duration: I **Damage:** P **Drain:** F – 2

By exciting the blood in the body of a living host, the spell causes the target to sustain burning damage from within, bypassing armor. This spell deals Fire damage (p. 171, *SR5*) and is resisted with Body (+ Counterspelling). If the target has taken

Physical damage previously that left open wounds, the blood ignites on contact with air and may ignite flammable materials it touches. The spell has no effect on targets without a circulatory system.

CORPSE EXPLOSION

(Blood, Direct, Elemental)
    Type: P   **Range:** LOS
    Duration: I   **Damage:** P   **Drain:** F

The most brutal (and gross) of the Corpse spells, this spell targets a corpse, violently exciting its blood and causing the body to explode, throwing super-heated flesh, organs, broken bone, and gear fragments with the force of a frag grenade. The Damage Value of a successful Corpse Explosion spell is the spell's Force + net hits, with an AP equal to – (Force). The radius of the effect is equal to the corpse's Body in meters. Damage from this spell is resisted with Body + Armor (adjusted for the spell's AP). The Force of the spell must be equal to or greater than the Body of the corpse affected. If the caster mistakenly targets a living being, the spell fails. The rules for blasts against barriers (p. 183, *SR5*) apply to the spell's effects.

EMBOLISM

(Blood, Direct)
    Type: P   **Range:** LOS
    Duration: I   **Damage:** P   **Drain:** F – 2

By breaking the steady flow of blood, the caster causes the target to suffer damage and crippling pain in the body part affected. Roll a 1D6 to determine where the embolism occurs:

GIGER SPIT

(Blood, Direct, Elemental)
    Type: P   **Range:** T
    Duration: I   **Damage:** P   **Drain:** F – 4

Biting their tongue or cheek, the mage spits a gob of acidic blood. The caster deals 1P damage to themselves, generating the Blood Magic Point required to cast this Blood spell. This attack has a range of (Magic) meters and deals Acid damage (p. 170, *SR5*).

EMBOLISM LOCATION TABLE

ROLL	BODY PART*	EFFECT
1	Head	Stunned (Body + Willpower (4) Test to resist or target receives a –10 penalty to Initiative Score)
2	Right arm	Broken Grip (target is unable to maintain their grip on anything in their hand, suffers a –1 dice pool penalty per injured arm for all Subduing or Clinching attacks, and drops any item in their hand for a number of Combat Turns equal to the DV of the attack
3	Left arm	Broken Grip (target is unable to maintain their grip on anything in their hand, suffers a –1 dice pool penalty per injured arm for all Subduing or Clinching attacks, and drops any item in their hand for a number of Combat Turns equal to the DV of the attack
4	Right leg	Slowed (target's Movement, including both Walk and Run rate, is halved, and no Sprint tests are allowed)
5	Left leg	Slowed (target's Movement, including both Walk and Run rate, is halved, and no Sprint tests are allowed)
6	Torso	Winded (target is unable to perform Complex Actions for a number of Combat Turns equal to the original DV of the attack)

* If the result of the random roll results in the spell targeting a body part that is missing or not biological (for example, a cyberarm), the spell has no effect. The spell has no effect on targets without a circulatory system.

ICE VEINS

(Blood, Direct)

Type: P **Range:** LOS

Duration: I **Damage:** Special **Drain:** F– 3

By lowering the target's blood temperature, the mage causes the target to slow down and take damage. Targets take Stun damage and suffer a –2 dice pool penalty to all actions performed with their extremities. Along with the normal uses of Blood Magic Points (p. 90, *Street Grimoire),* the caster may spend one point to add the following effects to the spell: Make the damage Physical, and the target's Agility is treated as 2 lower for the purposes of determining Movement. The spell has no effect on targets without a circulatory system.

PYROHEMETICS

(Blood, Indirect, Elemental)

Type: P **Range:** LOS

Duration: I **Damage:** P **Drain:** F - 4

The mage flings a spatter of ignited blood, doing fire damage. The caster deals 1P damage to themselves, generating the Blood Pool Point required to cast this Blood spell. This attack has a range of (Magic) meters and deals Fire damage (p. 170, *SR5).*

RUPTURE

(Blood, Direct)

Type: P **Range:** T

Duration: I **Damage:** P **Drain:** F - 6

With this particularly traumatic spell, the caster seizes control of the blood of the target, forcing it to evacuate his body by whatever egress it can. The target begins to bleed from their eyes, ears, nose, and so forth, while thinner patches of skin first contuse, then split open as blood shoots out in a scarlet geyser. This spell can only affect targets with a circulatory system. The damage caused by this spell can be used with the Sacrifice metamagic and to charge an athame.

HEALTH

CLOT

(Blood, Essence)

Type: M **Range:** T

Duration: S **Drain:** F - 2

A simple spell modifying the blood's clotting ability, Clot causes the improved stabilization of bleeding wounds, which can greatly assist in stabilizing a dying character who is bleeding out.

Any time you would take two or more boxes of damage to your Physical Condition Monitor, reduce the damage by one box. The Force of the spell must be equal to or greater than the Body of the target. Any attempts to stabilize a character who is into overflow damage while under the effect of this spell gain a +1 dice pool modifier for every 2 hits on the spellcasting test.

SHARE DAMAGE

(Blood)

Type: M **Range:** T

Duration: S **Drain:** F - 4

With this sympathetic spell, the blood mage joins his life force to another willing person, causing all Physical damage either individual takes to be shared between them, diluting the severity for the receiver. In the event of an uneven number of boxes of damage, Physical damage gives the extra point to whoever directly received the damage, but magical damage always gives the odd point to the caster of this spell. Stun damage is taken normally and cannot be shared. Damage already received by the target or the caster of the spell before the spell is cast is unaffected by the spell.

SOMATIC HEALING

(Blood, Essence)

Type: M **Range:** T

Duration: P **Drain:** F - 4

The noblest of uses for blood magic, the caster transfers some of their life essence into the target, taking their wounds for them. The target heals a number of boxes of Physical damage equal to the spell's hits from the Spellcasting test, while the caster takes the same amount of damage. This damage cannot be healed magically and must be recovered with mundane rest and care. Hits can

also be used to reduce the base time for the spell to become permanent; each hit spent this way shaves off 1 Combat Turn (you can split hits between healing and reducing time).

SYMPATHETIC REPRISAL

(Blood)

> **Type:** M **Range:** T
> **Duration:** S **Drain:** F - 2

A more dangerous version of Share Damage, Sympathetic Reprisal curses a target so their melee attacks against the caster cause the target to take damage in kind. This spell is cast with a Spellcasting + Magic [Force] v. Body + Willpower Opposed Test. Any successful melee attack the target makes against the caster has a number of points of damage equal to the net hits of the Spellcasting test immediately removed from the caster and

transferred to the target. If both Stun and Physical damage are dealt with one attack, Stun is transferred first.

MANIPULATION

BLOOD PUPPET

(Blood, Mental)

> **Type:** P **Range:** LOS
> **Duration:** S **Drain:** F - 1

Similar to the Control Actions spell, you control the physical actions of your target like a puppeteer pulling strings by seizing control of the blood in their body. The victim's consciousness is unaffected, but you control the victim's body. Use your own skills when forcing your target to perform actions. It takes a Complex Action to make the target perform any action. Blood Puppet only affects a single target. If the target of the spell successfully resists your control with a Willpower + Logic test (p. 292, SR5), they take (Force)P damage resisted by their Body as veins tear and capillaries burst under the stress. This spell can only affect targets with a circulatory system.

CORPSE SPIKES

(Blood, Environmental, Area)
Type: P   **Range:** LOS (A)
Duration: I   **Drain:** F

Targeting a dead body, this spell draws the blood out of the corpse and freezes in into a slippery sheet studded with sharp, almost crystalline spikes that jut out violently, forming a dangerous obstacle to those around it and potentially impaling anyone who slips on the ice. The affected area has a radius in meters equal to the Body of the corpse, with the corpse at its center. Characters crossing the frozen blood must make an Agility + Reaction Test with a threshold equal to the hits you score to avoid falling prone. A character failing this test falls prone and takes (Force)P damage resisted by Body + Armor. The sheet melts at a rate of 1 square meter per minute at room temperature (faster when it's hotter, slower when it's colder, or not at all if it's below freezing). If the caster mistakenly targets a living being, the spell fails. The Force of the spell must be equal to or greater than the Body of the corpse affected.

CORPSE LASH

(Blood, Environmental, Area)
Type: P   **Range:** LOS (A)
Duration: I   **Drain:** F - 1

Targeting a dead body, this spell causes the blood to burst forth in a swarm of tentacles, violently lashing out and grappling anyone nearby. Characters within or attempting to cross the affected area have their Agility reduced by every net hit on the Spellcasting test. If Agility is reduced to 0, the target is bound and unable to move his limbs. While bound by the spell, the target may attempt to crawl or hop short distances (at one-quarter their normal movement rate). Entangled targets may still defend and dodge against attacks, but they suffer a dice-pool modifier equal to the caster's net hits. A bound target may attempt to break free of the bindings by making a Strength + Body

[Physical] or Escape Artist + Agility [Physical] vs. Force x 2 Opposed Test. The Force of the spell must be equal to or greater than the Body of the corpse affected. The affected area has a radius in meters equal to the Body of the corpse, with the corpse at its center. If the caster mistakenly targets a living being, the spell fails.

BLOOD WHIP

(Blood, Physical)
Type: P   **Range:** T
Duration: I   **Drain:** F-2

With a slice of the blade across the wrist, the mage causes some of their blood to erupt out in the form of a magical whip. The caster deals 1P damage to themselves, generating the Blood Pool Point required to cast this Blood Spell. The blood whip functions as a bullwhip (R&G p21). For every two hits on the Spellcasting test, the lash gains +1P and -2AP. The whip has an Accuracy equal to the Force of the spell, and persists for that number of minutes. When wielded by the caster, attacks use Spellcasting +Agility. Any other person using the blood lash uses Exotic Melee Weapon (Bullwhip) + Agility.

BLOOD BLADE

(Blood, Physical)
Type: P   **Range:** T
Duration: S   **Drain:** F - 1

Slicing open their palm or conjuring from a "donor," the mage crystallizes blood into a blade, anything from a knife to a long sword. The blade has an Accuracy equal to the Force of the spell, and persists for that number of minutes. One hit on the Spellcasting test produces a small blade that deals damage as a knife, three hits on the Spellcasting test produces a medium blade that deals damage as a sword, five hits on the spellcasting test produces a large blade that deals damage as a combat axe.

VISCERA WEB

(Blood, Physical, Damaging)
Type: P   **Range:** LOS
Duration: S   **Drain:** F + 4

A horrific spell, this causes widespread rupturing across the target's body as their veins shoot out to adhere to the environment surrounding them. This incapacitates them with extraordinary damage and pain, plus the fact that their living veins stick to the floor, walls, and ceiling. Any damage caused cutting them down may cause them to bleed out—assuming they survived the initial spell. The caster must win a Spellcasting + Magic vs. Body (+ Counterspelling) Opposed Test. Additionally, the spell's Force must equal or exceed the target's Body. Non-living material—including clothing, gear, and cyberware—are not affected. The target's Agility is reduced by every net hit on the Spellcasting test. If Agility is reduced to 0, the target becomes fused to the nearest solid surface and unable to move their limbs without causing further damage to themselves. The target can painfully tear themselves free, though this causes additional damage equal to the net hits on the Spellcasting test and one additional box of Physical damage every (Body) minutes until they receive medical attention to stop the bleeding.

BLOOD RITUALS

The following rituals all require the Sacrifice metamagic to perform.

BLOOD BATH

(Adept, Blood)

The blood adept knows that blood within is life, and blood without is protection. Every scar was a wound that has grown tougher. But not all such armor need come from them. Adepts covered in blood can cause it to harden into a natural armor. The more blood, the tougher the armor. This armor stacks with standard armor for the purposes of determining encumbrance penalties (see **Armor and Encumbrance**, p. 169, *SR5*), but only if it coats the same regions covered by armor. For example, a blood adept might wear an armored vest and pants, but paint their face, arms, and exposed flesh with blood to harden into a sheath without adding to their armor encumbrance.

To perform this ritual, the adept makes a Arcana + Logic [Force] Test. This ritual takes (Force) minutes to complete. The adept paints themselves with fresh blood from a sapient being. Each hit on the test grants +1 Armor or Astral Armor (either one or a combination of both can be chosen). The benefit ritual decreases by 1 every 2 hours as the blood degrades until it offers no further benefit. Washing off the blood ends the effect prematurely. Needless to say, walking around covered in blood is quite conspicuous and may draw unwanted attention.

BLOOD OATH

(Material Link)

In this ritual, the subject swears that they will perform a specific task and receives greater ability to achieve that goal in return. Appropriate oaths would include swearing to defend a specific individual or to find a specific object. This oath must be taken freely, or the ritual fails. As part of the ritual, the leader inflicts a number of boxes of Physical damage to the subject equal to or less than the Force of the ritual. For every 2 boxes of Physical damage inflicted, the subject chooses one skill that they will use to achieve the goal of their oath. They receive a +1 dice pool and +1 limit modifier to the chosen skill. This modifier only applies when the subject is directly working to fulfill their oath. For example if a player chose Pistols as a skill for an oath to protect an individual, they would get the benefit of the oath if they were attacked while guarding the individual but not if they were attacked while alone. Once the ritual is complete, the leader may spend Karma equal to (2 + Willpower of the subject) to make the oath permanent; otherwise it lasts for (Force) days. If the subject achieves the goal of their oath, the effect of the ritual ends. If the subject of the oath intentionally betrays that oath, they suffer twice the damage they had inflicted on them during the casting of the oath ritual. Even if the subject survives this damage, the injuries leave severe scars, forever marking them as an oath breaker to those who know the signs. This damage only occurs if the subject breaks their oath, not if they fail to achieve its goal. The leader can hold active oaths with up to his Charisma in subjects. The ritual takes (Force) hours to complete. An individual can only have one active oath at a time. A blood oath does not require a blood magic Addiction Test, as it is purely voluntary and the required damage represents commitment rather than suffering.

DEATH CURSE

(Material Link)

This ritual allows the magician to exact final vengeance on anyone who slays them. If the subject of this ritual dies, they burn all their Edge, and a blood spirit is automatically summoned from their corpse. The Force of the blood spirit summoned is equal to the hits on a Magic + (number of Edge burned) test.

The Force of the ritual sets the limit. Because the ritual does not actually use the Summoning skill, any Awakened individual can be the subject.

The spirit has no master, but it has a burning desire to destroy the one who killed the subject of the ritual. The violence of the death is enough to create a brief metaphysical link between the subject and their killer, allowing the blood spirit to recognize them on sight. Once the blood spirit exacts its revenge, it is free to return to whatever dark metaplane it came from, or more likely to continue on a killing spree. Because of the high potential to set a rampaging blood spirit loose, this ritual is taboo even in areas where blood magic is tolerated.

GUARDIAN BOND

(Material Link)

A benign variation of the Blood Bond ritual (p. 125, *Street Grimoire*), this ritual bonds the magician to a genetically related subject. Unlike a Blood Bond, a Guardian Bond protects the subject, not the caster. The minimum Force of the ritual is equal to the subject's Willpower. Once the ritual is complete, the leader may spend Karma equal to 2 + Willpower of the subject to make the bond permanent, otherwise it lasts for (Force) days. This bond creates a low-level telepathic link between the leader and the subject (they know each other's emotional state and general whereabouts). The magician may use a form of Empathic healing (p. 171, *Street Grimoire*) to transfer physical damage from the subject to himself, if the subject is within (100 x Magic Rating) meters from the magician. The leader can bond up to their Charisma in subjects. This ritual takes (Force) days to complete. This ritual requires the Sacrifice metamagic to cast, however any Blood Magic Points spent must originate from the leader of the ritual. This ritual does not necessitate an Addiction test for the use of blood magic.

METAMAGIC

PREDATOR FEAST
(ADEPTS ONLY)

PREREQUISITE: CANNIBALIZE

The adept has tasted the flesh of its own kind and found it appealing. The life force, blood, bone, sinew—all are the same components which compose the adept's body. By committing cannibalistic acts, they can gain temporary regeneration of their own wounds.

Note that corporations and other groups will gladly hunt down such an aberrant individual for the DIMR bounty, and DNA from their saliva and dental patterns from multiple victims can be used to hunt them down. Being a cannibal in the Sixth World isn't easy.

Predator feast is an advanced metamagic technique that builds upon the Cannibalize power (p. 90, *Street Grimoire*). Predator feast functions the same as Cannibalize, except that instead of generating 3 Blood Magic Points, the adept gains the Regeneration critter power (p. 400, *SR5*). The effect lasts for (Magic x initiate grade) Combat Turns, but the adept may immediately spend 3 Karma to extend the duration to (Magic x initiate grade) days.

SOUL TETHER

PREREQUISITE: SACRIFICE

Instead of absorbing the life energy of a slain opponent, the blood mage channels the energy into a kind of temporary battery to power a sustained spell. In addition to the usual uses of Blood Magic Points, they may now be used to sustain a spell, much like a sustaining focus. The Blood Magic Points used to power this ability must have been drawn from a victim that died in the process. A number of Blood Magic Points equal to the Force of the spell must be spent to sustain a spell in this way. However, the process slowly eats away at the bound soul, consuming it to fuel the spell. Each hour, the spell loses one point of Force, until the soul, screaming, is snuffed out completely. This kind of magic is incredibly destructive on a spiritual level. Assensing tests against a blood mage sustaining a spell in this way receive a +2 dice pool modifier to recognize the nature of the mage's magic. Spirits react in an especially negative way. If a blood mage with a spell sustained through soul tether attempts to summon any type of spirit other than a blood spirit, the spirit gains a +4 dice pool bonus to resist the Summoning test. Other spirits encountering the blood mage will act with hostility, including attacking them preferentially if free to do so.

SPIRITUAL SACRIFICE

PREREQUISITE: SACRIFICE

This technique was thought lost around the time of Crash 2.0. The blood mage has learned to tap into the inherent link between the flesh and a possessing entity. Invested flesh forms, ally spirits

BLOOD ALCHEMY

By using the Sacrifice metamagic, an alchemist can enhance their alchemical preparations in the following ways:

- Increase the Force of an alchemical spell being cast by one per Blood Magic Point; this can exceed twice the caster's Magic Rating.
- Increase the caster's Magic Rating for the purposes of determining if the alchemical spell's drain is Physical or Stun, by one per Blood Magic Point.
- Reduce the amount of Drain the alchemical spell inflicts by one per Blood Magic Point, to a minimum of 0.
- Increase the duration before the preparation begins losing power to (Potency x 4) hours by spending Blood Magic Points equal to the Potency.

that have a living physical body, such as an animal familiar, and possessed hosts (loa, shedim, etc.) may now be used in sacrifice. This can be used as a kind of violent exorcism in the last instance.

BLOOD CRYSTAL QUALITIES

Blood crystal qualities do not count as standard qualities. They do not count against your maximum quality limit at character creation, nor does their Karma cost double after character creation. These qualities come in two forms, one representing the implantation of a blood crystal and another representing growing mastery over an implanted crystal allowing enhanced abilities related to it.

Like cyberware or bioware, implantation of a blood crystal reduces a character's Essence. Normally this would result in a reduction of the character's Magic rating, but the blood crystal replaces the lost Essence with a magical enhancement in the same amount, leaving the Magic attribute unaffected. The enhanced Essence only prevents MAgic loss; use the lower value for al other purposes (e.g., calculating the Social limit or surviving an Essence attack). For example, if the character had 6.0 Essence, but 1.0 of that was augmented Essence from a blood crystal, and the individual was subjected to an Essence Drain attack, they would die when 5.0 essence was drained.

If the blood crystal is removed, the augmented essence supplied by the crystal is removed as well, and the individual suffers the effects of Essence loss on their Magic as normal. During bonding, the blood crystal grows and takes the shape of any missing or severely damaged limb or organ, replicating its natural function perfectly. In the case of limbs, unaugmented Physical Attributes are replicated as well. Magical enhancements such as an adept's Improved Agility power or a mage's Improved Strength spell function normally, but mundane enhancements such as muscle replacement cyberware are not replicated.

Anyone bonded to a blood crystal has their Physical and Stun damage tracks reduced by 1 box each for as long as the crystal is bonded to them. Additional implantations increase this loss further. Implanted blood crystals can be damaged almost as readily as the flesh it replaced, but it can also heal just as if it were a natural body part. Mundane medical techniques cannot aid this healing, but magical healing works normally.

In spite of their highly magical nature, blood crystals are relatively difficult to notice on the astral. The inherent nature of their bonding and the replication of essence only shows slight disturbances in an individual's aura. It is about as difficult to detect a blood crystal through astral perception as it is to detect high-grade bioware (4 hits per the **Assensing Table**, p. 313, *SR5*).

CRYSTAL BREATH

COST: 5 KARMA, 1.0 ESSENCE

Your lungs have been replaced with blood crystal. You receive a +2 dice bonus against inhalation vector toxin resistance tests and a +1 dice pool bonus to resist fatigue.

CRYSTAL EYE

COST: 10 KARMA, 1.0 ESSENCE

One or both of your eyes have been replaced with blood crystal. Essence loss is the same whether one or both eyes are replaced, and later replacement of a second eye would require further loss of Essence. You can see as well as the average individual of your metatype, but you lose any special vision types granted by your metatype if both eyes are replaced. In addition, you receive low-light vision, and +1 die per eye replaced on visual Perception tests (not cumulative with any technological vision enhancement). You can no longer wear contacts, as your eyes have become faceted gems.

CRYSTAL GUT

**COST: 5 KARMA AND 0.5 ESSENCE;
MUST HAVE HAD YOUR LIVER, KIDNEYS,
STOMACH, OR INTESTINES REPLACED.**

One or more of your internal organs has been replaced with a crystal that assumes the function of the organ perfectly. When the liver is replaced, you gain +2 dice to ingestion-vector Toxin Resistance tests. When the stomach is replaced, you gain a ten percent reduction to Lifestyle costs. When the kidneys are replaced, you gain +2 dice to injection-vector Toxin Resistance tests. When the intestines are replaced, you no longer defecate or urinate and can go twice as long without water. For each gut organ replaced, you gain a +1 dice pool bonus to resist fatigue. Multiple damaged or failing gut organs can be replaced at one time with the application of one inert blood crystal, though the Karma and Essence cost must still be paid for each gut organ.

CRYSTAL JAW

COST: 10 KARMA AND 1.0 ESSENCE.

A bonded crystal rarely found among particularly vicious blood adepts, the crystal jaw supplants the jaw bone and replaces the teeth with sharp crystal shards. Attacks with a crystal jaw use the Unarmed Combat skill with a Natural Weapons specialization and the following weapon stats: (STR + 2)P, AP -4, Reach -1.

CRYSTAL LIMB

**COST: 10 KARMA AND
1.0 ESSENCE PER LIMB.**

Bonding a crystal in this manner will allow for a functional replacement of a damaged or lost limb. It will match the Strength and Agility of the individual's normal limb. The limb will benefit from any magical enhancements to Strength or Agility, but not any bonuses originating from cyberware or bioware augmentations (for example, muscle replacement). Limbs replaced by a blood crystal provide +1 Armor. Limbs that are severed can regenerate with time, provided at least fifty percent of the blood crystal still remains. Such regeneration takes (6 - Body) weeks (minimum 1 week). During the time while a crystal limb regenerates, the limb's ability to augment the player's Essence is hampered, increasing all drain values by 2.

CRYSTAL SPINE

COST: 10 KARMA AND 1.0 ESSENCE

Able to cure paralysis from a wide range of spinal injuries and neurodegenerative disorders, this type of blood crystal is often seen as a miracle for mages who struggle with the decision whether or not to cripple their magic to regain the ability to walk. The bonded crystal replaces the spine itself, as well as core of the central nervous system. Though the body system being replaced is naturally fully internal, this type of crystal bonding grows to show small crystalline protrusions on the back running along the spine. Upon bonding this blood crystal, you receive a +2 initiative bonus and +1 Armor. This initiative bonus does not stack with any other initiative enhancement, whether it's magical, chemical, or mundane. Individuals with this type of blood crystal are particularly prone to hearing voices.

CRYSTALLINE BLADE

COST: 10 KARMA

Prerequisite: Crystal Limb (Arm), Crystal Claws.

You have gained greater control over your blood crystal arm, allowing you to shape it into a formidable blade. As a simple action, you can shape your entire forearm into a long, sharp crystalline blade (DV (Str+3), AP -2, Reach 1). If you have more than one blood crystal arm, this ability can be used with either.

CRYSTALLINE CLAWS

**COST: 5 KARMA
PREREQUISITE: CRYSTAL LIMB.**

You have consciously learned to exert a small degree of control over the shape of your crystal limb. As a free action, you can shape the fingers or toes of your crystal limb into sharp claws [DV(Str + 1), AP -1]. If you have more than one blood crystal limb, this ability can be used with any limb you possess.

CRYSTALLINE DIVER

**COST: 10 KARMA
PREREQUISITE: CRYSTAL BREATH**

You have realized that your lungs are no longer flesh and blood and are not held to the limits of flesh. You can breathe underwater as well as you can in open air (you still suffer the normal penalties for pressure and cold while underwater).

CRYSTALLINE GRACE

COST: 10 KARMA
PREREQUISITE: CRYSTAL LIMB
(BOTH LEGS).

You have learned to push your new legs beyond the capabilities of flesh and bone. You gain a +2 to Jumping tests and can run for twice as long before suffering from fatigue.

CRYSTALLINE REFLEXES

COST: 15 KARMA

The blood crystal has further integrated into your central nervous system, facilitating rapid innervation of major muscle groups. You receive a +2 dice pool modifier to all Defense tests.

CRYSTALLINE SHARDS

COST: 10 KARMA
PREREQUISITE: CRYSTAL LIMB (ARM)

By learning to harness some of the innate regenerative and shape-changing capabilities of your crystal arm, you can cause the growth of needle-like crystalline shards and fling them as a hail of deadly projectiles. This attack is a standard action of Throwing Weapons + Agility [Physical], dealing (STR + 3)P damage, AP +4. They have the same range as shuriken (p. 185, SR5). Due to the similarity of the attack to flechette ammo, defenders receive a −3 modifier, and the attack cannot be used with Called Shots. The rapid growth of these crystals is taxing on the body as the crystal draws on your blood to fuel itself. Each time this ability is used, the bearer takes 1P unresisted Physical damage that cannot be healed by magic.

CRYSTALLINE VISION

COST: 15 KARMA
PREREQUISITE: CRYSTAL EYE.

Further attunement to your blood crystal eye (or eyes) has allowed you to peer beyond the mundane world. You gain the ability to perceive astrally, and you may take ranks in Assensing if you were not already able.

NEW SPIRITS

BONE SPIRIT

If blood is passion, then bones are reliable. Bone spirits must be assembled from a great pile of raw material; they never drop with gore and gristle but always appear clean and polished. They have no particular opinion regarding anything at all, lacking the rapacious appetite of blood spirits, and even the desire for freedom that normal spirits exhibit. A bone spirit is happy enough to perform any service it is able without complaint, though it makes for a poor conversationalist. They are not stupid; they simply appreciate simple directives. Its form depends on the bones it's made from: if it consists of the large skeletons of bulls, metahumans, and similar ilk, it takes a stable, firm form. Made from the bones of smaller animals, such as alley cats and devil rats, the bones rustle and rattle as they shift around one another in an almost amorphous, roiling mass. Larger bones, such as those from elephants, may break to conform to the spirit's size, while exoskeletons such as those from giant insects like the wyrd mantis will shift about over the others, sliding over the mass. Note that bone spirits will not possess the bones or exoskeletons of bodies that have been used by other blood spirits, bug spirits, or have served as corps cadavres. If asked, they will say, "Those bones have earned their rest."

Bone spirits have no incorporeal form; they are always formed from a mass of bones as per a possession spirit (use the same quantity rules as for a homunculus). Less prone to escaping control than other types of spirit, it can be maintained with a steady diet of bones added to its roiling form. These spirits act much like a homunculus in this way, showing little initiative or free will of their own, simply doing their duty until they run out of power, are destroyed, or their summoner is killed. Left to their own devices, these spirits simply sit and wait. If attacked, they will simply look at their attacker without offering resistance. If they are questioned, they simply reply, "I wait to rest."

B	A	R	S	W	L	I	C	EDG	ESS	M
F+3	F	F	F+2	F	F–1	F	F–1	F/2	F	F

Initiative	(F x 2) + 2D6
Astral Initiative	(F x 2) + 3D6
Skills	Assensing, Astral Combat, Perception, Unarmed Combat
Powers	Astral Form, Engulf, Natural Weapon (DV=(Strength) Physical Damage, AP—), Possession (Bones), Sapience
Optional Powers	Enhanced Senses (Hearing, Low-Light Vision, Thermographic Vision, or Smell), Guard, Noxious Breath
Special	A bone spirit can consume the bones of a dead creature to heal itself. The total Body of creature whose skeleton is being consumed determines the healing; the spirit restores 1 Physical damage box per 2 Body worth of bones consumed.

BLOOD SHADE

A horrific specialization of a blood spirit, this entity is siphoned exclusively from the blood and spirit of a single individual. The blood spirit binds with the body, much like a "good merge" bug spirit, gaining access to all of the sacrifice's skills, memories, and mannerisms. They can take the form of the host as they were when they were alive, passing all physical tests to determine their identity and masking their aura to fool cursory assensing. They can offer their summoner any secrets the sacrifice had and can get close to their victims with ease.

Its true form is the same shape as its host, but composed entirely of blood, with eyes that appear to be pitch-black pits and perfectly white teeth. It often smiles when it anticipates feeding, and it will play mind games with its prey, enjoying their fear when it feeds. If/when it goes uncontrolled, it will usually stalk and kill those related to the victim, finding their blood and Essence sweetest. For every six points of Essence it draws from genetic family, it gains one Force.

B	A	R	S	W	L	I	C	EDG	ESS	M
F	F+2	F+2	F–1	F	F	F	F+1	F/2	F	F

Initiative	[(F x 2) +2] + 2D6
Astral Initiative	(F x 2) + 3D6
Skills	Assensing, Astral Combat, Counterspelling, Impersonation, Perception, Unarmed Combat
Powers	Astral Form, Aura Masking, Deathly Aura, Energy Drain (Essence), Fear, Magical Guard, Mimicry, Possession (Blood), Realistic Form, Sapience
Optional Powers	Accident, Banishing Resistance, Compulsion, Paralyzing Touch, Search
Weaknesses	Evanescence

THICKER THAN WATER

The risks of blood magic. This isn't a tool chest of new ways to frag the rent-a-cops. This is playing with fire. It's potentially addictive, almost always harmful, and can stain your aura in ways that may affects spells and summoning for a long time—maybe even forever. Everything has a price, and blood is the coin of sacrifice.

BLOOD MAGIC AND ADDICTION

The use of blood magic has a high potential for addiction. The psychological effects of receiving such a rush of magical power with no cost to oneself is a temptation that only the strongest-willed individuals can resist. However, benign blood magic is possible. It is sometimes called martyred blood magic—as opposed to sacrificial blood magic—in which the caster damages themselves in order to generate Blood Magic Points. When these points are generated in this way, no Addiction test is necessary, regardless of how they are spent. In such cases, a blood mage can cause physical damage to themselves in order to generate and immediately expend Blood Magic Points as part of the action of casting a spell without suffering any applicable penalties due to the damage inflicted until after the spell has been completed. Casting a spell or performing a ritual in such a way is not addictive.

The addictive potential of blood magic is psychological. It has an Addiction Rating equal to the character's Magic and an Addiction Threshold of 2. If more Blood Magic Points are spent on a single effect than the character's Magic, the Addic-

OPTIONAL SACRIFICE RULES

The following rules cover different ways blood magic can be used, and can be employed if gamemasters and players wish to add more details to how blood is shed in the Sixth World.

- **Non-sapient Awakened:** This requires the death of a paracritter, adds half the sacrifice's Magic rating in Blood Magic Points.
- **Metahuman:** The standard for sacrificial metamagic. Use standard rules.
- **Awakened Metahuman:** As sacrificial metamagic, but add Blood Magic Points equal to the victim's Magic attribute if they are killed.
- **Self Harm:** A lesser sacrifice, but the bread and butter for the benevolent blood mage. That being said, it cannot be healed by any magical means and requires time and potentially medical attention. Overcasting in this fashion causes a multiplier to the healing time, as the body's life energy has weakened and cannot assist in natural recovery.
- **Permanent Maiming:** This is putting out an eye or slicing off a hand. You or the target gain a negative quality or lose an attribute point, as determined by the gamemaster. Two Blood Magic Points are generated for every 1 point of Physical damage dealt in this manner. The negative quality or attribute point cannot be countered with cyber. This can only be performed with an immobilized victim or by a character maiming themselves.
- **Loved Ones:** Indisputably evil, and yet has the greatest possible return on investment. You can conduct grand rituals with astounding success if you're willing to do this. You're also guaranteed to be twisted by the experience. This kind of sin stains the soul forever. Gain 3 Blood Magic Points for every 1 box of Physical damage inflicted. If the loved one is killed, increase the Addiction quality by one step with no chance to resist.
- **Essence:** Standard sacrificial metamagic on yourself. Carries the same Essence problem as Permanent Maiming, meaning you can't leap to have the lost Essence replaced with cyberware. After the maiming, receive 9 Blood Magic Points for each full point of Essence sacrificed, rounded down.
- **Pre-packaged Blood:** No good at all. Might be used as summoning material for a blood spirit to give it mass, or to set the mood of a ritual, but it has no mechanical use beyond that.

tion Threshold increases by 1. Blood magic functions similar to any other addiction (p. 413, *SR5*) but differs in a few ways.

Mild addiction still feels like having total control. The individual will feel the urge to turn to the power without questioning if they need it. They begin losing the perspective of the cost others pay for their power.

Moderate addiction marks an increase in the desire to use the power and doubt that they can function effectively without it. The pain and deaths they have caused mean less to them, and they feel increasingly disconnected from the rest of humanity. They begin acting cruel and vicious toward their allies, suspecting them of being envious of their power.

Severe addictions represent the stereotypical maniacal blood mage. They kill without hesitation or compunction. They see themselves as superhuman, and other metahumans are just fuel for their addiction. Using any of their magic without enhancing it with blood magic is unthinkable.

Burnout blood mages are an out-of-control freight train of death. They cannot go a day without killing and do not hesitate to dump as much power as possible into every spell or set powerful blood spirits loose to massacre anyone within reach. Causing death has become their only purpose. If a burnout blood mage fails an Addiction test, they must kill the next sapient being they come in contact with (rather than losing Body or Willpower as usual).

Blood magic use triggers an addiction roll under the following conditions:

- Overcasting while expending Blood Magic Points.
- Expending more than twice your initiate grade in Blood Magic Points toward one effect.
- Killing a sapient being purely for the purpose of generating Blood Magic Points or as part of a ritual.
- Inflicting damage to a sapient victim unable to defend themselves in order to generate Blood Magic Points.
- Generating Blood Magic Points from a victim and using them on a spell to harm that same victim (you gain +2 to the Addiction test if you are defending yourself).

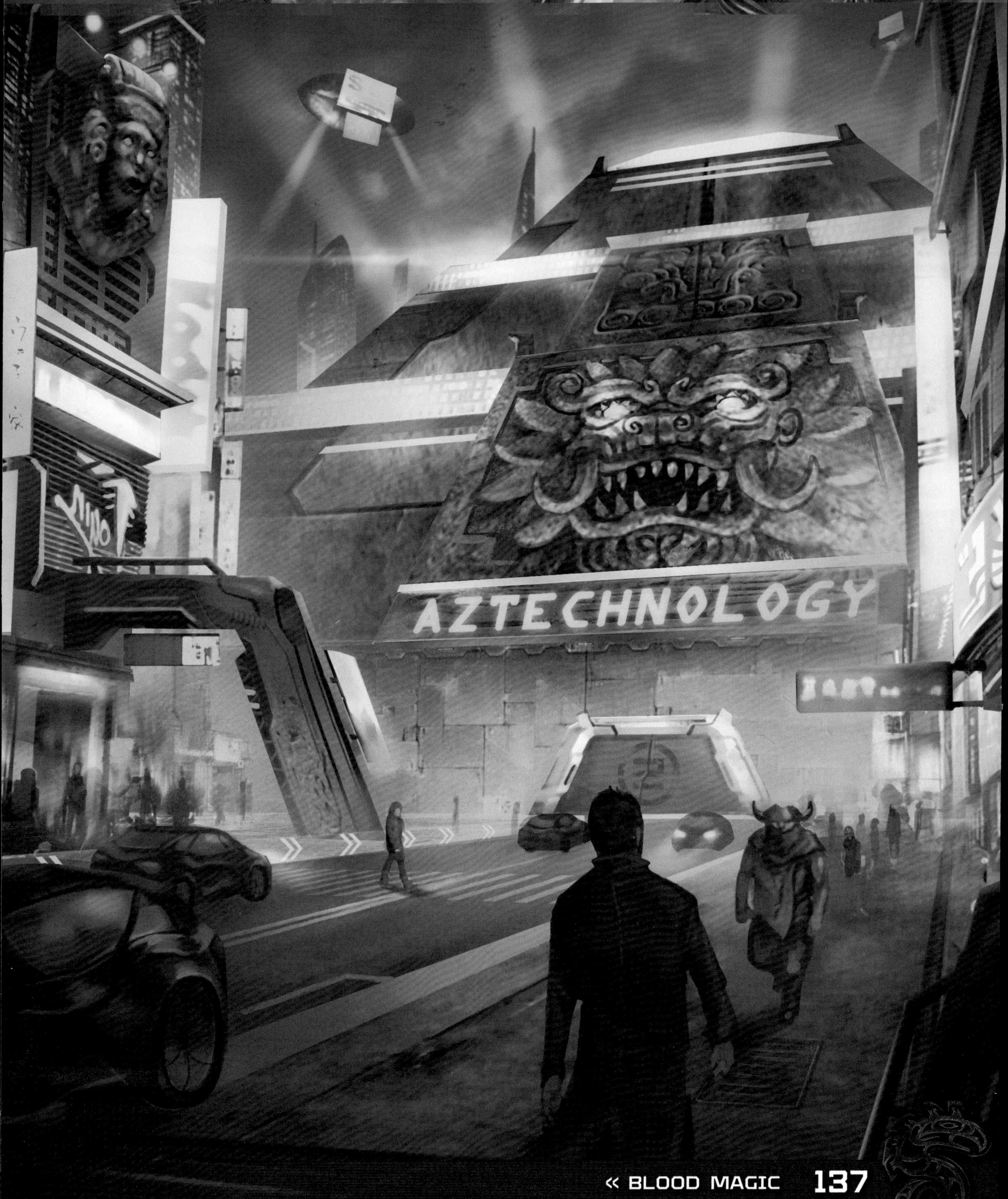
AZTECHNOLOGY

BREATH OF THE WILD

The man born seventy-odd years ago as Cecil Mains but now known as The Wolf That Walks as a Man peered deep into the snowfall. The red-tinted black-out light of his ancient Skidoo snowmobile showed the few traces of the game trail he and his fellow poachers were following, packs loaded down with fresh meat, hides, bones, and other items to smuggle from the Algonquin-Manitou Council lands and back into his native UCAS. The forest closed tight around the small vehicles and their riders, the evergreen and bare branches hiding them at least partially from view above, magic and spirits hiding the rest. This was his element, the middle of winter, in snowfall, moving in ways that even magicians could not spot. But there were worse things in the woods of what had once been central Manitoba, and shelter was needed for the night. *A handful of kilometers,* his thoughts ringed in a constant tolling. *We can do it.*

But that cycle was interrupted by the on-and-off blinking of a light just like the one on his own snow-mobile. It came from behind him, similar to the way a person in the city might flash some high-beams to get someone's attention. The AMC military's search-and-rescue teams might just be out on a night like tonight, and anything that would attract their attention was forbidden to the group outside of what was necessary to travel, unless it was a true emergency. Even magic could only do so much to keep them concealed when someone was shouting and waving lights, and the group only had meager magical powers available to them to begin with. The AMC was literal death on poachers, and Wolf knew his team wanted to live to realize and enjoy their meager gains. It would be a brief respite—it always was—and then they would head back into the forests that made up their real lives, the spot that gave purpose to the skills and abilities they had. Most modern metahumans had thought their particular set of skills to be obsolete, long unnecessary in the tech- and Magic-aided Sixth World. Wolf lived to prove them wrong.

The four circled the halftracks, killing the engines, and huddled close together so they wouldn't have to speak loudly at each other through the blanketing snow. Betty was the easiest to notice, being a troll and all, a fact that was clearly visible as she was the least bundled up. Also, she was huge. But she was used to weather worse than this in the Northern Winnipeg Barrens that had been her home. She was

BY RAYMOND CROTEAU

steady as can be, never talking when a grunt would do, and rarely even grunting. Charleen was her opposite, needing to tell at least one tall tale per day, and bundled up so tight that only her eyes and tusks could be seen. The fourth member was Fred, the dwarf who gathered them together and led them. He was an expert in trapping small game—and he had heard all the "small game" jokes as well. At the moment, he looked very, very worried. "Checked the astral plane when I felt a chill," he said. His ability to astrally perceive was his only magical ability, but a very useful one. "I saw a herd of windmares coming, and"—he swallowed hard—"a windstallion."

The Wolf thought hard, not wasting any time asking for a confirmation, for windmares were bad news. Their cold chill when they went through a person was horrific, especially in a cold place like this, and no shelter stopped them. Their chill went deep, right into the core, leaving your soul frozen. The much-rarer windstallion would pick up that soul, taking it with them as they ran through a metahuman. No shelter other than a proper home would protect against them, and no quickly summoned spirit would be strong enough to protect people. He needed something stronger,

more dangerous. More dangerous to the windstallions and himself both

"Set up a quinzhee," The Wolf ordered the others, "I'll see about getting us the protection we need." The other three looked at each other, wondering what was going to happen, but just as quickly set to the snow-hut shelter, the snow absolutely perfect for just such a thing. The wind was dying down; snow starting to stave off, but it was the calm before the stampede, before the ill meaning creatures of the Sixth World came forth to strip from them the ability to gaze upon yet another day.

Picking through his meager supplies, Wolf carefully picked out a few pieces that meant a lot to him and to the area in general—all things he made from these woods and were used for hunting. Tools and small traps, handmade and natural items, the last of his homegrown tobacco, and a locket with a picture of his long-dead parents, who had been in the woods of former Northern Ontario during the Great Ghost Dance and never had their bodies recovered. He also brought out the hand drum he had crafted many years ago. Finally, he pulled out the last of his smudge pack, lighting it up and having the smoke go over him while he concentrated. He worked hard to not curse himself for running out of his usual supplies for summoning and dealing with spirits of all types. But the patrols were thicker in their area than ever, apparently hunting after some lost civilians. Prepared, he found an area of snow that he was able to quickly shift away, finding a few rocks and frozen hard dirt to hold his objects while he sat down on a hard piece of ice. He then made a tiny fire in the center.

Wolf chanted low, centering him as he started to shift his perception, seeing what was not really there, things the vast majority of people in the world could never imagine. Wisps of mana flowed out from him. As he mentally pleaded for one of the local spirits to arrive and talk, the fire twisted, broke free and wandered over to make a deal. He started sweating, and he paused in his drumming to wring out his headband by instinct, adding his own personal scent to the summoning. Minutes passed. Ten. Fifteen. Twenty. He tried all the languages he had learned in his long life, English, French, Cree, Ojibwe, Inuktitut, Spanish, Portuguese, and Newfie. But the spirits only watched, staying silent in the trees and under the snow. His fellow travelers were making progress building a four-person shelter, similar to a cheap and knocked-together igloo that wouldn't last long. It only needed to stay upright for a night or two. A shanty shack made of snow, essentially.

"Sing," he ordered, wanting their physical voices to join his mental chant. They looked at each other in confusion, but the snow started to fall harder again, and they broke into the ancient classic rowing song "Alouette," which had been sung by their hunting and traveling forbearers, Le Voyageurs, as they used the song to time how they worked on the quinzhee. This song attracted attention—many old spirits had heard it time and again as they slept through the time of low magic that was the Fifth World, and now they came closer, to see what voices were bringing back this simple tale.

Their interest was piqued, but still none of the spirits came forward to engage. The trio shifted to "En Roulant Ma Boule," as Wolf threw a few more items into the little fire. Spices and herbs to make the bland trail food more interesting, a hand-rolled Cuban cigar he had planned to enjoy when he got back to the UCAS, a piece of jerky that was originally intended to be part of dinner. Finally, as the snow and wind rose to skin-cutting levels, he sighed and rolled up his sleeve, pulling out a small flint knife he knapped himself. He cut deep into his leathery skin, next to the many, many other scars that had come from a far-too-long

life in rough situations like this one. Some were ancient and nearly faded, others fresh enough to still be red and sore. He got a little blood flowing, sprinkling drops of it into the fire, sizzling and bringing forth the smoke to the entire crowd of collected wild spirits, making him easy prey. If the spirits here decided he was unwanted, they could track him long and far for however wide an area they wanted. Some of them might well decide he would never be free of them.

But it worked. A spirit emerged from the smoke, whirling around like a small tornado that grabbed pieces of wood and clumps of dirt from all over the forested area, forming itself from the environment. Smoke, sticks, snow, rocks, ice, and an elk's skull, glowing in the empty sockets that shined with the age of countless centuries. It towered over the small group, then settled down, hunching over as if to talk to a small child. It inclined its skull and motioned with a hand made from twigs and small bones. Lightly glowing sap could be seen between the cracks of the materials that made up his form. The source of the glow was unclear; if Wolf were pressed, he would say it was the glow of life. A heat came off the spirit's physical form, warm for now but threatening to burn. There was magic here that humanity had long forgotten, some elements that perhaps were best left that way. The spirit gave a cough—as if it somehow had lungs and a throat that were coated with dust from long years of disuse.

"You have caught my attention, mortal, but only briefly. Not all who have done so have survived the experience. I smell the blood of much game on your soul, and the blood of more than one of your own kind, but little accomplishment in your scent. You are unlike most hunters I smell in this age. None have I spoken to know of you killing for sport. This and this alone gives you a splinter of my time." The spirit made no physical sound as it "spoke." Its words went to the hearts of the gathered group, resonating in their blood. It spoke the language of mana, meaning Wolf was in the best position to understand its nuances and inflections.

"We are, as you see, four hunters, oh spirit of this land. We follow—or try to follow, for none are able to succeed at all times—the old ways, ways that had been half-forgotten before we were born. We take the old, the lame. We devour them in thanks. All of their body is used, none going to waste. But now, this changed, fallen world would hunt us like those others you speak of, bringing death for sport and pleasure. Please, great spirit, I beg your aid so that I might continue to teach these ways to others, and the ones teach to teach their youth." Wolf calibrated is tone carefully, keeping it strong without crossing into arrogance. Weakness may get all of them killed by the wild spirits here, before the windmares and the windstallion got to them. And death might have been a blessing compared to what some of these wild spirits were said to be able to do.

The skull looked the group over, somehow making its skull mouth frown at the snowmobiles. It then shrugged. "If my cousins wish you, why should I stop them? You have no hold over me. I am not some mere tiny spirit to be summoned and commanded, even if you try to twist your orders into questions."

Wolf slowly reached into some pouches in his belt. "I bring offerings, freely given. I can provide candied maple syrup from the French lands to the east. Or bear pemmican with blueberries and honey from a reclaimed and re-greened valley. Cane sugar harvested by my own hand, grown far beyond its native lands on farms that use special waters and no soil." He offered each in turn as he pulled out Québec maple cookies, preserved meat and dried berries coated in honey to make them last longer from Blezard Valley, and plain sugar cane stolen from one of the many Saeder-Krupp hydroponics facilities situated around the city of Winnipeg, feeding the various soft drink factories and canneries in that same area.

The spirit pawed at the items, which were laid down carefully in front of it as the fire sputtered. Rather than go out, however, it spat for a few seconds, then erupted into an even more powerful flame in a color that defied description, fueled by something beneath the dirt and behind the air, something more elemental than the elements. Wolf didn't jerk back, but his companions did, wondering if they'd survive to see the coming threats, and if they had blundered from the frying pan into the very oddly colored fire. The storm was coming, visible now, slowly moving forward like a huge wave of wind and snow. The windmares were now visible to the naked eye, horses made of rapid, chill winds and bad omens. The herd had been let loose upon the former prairie provinces and states during the Great Ghost Dance, and Halley's Comet had multiplyied their numbers. At their head wasn't a windstallion, larger and meaner than the windmares, but a beast of blood-red snow and rage—a windmustang. Mares and stallions were deadly but generally indifferent to the people they ran through. Windmustangs, though, actively hunted, seeking new blood to shed and new souls to devour. They were creatures constructed from nightmares,

dread and fear given form if not flesh. A living nightmare that existed only to kill.

"Have you any more of this, the cane sugar?" the summoned spirit asked. It attempted to hide the interest, but it was too apparent in motion and voice. This was a new thing to it, something different after millennia of similarity.

"Two more pieces, about the same size." Wolf answered quickly, his skin not quite turning pale only due to the leathery nature of it. It had been too tanned for too many years to lose any color. The weathered nature was intrinsic. He quickly brought out the last two items in his offering pouch and hoped it would be enough.

"Cuddle in your shelter, then. None shall enter while I watch it." The spirit's words carried the force of an order, and it violently ripped the stalks of sugarcane out of Wolf's hand. The four metahumans happily dove into the little snow hut. Wolf went in last, offering a nod of thanks to the spirit that now towered over all the area. He barely got his windproof outer coat off to act as a door for the entrance when the horse-like screaming winds started. Each form inside the quinzhee shuddered and collapsed inside themselves, trying to make as small a target as possible, but it was unnecessary. The windmares were unable to get in, just as the spirit promised, and a sigh of relief came from all as Wolf started to bandage his arm. All that would attack them this night was the sound of the wind and the cold around it. That was bad enough, but not life threatening.

"Last time I let myself run out of tobacco, sweetgrass, cedar, and sage." Wolf grumbled, shifting his remaining outfit to get warm and comfortable. He soon drifted off into a dreamless sleep.

Above the little shelter, the spirit sat upon the hut lightly, legs astride the entrance. Somehow the animal skull smiled and slowly chewed. The traditional offerings were good, indeed, and maple syrup was an old-remembered treat, but this new thing, this cane sugar was far, far more suited to its personal tastes indeed. It might be time to move beyond the trees that had long bound its entire existence, and see what these tiny creatures had been doing in this world. And discover where this cane sugar could be found in abundance.

WHERE THE WILD THINGS ARE

POSTED BY: ELIJAH

UNIVERSAL MAGIC THEORY

The single most influential publication of the past twenty years in the magical community, is undoubtedly Unified Magical Theory: The building blocks of magic and the applications therein, a paper published first in the *Thaumaturgia Universalis*, then given wide distribution via the *Thelluric Quarterly*. Introduced in Prague in 2060, it exploded in the wake of Halley's Comet and the magical effects that spiraled from that event. By 2070, it had become the leading magical theory in the world, transforming how magic was performed across all traditions, though some were slower to adopt its methodology than others.

- We often talk about how it rewrote the books for hermetics, moving them from an understanding of elementalism to one where more natural spirits were called forth, most impressively with the calling of spirits of man, formally an action exclusive to shamanic traditions. More interesting, I feel, is the ripple effect in the shamanic community, leaving behind the old ways of whistling up local spirits for bringing in those less bound by rules of location.
- Winterhawk

- Not all of us walked this new path.
- Man-of-Many-Names

- The biggest change was the acceptance in corporate circles, I think. Previously, shamans were a rare thing in the megas, who preferred hermetics, while shamans took to the treeline or the streets. UMT made shamans ... presentable. They weren't beholden to some unknowable entity, like some totem or another, but instead, it was simply how they shaped magic. Without that wedge, the corporations found that they could work with shamans, treating their ... eccentricities ... as they would a hot young decker. Suddenly, shamans were hip, cool, and socially acceptable.
- Sunshine

- It went further than that! Corporations started establishing "house styles," trying to direct young shamans to follow ... well, they used to be called totems, but they were re-branded as "mentors" to sand the mysticism off the term. At any rate, they wanted them to follow corporate-approved mentors, like Fire-Bringer or Cat, rather than a more disruptive element like Bull or, Ghost save us all, Coyote.
- /dev/grrl

- As word got around, and former street shamans started popping up with shiny new SINS, a corporate ID, and a support network, the shadows were hit hard. We'd taken the basic "us vs. them" divide as simply a Thing that would always be there, a dividing line that meant that we'd always have magical parity with the megas. I wasn't surprised that money talked, but I was disappointed. We were supposed to be better than that.
- Bull

Universal Magic Theory, at its core, is simply this: All magic draws from the same source; it's how the individual magician shapes it that defines their tradition. Ultimately, a spirit is a spirit is a spirit. There are levels of complexity beyond this, of course, and I can show you terapulses of debates about the *true* nature of spirits, but that simple theory is the core. It's important to note, here, that it's a theory, not a law.

- Wait. It's just a theory? Who cares then?! It's just a guess.
- Slamm-0!

- How I weep for the eradication of our education system. Right, in science, there are three levels of thought: A law, which is a proposal that has stood against every challenge and has reached a point where the scientific community

decides that it is a true thing and names it law; a theory, which is a leading thought about how something works but is still being tested in an attempt to disprove it; and a hypothesis, which is an idea someone has about why something happens but that has yet to be rigorously tested. When the layman says "I have a theory", they really mean that they have a hypothesis, or even just a guess, which is not at all the same thing as when we say it.

> Beaker

> Then why do we say "theory"?
> Riot

> Because "hypothesis" is a big word that's hard to pronounce and harder to spell.
> The Smiling Bandit

> Hey-oh.
> Slamm-0!

If you check the backlog in the magical discussion areas, you'll see that I've been one of the leading proponents of UMT here on JackPoint, and I've battled in academic circles as well. I'd show you a series of messages that the Atlantean Foundation and I have bounced back and forth for years, but it's a tad dry for these parts. My quandary is that, over the past ten years, I've found too many areas where the accepted dogma wasn't able to explain what I was experiencing. I'd always assumed that a solution to this would be found, but in my questing for answers, I've only found more questions. At this stage, I'm prepared to say this: I think that Unified Magic Theory is wrong.

> Will someone check my DocWagon monitor? I believe that I might have just died.
> Man-of-Many-Names

> OMG MOMN just made a joke
> /dev/grrl

> I've made several. I'm not to blame for your lack of comprehension.
> Man-of-Many-Names

That is to say, I believe that the core concept is still sound, but that there are, in fact, more sources of magic UMT accounts for. Perhaps this can explain the anomalies. It's still far too early in my research to publish, and I'm loathe to share even these early thoughts here, but I had a very close encounter near the Rio Grande, and had I not survived, all of these notes would be lost. As such, I'm uploading some notes into a virtual locker here, with Glitch's permission, with some standard deadman clauses. This isn't the entirety of my journal, but it contains those thoughts that I'm confident enough in that they won't risk my reputation. I'll share of them here now, since I'm certain that several of you will try to crack the code just to satisfy your own curiosity.

> I would advise against it. Strongly.
> Glitch

WHERE DOES MAGIC COME FROM?

It sounds like a basic question, doesn't it? Many would say "It doesn't come from anything. It's magic. It just *is*." But that isn't enough for myself or for many other researchers in the magical fields. Magic follows rules, rules that we might not yet understand or even known of, but it follows them all the same. Magic cannot return the dead to life. Magic cannot teleport matter, or energy, from one location to another instantaneously. Magic cannot break time. We have tried to break all of those rules, and in some instances have gotten somewhat close, but in each case it was bending, not breaking, those rules. Cybermancy can't return the dead to life, but it can keep those who should be dead from leaving their body behind. Several magics can animate a dead body to movement like a marionette, while replacing the body's spirit with another is the core underpinning of insect shamans. Shedim follow a path between those two options. We watched magical transportation whisking Aztechnology employees away from Ghostwalker's claws in Denver at a speed so great as to resemble teleportation but that, we later learned, was not, and seems to have been so costly as to squelch any desire to repeat it. Was it calling in a spirit's aid? Some long-bound magic that could only be triggered once? Like blood magic, did the effect draw some life energy from the caster, but in such high levels that it's simply unreproducible? As with much dragon magic, we don't know, but we *do* know that it wasn't teleportation. Magic follows rules.

One leading indicator of this is an examination of energy conservation. This flies in the face of many people's understanding of magic, since a magician is clearly forming, for example, a fireball out of thin air and unleashing it on a target with explosive results. Clearly, they just created energy. Those who study magical science, however, will tell you otherwise. That energy was gathered up, shaped by the caster's will and Art, and given existence as a ball of fire, true, but that energy was not generated within the mage's heart or mind but, instead, was drawn from an outside source—in this case, the ambient astral energy that surrounds us all. Astral energy permeates the world, generated by living creatures, be they plant, insect, animal, or human. It connects us all to one another, and we leave traces of this energy in our wake just as we leave flakes of skin and hair behind. This energy even imprints on non-living objects, and when you take up, for example, your grandfather's harmonica, his astral signature is wound through it, and even the mundanes of the world can feel that connection, the echo of the owner's energy and being.

- Seriously? Crystal-waving? I came here for science and I get New Age dogma? Pathetic.
- Clockwork

- This from someone who talks to his cars? Come on, Clocks, hold your venom until he's done. I mean, what do you think astrally aware people are talking about when they read an object? They're sniffing out those echoes

that the person who touched the thing left behind, sifting through however many astral signatures have brushed over it, tracking down the strongest, and trying to identify them. It's not far removed from smelling something in the kitchen and knowing it's spaghetti instead of onion soup. The Aware who focus on this area can read emotional states and even assemble strong thoughts that were felt while the object was held, learning information about the previous owner. This is established science and Lone Star's been at the leading edge of object reading for decades. Drek, there's probably a whole evidence locker of things you've left behind, from shell casings to dropped change from your pocket, that someone's assembled to make a case study of you.
- Hard Exit

- Thank you for stepping up for the defense of my secondary application, HE.
- Arete

- That said, there are plenty of fakes out there, or those with some Talent who aren't anywhere near as good as they claim. It's a basic scam, and you prey mostly on the vulnerable whose kids have run away or who recently lost a loved one. But at the end of the day, it pays the bills, so people fall into it.
- Lyran

Several ancient cultures tell similar stories, such as the Sioux Sacred Circles or Japanese Shinto, as well as more modern versions such as the Jedi in England who talk about an energy that connects everyone together. (Happy one hundredth anniversary to you lot!) Religions talk of souls and where we go after we die, as well as where those souls come from. We look to the stars, we look within ourselves, and we turn to holy books, all in the search of answers. I won't pretend that I know everything (as Man-of-Many-Names is oh so happy to remind me of on a regular basis!), but I can draw enough from the similarities in these beliefs, and what we know after nearly seventy years of thaumaturgical research, to know that the manasphere is constantly refilled by living creatures, and that it's the source of much of our magic. The question of why this happens has yet been approached with any serious inquiry (due to the lack of marketability philosophy has compared to the practical application of spell research, one would assume) or precisely how, but enough is known that we take it not unlike gravity or magnetism, forces that function even if we have yet to unlock all the secrets that drive them.

- Fraggin' magnets. How do they work, anyway?
- Glowin' Jugs

- Fred, what have we told you about sockpuppet accounts?
- Glitch

- Uh. Actually, it was me. Old joke.
- Bull

- Similar to the modern Matrix and the Foundation. You know that it works, but not how, but it's good enough to harness, so you're off and running while a few eggheads keep picking at it in the background.
- Turbo Bunny

- You honestly think that They don't know? They do, they just aren't telling you.
- Plan 9

- For once, I have to agree with Plan 9.
- Icarus

- Who're "they"?!
- Riot

Of further note is that mana pools in areas, or travels in a sort of astral stream. These are power sites and ley lines, respectively, and they come in both pure forms and aspected. Pure forms are exactly what they sound like and are far more rare than you might imagine, while aspected mana is attuned to a particular style of magic. The dragon lines around the Ring of Fire, for instance, or the Ley Lines (note that capitalization, since these ones are special) across Tír na nÓg or Great Britain are two well-known examples, while toxic dumps are another. The more rare ones are permanent, a source of renewable magical power that people are willing to struggle, fight, or even kill over, while temporary ones form and vanish on a regular basis based on a great number of factors including, but not limited to, unified thinking, emotional response, pollution, trauma, and sudden additions of energy, be they magical or otherwise. Rock concerts are famous for it, but the scene of a brutal murder, a joyous marriage, or an area often struck by lightning can be equally powered up for a time. A smaller level of any of the above, over an extended time, can also generate power sites, or aspect the overall mana generated from an area. You'll find this in Redmond and similar areas where the daily grind of life colors the astral space in pain and frustration, or in high schools where the con-

stant turmoil of being a teenager creates an intoxicating blend of emotional resonance even if no individual moment stands out.

- Um. Wizards get high sniffing locker rooms? Ew?
- /dev/grrl

- Less wizards (other than Haze) and more spirits. Spirits flock to this kind of energy source and seem to feed off it.
- Glasswalker

- I don't know if that's less creepy or *more* creepy.
- /dev/grrl

Mana is also created by natural life. A wooded area is filled with pants, trees, and small animals, each of which generates small levels of mana with each breath they take. It's interesting in that some areas that are protected will have a sense of peace and tranquility that permeates them, but areas set aside for hunting will have a reduced peacefulness to them while the fear and pain of hunted animals will permeate the astral, right alongside the more powerful feelings of joy and conquest that the hunters generate. These areas are stronger in the right seasons, of course, but never fully vanish. Mating season also fills these areas with a sense of lust. The research is as yet unsettled if this is why lovestruck teens flock to these areas to explore, or if those explorations simply further color the air.

- So, how does somebody sign up for this research? Asking for a friend.
- Slamm-0!

- One of the largest sources of ambient astral energy is the ocean. It's positively teeming with life, from whales and sharks to fish and seaweed to plankton and bacteria. I've taken a few mages out from the city for the first time and every one of them, without fail, will take a few hours to sit on the edge of the boat, switch to seeing the astral, and will just .... marvel. Wish I could see it myself.
- Sounder

- Tempo's long gone, but deepweed can do the job in a pinch. Drop me a line, I'll hook you up.
- Lyran

The last notation about this is that these sources of mana, no matter if they have a positive or negative flavor, can carry over into nearby objects. Living things, like plants and trees, are the best for soaking it up, but crystalline forms and minerals are right behind and, in some cases, even better, at doing so. This is the foundation of reagents and, from them, assorted talismans and fetishes. It's easier to find raw materials that you can then adapt to your particular style, but you'd be surprised by what you can gather from finished goods that were exposed in the right way. Spent bullet casings (growing quite rare with caseless rounds being the norm) sometimes catch a whiff of violence, while some concert T-shirts start off bland corporate merch before a show but soak up so much crowd energy that they glow on the Astral for a few days and retain a trace of the event for a decade.

We're still uncertain as to how the exact mechanism works, but in general an item focused on, like the statue of a saint visited for centuries, a sacrificial altar stained by the blood of hundreds, or the ratty old guitar a star's used starting when they were an unknown burger flipper at McHugh's, are all more likely to gather this energy and will hold more of it, but it doesn't always work. Several corporations have experimented with creating focal objects in this way, without any result, while a crayon drawing a datapusher's kid gave him before work winds up bubbling over with power. There's even some experimentation with people serving as magical focus points, such as the lead singer of a band, a heroic police officer whose story is distributed nationwide, or even a corporate CEO, with an effort to gather magical energies around them, but we're still in the very early days of observation and experimentation. The entire field remains esoteric.

- The leading fonts of knowledge in this area are Aztechnology and Wuxing, as you'd imagine, plus Renraku, who're known for anemic levels of magical research. Strange that they'd focus on this side of things.
- Axis Mundi

- Mitsuhama has a weird view of it all. They're the largest producer of magical goods and telesma, but their environmental policies are horrible, and they tend to devour an area rather than nurture it as a sustainable resource. They like to quash research that shows pollution is bad or anything that shows magic is generated by natural areas. You can make a whole MCT-subsidized career just debunking those theories on public trideo or in book deals, if you can stomach it. Whatever research they have about this angle, they never publish; it's in-house use only. Needless to say, there're tons of run opportunities that fall out of everything I just said. In fact, I have open contracts right now. Call me.

◉ Am-Mut

◉ Hey, while we're doing business in here, I should say that ever since Hestaby got kicked out of Shasta, there's been a surge of talismongers and shadowrunners sweeping into the area to gather up resources. While she's gone and her shamans were wiped out, there are still loads of magical defenses in place that have keep anyone from moving in to claim the area. California and Tír Taingire are both daring one another to make the first move, while Mitsuhama is still smarting from the bad press that came out of the Vegas protests and is operating via hired runners rather than just unloading corporate-branded soldiers everywhere. The stiff defenses shouldn't have been a surprise, but there've been several 'mongers who never came back, and it's chilled the moves from the smaller operators. You hire bodyguards or don't go. There's also a huge market for people who will claim that some reagent is fresh and smuggled out of Shasta, touched by a dragon, blah blah blah. It's just a scam to gouge money out of a mark, but if you sell it right, they'll shell out top nuyen for average junk.

◉ Lyran

◉ Well that explains your papering the Hiring Hall with guide requests last year. Sorry I couldn't help you out but—you know how it goes. Did you have any luck?

◉ 2XL

◉ As a matter of fact, yes. Most of them were the usual thing—flowers here, roots there, some crystals and lake water—but all of it was hyper-pure and unaspected. Anyone could use them, and they were *strong*. I even got a few things from right at the entrance to her lair, and they're dripping with juice. Anyone interested, I'll cut you a deal.

◉ Lyran

◉ Do tell.
◉ Orange Queen

◉ ... eep
◉ Lyran

◉ **USER LYRAN HAS DISCONNECTED**

WHERE DOES MAGIC GO?

A question more rarely asked than where magic comes from is this: Where does magic go? If it's constantly generated by living things, and we couldn't access it until the Awakening, where did

it all go before today? Some of it seeped into the ground, the Earth itself being a kind of living thing as anyone who can astrally project will tell you, where it pooled into hidden reserves of magic. It's theorized that these areas were where dragons hibernated during the downcycle. As you might guess, the main proponents of this theory are those who believe that magic comes and goes in cycles and that dragons were alive in the past, possibly carved out and channeled for that exact purpose for centuries, to provide a cocoon of mana that would keep them alive when magic, as a whole, vanished. There are problems with those theories, but the largest is this: If energy cannot be created or destroyed, magic couldn't vanish. It had to go somewhere, and those small lairs wouldn't be enough to drain ten thousand years of planetary production. The leading theory at this time is that the astral plane and the material world are not perfectly synchronized and, like the sun, moon, and Earth, interact in an eclipse-like fashion. That is, when they're aligned, energy flows between them, but when they separate, the energy spills into the astral but doesn't spill back out, cutting off our ability to harness it. This energy would generate the metaplanes, shaped by the thoughts of humanity like a dream. There are numerous problems with this mindset, and scholars produce gigapulses of papers arguing and exploring every year. The interactions of Halley's Comet with our manasphere multiplied these papers a hundredfold, and the writings about the magical transformations under and around Los Angeles still come hot and heavy. How does a city above sea level, on a tectonic plate moving north, east, and upwards due to forcing against a stationary plate, wind up flooded after an earthquake and with spiderwebs of caverns where it used to be solid rock? If you look at GPS coordinates, the city's actually higher than it used to be by over sixty centimeters, yet many areas are flooded even today despite being higher than sea level. It's a magical effect that's broken here or there but, in general, the mindset that LA would "fall into the sea" happened despite being scientifically impossible.

◉ Hang on. Is that true?
◉ Dr. Spin.

◉ Weirdly? Yes. The effect is magical in origin, and if you have someone with exceptional astral vision they can even see the aura, which is spread over the city in a convex shape, like a contact lens. The deepest water is at the center while the edges are shallow. If this worked like normal water, a universal depth would be established or, in this case, it would all drain back into the ocean where it belongs. I'm told that the effect is weakening since the Comet left, and some water has drained back as the effect cracks. Don't get me started on the caverns.

◉ Snopes

◉ The Lacuna is a gateway to the realm of Earth, where spirits cross over into our world. They're mostly interested in pottery and the Walk of Fame.

◉ Plan 9

Which brings us to nana ebbs and voids. These are areas that are lacking in magic, such as in space, where there is a weak or non-existent manasphere, but it also covers a more uncommon situation where magic bleeds from the astral to somewhere else. You're familiar with a handful of these, but the one that stands out is Crater Lake in Tír Taingire. At one point in time, it was a simple lake, but on May 2, 2054, it changed. Mana began to bubble out of it in great volume, famously floating some of the local landscape around it like some music album cover from a century ago. Tír elves went into lockdown mode, going so far as to blind satellites that flew overhead while allowing no one to enter or leave the area. It's hard to know exactly what happened here, as the information was hard to access in the first place and what little got out was lost in the second Crash, but some extrapolations do still exist. The most interesting of those, in my opinion, was a spike in Awakened births for several years, with a high number of elves and dwarves being born no matter the race of the parent. (And if you think it's odd for an elf to be born to human parents in the UCAS, it's even stranger when orks are birthing elves in the Tír!). Additionally, those born in that period have shown to be both more likely to have the Talent and to be stronger in magical arts than those born in other times. This resulted in a rate of nearly fourteen children out of a thousand being magically active, a number that seems small to you but for those who study such things is an impressive spike.

Soon after President Dunkelzahn's assassination, we became aware that the situation at the lake had changed. Word slipped out that the flow of magic from Crater Lake had stopped, then reversed course, turning it into a mana ebb. The lockdown, which had loosened somewhat, snapped tightly together again, starting a whole new round of rumors. The investigation by the Tír government focused on Teseteoinestea, or Wizard Island as it used to be known, a small island inside the crater itself.

◉ Shadowland was brutal in May and April of '54. Tír deckers were working their collective asses off to track down and quash any scrap of information that had slipped out, while talking heads were on trideo urging everyone to remain calm and assure us that nothing unusual was happening. It was two months of hell, but if you were brave, you could make some serious nuyen by sticking your nose where it didn't belong. As other things caught the public eye, pay fell off, and fewer people went for it. By the time we finally got easy access, it was scarcely remembered. Shame.

◉ Bull

◉ First I've ever heard of the place.

◉ Riot

◉ Back in '71, footage of a small group of sleepwalkers advancing on the military cordon, refusing to stop, and being gunned done went viral on the Matrix. The Princes went into denial for a while, but eventually public pressure became too strong and they talked about "altering procedures" and quietly replaced some personnel that were on site. If there have been any more incidents, I've not heard of them, but the original incident was never explained.

◉ Turbo Bunny

◉ Everyone looks for magical reasons for that, but from what I hear, the only thing that they all had in common was that they'd attended a job training siminar together. And who hosted it? A group known as Collective Solutions who, though hidden under six levels of ownership, is ultimately a Horizon branch. Coincidence?

◉ Plan 9

Since then, Crater Lake has served as a mana ebb, gradually draining magic from the area. It started small, with spirits being uncomfortable there and wanting to leave or magic being more draining to call upon, but eventually it got so bad that spirits couldn't be formed and spells simply fizzled. Mages who opened themselves to the astral were nearly sucked out of their bodies by the area being so hungry for magical energy, and at least two didn't survive the exposure. The High Council insists on keeping any information gathered there tightly clutched to their chest and have turned away multiple requests by the Draco Foundation to help. Hestaby was a leading voice in getting outside aid, but High Prince Zincan was as intractable on the matter as the first High Prince. Since she lost her seat on the council, I'm uncertain if anyone has brought the matter to High Prince Telestrian. The leading theory, based on what little we know, is that magic is being sucked through the lake, removed from here and put somewhere else; we just haven't been able to solve the question of where it's going.

More worrisome is the data that has been slowly rolling from the study, information that's given directly to the Council of Princes, bypassing the Star Chamber entirely. The ebb has been growing. It's still contained inside the crater itself, but it's gradually filling the space and, should it reach the rim, they're uncertain if it will spill over like some kind of astral lava or if it will continue to expand upwards like some kind of mana vortex. As it's grown larger, it's been pulling more magic into it. How much, you ask? We can't measure that yet, but we can measure the effects. The birthrate of magicians has dropped over the past decade and a half, and in 2076 (the last year for which I've gotten hard data), it was down to nine out of one thousand. Tellingly, if you combine birthrates with birthplaces, you'll see that areas furthest away from the lake continue at the traditional TT rate of twelve out of one thousand, with the number shrinking as you grow closer to the ebb. Those born within ten miles are showing a rate of only six out of one thousand, while there's only a single recorded birth of a magician within a kilometer. More worrisome is that the national birthrate of elves has been falling. Both elves and dwarves are being born at a rate below UCAS standard by a noticeable degree, and it may be affecting orks and trolls as well. Human birthrates are higher, as well as "revision births," where metahuman parents give birth to ordinary human children. Again, plotting births with nearness to the ebb points to it being the reason for this, with more humans born close to it while meta births are at the standard Tír rates once you've gone thirty kilometers miles from there. As you might imagine, this is a source of quiet concern atop the nation, but that information has yet to be shared with the populace at large.

> I'm quite curious as to how you saw those conclusions.
> Frosty

> If demand for data exists, that demand will be met. The supply defines the cost, of course.
> Icarus

WILD SPIRITS

Which came first, the chicken or the egg? There are two general answers to this. The first is, "The chicken, as God made all living things." The second is, "The egg, which existed in birds before the chicken, as well as reptiles, amphibians, and so on." You can break this down with quoted passages and rough dates, but those two answers sum up most answers fairly well. When it comes to magical creatures, you face a similar question: Have we always described the unicorn as they now look, due to remembering how they were when they existed in the past, or have they taken the shape that they have in response to our belief that this is how they should look?

> Third answer. I dunno. Who cares?
> Slamm-0!

> Wait. "When they existed in the past"? What?
> Riot

> Oh yes—we haven't gone into history, have we, kiddo? The theory is that magic is a cycle, rising and falling in ages that are around ten thousand years in duration. If that theory's true, then there used to be unicorns and dragons and whatever, but they went away when magic did. If you believe that. Which I don't.
> Butch

> I'd be happy to educate both yourself and your apprentice, Butch. The two of you should come by the magic discussion area later. We'll chat.
> Winterhawk

I tend to find evidence in the latter, personally, and it's reflected in a few areas, such as the varied appearance of any particular dragon when comparing images taken of them over the years, as well as the general understanding that comes from aspecting mana lines. Mana, in a raw form, can be shaped and "flavored" by those who can use magical energies. If these magics can thus be "cooked," then it stands to reason that they can resonate with our thoughts. If magic is a reflection of us, then by simple extension, it becomes what we wish it to be. As such, a magical being is a

formless, shapeless void until we will it into being, binding it down as a concept with a name and a shape—an essence, if you will.

- Heading this one off at the pass. Philosophical debate goes elsewhere. Focus on the data.
- Glitch

- Coyote cares not how you wish him to look.
- Man-of-Many-Names

- What did I *just* say?
- Glitch

The reason that I bring this up at all is due to the re-emergence of wild spirits. They've been around, in some capacity or another, since the return of magic but they have had periods of greater or less commonality. The most telling was that most seemingly vanished in the mid-'60s. The exact reasons for this are much debated, but the fact that they began to disappear as Halley's Comet drew near is, in my opinion, important. The comet disrupted mana lines across the planet, with the dragon lines along the Ring of Fire particularly hard hit. They might have gone dormant at this time, to wait out the manastorms, or due to one of the general upheavals of the decade. It happened to coincide with the publication of UMT, which is when both hermetic spellcasters and shamans changed their summoning methods. Mages found themselves summoning more strong-willed spirits, smarter and more capable than before, while shamans stepped away from calling for wild spirits and, instead, gathered a less-flavorful, but also untethered, spiritual type.

- Not all of us followed the new way.
- Man-of-Many-Names

- Untethered? What's that supposed to mean?
- Lyran

- There used to be a thing where spirits couldn't cross certain boundaries. Somebody sics a forest spirit on you, you could run for the edge of the woods and, if you made it out, they couldn't chase you. Saved my hoop more than once, but one day that just … stopped working. Huh. Never really thought about it.
- Bull

- Hey yeah! Mom used to talk about that! Her team had a rat shaman that could whistle up spirits, but he had to call up new ones each time they moved around from the sewers to the streets, to inside a guy's house, whatever. The only magician I ever saw as a kid was a hermetic, and his spirits went anywhere that he wanted.
- Slamm-0!

- What happened to your mom's rat-friend?
- Netcat

- Lone Star. He jumped off a roof rather than be taken in. He knew what they do to mages in lockup.
- Slamm-0!

Whatever the Yellowstone Incident was, it's woken these spirits back up in a big way. Where there were only a few, and even then only found in rich magical areas like the Mojave Crater, the number out in Pueblo country has exploded. As the aftershocks of the Incident continue to move around, more effects seem to activate in a range of locations. We haven't yet found a pattern to it, we don't know why it happens, we don't know *how* it happens, but we can see the uptick in every area that it passes through. Once it's moved on, the spirits remain active, and if it visits again, even more are found.

- Interesting exception: Salt Lake City hasn't had a single spirit awake there, despite three visitations.
- Stone

- Well now *that's* interesting.
- Frosty

NATURE SPIRITS

All the information out there is nearly twenty years old at this stage, and the second Crash was unkind to much of it. As such, I've assembled a small primer for you on the matter of domains, with a discussion to follow.

DOMAINS

A wild spirit is tethered to the land, in some ways a reflection of the magical potential to be found therein, a "living avatar," for lack of a better term, for the local manafield. Again, there is discussion about whether the reflection of the land creates the spirit, or if the spirit creates the reflection in

the land (for example, is it the psychic scar of a vicious murder that creates a terrifying spirit there, or did the spirit's presence drive someone to murder?) but the more important aspect for you to remember is that the spirit's reach is only as far as the manafield itself. We call this a domain, and it defines the boundaries of a wild spirit's power. Within this area, it is more powerful than you would think, able to draw upon the environment itself, but only the strongest can leave their domain, and even those find their power diminished greatly in the process. In most cases, the spirit stops where its domain does.

- Not unlike the vampire myths of old. A vampire is powerless to harm you unless invited across the threshold of your home.
- Winterhawk

- Or the Nightmarchers, Hawai'ian spirits who cannot harm you if you lie face-down on the ground, humbling yourself before them.
- Sounder

- Or the monsters that hide under your bed. If you pull the sheets over your head, you're safe. Sprout-0! knows this well.
- Slamm-0!

- I'm going to cry when he stops doing that.
- Netcat

- Oh, Winterhawk, about that ...
- Red

There are four general domains, with the Land, the Waters, and the Winds being fairly obvious, while the domains of Man are somewhat fuzzier. Interestingly, while there are numerous wild spirits of beasts, they never have a domain; they, and they alone, may travel where they wish, but as a consequence, they lack the power that other wild spirits can draw from.

SPIRITS OF THE LAND

There are four segments to the domain of Land, and a wild spirit of the Land will be tied to one, and only one, of them. These segments are the desert, the forest, the mountain, and the prairie. A spirit of the forest cannot enter the prairie or the desert, despite being of the Land, for example, nor may the forest be entered by the others.

While to metahuman eyes there would seem to be areas that merge the environments or that have aspects of each (for instance, heavily wooded hills that blend into low mountains), the spirits know precisely where their domain begins and ends, and what boundaries they cannot cross.

> Cannot, or will not?
> Aethernaut

> Yes.
> Man-of-Many-Names

Desert spirits have a varied appearance, based on the land in which they're born (a rule that runs true in all landed spirits, really). The traditional sandy deserts produce small dust devils in most locations but, on occasion, they form as small rivulets running beneath the sand, unseen save the wake of their movement. Those in rockier areas take the form of, well, rocks, or flash about as echoes, figures seen from the corner of your perception, or simply eyes peeking out from shadowy areas. They tend to wait for you to make the first move—always near, always watching, but simply waiting. It's up to you to prove that you're worthy of anything beyond them allowing you to die beneath the sun.

Spirits of the forest are often attended by beast spirits (see later in this upload), which has created some level of confusion in the layman, but once you've seen one in person, you'll know. They're formed of the woods themselves, taking the form of trees, entwined greenery, or, a personal favorite, a vaguely metahuman-shaped mound of earth, covered in grass and flowers. They tend to be somewhat friendlier if someone's been respectful of the area and the life within it, but they have a terrible wrath for those who despoil it.

> In Germany, they often appear as wicker stags.
> Lyran

Mountain spirits are, to a one, old. Old old old. Few bother taking a material form, instead letting their basic presence settle heavily over an area; even the mundane can feel it in their presence, a true weight bearing down on them without remorse. When they do deign to take a physical form, it's a troll-sized figure of stone, striding out of the face of the mountain, which it will eventually return to, melding back as if it never left. Interactions with them can be frustrating—not from the manners that they expect so much as their view on time. The mountain answers as it will and you must ... wait. At least take a lunch, but a tent and backpack are more likely needed. (And it should go without saying, but leave the area as pristine as you found it. Mountain does not care for your NumNum wrappers.)

Spirits of the prairie seem to be in a state of flux, giving rise to certain theories of magical echoes drawn from the people. More primal spirits are little more than the wind rustling through the grass, cousins of the sky above. They take a spiraling dust-devil visage not unlike those of the desert, but there are reports (which I have sadly never seen in person) of them taking the form of Amerindians or Mongols in miniature. More often, they simply refuse to materialize, bringing with them an uplifting aura of freedom and possibility, opposite of the mountain. Also in opposition of mountain, they feel young and vibrant, but they lack deep wisdom or any significant knowledge of current events.

> What about bison spirits? Or horse?
> 2XL

> Those spirits are of the beasts, not the prairie. Like the spirits of the forest, it is easy to think of one as the other.
> Man-of-Many-Names

SPIRITS OF THE WINDS

The four segments to the domain of wind are the breeze, the clouds, the mist, and the storm. It's interesting to note that these are winds, not air, and movement is innate in them one and all. An area becalmed most certainly has air in it, but wild spirits won't be found there, nor will they be found in areas where the air is stagnant. It's also fascinating to see that there's a delineation between the domains, such as the forest or the mountain, which clearly have air running through them, yet are impossible for these spirits to enter. Wind might blow through the trees, but Spirits of the Winds will stay just above the treeline, dipping into a clearing, then rise above the trees once more, never actually interacting with the "wrong" domain.

Breeze spirits tend to be the smallest and most peaceful of the Winds, fond of music and playful with metahumans. In the astral, they often take the form of classical faeries to dance and swirl about the hair and clothing of visitors. There are older, more powerful breezes as well, found near areas where wind blows hard. Several urban towers, for instance, have stronger breeze spirits that swirl about the updrafts and dance in the castoff debris of the city that is caught in the winds, while cliff faces and natural rock tunnels provide homes for truly ancient spirits.

Cloud spirits are the most aloof spirit, as you might imagine, content to laze about, high in the sky. They rarely interact with mere mortals. They have great vision but retain little knowledge of what lies below due to a casual indifference to such matters. They're far more capable of discussions about aircraft and drones, however, who they see as invaders into their world. A cloud spirit can identify which drone was present beneath it when the sun was in a certain position, but it will first take the time to give you quite a lecture about the temerity of it to try to touch the heavens and how your kind should really be satisfied with the dirt and should leave the sky to them. Cloud spirits that are found near the tallest mountains tend to be more understanding and gregarious, but that's a relative measure at best.

Mist spirits are quiet poorly understood at this time. After all, by scientific reasoning, a fog is nothing more than a low-hanging cloud, yet mist spirits are quite different than their high-flying cousins. Rather than be aloof, they're quite curious about metahumanity. They are also shy, though, so they tend to creep about, ever-watching and observant but never daring to approach. This can be disconcerting for those who can perceive the astral, and it's given spirits of the mist something of a sinister reputation, associating them with vampires, wolves, and other harbingers of disaster. In truth, spirits of the mist often possess some limited form of precognition, which leads them to gather to observe the event in question, rather than causing it.

Storm spirits are the least common of all, created in large numbers with any powerful storm, then vanishing soon after. Some magicians speculate that they are simply another face of cloud spirits, releasing pent-up anger before returning to normal, while others believe that they're distinct, if short-lived, spirits. Cloud spirits that I've talked to consider them cousins, not brothers, so I'm inclined to accept the definition myself. Spirits of the storm are no more powerful than any other spirit of the wind, but they push themselves to use up all of their power in their brief lifespan, expending in an hour what a spirit of the breeze might use in a thousand years. Interestingly, spirits of the storm that spend themselves to dissipation sometimes return during the next storm or activity. If you find an area notorious for frequent storms or lightning activity, such as the lightning rods gracing the tallest skyrakers of the sprawl, you can meet the same spirit a dozen times in a year, or at least meet one who uses the name and recognizes you from previous encounters. I confess to being terribly curious about this, and intend on doing more research as time allows.

SPIRITS OF THE WATERS

The four segments of the spirits of water are lake, river, sea, and swamp, with some debate in scholarly circles about the variation of lake and sea in regards to large ponds or oceans. The general consensus is that rivers have a stream subset, lakes have pond, and that oceans are so large that a multitude of sea spirits share it, but, research is only beginning to restart on that. For now, we will focus on the currently understood aspects with notes as appropriate.

Lake spirits tend to form in a large body of water that's free of commercial pollution. This is, obviously, less common than it was in the distant past, but I've been told troubling stories about toxic versions forming from impure lakes. As with most spirits, they prefer to appear as just a presence, either ripples in the surface of the water or in larger bodies, as an area of preternatural calmness. In smaller ponds, they're fond of taking the form of a person's reflection, which can be unsettling when they begin to move in ways the viewer did not. If called into a physical form, lake spirits almost always choose a female body, ranging from lovely women with ankle-length hair and white gowns to a more terrifying look of a drowning victim covered in weeds. The nature of the local legends about the body of water will often tell you what to expect before you get there. Most lake spirits are content with metahumanity, or even supportive, unless mistreated. The spirit of Central Park's Duck Pond is rumored to take a physical form and stroll about, looking kindly on children and feeding the birds from time to time. Spirits in Lake Michigan, in contrast, embrace metahumans with cold arms and sink to the bottom of the water, never to rise again.

> ◉ Ghost above! Remind me to stay out of the water!
> ◉ Riot

> Oh girl, the stories I could tell you ...
> Sounder

Spirits of the river are tricksters with a rough sense of humor. They often take the form of translucent fish made of water, gabbing with someone on shore, or mossy frogs that could easily be mistaken for rocks who croak at inhuman volume to startle hikers, laugh, then dissipate with a splash. Angrier spirits are as rough as rapids, made of gravel and sharp rocks, tumbling white foam, and sand. All of them are curious, exploring the length of their domain time and again, seeking new locations, sometimes pushing the path in new direction, and witnessing those creatures who interact with their flow. I'm told that some in California can be found with gold-producing abilities, but if they exist, those spirits are likely to defend themselves. Smaller bodies of running water, such as creeks or streams, sometimes produce weak river spirits, while the mightiest ones, like the Amazon or Mississippi, are filled with uncountable numbers of spirits, both weak and strong, including some great forms.

> I wonder if there are any spirits of canals?
> Netcat

Sea spirits are the strongest known, in general, and like the spirits of the mountain, they tend to be *old*. In a more natural form, they tend to reverse the local conditions by appearing as a bubbling area in a calm sea, or a strangely becalmed area in otherwise choppy waters, but when taking a more interactive form, they choose either a classical merfolk look of half-man, half-fish, or a more terrible form of the drowned dead whose mouths ooze black water when they speak, eyes long ago plucked out by the crabs that sometimes crawl along their bodies, which are covered in barnacles, starfish, and/or chains. They have a strong dislike of interlopers but will allow passage for a price. Those who pay are given safe passage while those who refuse ... well, the template of the drowned has to come from somewhere. They care little for the affairs of mankind, who dwell on only the surface of their domain, but know of all who pass through it; if you want to know who or what's come through, they're unmatchable sources of information, but most of their other knowledge is of little use to people like us.

> Not all of them accept payment against trespass. I've lost two ships in the Bermuda Triangle due to this.
> Kane

> It's important to remember that they know what lurks below, and while they are loathe to give up the treasure that they've collected, they're even more against the presence of metahumanity in the depths "where they don't belong," and they put a much higher price on their presence. Those who are unwilling to pay, or worse who simply arrive and begin to craft structures, will find themselves beset by calamity, leaks, and hostile life forms.
> Sounder

> Like sharks?
> Riot

> Like kraken.
> Sounder

> Ghost!
> Riot

> Hey Sounder! Know how you keep wanting to hang out with Butch? September 19th. You, me, Butch, and the new kid.
> Kane

> Anchors aweigh!
> Sounder

> ... what the f... RIOT! Get in here!
> Butch

Spirits of the swamp are the mystic, mysterious entry of the water set, and one that I have yet to meet in person. Most are content to be seen as simple balls of light, perhaps the source of will-o-the-wisp legends, but others take a shaggy humanoid form made of muck and rotting vegetation. Talk of "swamp apes" might be sasquatches or swamp spirits, but most of them aren't good enough to hold a solid form like this and, instead, are slumping mounds of mud that are only called humanoid out of generosity. Swamp spirits are not at all fond of metahumans and are all too happy to lead them to a terrible death within the fetid waters of their domain, even if they don't take a direct hand in the matter. Like other water spirits, they accept payment for passage, but unlike the others, they sometimes betray a charge and let them die. These spirits have a tangled and idiosyncratic system of rules, so the death might be due to the individual breaking some rule that they did not know about, rather than swamp spirits being uniquely treacherous.

SPIRITS OF MAN

This is where things start getting interesting. Nature spirits and beast spirits make sense to even the average layman, but spirits of man are expressly connected to mankind and to the social constructs that we form with one another. This is a note toward the chicken, or "We tell unicorns what to look like" side of the overall magical equation, versus the egg, or "We just remember what unicorns are supposed to look like" side of things that you find with the more natural spirits. Does one invalidate the other? Unified Magic Theory says no, but it threads the needle in a way that I'm not comfortable with. Perhaps there are two sources of magic? Or more? There are simply too many as-yet unknown factors preventing me from forming a hypothesis, let alone set up a true theory for peer review. But, I'm off topic. Spirits of man, like the nature spirits above, come in four categories; city, field, and hearth, capped with the newest addition to the family, corporate.

> ⊘ Wait, what? When did this happen?!
> ⊘ Arete

> ⊘ You're behind the current pulse, I'm afraid. There have been scattered reports over the past few years, but it's not really been taken seriously until the elevation of Inazo Aneki to be the Corporate Kami of Renraku, Aneki-sama, or, more properly Aneki-no-Kami, developed a large enough following that his spirit, or at least spirits claiming to be him, have been popping up at shrines in Renraku facilities worldwide. There have long been rumors and one-off encounters with corporate-ish spirits that were generally considered hearth spirits, but we're starting to see them as distinct entities now, with Aneki being the first officially recognized with the designation. Now that we know what to look for, I'd imagine many more will follow.
> ⊘ Winterhawk

Spirits of the city were the youngest until the new corporate type were officially named, forming up in large communities of metahumanity that have existed long enough to create a "flavor" for the area. The standard city spirits are reflective of the city's urban nature, taking the form of stray garbage, or possessing iconic materials of the city

(a street car in San Fransisco, a subway turnstyle in New York, and, I kid you not, a cheesesteak in Philadelphia) when asked to materialize. The stronger spirits take a metahuman shape based on whatever race is most common in the city (human, ork, or, in the Tírs, elf) and always have a thick regional accent. Great forms also exist, with the city of Atlanta being one of the most famous, a real beauty of a Southern belle wearing a charred dress from the fires in the nineteenth century. These days, she's also seen wearing a pair of smart goggles and producing AR feeds with a gesture, reflecting the city's technological status as well as its history. (And before you ask, those technological features are pure spirit illusion and non-functional. No spirit can interact with the digital world.) London, Paris, Neo-Tokyo—each and every major sprawl in the world has them, as well as most smaller cities whose spirits are, in turn, weaker. There seems to be a threshold of a hundred thousand people before a city spirit can manifest, with a million needed for a more powerful one. The biggest cities in the world have the most powerful while the oldest cities seem to have the wisest. Make of that what you will. Most of the time, you'll be dealing with minor versions of city spirits, "splintered" off of the main. Thus, in Seattle, you probably get the spirit of Third street when you put out a call, rather than Seattle herself.

> ⊘ Interesting. I wonder if this "splintering" technique is what caused the spirit of Denver's problems?
> ⊘ Lyran

> ⊘ I don't suggest asking Zebulon. Or Ghostwalker for that matter.
> ⊘ Frosty

> ⊘ Why are so many city spirits framed in the female?
> ⊘ Plan 9

> ⊘ [Bad French accent filter] Because, mon ami, you fall een LOVE weess ze city, no? [/French accent filter]
> ⊘ Slamm-0!

> ⊘ More Fred code to remove ...
> ⊘ Bull

Field spirits are arguably the oldest of the spirits of man, seemingly created as we moved from hunting and gathering to actual agriculture. Ritual sacrifices to stave off blight, to bring a good harvest, to burn animals to ensure that more would be born in the spring—all manner of ancient rituals were shown to be effective in the modern world, and even today there're dozens of "farm mages" enlisted to keep them happy, from the water witches and dowsing specialists in the Midwest to the hog callers of backwoods Alabama to the blood sacrifices of condemned prisoners in Aztlan to combat the Atlacoya Blight, all drawing on spirits of the field in some manner to ask for help. These spirits come in as many shapes as any other, from simple doll-sized farmhands wearing overalls, a straw hat, and nothing else, to warm sunlight to shuffling piles of cornstalks that twine around one another and walk the land. Across the world, they dislike birds and most rodents, and insist that the croplands be carefully tended.

- I've never seen one on a corporate-run industrial farm. Not one.
- Winterhawk

- Count yourself lucky. The high pesticide levels and machinery runoff causes the few that are formed to go toxic as a rule.
- Chainmaker

- One time in Iowa, I got chased by one that had materialized as a giant scarecrow, complete with scythe that cut the front of our SUV off clean with a single swipe. Had a pet crow that served as eyes in the sky to help it track us down. If it hadn't been for the farmer's daughter letting us inside, a handy supply of gasoline, and grandpa's old flint ring, well, things would've been pretty hairy
- Stone

Spirits of the hearth are the middle child of these spirits, forming in the home of families who follow the old ways, respect the home, and are willing to leave out the right things to attract the spirits. Hearth spirits most commonly take the form of mouse-sized humans, akin to mythical brownies, or cat-sized gnomes wearing human-like clothes and hats. They rarely show themselves to the home's occupants but work hard all the same, keeping things from falling apart, repairing broken table legs or chipped plates, mending shoes, and so on. In return, they need to be supplied with small saucers of food or drink and given respect. If they don't get it, they'll stop helping, curse the home, and leave to find some other family who will treat them better. In some cases, in modern homes that are lacking a true hearth, the spirits seem to be anchored to a treasured family item, such as one of grandmother's best plates, the family holy book, or an ancestor's iron tools that have been passed down for generations. These spirits are restricted to the domain of a house and yard, but their icons may be carefully moved to a new location, where they will reform after a month.

- Had a job about that, once! Couple had a bad divorce, but she got his family Torah in a bitter, bitter bit of court maneuvering. He hired my guys to get it back. Low pay, but an easy job, right? Turns out that there was a hearth spirit bound to it, which explains why he shelled out for a professional in the first place.
- Stone

- How do you keep getting these jobs, anyway?
- Chainmaker

Corporate spirits are the new kid on the block—not yet fully understood, but recognized all the same. Aneki-no-Kami is the most famous, but Renraku as a whole seems primed for them thanks to their views on cultural touchstones and integration levels. Ares and Shiawase have also reported them, and I can't imagine that the other corps don't have research teams investigating reports of their own. Most of them take on a form akin to a sarariman wearing the corporate logo, but Ares spirits have been found both in military uniforms and wearing denim shorts, a tank top with the old American flag on it, and sunglasses while twirling around a gun and a six-pack of beer (if certain reports are to be believed). Smaller corporations are too sterile, lacking the critical mass of population that seems to create, or at least feed, these spirits. On the upside, there's no spirit whose domain is quite so well-defined as a corporate spirit; if you're in an extra-territorial corporate area, other than living quarters (that's hearth territory), then you're inside their zone. Step a millimeter past the signs, and they can't touch you. Luckily, they're still quite, rare so you're unlikely to encounter one, but the Yellowstone Effect continues to spread, so it's only a matter of time.

- The first of these were likely to be Aztechnology, but so many are conflated with blood spirits that it went unreported.
- Haze

- Oh God.
- Butch

- Since when do you believe, Butch?
- 2XL

- I don't, shut up. Just the sudden dawning on me that the ACHE probably has one asleep inside it.
- Butch

- Jesus. If that thing ever wakes up ...
- 2XL

WILD BEAST SPIRITS

These are the wildcards of the wild spirit set. Scholars have gotten complacent, simply putting them into the broader of "beast spirits," a wide array of spirits who resemble beasts and who share common characteristics. This, though, is more of a hermetic oversight than a true-ism. Wild beast spirits are the only ones unbound by the concept of domains, freely scampering anywhere that they wish to go with only a token nod to the idea of belonging anywhere. The exception is a rural versus urban divide, with rural spirits such as Deer, Bison, or Elephant being found almost exclusively away from civilization while Rat, Pigeon, and Sheep are almost exclusively found in urban settings. A few, like Dog, Cat, Fox, and ever the rule-breaker Coyote, can be found in either spot but are more common in one or the other. Outlying areas, like suburbia, are where both sides seem to mingle. There's no restriction saying that you can never find Whale hanging out downtown or Rat in the Arctic Circle, but as you can imagine, the further away they are from where they fit, the more rare they become. Lacking a domain to call their own to draw power from, these spirits are weaker than the other wild spirits, but that freedom of travel gives them some options the rest lack.

The most telling aspect of a beast spirit is their versatility. It's a rare hermetic who can whistle one up, and as rare as corporate shamans have always been, a wildcalling corporate shaman is even more unknown, which has left us lacking good documentation on the assorted substrata of beast spirits. There are differences between, say, Bear spirits and Rat spirits, as you might imagine, but there are also subsets within those areas, with Black Bear, Brown Bear, and Polar Bear having different power sets and personalities than one another, as do Sewer Rat, Lab Rat, and Country Rat. There's further differentiation within *those* subsets by cultural expectations. Rat spirits in the UCAS are often filthy, craven, and cruel, while those in Asia are often clever risk-takers with no association with disease. These cultural aspects are carried over to the spirit forms (or, again, the spirits innate differences influence the perception of them in those areas), creating a vast set of differences in each type of wild beast spirit.

- Man-of-Many-Names, you've been holding out on us! This is fascinating!
- Winterhawk

- There are certainly some interesting matters that I'd like to know more of here. Do all Rat spirits share the same metaplane of origin, for instance? Will projecting from Tibet take you to the same metaplane as from London if you're following a Rat spirit native to those areas? You've got my nose itching.
- Ethernaut

- Before you accuse me of "holding out," perhaps you would like to review the many occasions where you have spoken about fire spirits and the innate differences that they have with one another, despite everyone knowing such things intimately?
- Man-of-Many-Names

- Man's got a point.
- Glasswalker

- Wait. Most of you think of Rat in a negative way?!
- Jimmy No

Wild beast spirits are often found in the service of other nature spirits, sharing in the protection of the other spirit's domain in exchange for sometimes performing errands for it. Taking messages about, investigating things beyond their senses, leading wayward explorers off in a stray direction, and so on. Some are also both curious about metahumanity and genial by nature, so they find themselves hanging out around populated areas, engaging in people-watching and following those who give off interesting emotional auras. If you get a feeling like you're being watched but no one's there, a wild beast spirit might have just checked out your aura.

- Is *every* spirit creepy now?
- /dev/grrl

Since there's a good chance that a wild beast spirit might seek you out, they're a great way to start talking to the wild spirits in your area, serving as a gatekeeper that can figure out who can be trusted and who can't, guiding the deserving deeper into the wild world. I have some idle thoughts about connecting these to the first mentors, but it's more of a free-association of thoughts than a true hypothesis at this stage. Regardless, many places have legends of white hounds or red bulls, which are good starting locations for tracking down places that a wild beast spirit might frequent. Otherwise, find a friend with the ability to see astrally and walk around for a few days. Odds are, you'll run into one somewhere once you know what to look for.

WILD URBAN SPIRITS

One of the things that's most caught my eye after the Yellowstone Incident was the introduction of true urban shamans. "But Elijah," I hear you say, "We've had shamans in the city for sixty years! How is this new?" Glad you asked. The original urban shamans were little more than city-dwellers who aped the Native Americans in the wake of the Great Ghost Dance. They had magic that worked after all, and those with the Talent weren't going to let a little thing like a three-meter-by-three-meter apartment stand between themselves and whistling up Grandfather Rat. Urban shamans were at the head of discovering the urban domains of spirits of man, as well as expanding the animal spirits that the more traditional shamans were known for, but true research in the field leveled out in the '30s and never really went anywhere. Corporations just weren't interested in shamans (Or, more accurately, found them unreliable, while most shamans had environmental interests that flew, hard, into the pollution wall), dedicating few resources to the issue, while the more "normal" shamans considered their city cousins sadly lacking in The Truth and rarely reached out. It was the SINless community, especially orks, who tapped into this magical style. Unfortunately, the SINless tend to have poor access to materials, low, or non-existent, literacy, and they are more concerned with surviving than getting involved in deep experimentation and peer-reviewed theory. You would find a bright mind here or there, but there was simply no support network to share findings, other than rumor and gossip shared by talismongers. Those of us in academia dismissed them.

That was a mistake.

There was a spike in urban magicians during the passage of Halley's Comet, but what most of us missed in the general comet madness was a rise in urban spirits as well. As was so common, we mislabeled many as "spirits of man," rather than understanding what they truly were, and talk of cars, streets, or even streets Awakening were attributes to "too much deepweed." For a supposedly educated lot, my people can be fools.

* There is no shame in ignorance. A child does not know that a fire will burn them until they touch it. Shame follows only when you have an opportunity to learn and choose to close your eyes and ears.
* Man-of-Many-Names

* There's a disturbing trend in this nation, where people take pride in not knowing things. "Economics? I don't know drek about that! Keepin' it real!" Yeah, real ignorant. A real problem in my community is that you get more respect returning from prison than from college. Finding someone open to sitting down and *thinking* is rare.
* Butch

* That said, there's more in the world than you can learn from a book.
* Stone

The Yellowstone Incident changed everything. Whatever this energy is, when it crosses an area, spirits tend to wake up. They were slumbering so deep that we had no idea they were there. Not everything wakes up, of course; the idea of a city street erupting into dancing cars, wacky fire hydrants, and flapping pizza parlor awnings is the stuff of cartoons, but even one or two new urban spirits in a city block is enough to make us wonder how many others there could be. This is when we found that certain urban primitives had been waking up and communicating with urban spirits since '61, and their techniques were absolutely applicable with these fresh births. When I'm able, I want to invite one of these fellows, named Drummer, to swing by JackPoint for a discussion, but for now, allow me to share one of his more salient quotes: "There's a spirit in everything, chummer. The city's alive. There's a pulse, a rhythm, a heartbeat to every city, and each back alley has a story to tell. You just have to listen for it." One of the key elements in this urban awakening comes from music. Just as traditional societies would dance and sing to celebrate, and in the process pour out astral energies to the spirits, so to do the urban shamans bring music to the people and, through them, energy to the astral. You wouldn't think of turntables and stretched-skin drums as being the same thing but, whatever the method, a good underground rave is as much of a feast for spirits as a shamanic drum circle.

- Wait. Spirits eat astral energy? Like, when I get my dance on, something is gnawing on my leg?
- SeaTac Sweetie

- I don't think I'm comfortable with the idea of spirits as parasites.
- 2XL

- Not exactly. It's better to think of a dance as a fish tank and spirits as fish. When you let your emotions pour out, it's like sprinkling some food into the tank. The fish ignore you entirely but scoop up these small bits that are floating around due to your action. It's much easier if I can show you in person with an illusion.
- Haze

- Speaking of parasites ...
- Pistons

I ask you to keep in mind that research into this area is still *very* thin and that many of these classifications are subject to change as more empirical evidence is found, methodology perfected, and, in general, research completed. Again, I'm loathe to put this out in this state, but the pressing need of these unfolding situations requires a looser form than I prefer.

SPIRITS OF CERAMICS

The oldest of the urban spirits, as far as we can tell, are the ceramic spirits. Clay, concrete, and glass spirits have all been placed here for now, as they all seem to fit the proper criteria. (That said, some replace glass with porcelain. This is bleeding-edge material, and university studies are hot datasteals, while extraction of researchers and students is right behind.) All these spirits are closely tied with Earth, and some insist that they're just subsets of ordinary spirits.

Clay spirits are the oldest and most friendly to metahumanity. They tend to take the form or short, overweight metahumans, jolly by nature and with a ruddy skin that reflects their roots. They're quite community oriented and are fonts of wisdom in terms of cooking and, by extension, herbalism. Most are natural historians, and all of them have a

good eye for art in all its forms.

Spirits of concrete are more businesslike and orderly than clay, with more mathematical-oriented minds. As you would imagine, they enjoy engineering and construction, taking pride in their work. Most have a modern metahuman look to them, save for the grey, abrasive skin that defines them, complete with hardhats and toolbelts. I have reports from Europe that says they instead resemble Roman soldiers over there. What I find most interesting is that concrete spirits talk about being part of a "union" and will speak of being from a local organization tied to that union. For example, "The Union of Pebbles, Gravel, Limestone, and Debris, local 414." We have yet to find evidence of this higher-level organization, but it can't be ruled out, either.

Glass spirits are sometimes reclassified due to their flexible nature, but, the majority of this area of research, such as it is, groups them with ceramics. Glass spirits are usually willowy and graceful, sliding between shapes as easily as you or I breathe, while speaking in a very musical, vibrating tone. Those who were born in a more violent environment are instead jagged and angry, ten thousand shards that have been roughly shaped into a humanoid form, creatures that screech in agony and hate as they lash out. Are these toxic glass spirits or pure ones? It's too early to know, but if you encounter one, please try to take notes.

- Oh yeah. Top of my list of things to do when a glass whirlwind is trying to slash my throat open is to grab a pen.
- Kane

Spirits of asphalt may also be in this area but I personally consider them toxics, so I haven't included them in the general ceramic notation other than placing this here. Blazing hot, giving off toxic fumes, and being both heavy and abrasive, asphalt spirits are combat machines with little to offer beyond fighting ability. Each one I've read about is foul-tempered and lashing out in some way, with not a single one holding a conversation or negotiation. Approach with caution.

- Ceramics are interesting, as they aren't purely Earth. Water is used in concrete and clay, while fire is needed for clay and glass. Wonder if that influences them to be so communal?
- Lyran

- More interesting, I think, is the lack of modern ceramics and compounds. Refined materials, we know, are largely inert when magical forces attempt to influence them. One would imagine that they are similarly difficult to Awaken. The question, then, becomes this: Is it difficult or impossible?
- The Smiling Bandit

SPIRITS OF METAL

Nearly as old as the ceramics are the spirits of metal, but they're more common in certain urban environments. Interestingly, the Seven Metals of Antiquity have all been seen in spiritual forms, but none of the modern metals have similarly been discovered. I would imagine that arsenic is only a matter of time, being the eighth metal, but that's pure speculation on my part.

Noble spirits are gold and silver. These are obvious icons of wealth and jewelry, but they are also known for being entirely nonreactive (gold) or almost entirely nonreactive (silver) with metahuman physiology. Silver is particularly notable for its antiseptic properties and being a "cure" for certain magical monstrosities, such as the silver bullet that ends a werewolf. Noble spirits take a metahuman shape that's perfectly formed but made of their metal and clothed in rich fabrics. Like most spirits, they prefer classic attire (Roman robes and Egyptian finery both rate highly), but some can be found emulating the newest high fashion as well. Noble spirits have an arrogance about them due to their perceived superiority over other, common metals, but they also possess a *noblesse oblige* to help when asked.

- It isn't arrogance if you can back it up.
- Kane

Spirits of construction include both coper and iron, metals with a very martial history. Copper is the core of bronze, while iron eventually gave way to steel, but each has thousands of years of use in tools of all kinds that is reflected in their general handiness. Spirits of construction are builders, creators, and engineers (and get along with concrete spirits mentioned earlier), but they are equally at home in in agricultural or militaristic setting. Despite, or perhaps because of, their usefulness in so many areas, these spirits have very poor initiative and prefer to serve others. They enjoy working but have little imagination for design.

Supportive spirits are lead and tin, often found alongside other, more useful, metals. Tin makes up the other half of bronze, while lead was generally discovered alongside silver and gathered up due to having such a low boiling point. Lead and tin have been conflated in many cultures as "grey lead" and "white lead," and this may be why they were grouped together in classification. These spirits take a compact metahuman forms, with lead invariably rounded and "plump," while tin tends to being thin, easily reminding you of a classic comedy duo. Lead spirits are notoriously dull-witted, however, and you shouldn't expect them to respond well to jokes, let alone know any. Tin spirits are more curious in that, for while most of metahumanity's existence tin has been thought of as a strong, useful metal, the modern world has come to think of "tin cans" as shorthand for fragile and weak, and this modern perception has influenced spirits of tin to sometimes be laughably fragile.

- Wonder if copper and tin spirits can combine themselves into Bronze and fight better?
- Riot

Mercury bears a mention all its own. Mercury has a reputation for being energetic, wild, and temperamental, an ignoble metal that's reflective of many of man's most base features. It's also the first substance found which would react to the noble metals of silver and gold, melting them and allowing for amalgamation to take effect. Mercury spirits should be treated with caution, as their emotional picots come quickly and with strength, causing them to lash out over minor incidents but, just as quickly, to calm down and apologize. Mercury spirits flow through new shapes as often as a person's heart beats, chaotic spirits who simply cannot keep the same shape for any length of time. Curiously, despite the fact that mercury is a silvery metal, many mercury spirits are red.

- Oh hey, one that I know! A long time ago, thermometers used to be filled with mercury, but the silver was hard to see, so it was often colored red to stand out. When people found out that mercury was bad for you if you swallowed it (always a risk with oral thermometers), it was removed and replaced with alcohol, which was still given the bright-red coloration. This lead to generations of people being born who believe that mercury is red and who are always shocked to find out otherwise. If this psychoreactive theory of magic is correct, since so many people believe the color is red, then the spirits who are influenced by that would be red. Ta da!

o Bull

o There're so many small errors in here that I'm twitching. I understand that you're not a metallurgist, but … gah.
o Beaker

SPIRITS OF ENERGY

Now we start getting a little more out there. Spirits of electricity are known to exist, and they make up the only real type of spirits in this category, but there are several more contenders who want in. Should fire be classified as energy? Radiation? What about magnetism? In all honesty, this category exists to be the "fire" of an earth/water/fire/air wheel for urban spirits that I'm not certain is appropriate. Certainly electrical spirits exist beyond the more storm-like lightning spirits of nature, but are they an entire category unto themselves or simply one aspect of a greater whole? I tend to believe the former but, as always, this is a young school of thought and there is a *lot* of research yet to do. For now, I'm using energy as a grouping, but I know that this classification could change more than most.

Electrical spirits are cousins of storm and lightning, but they are harnessed by metahumanity into doing something useful. Most people think of electricity as dangerous, but that's a lower-case "d." Much like the difference between burning your hand on a pot is "hot" while a raging house fire is "Hot," so too is house current "dangerous" while a downed power line is "Dangerous." Electrical spirits come in both flavors, from the small useful ones who can charge your commlink in an emergency to Old Sparky, the spirit of electric chairs who can, and will, end you. Electrical spirits are curious, poking around anywhere you call them up, and flighty; you'll have to work to keep them focused on a task at hand. Most take a cartoonish, vaguely humanoid look when they manifest, not unlike fire spirits but more adorable. I'd offer a picture but, you know … spirits.

o Wait, that's it? One type of spirit? Why is this not just "Spirits of Electricity?"
o Sounder

o He mentioned it's a work in progress. It's good to leave some room for expansion if your hypothesis starts showing legs.
o The Smiling Bandit

SPIRITS OF THE AIRWAVES

If you were thinking in pure scientific terms, you'll be blowing a gasket right about now. "Radio waves are just a form of energy!" True, but the metaphysical aspects are more important than the physics, here. Airwave spirits echo broadcasts of modern trideo, older flatvids, and even radio broadcasts, but not AR or wireless Matrix signals, which is a fascinating subsection I want to investigate someday, but I digress. Airwaves rarely manifest in the traditional sense, instead choosing to form on broadcast devices, such as a nearby trideo screen (regardless of if it works or not!), or buzzing into your headphones. The few who take a physical form invariably mimic some kind of broadcast icon, from a film noir detective to Dracula to Santa Claus, reproducing the sound and pattern of whatever icon they're impersonating. The ones who reach back far enough often have a grainy, black-and-white appearance. The rest flit frequently between characters, speaking snippets from commercials or movie lines, resulting in a spliced together conversational string. The first few times it's jarring and you wonder why they can't simply say "Don't trust that guy" and instead move from one source to another as they piece together phrases. Let me call one up. Hang on.

o **UPLOAD: VIDEO_CLIP_STAGGERED_01>**
  "Don't buy" "ANYTHING!" "this guy" "says about" "need" "the cops!"

Six different sources, three off flatvids, one from that annoying Juan commercial, a radio broadcast, and one I don't know, just for a single sentence. It's annoying, but you adapt to it soon enough. Most of what they say you can physically record, since they're transmitting via ordinary electronics, but every now and then, they'll talk to you through an old broken vid screen, crackling it to life and putting on a performance through it. Those are pure astral energy and unrecordable. Oh, and before you ask? They can't interact with anything Matrix-based. They can hop onto your commlink's video feed or through the headphones to buzz your ear, but they can't access any data on it, activate any AR controls, or even sense AR or VR constructs. The Matrix remains a hard line drawn between metahumanity and spirits.

o Discounting free sprites and other Matrix entities, which are very much alive.
o Netcat

- Or e-ghosts. Not that I know anything about those.
- Icarus

- I'm going to head this one off now. "Are sprites Matrix spirits?" is a whole other chatroom two doors down.
- Glitch

Regardless of the limitations, I'm finding some small differences between reports of video spirits and radio spirits, and there might be others as we dig deeper into this one. Much like Energy above, I'm willing to give them a category of their own, for now, until we can properly assign them taxonomy. There are others which may wind up in these categories, or reshuffle the entire deck, now that we're starting to see them wake up and begin embarking on their own agendas.

VEHICLE SPIRITS

- Wait, what?
- Slamm-0!

I'm willing to bet someone just went "Wait, what?" under that title.

- Drek.
- Slamm-0!

Truth is, there have been legends of spiritual vehicles for a thousand years, with ships being the first of these "ghost vehicles," then trains, cars, and now aircraft as well. These spirits are somewhat harder to classify, with most having simply called them spirits of man and moved on, but they're distinct enough that I feel that they deserve their own classification. I've further separated them into four subcategories, matching a more traditional spiritual class. I'm blazing a bit of a trail here, and we're a long way from a proper peer review, so understand that there are some areas that will need to be amended over time.

VEHICLES OF THE SEA

The oldest of the vehicular spirits—those of the sea—are almost entirely based on sailing vessels, drifting about the oceans of the world, and some smaller navigable bodies of water, like abandoned craft. Indeed, many legends of unmanned ships at sea are early viewings of these spirits which had Materialized, showing them operational but without a living soul on board. The first post-Awakening report of these was from January 1, 2012, when an old Spanish galleon wandered into Havana. It was approached by authorities and boarded, found empty, but it resisted attempts to take the helm. Once it had docked itself, it melted away into mist, leaving puzzled agents in its wake. Similar ships have been seen all around the Bermuda Triangle, the Sargasso Sea, and in the South China Sea, of all places. (These are likely mis-identified Portuguese ship designs, of course.)

More worrisome are the "ghost pirates," ships that carry a number of spirits aboard them, attacking small vessels on the high sea. Akin to the Flying Dutchman legends of old, these ships come seeking the treasurers as they did in life, but sometimes take a single metahuman on board instead. While all spirits of sea vehicles have terrifying properties, these crewed vessels seem to have a much magnified version of this, as every eyewitness report differs. And each is seemingly more horrible than the last.

- Rumor has some of these vessels as being populated with half-man, half-creature abominations, some of skeletons or ghosts, while others are said to be humans through and through and unfailingly polite to those who follow their rules. Those who don't have their skin flayed from their bodies, then the meat pulled away, torturing someone to death over failing to say "bless you" after a sneeze. The worst monsters hide their nature.
- Sounder

- I should point out that Elijah is using "ghost" in a loose way here. He knows well that there are no confirmed reports of an afterlife, only some spirits who claim to be the spirit of a deceased person and who have some ability to tap into some, but not all, of their memories.
- Winterhawk

- Just because it hasn't been proven, don't think it isn't real.
- Thorn

- The Caribbean is full of people that are terrified of these things, and any port you pull into will serve up a hundred stories. Never seen one myself, but I've used the reputation a few times. Stick a fog machine on your ship, play some spooky sounds and flash some lights, and people wet themselves thinking you're the *Flying Dutchman*. Bunch of idiots.
- Kane

- They're not all sailboats. Plenty of gas-powered yachts or warships are out there, but none dating from after the twenty-first century. The scariest, by far, are the submarines. Friend of mine was on board a ship that was sunk by some kind of German sub that looks to be from the middle of the twentieth century. One whole side caved in, skeleton soldiers wearing old uniforms and armbands, seawater and weeds pouring out when it surfaced to fire on the sinking ship with a deck gun … just horrible.

- Sounder

- Bet your friend was drunk of her ass when she shared that story.
- Kane

- He, actually, and yes. What does that have to do with anything?
- Sounder

- Hey, while we're here, anybody know about that Azzie missile cruiser that vanished? Reports have been sketchy.
- Snopes

- Three weeks ago, the C106 Atzcapotzalco was on a maiden voyage, intending to bring some pushback to the CAS by strutting their latest and greatest in the Gulf of Aztlan. A storm appeared and blew the escort ships off course, and it took nearly twenty-four hours for them to reconnect. Everyone was found … except for C106. Search efforts have continued, but now they're looking for scrap, not survivors. The interesting thing is that it's the third cruiser they've lost in the area.
- Icarus

- Once is an accident, two a coincidence, but three is enemy action. All three lost ships were constructed in San Diego, and after this latest incident, Aztlan is combing every inch of that yard to ferret out whomever's responsible. Fingers are pointed at CAS, the PCC, Horizon—you name it, they're accused of it, and each of those pointing fingers it tipped with a hand full of money for anyone that can prove it. Needless to say, jobs a-plenty for us.
- Fianchetto

- Curious what made you ask about that here, Snopes.
- Sunshine

- Because I have some rumors about a ghost ship being seen off the coast of Texas that sounds similar, but no one has any actual evidence for me yet. I'd hoped that some of you might know more.
- Snopes

- Give that kind of thing away for free?
- Icarus

VEHICLES OF THE LAND

The ones you're more likely to see (in a relative sense; most people will go their entire lives without seeing one of these things) are the land vehicles, simply because you're more likely to be there than anywhere else. The first thing you may notice is the age of these things; not a single one has been spotted that dates after the Awakening in terms of emulated design, which is rather surprising due to magic not existing when these cars did. There are some working theories about this, the largest being that modern designs are somehow lacking the right "soul," while others think it's tied in with the spread of plastic and other unnatural materials in their construction. I hope to investigate this further at some stage but, for now, my research keeps me otherwise engaged. Then again, a few of them are fairly close to my current location …

Trains come in two flavors: The more common is the ghost train, which runs along the tracks it once traveled, despite those tracks having been gone for a century or more. They seem to be mostly harmless, simply passing through and whistling, which has some researchers rating them more as phenomena than true spirits. There are also those who have seen them stop to pick up lone passengers who have never been seen again.

- Not entirely true. Normally they only pick up the dead or dying, but if you have the right ticket, they can take you through the astral to other locations. Friend of mine knew a guy who could buy tickets from (and, brother, they weren't cheap) who was able to get from New York City to LA in under an hour thanks to this.
- Stone

- That's amazing! Do you have his contact information?
- Winterhawk

- I wish. Last time he, wound up with the wrong ticket and went somewhere into the metaplanes. His body came back, but his mind? Not so much.
- Stone

While ghost trains can be found all over the world (along with headless rail workers who search for a replacement by lantern-light), there's a specimen that's exclusive to North America. The Iron Buffalo is said to be a crazed combination of locomotive, fire, and a buffalo, mystically placing tracks before it that vanish into ethereal flames in its wake. It screams as it travels, sometimes chasing down living people, which it swallows into its furnace for power. I've never seen this one, but I think I heard one near Roswell. The fear was paralytic, and despite my curiosity, I wasn't able to force myself closer to witness it firsthand.

- ⦿ From what I'm told, these things were created when a bunch of trains found out that mummies were cheaper than coal around two hundred years ago and used to toss them in as kindling. Commoners burned okay, but a prince could really give you a boost.
- ⦿ Stone

- ⦿ Do you want haunted trains? Because burning cursed Egyptian royalty is how you get haunted trains.
- ⦿ Slamm-0!

- ⦿ That's an urban legend, a tale spun by notorious talespinner Mark Twain, with zero corroboration.
- ⦿ Icarus

- ⦿ Maybe so, but one of the thoughts Elijah has been setting down is that belief in something is enough to shape magic, regardless of the truth.
- ⦿ Jimmy No

- ⦿ Wait, are you telling me that if I lie hard enough to make myself believe it, it'll happen?
- ⦿ Lyran

- ⦿ One person's not enough. You'd need hundreds if not thousands, of people all focusing on the same thought at the same time, binding it with emotion. This is why rock concerts or sporting events are so addictive to magical forces. The energy that these events unleash is focused by that shared thought and emotional base, emerging in waves of astral energy.
- ⦿ Akuchi

- ⦿ Confession time: I hit Flipside a few times myself to check out some performances and, woo, let me tell you, I understand how Haze got addicted.
- ⦿ Kat-o-Nine-Tales

- ⦿ I'm not an addict, dammit!
- ⦿ Haze

Lastly are the car spirits, which again always seem to be based of designs before the twenty-first century. Most are racers or sometimes muscle cars, but all of them are big, loud, and fast. Flames and skulls are common. Some have ghostly drivers, others don't, and they seem to exist just to test themselves against metahuman drivers. I'm told that some are cautionary, some take the soul of those who challenge them and lose, while others just go through the motions and vanish before reaching the finish line. Not all ghost cars race, of course, but even those with other goals tend to ride the roads for adventure. Interestingly enough, they're one of the easiest vehicular spirits to research due to a reliable timing and location. Ask the locals of any small town about "Dead Man's Curve" and you're sure to hit a legend of a driver who'll accept challenges under the full, or new, moon, or who shows up once a year on the anniversary of some local boy's death, looking to run the race he never got to when he died the night before. Sadly, there's a shortage of people with both the Talent and a deep fascination with automobiles, so these rocks have been largely left unturned.

- ⦿ … so, who wants to join me for a road trip?
- ⦿ Turbo Bunny

VEHICLES OF THE AIR

As you might suspect, these are the newest, and least-common, of the vehicular spirits. Not only are they pre-twenty-first century, but most of these are subsonic planes that use propellers, of all things. They're mostly seen in North America and Europe, with Germany and England having numerous incidents of World War II-era planes in their skies, while France sees planes from World War I. The UCAS has a few from the era of barnstormers, and there have been sightings of a ghostly Hindenberg which may be a spirit or may be an astral phenomenon; sightings are rare and investigation has been in the singular. There have also been numerous sightings of UFOs which is a whole area of discussion I don't want to enter.

- ⦿ They aren't aliens. There's no such thing as aliens. They're psychic echoes of the fear of aliens, manifested in spirit form drawn form ambient astral energies.
- ⦿ Plan 9

- ⦿ … can someone find my jaw for me?
- ⦿ Snopes

- ⦿ The astral energies are eddies left behind from the passage of Sirrurg when he was scouting Roswell during a brief upswing in magic, before going back to Aztlan for another sixty years of slumber.
- ⦿ Plan 9

> Ah, there it is.
> Snopes

AWAKENED VEHICLES

The last category are Awakened vehicles, machines which have somehow developed an astral form. Interestingly, none seem to be truly sentient while the mechanical part is still functional, but come to life after the "body" has "died." Some will tell you of waking up just before they died, possibly saving the life of their driver at the cost of their own, but most wake up in terrible pain, finding themselves unable to move and cast into a junkyard to rust away. I've personally only met one of these, but I'm told that there is a Parliament of Cars in the Pacific Northwest, where a dozen cars in a junkyard are Awake and speak to one another about fond memories. Needless to say, it's on my touring list for the near future.

> Treat your car right, it'll never let you down.
> Clockwork

> They'll never replace having friends.
> Netcat

> Fuck you.
> Clockwork

HERMETIC ELEMENTALS

One of the things I've mentioned here was the rise of UMT and how it's largely taken over magical trends in both shamanic and hermetic circles. We just went through a wide section on wild spirits, both natural and urban, and there's a section yet to go, but before we get there, I want to talk about elementals. For the youths in the mix, these are the four elements that you've seen with air, earth, fire, and water, as sat down by Aristotle, and the foundation of the hermetic tradition that you usually see bandied about as "true" magic. One of the largest unanswered questions of the hermetic elemental style was the lack of an aether, the fifth element known sometimes as quintessence. Hermetic magicians chased this for fifty years until it was finally unlocked by the students in Prague who also unlocked Universal Magic Theory. Unlocking that discovery changed the very nature of the spirits that they called, moving from a fire elemental to a spirit of fire, for one example. To you, that might not sound unusual, but for those who predated that discovery, the difference is massive.

So now you might wonder why all hermetic magicians now use the new method.

First, they don't, there are still several crusty old timers who refuse to change their ways and still whistle up elementals, but for the majority? It's all about being in the right place at the right time. When magic first returned to the world, people jumped quickly to the magical forms that they knew. For shamans, this was to call upon old dances and songs while for hermetics, it was musty tomes and scrolls. It wasn't until the '30s that the stubborn codgers started moving to a more digital format, and it was the generation that came of age in the '50s who well and truly embraced it, turning away from big thick books and reams of paper. The older magicians lived through the Crash and were always patting themselves on the back about having hardcopies and how they didn't lose their knowledge. The younger types made fun of them while flicking through digital spellbooks that they could fit into personal secretaries or even slot into headware memory. Costs for printing kept going up, demand kept going down, and by the mid-'50s, it was a massive moneysink for even Mitsuhama. They started moving away from physical tomes and moved fully to a digital grimoire in 2060. When they bought the rights to distribute UMT's core concepts, they waived purchasing the printing of physical media, which was scooped up by the Atlantean Federation. The AF was already one of the larger publishers of physical books in the market and the largest for dead tree versions of magical talk, and MCT would rather they have an outmoded option than cut into the digital sales. UMT, which unlocked the quintessence that so many had been searching for, was a huge hit and became their best-selling book, with requests for summoning formulae coming in from every direction.

> Wait. I thought Aztechnology was the largest?
> Butch

> Nope, it's MCT, of all corps. The Azzies are their primary rival in the field, with Saeder-Krupp never having as large of a slice as you'd expect a dragon-lead corp to have. Wuxing didn't even have a magical wing until getting that third A, but it has quickly shot up the ranks.
> Jimmy No

- In terms of physical publishing, the Atlanteans are third, behind Renraku and Shiawase, but they're tops in terms of publishing magical books. I have no idea how they went from a crackpot mailing list group to one of the world's most prolific publishers.
- Haze

Of course, this is when Crash 2.0 hits, wiping out virtually all digital data, eradicating the Matrix, and leaving the world unplugged for weeks—or months, depending on the region—and requiring two years of repairs and reboots to the underbelly of the system. During this time, all those formulae that Mitsuhama so lovingly sold via the Matrix or datachip services? Eradicated. Fifty years of magical research almost entirely gone in a flash. As people started realizing what had happened, paranoia set in. A magician without spells is hardly a magician at all, and there were several mages who were driven by desperation to commit some rather heinous acts. Once news of the first murder (or at least rumors of same) got out, those who still had the data went into hiding, pretending that they didn't have any in order to not be murdered for knowledge. I wish I could say that the community came together in love and understanding and started sharing their knowledge with their peers in the name of restoring lore, but no. While this is going on, the AF newsletters started arriving using good-old snail mail, pressing past the modern digi-saster with old-fashioned pen and paper. Hungry mages flocked to the information and started ordering copies at any price. Atlantean printing presses didn't stop for nearly a year, cranking out file after file, and what was the most ordered thing? UMT summoning rituals. By the time the Matrix was up and running again, UMT was accepted as the new way of doing things properly by both young mages and old, and those who lost their access to spells during the crash, then watched their brothers do amazing new things with the new theories, flocked to MCT once they were online again, ignoring the old and embracing the new. By the time the old elemental files were reconstructed, no one cared. By 2065, hermetic magicians were known for calling spirits of air, earth, fire, and water, topped off by spirits of man. The Quintessence and elementals had fallen into disfavor, but they still exist.

You don't see them often, but a few of the old timers still call them up instead of modern spirits, and they sometimes pass their forms on to younger mages. It's a dying art, but with the Yellowstone Incident straining the control that many magicians have over their spirits, and introducing wild spirits which yield to no one, the idea of a fully subservient spirit is growing in appeal once again. I'll provide a primer; you'll decide what to do with it. Let's go.

ELEMENTALS IN GENERAL

In the older hermetic tradition, elementals are formed of the basic building blocks of all matter, the essence of air, earth, fire, and water. All things are composed of these, in this theory, with a fifth essence, the Quintessence, or aether, being the unknowable energy of life itself. Call it a soul, call it a touch of the divine, whatever you wish, but it was a concept and a quest more than a known commodity. Hermetic magicians would call up an essence in a pure form, slaving it to their will, where they would serve willingly, if not exceptionally. This works differently than today's spirit summoning in subtle ways, and from shamanism in more overt ways, with the largest being that elementals were, shall we say, slow of mind. This stunted mental state left them easier to control but also easier to confuse, as well as lacking in any personality beyond the very basic. They were tools, closer to spells incarnated into physical forms than spirits as we talk of them today. Research indicates that some spirits seem to communicate with one another, establishing a sort of astral reputation for magicians who treat spirits well, or an astral notoriety for those who abuse them, not unlike the rumor mill and friend-of-a-friend system that shadowrunners use to keep tabs on one another, indicating what fixers and Mr. Johnsons are on the level. We've never seen any indication that elementals engage in such information-trading, which has lead to a rather unfortunate situation where mages who have burned all their astral bridges have scrambled backwards, pulling up elemental conjuring formulae to take the place that no spirit will fill. That means that, at this stage, most elemental conjurers are either quite old and set in their ways or immoral bastards who have a long reputation of abusing spirits. Still, with the Yellowstone Incident creating pushback in the spirit world, there's a throwback movement forming in hermetic circles to "take the astral back" and reclaim hermetic elementalism and spiritual subservience.

- Heremetic circles. Hah!
- Slamm-0!

- How can you laugh at this? He's talking about those who have so abused spirits that none will work with them and so they turn to buying astral slaves. There's nothing funny in that! These people are monsters.
- Netcat

- Yeah, I know, but ... wordplay.
- Slamm-0!

- For those curious, Mitsuhama has had a full suite of elemental formulae on the Matrix since June of last year.
- Haze

- You sick fuck.
- Pistons

- Hey, not my thing. I just wanted to help point out it's not an underground movement anymore.
- Haze

- Troubling.
- Man-of-Many-Names

ELEMENTALS IN PARTICULAR

I'd originally hammered out each in turn, but then I realized that writing "A vaguely metahuman-shaped column of (element)" over and over would bore my old professor to death. The four elementals are exactly that, with some subtle hints about their power level from size and structure. Hotter fire elementals are blue and cooler ones are red, for example, while weak earth elementals are mostly dirt and strong ones are more stone. Weak air are fluffy white clouds, strong ones are dark and stormy or tornado-like. Water elementals are ... well, water. Volume's the only thing I've seen to really tell them apart. The weakest ones are the size of kittens and can fit in your hand, normal ones are around human-sized, while strong ones are ork- or troll-sized. If you see them bigger than that? Get the frag out. As for personalities? Easy.

They don't have them.

Elementals are closer to programmed drones than spirits, undertaking whatever task that they're ordered to but not deviating from that very well. They don't talk as a general rule, but they can if commanded to; guards tend to give a warning or say "Halt," for example, but conversation? Forget it. They can't be bribed or seduced, and they ar-

en't easy to trick since they don't process things like a truly sentient creature would. But if you can go outside of their programming, they'll just stand there while you go about your business. Finding out how their orders are worded can turn a dangerous encounter into a cakewalk.

FOUR OUT OF FIVE AIN'T BAD

The last takeaway from this is that those following the hermetic elemental path only summon elementals in four flavors. Air, earth, fire, water, and that's it. The discovery of the fifth essence, the Quintessence, led to UMT and the summoning of "proper" spirits, rather than elementals. The magicians following this old path don't have that option. They only get four, not five, spirits to answer them. In addition to the most obvious lack this produces, it stands that, since one area of study has no spirit analogue that they tend to be weak in one area of study. For traditional hermetic studies, the lack of a spirit of man means that they don't have any spiritual support for Health magic, from healing to augmentations to water breathing. They can still cast those spells, they just don't have a spirit that can help them sustain spells, aid sorcery, and so forth.

- Hang on. Hermetic elementals can be called up by people other than hermetics? What?
- Lyran

- According to Mitsuhama, as long as the caster can call on the four elements, it doesn't matter what the fifth was or what the actual tradition is. They've managed to tie the summoning rituals to several traditions, but it's an either/or scenario. Once ordinary spirits learn that you call astral slaves to service, they refuse to work with you. If you turn your back on the elemental method, there's a chance that you can redeem your reputation with a lot of work, but it won't be easy.
- Haze

- Spoken like someone who's gone through the process.
- Bull

- No, but my reputation's been through the ringer here. I can relate.
- Haze

PLATONIC CONCEPTS

The final step in this journey is the bleeding edge of thaumaturgical research, where the very boundaries of scientific magic are pushed. In this case, we talk of Platonics. These are concepts, both in terms of social constructs via mindspace or philosophy, but also in terms of ideals or non-sentient objects. As an example, picture a chair in your mind. No, I'm being serious. This is important. Close your eyes for a moment, count to three, then form an image of a chair in your mind. Got it? Okay, good.

What was it made out of? Was it wood? Plastic? Metal? How many legs did it have? Did it have four? Three? One? Did it have rubber feet to hold it solidly in place, or did it have rollers? Or, perhaps, rockers? Was it padded or hard? Armrests or no rests? What color was it? Was it only a single color or more? Were there patterns in the design?

I would imagine that each of you, right now, have a different mental picture of a chair in your mind. Your chair is different then my chair, which is different than Bull's chair, which is certainly different than Slamm-0!'s chair, but at the end of the day, they're all chairs.

The reason I bring that up is that the thing we call the ultimate level of chair, the high chair (hah!) or, to use the technical term, the Perfect Chair, is all of those chairs at the same time. Your mind can't form it, your brain can't fathom how it can be a rocking chair and an easy chair and a beanbag chair all at the same time, but they all fit under the umbrella of "chair" and, as such, belong to this Perfect Chair hierarchy. The level below this would be the Platonic chairs, each of which are perfect examples of every chair you can imagine. There's the Platonic school desk, the Platonic office Chair, the Platonic throne, and so on, each of which is exactly what you picture when those words are mentioned, without also being the others that are all contained by Perfect Chair. In turn, each of those chairs spawns assorted chair forms, which are variations upon that Platonic chair. There are office chairs with or without armrests, some that are black and chrome, some that have fabric covering, some with a leather-like substitute, some with five casters, some with six, and some with four. Each of these chair forms is subservient to the Platonic chair above, which is in turn subject to the Perfect Chair. With me so far?

> ● I am not high enough for this.
> ● Stone

Replace "chair" above with "bear," and you start scratching at the easy-to-reach areas of this research. Polar bear, brown bear, black bear, and grizzly are all under the Perfect Bear in terms of capabilities, yet each is somewhat different. Beyond this are regional versions of these Platonic bears, or bear forms. Russian bear is not West Virginia bear is not California bear, yet each is still part of both Platonic Bears and the Perfect Bear. Totemic avatars fit in this band in some as yet-unagreed-upon way, as do mentor spirits, while below them are the more common Bear spirits that you might encounter in your daily life.

> ● I was wrong. I'm exactly high enough for this.
> ● Stone

We have a degree of research on this concept, and Axis Mundi, should he be around when this is uploaded, should be able to tell you more on the subject if you're curious, but where that data has led us is quite interesting. That an animal can be totemic is a given; we've had Wolf, Bear, and more since magic returned, but quietly a few other mentors arose that fell outside the lines. It started with The Adversary and Wise Woman, still iconic but not formed around a physical thing so much as an idea. From there we reached the mythical, Dragon and Phoenix, and then Sun, Moon, and further away. Research around religions is a very touchy subject for several reasons, but we know that there are spirits that embody concepts, such as Mercy or Healing, which are then revered when they appear and sometimes conflated with religious icons. We continue to push magical concepts further and further, extending our boundaries, and one wonders just how far it can go? Can pure concepts serve in this way? Could one take Art as a mentor, or Justice? Would spirits of these concepts arise fully formed as they were discovered or are they within us in some way, dormant and waiting to be awoken? If these bright and noble thoughts could be followed in that way, it would stand to reason that there are dark opposites that would also be slumbering, spirits of Hate or Torture. We have reports of spirits that feed off that sort of negative energy from the Azt-Am War, but as the war has ended, so to have the reports. Did they go back to sleep? Did they only exist in the maelstrom of energy that is war and fall apart afterwards? We need to know more. We continue to dig, we continue to explore, and we continue to learn.

- As I have said before, burn your books. Cast aside your old knowledge when new arrives.
- Man-of-Many-Names

- Wonder if those things are really gone?
- Kane

- Sixty-eight years. It has taken you only two-thirds of a century and you assemble this kind of magical theory. I should have paid more attention to Dunklezahn when he was still around. With the Matrix, with communications technology, with a culture that promotes the sharing of information, not greedily hoarding it in some sequestered tower, written in a secret code known only to you and lost at your death, with the sheer volume of population, several orders of magnitude beyond what once was, you learn so much, so quickly! He told those he respected (how he counted me in that number, I will never know) of this, and of how you had the potential to learn things that we never did. We dismissed those claims. It was in error. How could a monkey type *Romeo and Juliet* on a typewriter? The answer, it would seem, is that you simply have to gather enough monkeys. It's not that they will eventually type it at random so much as they will learn to communicate with one another, improve their works, and before you know it they will complete works on par with the Bard himself. And look! Even as the nobility is expressed, you understand the danger of the darkness, you see that it can appeal and that there are paths that must not be followed, yet some walk them no matter how many warnings you lift. The Big D suggested this was a possibility, but we brushed it aside. For one who wears the jester's face, I know what it is to feel the fool.
- The Laughing Man

- Uh, guys? Have you looked at the timestamp on that comment? TLM added that before we got it.
- Slamm-0!

- Or he got a really good hacker to change the code for him.
- Bull

- Or he's a good enough hacker to do it himself.
- Glitch

- I haven't been able to reach him directly in a while, or I'd ask him myself. Just something to keep an eye on.
- Slamm-0!

- Slamm-0! is taking a security issue seriously? Stone, pass me some of what you're having, because I know I'm not high enough for *that*.
- Glitch

IN CLOSING …

Assuming I make it out of here alive, I'll log in to JackPoint and talk about the file a bit. I'm still not comfortable with it and, as you can tell, it's more of a collection of notes and speculation instead of true scientific thoughts laid into a proper format, but, I've been guzzling tequila and some medical herbs that I don't quite recognize out here, so I'll be amazed if it comes through at all. Elijah, signing off, hopefully not for the last time.

- And for those who've been pestering me for the past week since the files dropped, I can say both that he made it through and that he's here to answer a few questions. Go easy on him, kids, he's been through some rough times, and I'm not sure how long he'll be able to stay. He's still recovering.
- Bull

- Hello everyone.
- Elijah

- **8.9 GP OF DATA DELETED BY SYSOP**

- Yes yes, we're all glad you're back/glad to see you etc. On topic, please.
- Glitch

- So, how'd you get banged up, anyway?
- Butch

- One of the areas I went to had a few Azzies around who hadn't gotten word that they lost the territory a couple of years ago. Extraterritoriality, how does that work? And of course, my history with the Big A didn't help things much. At any rate, I was putting my nose where it should not be, and while the bullet barriers worked wonders, I missed the grenade. Shrapnel is not your friend. On the plus side, I don't have any metal parts and my organs are mostly functional, but one kidney's done and there's some other intestinal issues that might require bioware replacement. I'm trying to decide if it's worth it or not. The debt's bad, but I've seen the impact even minor upgrades can have on a magician's aura, and I'm not sure if the tradeoffs worth it.
- Elijah

- I never thought about what it's like for you wizbangers. If somebody'd cut me that bad, I'd upgrade in a nanotick.
- Riot

- Says the kid saving up for her first cybereye.
- Butch

- Still in the PCC?
- Haze

- You'll understand my not answering that just yet? I know that our leak's been … dealt with … but I'm not in any shape to defend myself just now. I'll say that I'm in the Southwest and leave it at that.
- Elijah

- When you need an extraction, I've got you covered. Gratis.
- 2XL

- So, here's the million nuyen question: Was it worth it?
- Haze

- I'll let you judge yourself when the paper hits peer review. Looking over the notes I sent you is just painful to read now. They're jumbled, out of sorts, lacking proper attribution and footnotes—academics would dismiss these rambles without even consideration. Getting things together properly will take months. Still, I'm glad that the data got out. If the worst would have happened, I needed this to get out.
- Elijah

- I appreciate the risk and all, but honestly, most of this is information that we could have gathered up on our own, over time. Where's that Elijah I used to know? The one with cutting-edge theories and who talks about angles that no one else perceives? Surely this isn't the whole of it.
- Winterhawk

- Wait. You knew this drek already?
- Riot

- Elijah?
- Winterhawk

- Butch? Can you check his vitals remotely?
- Winterhawk

- No need. I'm here. I was just. That is. <sigh> T h e r e ' s one part I haven't detailed yet.
- Elijah

- Here we go.
- Glitch

- The entire reason I was down in the Rio Gambit territory was to get my astral eyes on the prize. In this case, that's the fovae, magical nullspace that's only been found in Aztlan. I can confirm that they're real, which we essentially knew. They're not mana voids, or at least they aren't in the traditional way.

Magical energies that enter them are snuffed out, and paranormal animals that are forced into them don't die as they would in a true magic vacuum. Instead, they lose their paranormal abilities while they're in them. Spirits won't go in them no matter how well bound, but elementals will.
- Elijah

- What happens?
- Winterhawk

- They get pulled through and vanish. No matter how large the elemental, no matter how small the fovae, the elemental just … breaks apart… and the pieces are sucked through. It's so fast that you can barely process it, and you can't see the damn hole that they fall through. From a distance, it's the same as everything else, both in the material world and the astral, but when a spell hits it? Poof. Gone.
- Elijah

- That eradication of magic is expected from a mana void, but it should kill the paracritter. I'm puzzled.
- The Smiling Bandit

- Well, I wasn't worried before, but if Smiling Bandit's at a loss for words, I'm fraggin' terrified.
- Bull

- The magic isn't eradicated.
- Elijah

- Say on …
- Winterhawk

- It's moved. I want to say "flushed." It leaves here and goes somewhere else, akin to a metaplane but different. If an astral form glances it, your perception goes wonky for an hour or two and you won't really understand what happened, but you don't die. You can even switch to astral perception inside of one and you won't empty out like you do in a true void. It feels like you're being sucked out of your body through your eyeballs, but you're still inside your body, so you don't leave, but …
- Elijah

- Wait. You didn't try that, did you?
- Winterhawk

- Elijah?
- Winterhawk

- … you did, didn't you?
- Winterhawk

- Yes.
- Elijah

- Jesus
- Winterhawk

- Is that bad?
- Riot

- In a mana void, where there's no astral energy, the empty space is "hungry," for lack of a better word. Turn your astral energies on inside of one, they get torn from your body. Think of what happens when a person goes into the vacuum of space in their birthday suit.
- Jimmy No

- Pop.
- Riot

- Right. Pop. Only in space, it takes a while. You have a minute, give or take, to get back inside before the damage is too great. Turns out that skin and meat are both quite good at keeping your important bits inside where they belong. Amusingly, if you hold your breath, you're in greater danger than if you exhale. There's … well, I'm going into lecture mode. The important thing to remember that, in space, the metahuman body has a small window. For the astral form, lacking any of that protective shell, the situation is dire.
- The Smiling Bandit

- Measured in nanoseconds.
- Winterhawk

- Ghost!
- Riot

- For the record, it wasn't as bad as when my astral form dove in.
- Elijah

- !!!
- Winterhawk

- In the name of scien—
- Elijah

- HELL NO.
- Haze

- There's no record of—
- Elijah

- THERE'S A REASON FOR THAT!
- Winterhawk

- Calm down, everyone. He broke every rule of research with this, but if I can mix my metaphors, it's too late to appeal to reason after Doctor Marshall has injected himself with the serum. All we can do now is record the results.
- The Smiling Bandit

- I don't condone this.
- Winterhawk

- I didn't ask you to.
- Elijah

- You can talk about it later. For now, Bandit's right. What did you learn, Elijah?
- Glitch

- It was hard to handle when it happened, and once you add the drugs and the alcohol, the pain medication …
- Elijah

- Stop stalling.
- Haze

- There was something there.
- Elijah

- So, they're gateways to the metaplanes after all?
- Haze

- Yes. No. Maybe. It's like a one-way mirror, but not.
- Elijah

- No pressure, Elijah. You can write it up in more detail later.
- Bull

- No! No, it … I can't. Every day, it fades. Some of it's burned into my retina and I can never unsee it, but most of it gets further away. Like a dream, but … if I don't get this out, I might swallow it all. There's something on the far side, a metaplane, but not. There's a pathway, but it's blocked. It feels like a membrane, but my mind constructed it as a sort of canyon, if that makes sense. A canyon with the astral on one side, with me, and I could feel the other metaplanes, the more traditional ones, beside me, but across that canyon was something else. Something alien.
- Elijah

- Oh drek.
- Bull

- Whatever it was, I can't even … eyeballs. Eyeballs and teeth and tendrils and … it… the shapes. There aren't words for the shapes, but I remember the eyes. I'll always remember the eyes. And it talked.
- Elijah

- Was there a bridge?
- Bull

- Yes! But it was broken. That's the thing. Whatever was on the other side couldn't reach the bridge. It couldn't repair it, it couldn't approach it, but I could. It wanted me to do so. It made offers … knowledge. So much knowledge …
- Elijah

- Drek drek drek
- Bull

- Something you want to share with the class, Bull?
- Glitch

- Gotta call Frosty.
- Bull

- **ADMIN BULL HAS LOGGED OUT**

- Well this went from interesting to *very* interesting! Popcorn?
- Haze

- For the record, thanks to Glitch, I *can* get some readings from here. Elijah, I'm not happy with your heart rate or your blood pressure right now. Have you had your medicine?
- Butch

- Later! Later, I swear. This needs to be said before I forget. Please, a moment.
- Elijah

- **ADMIN BULL HAS LOGGED IN**
- **USER FROSTY HAS LOGGED IN**

- Well, this should b-
- Haze

- **USER ORANGE QUEEN HAS LOGGED IN**
- **USER WORDSMYTH HAS LOGGED IN**

- … oh shit.
- Haze

- **USER LAUGHING MAN HAS LOGGED IN**

- OH SHIT
- Haze

- This is a most unexpected invite, Mr. McAllister. My dear former apprentice was ever so insistent that I—
- The Laughing Man

- Frag you now and forever. I'll bathe in your blood later you bastard, but this? You need to hear this.
- Bull

- So many things I was offered, if only I'd help repair the bridge. Others had been there, others had lifted a rock here, a rope there, but they were only small steps of a marathon. They needed so much work to repair the bridge and they had time, they had so much time, but they were also wanting to cross sooner. They can't. They have to be invited. They have to be reached by us, they can't do it themselves. They need our help, but they can help us. They can send things. Knowledge. Whispers. Power. Answers. So many answers to so many questions!
- Elijah

- Can anyone tell me what this is all about?
- Glitch

- Silence! This is a thing which should not be!
- Wordsmyth

- Motherfucker, you're going to tell me to shut up? In my house?!
- Glitch

- Stand down! Glitch, please. You don't know how much this is costing me.
- Bull

- You're paying them?
- Glitch

- No, but there's a debt. Long story. Tell you later. Just … stand down, okay?
- Bull

- Daaaaaaamn.
- Haze

- The bridge. How far did it go?
- The Laughing Man

- The bridge? It's hard…. My eyes were closed, my hands over my ears but I could still hear… I could still see …
- Elijah

- How many steps?
- Wordsmyth

- Four. Four steps.
- Elijah

- That is more than two, Laughing Man.
- Wordsmyth

- But how many were there before?
- The Laughing Man

- Too many.
- Bull

- This one has seen the bridge?
- Wordsmyth

- One of them.
- The Laughing Man

- And it cost me my brother.
- Bull

- I'm so sorry.
- Frosty

- Did you repair the bridge?
- Wordsmyth

- Why the frag would think that?
- Bull

- Not you. Him.
- The Laughing Man

- I ... don't ... it's so hard to focus ...
- Elijah

- You must! Did. You. Make. Any. Repairs.
- Wordsmyth

No. There was so much knowledge there, so many answers, but ... the rope was made of entrails and the rocks were skulls. I couldn't ...
> Elijah

Then there's salvation possible for you. I will come to you soon, Elijah. Help is on the way.
> The Laughing Man

Impossible. No one knows where I am.
> Elijah

Difficult is not impossible, only difficult. Wordsmyth. Frosty. Mr. McAllister. *tips hat*
> The Laughing Man

USER LAUGHING MAN HAS DISCONNECTED

Elijah? I need you to look up for a moment. Look up, and think of your shoes.
> Wordsmyth

What?
> Elijah

Look up and think of your shoes. What color are they?
> Wordsmyth

White. I had to buy new ones after the last ones were ruined form the mud. Those were quality boots.
> Elijah

What the hell? Vitals just dropped halfway to normal.
> Butch

If you'd like to keep it that way, avoid this topic for the next day or so. Once Laughing Man arrives, your friend will recover completely. For now, he needed to think about something mundane to bring his mind back from somewhere it has no business being.
> Wordsmyth

What the hell is going on?
> Glitch

USER WORDSMYTH HAS DISCONNECTED

Sorry guys. There are rules.
> Frosty

USER FROSTY HAS DISCONNECTED

Can I tell you how happy I am to be here right now?
> Haze

Listen, my head's back for a minute, but here's the thing. I mentioned I couldn't trust Universal Magic Theory anymore?
> Elijah

More important things are brewing.
> Winterhawk

I'll deal with that, but you have to listen. The core tenet of UMT is that all magic flows from the same source. That astral energies are formed by living beings, and all of us—hermetics, shamans, voodoo, psionics, whatever—draw our power from the same place. It's wrong. There are other places. Deep in the metaplanes, not connected to us at all, not connected to astral space, full of inhuman things, inhuman shapes, inhuman thoughts. Magic can come from other sources.
> Elijah

Impossible.
> Haze

There are reports of mundanes being discovered to have magic later, but they were considered to have always had the Talent, just having been missed in testing. A few have later been discovered to be the result of spirit pacts, but even then, that's an astral construct. It falls inside the paradigm.
> Winterhawk

There are some insect shamans that were mundane. They received power from the Queens. I'd always thought it was a spirit pact, but maybe this is bigger than that?
> Haze

Yes. The power's there, but they have trouble connecting to us. It's too far to reach. Someone has to step near enough that they can speak to them. Once they have one, then they can bring others. I don't know how many can go there. I got lucky.
> Elijah

Unlucky.
> Haze

There're more places. The bridges were destroyed more than twenty years ago. Or, well, one was. There were supposed to be others, but I only saw the one.
> Bull

This is going to be a great story.
> Haze

- Later. For now, I have to get the taste of asking that bastard for help out of my mouth. Elijah, you good? Wiz.
- Bull

ADMIN BULL HAS LOGGED OUT

- There's a lot to unpack here, Elijah, and I'm not feeling confident. Send me your location. We need to talk in person.
- Winterhawk

- Yes. No. Maybe. I need some time. Help is on the way.
- Elijah

- I don't trust him. Let me at least join you astrally. I can be there in five minutes.
- Winterhawk

- Shit. Injured rolling in. Riot? We gotta roll.
- Butch

- Hai, sensei.
- Riot

USER BUTCH HAS LOGGED OUT
USER RIOT HAS LOGGED OUT

- Actually, I'm going to close this down. Last time those damn pointy-eared bastards dropped in, they rebooted the place in the process. I want to make sure these files get saved. Everybody out.
- Glitch

- Elijah?
- Winterhawk

- Check your PMs.
- Elijah

USER WINTERHAWK HAS LOGGED OUT
USER ELIJAH HAS LOGGED OUT
USER 2XL HAS LOGGED OUT

- Thank you for a very enlightening evening, everyone. I need to make certain I'm on certain mailing lists. Taa!
- The Smiling Bandit

USER THE SMILING BANDIT HAS LOGGED OUT

- Save, reboot, and restart on the way once I get into command.
- Glitch

- **ADMIN GLITCH HAS LEFT THIS NODE**
- Well damn. Guess I'll turn out the lights.
- Haze

- <munching animation> Who made this Slamm-0!-brand popcorn? It's delicious.
- Orange Queen

- Right. No one will believe this.
- Haze

WILD SUMMONING RULES

While wild spirits follow most spirit rules, there are a few exceptions listed below. An important note is that the rules embody what is known in the magical community as of 2079. Wild spirits are not yet fully understood, and as research continues, more types may be discovered and formerly unknown abilities or restrictions may make themselves known. Feel free to create your own wild spirits in your game using the ones shown here as a guide.

WILD REPUTATION

While Astral Reputation (p. 207, *Street Grimoire*) can tell you how notorious you are in the spirit world, your Wild Reputation will tell you how respected you are by wild spirits. Your Wild Reputation is based on both how well you treat the astral world and how well you combat the corrupted aspects of it, such as toxic spirits. It's important to note that characters will accrue a reputation whether they know it or not, and that word in the astral travels both quickly and widely. Those who are friendly will find themselves welcomed with open arms, while those who are known to abuse spirits or harm the environment will find themselves with a far more Faustian welcome.

The following chart is a guideline for the Wild Index, which is the basis of a Wild Reputatiom and a tool for the gamemaster to track characters' stats. Gamemasters have final say in how the index is applied; if they feel that the action undertaken is taking advantage of the system, rather than accurately reflecting the in-game world, they should feel free to deny any bonuses to the character seeking an advantage.

ACCRUING WILD INDEX

The following actions increase a character's Wild Index by the listed amount. A character may not increase their Wild Index with the same action within a single twenty-four hour period.

- Disrupting a toxic spirit: That spirits' Force
- Destroying disrupted toxic spirit in its native metaplane: That spirit's Force x 2
- Cleansing disrupted toxic spirit: That spirit's Force x 3
- Destroying a toxic power site: That power site's Rating x 5
- Cleansing a toxic power site: That power site's Rating x 10
- Releasing a spirit with services remaining: 1 per service lost
- Banishing a spirit controlled by a mage: 2 per service lost
- Temporarily awakening a slumbering wild spirit: 1
- Permanently awakening a slumbering wild spirit: That spirit's Force
- Creating an ally spirit: That spirit's Force
- Willingly setting an ally spirit free: That spirit's Force x 3
- Successfully calling a wild spirit: 1
- Accepting a spirit marker: (Spirit marker's Rating)
- Breaking a spirit marker: Subtract twice what was gained
- Binding a spirit of any kind: Subtract that spirit's Force
- Bringing toxicity to a natural area: –1
- Bringing toxicity to a power site: Subtract that power site's Rating
- Turning a spirit toxic: Subtract that spirit's Force x 2

- Destroying a power site: Subtract that power site's Rating x 5
- Turning a power site toxic: Subtract that power site's Rating x 10

The gamemaster is encouraged to keep a character's Wild Index secret until its effects begin to impact gameplay.

WILD REPUTATION

A character's Wild Reputation begins at 0. For every 25 points of Wild Index a character accumulates, their Wild Reputation increases by 1. When calling a wild spirit or conducting interactions with wild spirits that require social skills a character gains a positive dice pool modifier equal to his Wild Reputation.

A character can reduce their Astral Reputation by permanently sacrificing 2 points of Wild Reputation for every point of Astral Reputation.

CALLING WILD SPIRITS

Wild spirits may not be Conjured in the traditional way. They exist where they will and cannot be forced into service so casually by metahumans, but they may be called. Calling a Wild Spirit may be done in one of two ways. The first is to attempt to force them to appear via Conjuring. This is an Opposed Test using Summoning + Magic [Force] vs. the Wild Spirit's Force, requiring a number of hits equal to (1 + Summoner's Astral Reputation) to succeed. If the required number of hits are generated, the spirit appears, but it owes the summoner no services; it is simply present. The summoner may then address it as they choose. The second way is to travel to a location where a wild spirit is present and attempt to catch its interest. The social skills of Con, Etiquette, Negotiation, and Performance are all applicable, requiring a number of hits equal to the spirit's Force to cause it to appear to see what this mortal is all about. Intimidation may also be used with a similar target, but a success will cause the spirit to see the intimidator as a worthy foe, and it will be looking for a challenge when it appears. Lastly, a character may sacrifice 1 Karma, either with a small bit of their own personal matter (blood, hair, flesh) or while feeling strong emotion (hate, fear, grief), which will always attract the spirit's interest.

Regardless of the method used, if a wild spirit is not near the character attempting to call it, no spirit will appear.

Wild spirits are most often found around power sites, finding the area pleasing and drawing a level of sustenance from it. Others will claim their own astral territory, with more powerful spirits claiming a larger territory. A Force 1 spirit's territory could be as small as the space beneath a child's bed or a mushroom ring in the woods, a Force 3 spirit's as large as an apartment, garage, or clearing in the woods, while a Force 6 spirit could claim an entire apartment complex, the sewers of a city block, or a peaceful lake or hill in the countryside. The gamemaster has full control on whether a wild spirit is present or not. Rumors of where a spirit is frequently seen can serve as an adventure to find such an area where a wild spirit might be met, called, and related to in the future. Areas that have been touched by the Yellowstone Incident are positively crawling with wild spirits, while mana ebbs or voids are devoid of any.

DEALING WITH WILD SPIRITS

Unlike ordinary spirits, wild spirits are not beholden to any magician and have their own agenda, be it as simple as frolic in the sunlight or as complex as masterminding an expansion of corporate influence. Each wild spirit should be treated as an NPC in their own right, with wants, desires, and fears, and they should display all the agency that comes with these traits. The spirit will be willing to make deals, as long as it gets something in return, but it may value things in a way different than a metahuman. Deals are considered made when a wild spirit generates a spirit marker with someone. While the currency of choice when dealing with the spirit world is Karma (which always bears a small token cost of physical, emotional, or mental material), most are willing to bargain for other things. Some are fond of physical material, such as sugar and tobacco often coveted by Caribbean spirits of man. Reagents are useful almost anywhere in the world, while some spirits are fond of tasks, such as destroying a nearby toxic spirit or preventing a local garden from being paved over, while others have more exotic desires. Wild Spirits are perfectly willing and able to walk away from a deal and may be insulted if not given the respect they feel they deserve. In general, a wild spirit negotiates to discharge a debt first, get something it wants second, and to teach someone a better way to behave third.

A spirit marker comes with a Rating from 1 to 6. This spirit marker is linked to both the character and spirit's astral signature, and each party is always aware of how many services are remaining via the marker and whether the deal has been broken. A wild spirit is always considered present with anyone who holds a spirit marker with it and may be called as normal. A wild spirit decides what Rating of a spirit marker it will offer, which is usually equal to the character's Wild Reputation + 1. A character may negotiate for a larger spirit marker, but the spirit may refuse. A character may also negotiate for a smaller spirit marker, but they know that this is often seen as insulting to the spirit. A spirit marker requires that the character buy it, in effect trading a Service for a "service," with the spirit usually setting a price in terms of what the character must do, but a character may suggest similar payment using the guidelines shown below. The gamemaster, as always, is the final arbitrator of what's a fair deal.

WILD SPIRIT SERVICE TABLE

RATING	SERVICE
1	A Performance requiring a number of hits equal to the wild spirit's Force. A Status for twenty-four hours. Future favor.
2	A Status for a week. An immediate favor.
3	A Status for a month. Permanently awakening a slumbering wild spirit.
4	A Status for a year and a day. Arranging a temporary power site creation or attuning an existing one to wild.
5	A Status for life. Creating, then setting free, an ally spirit. Destroying a toxic power site.
6	Creating a permanent power site. Cleansing a toxic power site.

An offering of Karma equal to the wild spirit's Force, or a matching value in material goods that the spirit enjoys, is usually appropriate and certainly acceptable for a Rating 1 or 2 marker.

A Status can take many forms. Ultimately it's an agreement between the character and the spirit to either undertake a type of behavior or to avoid

one for the duration of the agreement. This Status is never the sort that would end a life, such as not eating or drinking for a year, but are intended to showcase the character's obligation and implied veneration of the spirit. Openly wearing a token of a beast spirit (tooth or feather, for example) when in public, greeting the sunrise with a loud song, never harming a certain type of animal (popular with both beasts of prey animals and vermin), or never talking above a whisper are all appropriate for Rating 1 or 2 markers, while larger markers are more demanding. To not cut your nails or hair is fitting for a Rating 4, for example; other possibilities are to not eat meat (including faux meat, like a soyburger), or to paint one's face blue for the duration. An even larger marker could require the character to tattoo themselves with the spirit's chosen glyph, only walk backwards, or to never bathe. This kind of Status has led to unusual behavior in mystics throughout history and a study of these mannerisms from Wujen, shamans, and more can give you many more examples. More powerful spirits will, of course, ask for greater boons in return for their favor.

In return, the wild spirit can be asked to perform a service, as if it were a bound spirit. It should be reminded that anyone, magician or not, may call a spirit and negotiate for a spirit marker. It's entirely possible for a street gang member that's wearing a dog collar around his neck is friends with a local wild dog spirit and can call on them for help, or that a scared child could attract the notice of a powerful spirit that will trade her tears in exchange for destroying the scary people hurting her family in the next room. Some wild spirits are noble, some sinister, and a wise person will get to know one before entering agreements.

Let the buyer beware.

WILD SPIRIT RULES

Wild spirits follow the rules for the type of ordinary spirit that they reflect (air, land, etc.), unless otherwise noted. Wild spirits can never be Summoned.

Wild spirits can be attacked with the Banishing skill. This is a Complex Action, making an Opposed Test of Banishing + Magic [Astral] versus the wild spirit's Force x 2. Add the number of net hits the banisher gets to the total he already had (starting at 0); when this total equals or exceeds the wild spirit's Force x 2 roll, the spirit is disrupted. The Drain Value for this attempt is equal to the number of hits (not net hits) on the spirit's final Defense test, with a minimum Drain Value of 2. If the spirit's Force is greater than the banisher's Magic rating, the drain is physical; otherwise its Stun.

If a wild spirit is disrupted, for the remainder of this round and until the end of the Banisher's next action, a magician, including the banisher, can attempt to bind the wild spirit in order to force it into serving them and generating services as per a normal binding attempt. It doesn't matter what type of spirit it is or what tradition the binder uses in this case. Wild spirits bound in this way are as furious about the situation as they are helpless to do anything about it. If the spirit has a domain, this bound state continues if the binder leaves the spirit's domain, but the spirit cannot leave the area, nor may it be summoned to another. It will simply wait, fuming, until the binder returns to command it again. When the binder's services expire, the wild spirit will be certain to look for opportunities to repay the magician for the treatment they received.

WILD NATURE SPIRITS

Wild nature spirits have the **Domain** quality. In return, they gain one additional Optional Power from their usual list.

WILD BEAST SPIRITS

Wild beast spirits are the most diverse type of wild spirit, and you should take time to adjust them in a way fitting for the type of beast that they embody. A beast spirit may take as many beast traits as its Force, but each may only be taken once unless otherwise noted. These beast traits help define the spirit in a way that aligns with the animal it represents. As always, the gamemaster is the final arbitrator in what is, or isn't, appropriate for a beast spirit to have.

BEAST TRAITS

Large: +1 Body, -2 Reaction
Powerful: +1 Strength, -2 Agility
Small: +1 Reaction, -2 Body
Quick: +1 Agility, -2 Strength
Beautiful: +1 Charisma, -2 Logic
Wise: +1 Logic, -2 Charisma
Clever: +1 Intuition, -2 Willpower
Noble: +1 Willpower, -2 Intuition
Aggressive: +1 Power on Natural Weapon or Unarmed Combat

DOMAIN QUALITY

A spirit with the Domain quality is bound to a location by their nature and may not leave it, but they may move between the material and astral versions of that spot as normal. If disrupted, the spirit lingers in an immaterial state in the astral, rather than travel to a demiplane, and it may be destroyed there as if it was on its home plane. When using the Accident, Guard, or Search powers, use the spirit's Magic x 2, rather than Magic x 1 as normal.

Vicious: -4 AP on Natural Weapon or Unarmed Combat
Durable: +3 physical damage boxes
King: +3 Charisma when using the Animal Control power.
Keen: +4 Magic for using the Search power.
Sneaky: +3 Magic for using the Concealment power on itself only.
Deadly: +2 Magic for using the Venom power.

The exact combinations will depend on the type of beast the spirit reflects. A wild beast spirit (rat) might take Small, Quick, Clever, Sneaky, or King, for instance, while a wild beast spirit (owl) might take Wise and Sneaky.

A wild beast spirit may trade two traits for a new skill if it's appropriate. A wild spirit (beaver) might take the Crafting skill, for instance, but not Repair Ground Vehicles or Automatics.

A wild beast spirit may also trade two traits to add an appropriate Power to the Optional Powers line, but it must still buy those powers as usual. (A spirit gains 1 optional power per 3 Force.) A wild beast spirit (rat) could add Pestilence (p. 197 *Street Grimoire*) to its optional powers, but an owl could not.

Traits, skills, and Optional Powers allow you to construct wild beast spirits that are closer to the way animals in assorted regions are perceived, making a Chinese rat quite different from a British one.

WILD SPIRITS OF MAN

Like wild nature spirits, wild spirits of man have the Domain quality and gain one additional optional power. Wild spirits of man are easier to find, due to their domains being rather clearly defined in the material world, and their effective reach is similarly known. Corporate spirits, in particular, can never cross from areas clearly flagged as belonging to their corporation of choice. The easy way to remember is if it's extraterritorial, it's in their domain.

WILD URBAN SPIRITS

CERAMIC SPIRITS

B	A	R	S	W	L	I	C	EDG	ESS	M
F	F+1	F+2	F	F	F	F	F	F/2	F	F

Initiative	((F x 2) +2) + 2D6
Astral Initiative	(F x 2) + 3D6
Skills	Assensing, Astral Combat, Exotic Ranged Weapon, Perception, Unarmed Combat
Powers	Astral Form, Concealment, Confusion, Engulf, Materialization, Movement, Sapience, Search
Optional Powers	Accident, Binding, Elemental Attack, Energy Aura, Enhanced Senses (Enhanced Vision), Guard, Skill (choose an appropriate technical skill)

METAL SPIRITS

B	A	R	S	W	L	I	C	EDG	ESS	M
F+4	F-2	F-1	F+4	F	F-1	F	F	F/2	F	F

Initiative	((F x 2) – 1) +2D6
Astral Initiative	(F x2) + 3D6
Skills	Assensing, Astral Combat, Exotic Ranged Weapon, Perception, Unarmed Combat
Powers	Astral Form, Binding, Guard, Materialization, Movement, Sapience, Search
Optional Powers	Concealment, Confusion, Engulf, Elemental Attack, Fear

ENERGY SPIRITS

B	A	R	S	W	L	I	C	EDG	ESS	M
F+1	F+2	F+3	S–2	F	F	F+1	F	F/2	F	F

Initiative	((F x 2) + 3) + 2D6
Astral Initiative	(F x 2) + 3D6
Skills	Assensing, Astral Combat, Exotic Ranged Weapon, Flight, Perception, Unarmed Combat
Powers	Accident, Astral Form, Confusion, Elemental Attack, Energy Aura, Engulf, Materialization, Sapience
Optional Powers	Fear, Guard, Noxious Breath, Search
Weaknesses	Allergy (Water, Severe)

AIRWAVE SPIRITS

B	A	R	S	W	L	I	C	EDG	ESS	M
F+2	F+3	F+4	F–3	F	F	F	F	F/2	F	F

Initiative	((F x 2) + 4) + 2D6
Astral Initiative	(F x 2) + 3D6
Skills	Assensing, Astral Combat, Exotic Ranged Weapon, Imitation, Perception, Running, Unarmed Combat
Powers	Accident, Astral Form, Concealment, Confusion, Materialization, Sapience, Search
Optional Powers	Elemental Attack, Energy Aura, Fear, Guard, Psychokinesis

VEHICLE SPIRITS

The nature of vehicle spirits makes them more comfortable traveling well-worn paths rather than branching out to new locations. When they are seen in the wild, they typically are traveling paths familiar to their type of vehicle, and left to their own devices they would likely continue following those paths. The result of this is that vehicle spirits are treated as having a version of the Home Ground (The Transporter) quality, only with a penalty for operating in unfamiliar environments. When operating in their their selected neighborhood, vehicle spirits receive +2 dice on both Evasion tests and Pilot tests for their vehicle type. When operating outside their Home Ground, though, they receive –2 dice on those tests. They may gain extra abilities in this area if they have the Haunt power (p. 192, *Howling Shadows*).

Vehicle spirits also tend to be somewhat simple-minded. While this can be a relief to summoners, in that they can sometimes avoid the arguments or debates that other spirits may engage in, they do not have a significant amount of creativity to apply to the services they are given, which means instructions for them must be clearly spelled out.

VEHICLE SPIRIT POWERS

Vehicle spirits have a few additional powers available to them: **Evasion, Maneuvering,** and **Stealth**. These function like the autosofts of the same name (p. 269, *SR5*), with a Rating equal to the spirit's Force. There is no separate Targeting power for vehicle spirits; any vehicle spirits with the Natural Weapon critter power are assumed to have the Targeting power equal to their Force, and this is what they use to fire the weapon, rather than the Exotic Ranged Weapon skill. When vehicle spirits have a Natural Weapon, it is a firearm with the typical stats for that weapon. Listed with the Natural Weapon is the type of weapon it should be; gamemasters may select which weapon from that class is used.

SHIP SPIRITS

B	A	R	S	W	L	I	C	EDG	ESS	M
F+4	F–1	F–1	F+2	F	F–2	F	F	F/2	F	F

Initiative	((F x 2) – 1) + 2D6
Astral Initiative	(F x 2) + 3D6
Skills	Navigation, Perception, Pilot Watercraft, Survival, Swimming, Unarmed Combat
Powers	Armor (F), Materialization, Sapience, Toughness
Optional Powers	Aura Masking, Haunt, Natural Weapon (any Cannon or Launcher), Storm

TRAIN SPIRITS

B	A	R	S	W	L	I	C	EDG	ESS	M
F+3	F−1	F−1	F+2	F+1	F−2	F	F	F/2	F	F

Initiative	((F x 2) − 1) + 2D6
Astral Initiative	(F x 2) + 3D6
Skills	Intimidation, Navigation, Perception, Pilot Ground Craft, Unarmed Combat
Powers	Accident, Armor (F), Materialization, Sapience
Optional Powers	Aura Masking, Haunt, Natural Weapon (any Cannon or Launcher), Reinforcement

AUTOMOTIVE SPIRITS

B	A	R	S	W	L	I	C	EDG	ESS	M
F+1	F+2	F+1	F	F	F−2	F	F	F/2	F	F

Initiative	((F x 2) + 1) + 2D6
Astral Initiative	(F x 2) + 3D6
Skills	Navigation, Perception, Pilot Ground Craft, Running, Unarmed Combat
Powers	Accident, Evasion, Maneuvering, Materialization, Sapience
Optional Powers	Aura Masking, Haunt, Movement, Natural Weapon (any Machine Gun; motorcycles and lighter vehicles can only have LMGs)

AIRCRAFT SPIRITS

B	A	R	S	W	L	I	C	EDG	ESS	M
F+2	F+1	F	F+1	F	F−2	F	F	F/2	F	F

Initiative	(F x 2) + 2D6
Astral Initiative	(F x 2) + 3D6
Skills	Free-fall, Navigation, Perception, Pilot Aircraft, Unarmed Combat
Powers	Evasion, Maneuvering, Materialization, Sapience, Stealth
Optional Powers	Aura Masking, Dive Attack, Haunt, Natural Weapon (any Cannon or Launcher), Search

AWAKENED VEHICLES

The spirit has the base abilities of a spirit of the type it is (automotive, ship, etc.), but is trapped as a dual-natured being, situated in the physical form of the vehicle it once was. In most cases, this will leave it immobile, or functionally so, but some vehicles have Awakened while still fully functional. These vehicles may be as mobile as they would ordinarily be. Some display unusual spirit powers, such as a car with the ability to drive up walls or a ship that sails through sand, but these are quite rare (as always, the gamemaster has final say on designing these unique spirits).

HERMETIC ELEMENTALS

Mechanically, these are simply spirits of air, earth, fire, and water, with one modification: the **Ele-mental** quality. Spirits with the Elemental quality have their mental attributes (Logic, Intuition, Charisma, and Willpower) reduced by a number equal to half their Force (rounded down). So a Force 3 elemental will have those attributes reduced by 1, while a Force 6 Elemental will have those attributes reduced by 3 (to a minimum adjusted attribute of 1, of course). Elementals are those slow-witted and poor thinkers who are prone to follow commands with little agency of their own. There are some benefits, however. Spirits with the Elemental quality are more easily bound, with any Summoning or Binding test that generates at least 1 service after being fully resolved gaining an additional service. Beyond this, actions taken on elementals never generates either Spirit Index or Wild Index, as they are loyal to a fault and do not spread information about their master. Lastly, in those areas where leashing is an issue, a spirit with the Elemental quality never tries to free itself from servitude.

Elementals should be portrayed as stoic servitors of their master, following orders instantly and having no care for mistreatment or any desire to be more than a simple tool. Wild spirits regard them with pity and their masters with scorn, but to those who control them, only obedience truly matters and the thoughts of untamable wild spirits is of no concern.

At character creation, any mage that can summon air, earth, fire, and water spirits may choose to be a hermetic elementalist, losing the ability to summon their fifth spirit, regardless of the type, but all spirits they do summon will have the Elemental quality. Any other mage that can summon those four spirits may become a hermetic elementalist via Paradigm Shift (p. 43) but will lose the ability to summon all other spirit types when they do so. When a mage is created as, or becomes, a hermetic elementalist, they gain an Astral Reputation score of 6. This may be reduced in the usual way. Taking Paradigm Shift again to leave this path will not reset their Astral Reputation, but it is the first step to take before they can.

SPIRITS AS CONTACTS

It should be noted that free spirits and wild spirits may be taken as contacts, like any other NPC. They will be unwilling to provide services without payment but may be as friendly and as handy for information as any other. Upkeeping these contacts will usually require a Spirit Marker, with a Rating equal to half their Connection rating, but this is required less often than a normal flesh-

and-blood contact, as simply being in their presence and talking generates low-level emotional energy that they absorb.

A particularly fun version of this is a wild beast spirit in the form of the character's Mentor, taken with Connection 1 but Loyalty 6. This contact can serve as a spirit guide, appearing before the character to offer some cryptic advice or to talk through problems while not seeming to offer any material aid at all. In a dire situation, they might take physical action, but by far their preferred course of action is to nudge the character toward a path, then let them walk it on their own.

OPTIONAL RULES

For those gamemasters that wish to see a more living world, here are some optional rules that you might add to your game to reflect these new spirit types and effects.

THE MENTOR'S MASK

Formerly known as the Shaman's Mask, the Mentor's Mask is a side effect that any magician with a Mentor spirit may chose. Once chosen, the mask is always in effect when they use magic and may not be switched off. A Mentor's Mask is a side effect of using magic, bleeding some energy off to create an illusion of the character's Mentor around them that can be seen on the material plane, making their magic more obvious but less taxing. Characters who have a Mentor's Mask effect reduce all Drain by 1, but the threshold for noticing them using magic is lowered by 3 to a minimum of 1 (see p. 280, *SR5*).

Adepts may also choose to have a Mentor's Mask if they have a Mentor spirit, which they will manifest whenever using an adept power. An adept who chooses to have a mask gains 1 bonus Power Point but generate a mask whenever using any of their adept powers. The threshold for noticing this effect is 6 - (4 x total Power Point cost of the power being used). Thus, a character using Critical Strike will have a threshold of (6 - (4 x 0.5)) or 4, while one using Improved Reflexes 2 will have a threshold of (6 - (4 x 2.5)) or 1 (which is the minimum for the threshold).

The exact nature of the mask varies based on the character, but at a minimum a glowing version of the mentor's head is imposed over the character's own (thus the "mask" name for the effect) but a second voice like the mentor's cry, fur or feather markings across their body, illusory claws or talons

on their limbs, and so forth are commonplace as the threshold lowers.

SPIRIT LEASHING

The connection between a controlled spirit and the controlled is called a leash. In most cases, this simply binds them together, and no real thought is ever given to it. In those areas touched by the Yellowstone Incident, however, spirits struggle against the leash with a desire to free. Gamemasters who wish to restrict the use of spirits in their own games may also use these rules anywhere as the concept of going free spreads like wildfire through the spirit world. When summoning a spirit, or calling on the services of a bound spirit, a magician will need to determine if they keep the leash in a state of being slack or tight. On their turn, a magician may change the state to the other as a free action.

When a spirit is controlled with a slack state, the controller pays it little mind and is not distracted. When a spirit is controlled in a tight state, keeping it under control counts against the magician in the same way as a sustained spell, a -2 penalty to all dice pools other than a Test the Leash roll.

TESTING THE LEASH

A spirit will sometimes Test the Leash, trying to see how tightly it is bound to service. Any time a spirit scores hits on a test equal to or greater than 6 - (Force/2), it Tests the Leash automatically. This means a Force 3 spirit will Test the Leash if it scores 5 hits or more on a test, while a Force 6 spirit will Test the Leash on only 3 hits. When a spirit Tests the Leash, it rolls an Opposed Test pitting its Force x 2 against the controller's usual Drain Resistance. For each net hit the controller scores, the spirit takes 1 Stun Damage. For each net hit the spirit scores, it erases 1 service. If the leash is being held tightly, the controller may suffer one box of Stun damage per service that would be erased rather than lose those services. If the spirit's Force is greater than the controller's Magic, damage taken is Physical instead of Stun.

If a spirit reduces its services owed to 0 in this way, it usually attempts to return to its native metaplane on its next turn. Those spirits that have been treated badly, or that are controlled by someone with an Astral Reputation of 4 or more, will instead attack their former controller. As a reminder, spirits with the Elemental quality never Test the Leash.

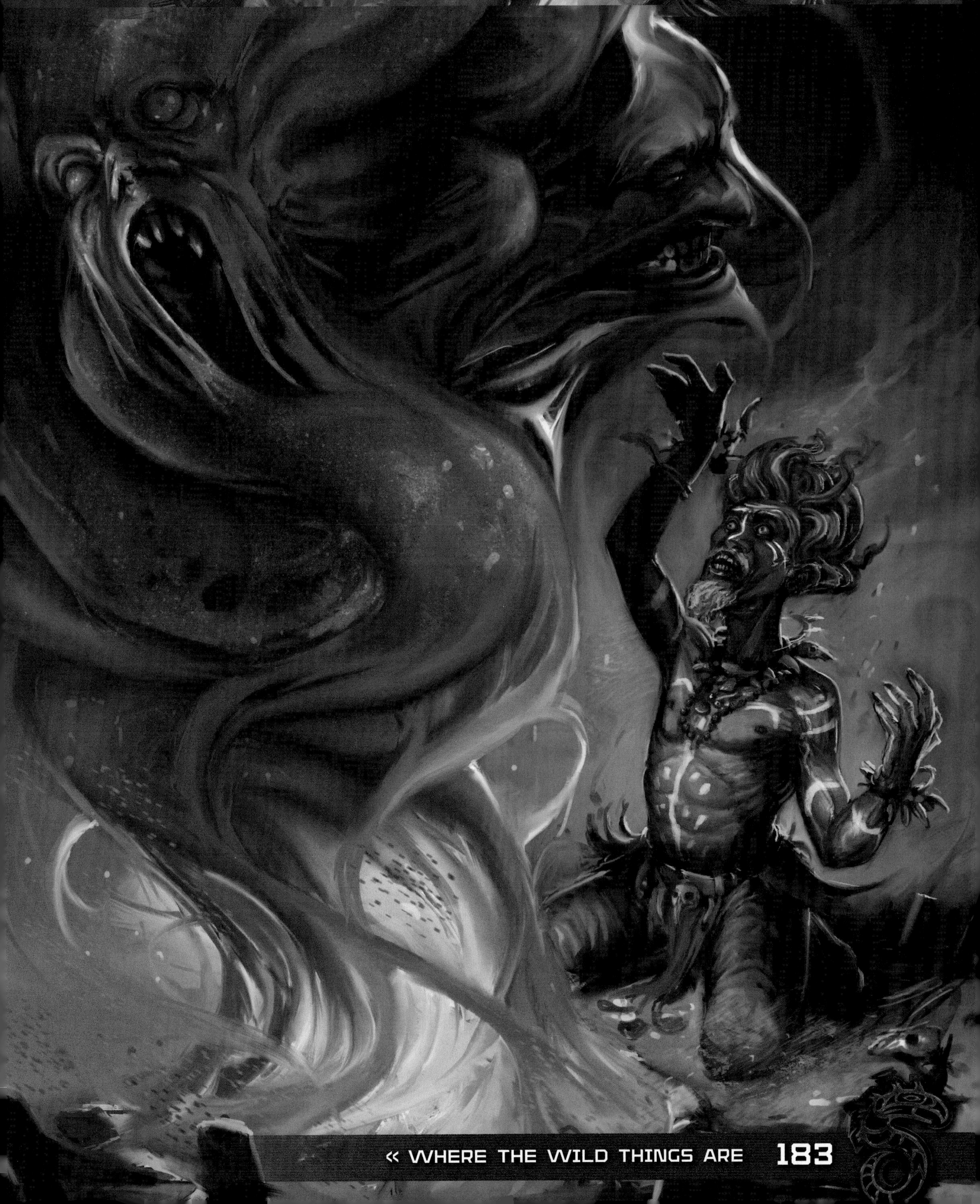

ADVANCED ALCHEMY

Alchemy is the amalgamation of primal mystical power and application of mana with the meticulous research methodology of science. This mystical art is believed to have been discovered during the Fourth World by magicians on the island of Thera, commonly known as Atlantis. The legends surrounding alchemy echoed in the human subconscious during the magical drought of the Fifth World, emboldening scholars to attempt to master the compound formula for transmuting lead into gold. These misguided would-be-magicians, trapped in a dark age devoid of mana and magic, failed to comprehend the essence of this lost art. They falsely believed that alchemy was merely the ability to transmute substances from one form to another; a means to turn simple lead into precious gold.

Mana naturally accumulates in plants, animals, objects, and places heavy with the weight of history. Alchemists harvest reagents from materials that have absorbed this ambient mana and refine them into mystical compounds and alchemical preparations to produce fantastic, otherworldly effects. Once a reagent is spent, the mana within dissipates, but the physical form remains, allowing an alchemist to harvest it later once it reabsorbs mana. The sad truth is most reagents are fairly common but take a good deal of time and skill to locate and harvest as needed. This process isn't cheap or easy, which is why most magicians seek out common reagents at their local talismonger, preferring to pay for the time and expertise over the drudgery of doing it themselves. For more information about harvesting reagents, see p. 304, *SR5*, and p. 209, *Street Grimoire*.

With the proper time and material, an alchemist might brew a potion that extends a magician's ability to astrally project, create a fetish that reduces drain when a specific spell is cast, or generate a manatech alchemical preparation that temporarily increases the limit of a weapon.

The quality of a reagent is measured in terms of drams of orichalcum. Refined and radical reagents can increase the potency and duration of the final product, and they can also decrease the drain cost for its creation. Once the proper formula has been discovered or learned, an alchemist might use a refined or radical reagent to create a mystical compound or alchemical preparation that charges mundane objects to release stored spells when triggered, infuse a torch with an oil that will repel bug spirits when lit, or even brew a potion that will heal wounds or temporarily retard the advancement of mystical illnesses, such as the Human-Metahuman Vampiric Virus. For more information about the quality of reagents, see p. 228, *Street Grimoire;* to explore new refined and radical reagents, see p. 187.

A magician may use any reagent in a pinch, but if it isn't directly from their magical tradition, then it only works at half-strength. For example, a hermetic alchemist can leverage a refined gris-gris bag, but it just doesn't work as well.

In the Sixth World, alchemy has once again captured humanity's imagination. This time it isn't gold for which they dream, but a cure to the plagues of the modern age, the promise of healthy life, and quick solutions for the elite who can afford it. Local talismongers serve as the apothecaries of ages past, curing those who can pay from the neighborhoods while the rich and elite pay for top corporate-generated formulas that keep them young and heathy.

LIFE OF A CORPORATE ALCHEMIST

Once, alchemy was the sole dominion of the elite magicians who prepared their brews and com-

pounds solely for their own benefit or to serve wealthy patrons. The megacorporations sensed profit to be exploited and began to apply their vast resources and knowledge of mass production to push talismonger shops to the edges of society. Why go through the hassle of harvesting a common reagent yourself, or pay an unsavory middleman when you can purchase from a trusted corporation that offers a warranty on their products made to special order? Most folks ignore the rumors about the corporations overharvesting Native land for the mana to produce alchemical preparations that line the shelves of expensive boutique stores promising youth, vigor, and extended life.

Discovering a new formula that remixes standard reagents into new, exciting compounds is a matter of the inspiration of genius mixed in with countless research hours and resources. It might not be easy to purchase inspiration or genius, but when you have unlimited nuyen to throw at a pet project, anything becomes possible. Those with magical talent and the scientific bent often have a strong independent streak, but corporate headhunters get big bonuses for finding young hopefuls with a lack of education and dire economic straits. With their heads filled with promises of a bright, upwardly mobile future, these poor bastards get roped into indentured servitude, hocking their potential for a comfortable present.

Corporate life feels like heaven to the conscripts from the wilds until the alchemists learn propriety information in terms of formulas or information about rare reagents. Success comes at a steep price for the corporate alchemist. The research and development of a new alchemical compound might cost millions of nuyen, but once the formula has been peer reviewed and can be duplicated for mass production, the actual cost for the final product might be relatively minuscule. If another alchemist—or worse, a rival corporation—

learns this formula, millions could be lost. Thus, the secrets of these formulas must be protected at all costs.

A good alchemist is as much an artist as a scientist, and that perfect storm is hard to cultivate. Good corporate citizens understand that privacy is sometimes a luxury that must be denied to protect corporate assets.

MANATECH: RISKS AND REWARDS

Manatech is the catch-all term to describe the alchemical processes that bridge the gap between technology and magic. This encompasses all spells and alchemical compounds that directly affect tech and machines (positively and negatively) to devices specifically engineered to enhance the use or creation of magic. Where there is nuyen to be made or power to be had, both runners and corporations will spare no expense and risk anything to remain on the cutting edge.

NEW SPELL: ALTER BALLISTICS

(MANIPULATION, PHYSICAL)

Type: P	**Range:** T
Duration: I	**Drain:** (F – 2)

The Alter Ballistics spell is a spell unique to the Alchemical Armorer that allows them to alter the ballistic properties of bullets or add helpful effects like noise reduction. This spell only works as an alchemical preparation that uses a bullet as the lynchpin. Bullets used as a lynchpin may only be fired by Single Shot weapons. The preparation must be activated before it is fired or the lynchpin will be destroyed by firing the bullet. When using a command trigger, a character may choose to activate a single preparation normally (with a Simple Action) or any number of bullets (including all of them) at a time with a Complex Action. When activated, the preparation lasts for a number of minutes equal to the Force of the preparation. When crafting the lynchpin, the character must specify and make a record of the effects they would like the bullet to have, in order, from most desired to least desired. When the preparation is activated, each net hit will add the listed properties to the bullet in the specified order until net hits or the list of chosen effects is exhausted.

LIST OF EFFECTS

- Double weapon range (changing all categories of range modifiers).
- –4 dice pool modifier to Perception tests to notice gunfire.
- +1 Accuracy.
- Deformation Resistance: –2 AP, –1 DV. Deformation-resistant bullets do not deform when fired or upon impact, which inflicts a –4 dice pool penalty to any Armorer tests to identify the weapon that fired the bullet. Cannot be used with hollow-point ammunition.
- Increased Deformation: +2 AP, +1 DV. Cannot be used with APDS.
- Astral signature fade time reduced by 50 percent.
- Impact Dispersion: Reduces the Physical limit of a character by 2 when comparing it to the DV to determine knockdown.
- Frangible: Treat any barrier the ammo hits as if its Armor were twice normal.

Mixing magic and technology can bring great rewards. Ask any spell slinger if they haven't considered an upgrade to their senses or body, and they will tell you the same thing. Sometimes it's worth the damage, but it better be important. Incorporating technology into the body of a magician or adept affects their Essence, the source of their magic. The more extensive the cyberware, the deeper the impact on the Essence of the magician or adept. While the more cutting edge and expensive versions of cyberware, or even bioware, can mitigate this damage, nothing can ever eliminate it completely. The same holds true for the effect of magic on technology. The more magic in an area, the more ambient noise. This can, in some instances, impact how technology works, making it more difficult to access the Matrix.

Alchemists are unfortunate in that they suffer in both these instances. Heavy use of magic can affect the tech they use to enhance their creations, just as too much tech can influence the potency of their creations. As such, they are very careful on what combinations they use. The key seems to be using tech to assist in the creation of their project, or as the target, but rarely both. Tools such as the crucible, vault of ages, or alembic are all examples of ways that clever alchemists have managed to leverage the power of technology to create faster and more powerful products. By ensuring that each aspect of the process is carefully balanced between magic and technology, powerful effects can be generated at low risk—something every talismonger or corporation will agree is always the best solution. The other option is to create magical compounds and preparations that have little tech involved in their creation, instead targeting technology itself through machines, the Matrix, or the cyberware of others. This tightrope is hard to walk, but alchemists are always willing to experiment.

The risks and rewards of manatech are myriad. Clever runners will maximize the power while minimizing the cost and risk, something even corporations can agree is the ultimate strategy. The true power of manatech is the constant progress it inspires. Each blending of magic and technology encourages others to take it to the next step. Go one further. Make it better, faster, or cheaper. The constant need sustains this continuing state of progress to remain one step ahead, staying clear of those who are right behind, waiting for a single mistake.

UPDATED REAGENT COST AND EFFECTS

REAGENT	COST (PER DRAM)	AVAILABILITY	EFFECT
Tainted	20¥	—	Increase time to refine by 100 percent
Inferior	30¥	1	Increase time to refine by 50 percent
Subpar	40¥	4	Increase time to refine by 25 percent
Baseline	50¥	6R	No change
Superior	60¥	14R	Reduce time to refine by 25 percent
Prime	70¥	20R	Reduce time to refine by 50 percent
Refined	Type x 5	+4	See **New Ways to Leverage Reagents** (below)
Radical	Type x 25	+8	See **New Ways to Leverage Reagents** (below)

NEW REAGENTS OF THE SIXTH WORLD

Gathering and refining reagents is the staple of the alchemist. Reagents are measured by the specific amount required to be equivalent in strength to a dram of orichalcum. For example, a physical pound of gris-gris dust from a less-refined reagent might only hold the mystical equivalent of a few drams of orichalcum. With the myriad of traditions and paths different practitioners of magic employ, there is always a high demand for reagents of different styles and types. As many traditions are careful to protect their secrets, a successful alchemist or talismonger seeks to provide a vast selection of reagents and takes careful notes about who purchases what.

HARVESTING REAGENTS

Mana flows and pools throughout the Sixth World, creating rich veins where alchemists and talismongers harvest reagents. Sadly for those aspiring entrepreneurs, the safer and better known the area, the less likely it is to find reagents that are rare or powerful and command the highest prices. This quest to find new locations to harvest has led to the discovery of some rare and exotic ingredients that are just now becoming known to alchemists in the shadows as well as their corporate brethren.

OVERHARVESTING REAGENTS

Once an area has been properly harvested of reagents, it can take forty-eight hours or more for the mana to replenish. Sometimes, though, you need what you need and don't have time to wait. It's possible to overharvest a specific area, but it's a desperate and dangerous maneuver. Overharvesting has the very real possibility of tainting the area enough to ensure it will never again be able to collect enough mana to enable the creation of viable reagents. This process also taints the alchemist, reducing the quality of any other reagents they may gather for the next forty-eight hours by one full level (Superior to Base, Base to Subpar, and so forth). Talismongers, corporations, and alchemists alike have no tolerance for those who would permanently destroy valuable resources. And chummer, someone is *always* watching.

To harvest a reagent from an already taxed area, make an Alchemy + Magic [Mental] Test. You gather one dram for every 4 hits on this test if you are in an area suited to your tradition, and one dram for every 6 hits if you're not. Glitching this roll results in the area being totally unsuitable for reagent harvesting for a full week. A critical glitch renders the area permanently dead to the possibility of gathering reagents.

NEW WAYS TO LEVERAGE REAGENTS

Reagents have more uses than just as a key component for different compounds. The different levels of refinement allow for differing and advanced effects depending on their level of sophistication. Below is a list of additional effects that reagents may be used for beyond those listed in *SR5* and *Street Grimoire*. The total amount of bonus effects may not exceed the user's Magic rating. Effects from a Radical reagent are not cumulative with effects from the Refined version of that same reagent.

RAW REAGENTS

These reagents are newly harvested or have yet to undergo refinement by an alchemist.

- Reduce drain by 1 for Ritual Spellcasting tests.
- Raise the limit by 1 for any tests using Magic.
- Create refined reagents (requires 10 drams to be refined into a single dram of refined reagent).

REFINED REAGENTS

These reagents have undergone the refinement process and have attained a new level of power.

- Reduce drain by 2 for tests using skills in the Sorcery group.
- Reduce drain by 1 for binding.
- Raises limit by 5 for all tests using Magic.
- Create Magical Compounds (p. 219, *Street Grimoire*).
- Create radical reagents (p. 210, *Street Grimoire*) (requires 10 drams to be refined into a single dram of radical reagent).

RADICAL REAGENTS

The most powerful version of a reagent, these have gone through the refinement process twice to reach their maximum potential.

- Reduces drain by 2 for tests using skills in the Conjuring group.
- Reduce drain by 4 for tests using skills in the Sorcery group.
- Reduce object resistance by 1 per dram.
- No Force limit for any tests using Magic (though Drain is caluclated as normal).
- Reducing Spirit Index (p. 207, *Street Grimoire*).
- Create orichalcum (Requires 10 drams each of the required reagents listed as per (p. 210, *Street Grimoire*).
- Create fetish (p. 212, *Street Grimoire*).
- Create inanimate vessel (p. 214, *Street Grimoire*).

NEW RARE REAGENTS

The reagents detailed in this section are considered rare and difficult to harvest. They are almost universally usable by different traditions and are in high demand. Their purity of mana makes them desirable, as the smallest amount can go a long way. They are also useful in several new compounds that have been invented to make use of the qualities inherent in each. Even the lowest quality of these are considered superior reagents. The danger in their acquisition can be high, but there are many who are willing to do far more for a few nuyen.

REAGENT: BONE OR HAIR FROM A BAOBHAN SITH

Known as the White Women, the baobhan sith are fae with deep ties to myth and legend (p. 114, *Court of Shadows*). Some believe they are the progenitors of the first vampires as the source of the human metahuman vampiric virus. Others claim they are the source of the tales of nymphs and sirens that lure men to their deaths with their beauty. The baobhan sith appear as hauntingly beautiful women with the terrifying power to alter their very bones into rending talons and razor-sharp teeth. These monsters live off humanoid blood and inflict a strange euphoria in their victims, creating an addiction to being their prey.

Restored access to the Sixth World through the metaplanes has freed the baobhan to once more hunt the mortal plane. A hunter, however, may find themselves prey if they are not careful, as the runners in the shadows are no easy meat. Prey alone is not the only reason the baobhan have returned to the mortal plane of the Sixth World. Status within their kind is based upon a meritocracy. Providing the most use to the whole earns value. In the course of hunting for sustenance, a White Woman may also be seeking to extend her personal network of spies and informants or gain access to a new and valuable skill that would increase her worth or standing back home.

Once properly refined, the bone or hair from a baobhan sith serves as a primary reagent for compounds and preparations that could enhance regeneration and heal physical wounds, or become

a tenacious poison that damages not just the body, but also one's ability to wield magic.

REAGENT: DROP BEAR SALIVA

The mass of jet-black fur and razor sharp teeth known as the drop bear (p. 60, *Howling Shadows*) is a form of Awakened koala. Known carriers of HMHVV II, these omnivorous predators are currently on the bounty list all over the Outback and other areas of Oceania. While they are able to survive on their preferred food source of eucalyptus, they are ambush predators that are always looking for a way to add easy meat to their diet.

Outside of captivity, drop bears are found primarily in the outback of Australia, as well as in forested areas of New Guinea. Recently, some zoos and corporations have begun importing or breeding the beasts, making it possible to find them in other areas, though under very difficult circumstances due to both the bounty and their innate ferocity. Recent discoveries on the alchemical uses of their saliva may rectify this situation swiftly, assuming a synthetic can't be manufactured first.

Alchemically, drop bear saliva has become incredibly popular. A corporate researcher discovered by accident the ability to refine the saliva and create a serum that inhibits the continuing mutation of HMHVV II. While it does not serve as a cure, it stops any progress of the virus as long as the serum is administered on a weekly basis. This serum is not generally known to the public yet, but the black market has erupted with the formula for the creation of the compound, and many willing test subjects have come forward. Other uses for this reagent have been explored but are unconfirmed at this time.

REAGENT: GHOST ORCHID PETALS

Ghost orchids are a particularly rare breed of orchid. They bloom at night by the light of the moon, and the white coloration gives them an otherworldly glow. Researchers into these matters agree that the very rarity of the flower makes it a natural accumulator of mana. When combined with the ambient mana of the Sixth World, this allows these delicate flowers to take on powerful characteristics when properly processed and refined by a skilled alchemist.

Ghost orchids are most commonly found deep within forested areas. They need exposure to direct moonlight to bloom, so they are difficult to obtain in the first place. There has been some limited success in cultivating the flower in greenhouses and such, but the ambient mana must be high in order for them to develop and thrive. Most commonly found in the UCAS areas, their very rarity is part of what makes them such a potent reagent.

When properly refined, ghost orchid petals are powerful reagents that are added into compounds and preparations designed to enhance vision-based perception. They also may be further refined into radical reagents that can allow for increased duration in the astral plane and enhancing one's Charisma.

REAGENT: GROUND KILLDEER ANTLERS

Killdeer (p. 97, *Howling Shadows*) were originally mutated whitetail deer that now breed true as their own unique strain. At first glance, they look similar to their original stock. The primary differences are the sharpened antler tips for goring prey and the elongated muzzle that contains sharp teeth for rending and tearing meat. These hardy creatures are omnivores, though unlike their whitetail predecessors, they subsist primarily on meat and supplement with vegetation when hunting is poor.

This species came into being after radiation mutated the whitetail population in and around the suburbs of Chicago. From there, they have spread to cover entire swathes of the CAS and UCAS, as well as parts of the NAN. Their omnivorous nature makes them strong survivors in most environments. They tend to breed swiftly and are constantly expanding their territory, pushing out the whitetail herds that provide an unwitting camouflage.

Killdeer are sturdy beasts, and alchemists have found many ways to distill that nature into various compounds. Killdeer antlers in particular are potent aids in healing, regeneration, and toxin-resistance compounds. They may also be used in poisons to sap these very characteristics, weakening targets or doing them injury. The rarity of this ingredient is reflected by the difficulty of obtaining the correct type of antler, which is challenging to distinguish from the whitetail, and as such, easily counterfeited.

REAGENT: KAYERI MUSHROOM

Deep within the forests of Tír na nÓg dwell a peculiar faerie known as the kayeri (p. 121, *Court of Shadows*). They are guardians and nurturers of the forest, along with the plants and animals within it. Resembling giant rabbits with extended jaws, carnivorous teeth, and mushrooms growing from their skulls, the kayeri are fierce protectors of their vegetative homes and require any outsiders who wish to access their lands to negotiate for the privilege.

There are only two places one may find a kayeri. Their natural habitat within the forests of Tír na nÓg or select aspected domains of the Sixth World while they hunt down those who have desecrated their protected charges or one of their kin. The second is rather uncommon, as no kayeri wishes to leave its charge or community for very long. It takes an act of desecration or a desire for revenge to lure these protectors from the forests. Once removed, they are fiercely devoted to achieving their goal and returning as swiftly as possible back to their home plane.

Kayeri mushrooms, once refined, are potent curatives for toxins, poisons, or diseases. Their healing properties are some of the most powerful available for alchemists to distill due to their inherent prime quality. While there is danger during the refinement process, the possible benefits that come from these curatives has outweighed the risk of vengeful rabbit fae descending upon the mortal plane. For now.

NEW EXOTIC REAGENTS

The reagents detailed in this section are considered some of the most dangerous and difficult to acquire. They are powerful items that can be used by nearly every known tradition. Due to their inherent flexibility, they are highly sought after and usually quite expensive. Many of them serve as required reagents in some of the more powerful or rare compounds and preparations an alchemist can learn. Only the most adventurous or powerful can harvest these items, as not only are they difficult to find but also deadly to claim.

REAGENT: DRAKE SCALES

Drakes (p. 162, *Howling Shadows*) are powerful metahumans, either born as such or possessing the latent ability to transform. These creatures are the preferred minions of dragons, and most are bound to one or another as servants to the mighty beasts. They do have other uses however, and not merely to themselves. Alchemists and other magicians have found that the different types of drake share a unique property. Their bodies are natural mana accumulators. This facility with mana makes the scales of a drake particularly potent reagents when properly harvested and refined. However, their sympathetic connection makes few drakes willing to part with their scales.

Wherever you find a dragon, chances are you will find at least a few drake servants. This is, however, an incredibly dangerous way of finding harvestable reagents. More common are those who manage to identify lairs of unbound drakes or are lucky enough to clean up after confrontations. Both scenarios offer a somewhat safer avenue to harvest the valuable scales.

Due to the different nature of each species of drake, their scales have been put to many varied uses once refined. Different traditions find varying degrees of synergy dependent on the breed of drake from which the scales originated. All agree they are powerful mana accumulators, and as such, their quality is never less than superior. A notable exception is that any breed of drake scale is useable in the compound formula recently uncovered to combat the physical damage of drain. Predictably, demand for these items has skyrocketed in the magical community and black market.

REAGENT: ORGAN OF INSECT SPIRIT HOST

The rise of the bug spirits and their shamans making deeper inroads into the Sixth World has not been totally without benefit. Alchemists have dis-

covered that the organs of a host of one of these spirits can be a powerful reagent in many types of compounds and preparations. The otherworldly mana within them makes them excellent alchemical agents. Viable even after the death of the host, different organs that have been subjected to the mana of these spirits take on interesting alchemical properties.

Chicago is still considered a hotbed of insect spirit activity, making it one of the most likely places to obtain an infected host, living or dead. The spread of these spirits has made it possible to find them in other areas as well. The corrupted mana of these spirits seems to linger after death, and grave robbing has been on the rise as industrious alchemists follow the age-old adage of waste not, want not.

The most potent use for this reagent is the alchemical compound that bonds the spirit and body of the astral traveler in such a way as to increase their ability to manifest themselves. Other alchemical preparations and formulas that focus on travel or communication have also benefited by the use of these organs steeped in the mana of spirits from another plane.

REAGENT: VEINS OF AN ADEPT

At the core of any type of reagent is its natural ability to accumulate and store mana. As such, some dark tradition alchemists have begun to experiment with the body parts of those known to be a conduit for mana. Thus was born the formula that uses the veins of an adept to negate the risk of drain. Whether from grave robbing or harvesting from captives, this reagent has tempted even the most noble due to the raw power granted by the compounds and alchemical mixtures that make use of them.

Adepts may be found all over the Sixth World and some other planes that connect to it. Finding one already slain, or harvesting the veins from one still living, is another matter altogether. The adept community finds the rise in demand for their body parts for alchemical experimentation abhorrent. They actively seek out those who would use such things for their own particular brand of revenge.

This particular reagent is often harvested by those of dark traditions, enterprising talismongers who have made quite the tidy profit in selling compounds without mentioning the ingredients

THE PHILOSOPHER'S STONE

Rumor, lore, and conspiracy theorists insist that there's an alternative method of harvesting orichalcum. Behind closed doors, they speculate that this is the true meaning of what was known as the Philosopher's Stone. The oft-told tales of turning lead into gold were merely allegory of harvesting the true "gold" of all reagents—orichalcum. None have been willing or able to confirm its existence directly, but legend holds a talented alchemist can discern the scent of the refined orichalcum via the Philosopher's Stone. Some say that the material somehow feels like pure mana. Others say it smells of roses. Ancient stories also say that the Philosopher's Stone is not found but made with exotic reagents and formula lost to the ages. Whether it is a secret rediscovered from the annals of the ancient past or an artifact recovered from some unknown tomb, none can be truly sure.

The legendary Philosopher's Stone grants the possessor virtually unlimited access to orichalcum by reducing the time and materials necessary to refine a dram. It is said that instead of ten of each ingredient as in the normal refinement of orichalcum, only a single dram of each is needed. If true, an alchemist could create ten times the normal amount of orichalcum in a single session. Unlimited riches for the lucky possessor, assuming they could remain in possession of such an artifact long enough to make their fortune. If such an artifact exists, it remains a closely guarded secret by necessity, as there's not an alchemist in the world who wouldn't kill to possess it.

they contain. Many care more about the effect than where it comes from. There are rumors that if the veins of an adept provide such a powerful reagent, perhaps other mana-wielding entities may have similar benefits, but alchemists are rarely willing to encourage that line of thought.

ALTERNATIVE USES FOR ORICHALCUM

Orichalcum is the professional standard across all magical traditions for reagents. This rare material appears as an ethereal golden-orange colored metal with the malleability of tin, and it can't exist without the presence of magic. During the passage of Halley's Comet, there were reports of orichalcum found by miners, alchemists, and researchers. Since 2061, this phenomenon has never been repeated. The only reliable means to harvest orichalcum is for an alchemist to refine ten drams of gold, ten of copper, and ten of cinnabar in a laborious process that takes twenty-eight days to complete a single dram of orichalcum.

Orichalcum is commonly leveraged to supplement power within a compound or preparation. It is universally compatible with any tradition, and as such, is ultimately useful for any alchemist or talismonger. Alchemists have experimented with this potent reagent since the dawn of the Sixth World and have uncovered many uses for it.

A single dram of orichalcum may be used to replace the need for any other specific reagent for a compound or alchemical preparation. Once the orichalcum has been created, an alchemist may now refine that dram further, to change and augment the aura to mimic another specific reagent. For example, when creating the poison known as Lot's Curse (p. 220, *Street Grimoire*), a properly prepared dram of orichalcum may be substituted for the normally required refined Gomorrah apple. An alchemist must have previously sensed the aura to be mimicked at least once in order to successfully transmute the aura of the orichalcum.

Orichalcum is such a strong conductor of mana that it may be used to enhance the effect of preparations. Any preparation that has a dram of orichalcum used within its creation retains full power for Potency x 3 hours, instead of the standard Potency x 2, before it begins to degrade. When used in the creation of items (other than compounds and the creation of reagents), orichalcum can reduce the object resistance by 4 for any Enchanting test. It can also enhance the magnitude of any Sorcery test by increasing the Magic rating by 5. No matter the use, adding orichalcum removes any Force limit involved, proving by this alone its incredible potency and value.

NEW ALCHEMICAL TOOLS

The lore of alchemy conjures images of bubbling beakers and strange apparatus that once facilitated failed attempts to recreate magic during the Fifth World. Some of these tools have been reinvented and repurposed in the Sixth World to help push the boundaries of alchemy. While the list below is not exhaustive, as additional tools are developed every day, several stand out in the field. Corporations and runners alike continue to develop any advantage they can to facilitate not just profit, but survival, within the Sixth World.

ATOMIZER

Developed during the early resurgence of alchemy as a practice, the atomizer is more a delivery device than it is an actual tool. The key to this device lies in its ability to take solid or liquid compounds and break them down into an aerosol spray without any loss in power or effect. This enables both healing and poison effects that would normally be command triggered to be created as contact triggers while retaining efficacy. The nature of the atomizer itself keeps contact with the device from activating the contact trigger. This enables the atomizer to spray out its payload which will then activate upon contact. Rumors exist about atomizers that may hold more than one compound "cartridge" at a time, though none can verify the truth of them.

Effect: One compound may be converted from a solid or liquid into an aerosol when inserted into the atomizer. Compounds made with a contact trigger are not enacted until they contact a substance after being fired from the atomizer. Atomizers can be used to make a ranged attack with a maximum range of three meters.

Price: 500 nuyen for the atomizer itself, 5 nuyen for an empty cartridge

ALEMBIC

The original distillery, the term "alembic" encompasses all three pieces required for the distilling process. Alchemists may use this device to increase the potency of the product their reagents produce. By distilling down to the important essence, more refined reagents are produced during the process from the same original amount of base ingredient. As such, the standard ten drams of reagent will produce two drams of refined, instead of one. The same process applies to further enhancement of refined reagents into radicals at the same ratio.

Effect: Using an alembic during the refinement process doubles the amount of refined or radical reagents created.

Price: 3,000 nuyen

ATHANOR

An athanor is a furnace used in the alchemical refinement process. It provides a constant rate of heat vital to the successful creation of refined and radical reagents. New technologies have allowed for the perfection of this device, a rare case where technology benefits the magical rather than hinders it. An athanor provides a strong and consistent flame that requires little maintenance. This allows an alchemist to spend more time on other projects without having to constantly attend to other reagents they are refining.

Effect: An athanor grants the alchemist leeway in the refinement and circulation process. During the refinement process of standard reagents, an alchemist may step away for up to one hour during the ten-hour process without ill effect. When undergoing the month-long process of creating orichalcum, an alchemist may check on the refinement process once every twelve hours, instead of every ten.

Price: 1,000 nuyen

CRUCIBLE

No matter how careful the alchemist, there are times when reagents become corrupted, or when the reagents are lower quality than desired. The crucible was reintroduced to alchemy to combat this effect. Careful use of this device can allow an alchemist to steam away the impurities found in some reagents and increase their potency. There are limits of course, and a crucible can't be expected to perform miracles. It can, however, allow a canny talismonger who is willing to take the time and effort to vastly increase their profit margin. By buying less desirable reagents and refining them with a crucible, they can scrape every nuyen possible out of a sale.

Effect: By using a crucible, an alchemist may upgrade the quality of a reagent one step. This takes the same amount of time as a standard refinement cycle of ten hours. A reagent may be upgraded from superior to prime in this manner, but it may not be enhanced any further than prime quality.

Price: 500 nuyen

VAULT OF AGES

The "vault of ages" is the most common name for this relatively recent innovation. Taken from the habit of secretive alchemists who hide their formulas and creations in secret vaults covered in traps, the preservative nature of this item gives it the name. First invented by a talismonger skilled in alchemy, the vault of ages helps mitigate the greatest flaw in crafted items. From the moment of creation, alchemical compounds and preparations begin to degrade. Dependent on the strength of the creator, they can quickly become useless if too much time passes, becoming a massive waste of resources and time. The vault stabilizes alchemical creations, halting the degradation process for the duration of time it remains within the vault.

Effect: A vault of ages may store a number of alchemical compounds or preparations equal to twice the Magic rating of its creator. The Rating of these items cannot be more than twice the rating of the vault. While within the confines of the vault, these items do not degrade. The degradation clock starts ticking as soon as they are removed.

Price: 2,000 nuyen per Magic Rating to a max of 5

ALCHEMICAL TOOLS

ITEM	COST	AVAILABILITY
Atomizer	500¥	4
Cartridge	5¥	2
Athanor	1,000¥	4
Crucible	500	2
Vault of ages	2,000 x Rating	(Rating +4)R

NEW COMPOUNDS

Alchemy is a constantly evolving field of mystical study as practitioners, from solo magicians to teams of corporate researchers, experiment and explore new uses for reagents. Their ultimate goal is to discover new compounds that will make them rich, famous, and/or powerful. Many who make such a discovery hoard their knowledge to corner the market and maximize their profits. There are also those who seek to reverse-engineer the newest fad, analyzing a compound and taking it apart to find how it was made. Whether it is undercutting a rival or finding new and cheaper ways to produce the compound, any talismonger

worth their salt always has their ear to the ground for the newest creation.

Persistent runners can find talismongers willing to sell some of these compounds, but it's neither easy nor cheap—due to the time it takes to create them versus the time they last before potency runs out, these compounds are not exactly sitting on store shelves. Still, runners are known for having contacts who might have unlikely items, and sometimes a talismonger friend might just have the item on hand that can provide important assistance to a runner team.

The lack of a standard market for these items leads to a lack of standard pricing. Still, there is a baseline to consider, and it looks like this: [(Force of spell involved) + (Current Potency)] x 500¥. Another factor that might raise the price is whether there is a current scarcity of required reagents (either globally or locally). Base availability for all compounds is 14R. Creating alchemical compounds requires advanced alchemy metamagic (p. 153, *Street Grimoire*).

ALCHEMICAL DUCT TAPE

Few things have endeared alchemists to riggers and deckers more than the creation of this compound. While on a run, there is never enough time to repair a damaged vehicle or drone to perfection. Sometimes you just need to get it working and get moving. That's where alchemical duct tape comes in. By slapping this on and activating the compound, complex repairs can be achieved in an instant. Use of this compound is the only magical repair possible, after which more mundane efforts are required to fix the machine.

- **Trigger:** Command
- **Effect:** When activated, this compound magically repairs a non-living target. Each hit upon activation repairs one point of structure or one box of damage, as per the spell Fix (p. 116, Street Grimoire).
- **Aftereffect:** Stunned side effect
- **Required Reagent:** Refined mallard fat

ASTRAL INCREASE

The limits on a magician's ability to manifest can seriously threaten the success of a run. Alchemists have finally created a solution for this problem thanks to the rediscovery of the ghost orchid. These ethereal flower petals enhance the magician within the astral plane. The careful and repeated refinement imbues the user with that dual nature, enhancing their physical and ethereal nature at the same time. Ghost orchids are incredibly difficult to cultivate outside of the wild. Doing so requires a level of care and concern that few are willing to put forth. Ghost orchids are most potent when harvested under the light of a full moon, especially in spots where the light may reach the petals unimpeded.

- **Trigger:** Contact
- **Effect:** Once ingested, this compound doubles the amount of time a magician may remain manifested while in astral projection.
- **Aftereffect:** Winded side effect
- **Required Reagent:** Radical ghost orchid petals.

ASTRAL BOND

Normally the bond between body and soul is not strong enough to invoke other prepared items in the alchemist arsenal. This compound resolves that issue, reinforcing that bond and allowing mana to flow to the prepared items. This compound mystically encases that elusive connecting silver cord in steel, conveying a stronger bond between body and soul while inhibiting neither. While under the effect of this compound, many users have spoken of the ease of travel and response while astral, almost as if their body itself was there instead of just their soul.

- **Trigger:** Contact
- **Effect:** While this compound lasts, the bond between body and astral form is much stronger. While manifesting, the target may activate command triggers.
- **Aftereffect:** Can't Speak side effect
- **Required Reagent:** Refined organ from insect host.

BAOBHAN'S TEARS

The worst nightmare of many a magician, baobhan's tears is a contact poison that deals damage to the body as well as to the ability to shape mana. While this compound does not share the addictive qualities of the real kiss, the blend of euphoria remains, even while at odds with the damage it inflicts on the body.

- **Trigger:** Contact
- **Effect:** Upon contact with the skin or inhalation, this poison deals 4P damage that may only be resisted by Body. If any dam-

age is not resisted, the target also loses 1 point of Essence for the next twenty-four hours. Repeated doses of this poison may inflict damage, but only 1 point of Essence may be lost during the twenty-four-hour period after initial infection.

- **Aftereffect:** Stunned side effect
- **Required Reagent:** Refined tears of a baobhan sith (p. 114, *Court of Shadows*)

DRAIN AWAY

Holding the ability to lower the damage caused by drain, this compound has become one of the most feared in the arsenal of dark aspect magicians. It can only be made with the mana-fueled veins of an adept, and producing this compound pushes past lines even most shadowrunners will not cross. Countless adepts perished before the formula was perfected. Now it spreads deep within the shadows for those willing to pay the price for power. Dark traditions and insect shamans are known to carry a dose as a trump card few could expect.

- **Trigger:** Contact
- **Effect:** Once imbibed, the next time the target would take physical damage from drain, that damage is negated.
- **Aftereffect:** Nauseated side effect
- **Required Reagent:** Refined veins of the adept

DULLED EDGES

When damage is inevitable, reducing the target's ability to inflict damage itself is a cunning tool. This poison dulls the edges of the target, lowering their reaction times, weakening their muscles, and sapping their strength. Even the mightiest street samurai fears the moment when their body is turned against them.

- **Trigger:** Contact
- **Effect:** Once it contacts a target, this compound decreases the target's Physical limit by 2 for 3 turns.
- **Aftereffect:** Fatigued side effect
- **Required Reagent:** Radical killdeer antler (p. 97, *Howling Shadows*)

FEEL NO PAIN

Known as FNP on the streets, feel no pain delays the need for sleep, food, or even water. While it doesn't eliminate these urges, it can delay them until the user is in a better place to handle these basic needs. Quite popular among corp workers who are closing in on a project deadline, since nothing gets you through it faster than a bit of FNP. There are very real dangers when it comes to this alchemical compound. More than three days of consecutive use of FNP brings risks of addiction as well as fatigue and disorientation (Addiction Rating 4, Addiction Threshold 2; see p. 172, 409, and 414, *SR5*).

- **Trigger:** Command
- **Effect:** When activated, every net hit counts as one hour of sleep for the purposes of resisting fatigue. It also allows a target to skip one meal per net hit with no ill effects. When the duration of FNP ends, the effects of dehydration and starvation immediately apply to the subject.
- **Aftereffect:** Fatigued side effect
- **Required Reagent:** Radical kayeri mushroom

FORCE OF PERSONALITY

For those who heavily engage in combat in the astral plane, this compound is a godsend. Alchemists have developed a gel that enhances the ability of a magician or adept to deal damage to astral creatures and constructs alike. The compound can also be helpful to non-magicians who wish to display enhanced levels of charisma and charm. Few are willing to endure the side effects without substantial reason, due to the risks it entails.

- **Trigger:** Command
- **Effect:** This compound must be applied to the target's skin and then activated. While active, the target's Charisma is increased by 2 for the purposes of astral combat only. Such an artificial increase manifesting on the astral plane requires a potent ability, and comes with an equally debilitating side effect.
- **Aftereffect:** Stunned side effect
- **Required Reagent:** Radical ghost orchid petals

HMHVV II INHIBITOR

Developed in secret by the Aztechnology Alchemy division, this compound is only sold and then administered to approved and vetted elite corporate citizens who sign a specialized NDA to prevent rogue alchemists from attempting to reverse-engineer it. A new and rare inoculation, this magical compound prevents further progress of HMHVV II as long as the compound is continually ingested.

- **Trigger:** Contact
- **Effect:** This compound must be consumed once every seven days. As long as the regimen is maintained, all progress of HMHVV II is halted. This is not a cure, merely an inhibitor. Failure to continue dosing will allow the virus to progress once more, often more virulent than before due to the repression. There is also a possibility of addiction when using the inhibitor; it has Addiction Rating 3, Addiction Threshold 1.
- **Aftereffect:** Fatigued side effect
- **Required Reagent:** Refined drop bear saliva (p. 60, *Howling Shadows*)

LAMINATE

Many traditions use writings or symbols painted or drawn upon an item for their alchemical preparations. These markings are susceptible to damage or accident, rendering the time and energy spent on them wasted. Recently, the infamous alchemist Megalith released this compound to spite the Aztechnology Alchemical division.

- **Trigger:** Contact
- **Effect:** An aerosol spray that when applied coats a layer of writing or runes in a thin protective gel. Unable to stand up to any real damage, (1 point of Physical damage destroys the layer) it will protect from accidental scuffing or blurring through inadvertent contact. For example, a sword with runes drawn upon the blade may be sheathed and unsheathed without damaging the inked writing.
- **Aftereffect:** Blinded (One Eye) side effect
- **Required Reagent:** Refined slug glands

PERFECT SIGHT

Perfect sight has hit the streets, and for the first time non-magicians have an inkling of what it's like to see the astral plane. Some use this just as a recreational drug, seeing sights they never imagined could exist from the comfort of their own homes. Enterprising runners and corporations have also made use of this compound. Guards can detect the dual-natured, or even warn their superiors about astral beings attempting to access secure locations. Runners can keep an eye on their astral counterparts without requiring them to waste time manifesting. This increased bond to the astral does come at a cost however, as use of this increases the noise (p. 441, *SR5*) in the local area.

- **Trigger:** Command
- **Effect:** When applied to the eyes and commanded to activate, this compound allows the target to perceive the astral plane. Throughout the duration of this compound, the ambient noise in an area is increased by the net hits achieved when activated as per the spell Interference (p. 117, *Street Grimoire*)
- **Aftereffect:** Stunned side effect
- **Required Reagent:** Refined ghost orchid petals

SHARPSHOOTER

One shot, one kill. The motto of the sniper, and harder to accomplish in this age of advanced magical and mundane protection. This compound returns some of that danger and ability to the sniper by removing the pesky impediments of range or perception. A cunning alchemist has managed to combine the spells of Hawkeye and Enhance Aim into one easy-to-use compound. Even the most experienced sniper or gunslinger likes to have a little Sharpshooter on hand to ensure they don't miss when they take aim.

- **Trigger:** Command
- **Effect:** Applied to the eyes or in a quickly digestible pill, Sharpshooter improves the target's aim as well as negating range modifiers in increasing increments. For each net hit, reduce Range conditions by one category (p. 175, *SR5*). It also grants a +1 dice pool modifier for any visual-based perception tests.
- **Aftereffect:** Blinded (one eye)
- **Required Reagent:** Radical eyes of a bird of prey.

UNSTOPPABLE VIGOR

Another powerful tool in the arsenal of the magician, this compound makes even the frailest mana worker more likely to survive extended spellcasting. Far more than the blades or bul-

lets of enemies, drain itself becomes an unwary spellcaster's greatest foe. This compound forces an unnatural stamina to suffuse the body of a magician in order to combat the physical damage that drain may inflict. It is a double-edged sword, as this increased hardiness can convince some to cast spells far beyond their power until they become addicted to it (the compound has Addiction Rating 6, Addiction Threshold 3). This forces them to continue consuming the compound to survive the repeated damage of drain.

- **Trigger:** Contact
- **Effect:** Once imbibed, the target gains a number of boxes on their Stun Condition Monitor equal to the potency of the compound. These boxes are only useful for resisting the damage associated with drain. Once the potency expires or the boxes are full from drain damage, they disappear and the effect ends.
- **Aftereffect:** Slowed side effect
- **Required Reagent:** Refined drake scales (any type)

WATER BREATHING

There are those who refuse to let such a minor setback as being underwater stop them in their quest for hidden riches. Use of this compound magically imbues the user with gills, allowing them to breath easily underwater. This is not some mystical conversion, but rather true gills, which can be problematic to the inexperienced user. While this compound remains in effect, the user cannot breathe air alone; they must take their oxygen from the water. As such, the truly innovative have taken advantage of this fact, applying the compound to a target and then watching their victim suffocate before them.

- **Trigger:** Contact
- **Effect:** The target is empowered with the Gills critter power (p. 192, *Howling Shadows*). While this compound is active, the target has real working gills and may only breathe underwater. Canceling this effect removes them and returns the ability to breathe air.
- **Aftereffect:** Winded side effect
- **Required Reagent:** Refined salmon scales

NEW ALCHEMICAL PREPARATIONS

Alchemical preparations are spells that rely on a physical conduit, called the lynchpin, to channel mana from the astral to the physical realm to activate them. Lynchpins are the weak spot in any alchemical preparation, as even the slightest damage to them will render the entire preparation inoperable. They can take many forms, from arcane writing on paper to the severed hand of a murderer mystically imbued with power. Tradition and imagination are the limit when it comes to alchemically preparing a vessel for a spell.

Rules for purchasing preparations follows the same outline as buying compounds (p. 194), namely that they are hard to find—in fact, even more so because of the shorter lifespan. The base price is [(Force of spell involved) + (Current Potency)] x 500¥. Base availability for all preparations is 14R.

ABANDON ALL HOPE

Another popular trap and defensive preparation, this preparation increases an aura of fear and helplessness in the entire area when activated. By setting this up in an area where other traps are located, it becomes much easier to deter any who seek to beard the alchemist in their lair. This preparation is often set upon something of value left easily found. As the magic is undetectable until activated, once a would-be thief touches the item, the fear aura ignites.

- **Trigger:** Contact
- **Effect:** When activated, this preparation enacts the Foreboding spell upon the area.
- **Required Spell:** Foreboding (p. 112, *Street Grimoire*)

BARRICADE

A few seconds can seem a lifetime, or make all the difference in the world. Upon activating this preparation, the structural integrity of a wall or door can be increased. Traditional-minded alchemists use runes written on paper, which is then applied to the target. Other, more innovative methods, such as a penny in the door seam, can work just as well when properly prepared.

- **Trigger:** Command
- **Effect:** Upon activation, the spell Reinforce is cast on the object the preparation has been applied to.
- **Required Spell:** Reinforce (p. 118, *Street Grimoire*)

BURN, BABY, BURN

Triple B is one of the most versatile trap-style preparations and can take many forms. A room filled with flammable gas, with a hidden rune upon the floor that ignites the entire room in flames. A grenade of flammable liquid, with a command rune inscribed upon it. There are myriad ways to capitalize on something igniting in flames on command.

- **Trigger:** Command
- **Effect:** When activated, this preparation enacts the Ignite spell upon the target.
- **Required Spell:** Ignite (p. 293, *SR5*)

DO YOUR BEST

Unleashing the limits of body or mind can make the difference in any battle. This preparation allows an alchemist to raise the effectiveness of herself and others. While this isn't a guaranteed win, it greatly increases the chance of success in whatever endeavors a runner might undertake. Coated pills are a common form for this preparation, and when the command word is spoken the spell activates.

- **Trigger:** Command
- **Effect:** When activated, this preparation enacts the Increase Inherent Limits spell upon the target. Only one limit may be increased at one time, and further activation of this eliminates the previous version.
- **Required Spell:** Increase Inherent Limits (p. 110, *Street Grimoire*)

GET AWAY FROM MY RIDE

A getaway vehicle is nothing if it can't help runners escape. It's a weakness in any plan, and as such, alchemists have devised a way to protect that key element of any good escape. Emblems and decals are popular forms for these preparations to make them blend in with the vehicle and hide their magical nature until it is too late.

- **Trigger:** Command
- **Effect:** When activated, this preparation enacts the Protect Vehicle spell upon the target vehicle.
- **Required Spell:** Protect Vehicle (p. 117, *Street Grimoire*)

HIGH AS A KITE

It's not always about solving the problem yourself. Some of the most powerful preparations are ones that set up the rest of the team to succeed. The use of this preparation lowers the target's ability to resist toxins and drugs. This can set up other teammates to deliver devastating attacks. This is most commonly prepared on projectiles for easy delivery.

- **Trigger:** Command
- **Effect:** When activated, this preparation enacts the Enabler spell.
- **Required Spell:** Enabler (p. 110, *Street Grimoire*)

NOISE ON THE LINE

Deckers, riggers, and other skilled Matrix users can present a unique problem for magicians. To prevent such issues before they can arise, this preparation increases the noise in the area, making the Matrix more difficult to use and access. Few things are more likely to incite the hacker population than frequent use of this compound.

- **Trigger:** Command
- **Effect:** When activated, enacts the Increase Noise spell.
- **Required Spell:** Increase Noise (p. 116, *Street Grimoire*)

NOMW (NOT ON MY WATCH)

Sometimes the difference between living and dying is so razor thin, even a spell will not be fast enough. For this reason, alchemists created a contact preparation to stabilize critically wounded individuals just long enough to get them the help they need.

- **Trigger:** Contact
- **Effect:** When contact is made, the spell Stabilize (p. 289, *SR5*) is enacted upon the target.
- **Required Spell:** Stabilize

LIGHTNING BLADE

Even with ceramics, plastics, and mystical armor, there are those who place their faith in a layer of metal between them and those who would do them harm. Alchemists have perfected a preparation to remind them of the error of their ways. By imbuing a weapon with the power of lightning, the protection of metal armor becomes nullified and the damage becomes resistible by the body alone.

- **Trigger:** Command
- **Effect:** Written upon a blade or other weapon, when activated this preparation makes the next successful attack unable to be resisted by metal armor.
- **Required Spell:** Lightning Bolt (p. 284, *SR5*)

SPIRIT ZAPPER

Spirits can serve as weapons both offensive and defensive, as well as the ultimate spies. This preparation is important for any magician wishing to guard their secrets against spirits trespassing on their astral domain.

- **Trigger:** Command
- **Effect:** This preparation comes in many forms, from candles made of exotic materials to runes and diagrams written out in different forms and languages. No matter the actual form, the effect remains. When activated, it creates a barrier just as the Mana Barrier spell, or the Offensive Mana Barrier spell, depending on the preparation.
- **Required Spell:** Mana Barrier (p. 294, *SR5*) or Offensive Mana Barrier (p. 117, *Street Grimoire*)

STINK BOMB

A trap to disable a would-be thief with gut-wrenching sickness, a tool to incapacitate enemies chasing a runner down a darkened alley ... there are myriad uses for the stink bomb, limited only by the cleverness of the user.

- **Trigger:** Command or Contact, depending on use
- **Effect:** On command or contact, dependent on the trigger chosen, the Stench spell is enacted over the area, affecting enemies and allies alike.
- **Required Spell:** Stench (p. 113, *Street Grimoire*)

STOP THIEF!

Quick to produce and relatively inexpensive, these preparations are incredibly popular with talismongers as both a deterrent as well as a demonstration. This preparation can be done on anything from a welcome mat with hidden writing to a throwable ball that bonds to whatever it touches when the command word is spoken. Stopping thieves in their tracks or marking them for later identification are common uses, though tagging people with an RFID that can be used for tracking or drone targeting are other possible options.

- **Trigger:** Command

- **Effect:** When activated, this preparation enacts the Glue Strip spell.
- **Required Spell:** Glue Strip (p. 116, *Street Grimoire*)

TRUTH SERUM

When you absolutely must get to the truth, nothing can beat this type of preparation. While it may require other types of coercion to get the target to actually speak, with this you can be assured whatever words come out of their mouth are the truth. Handcuffs and manacles are the most common forms of preparation, as they are easily locked on and activated. Some prefer to put this in pill form, just for the drama of making someone swallow a truth drug.

- **Trigger:** Command
- **Effect:** When activated, this preparation enacts the Compel Truth spell upon the target.
- **Required Spell:** Compel Truth (p. 114, *Street Grimoire*)

UP AND AT 'EM

It is always easier to help a comrade run than it is to haul an unconscious body. These occasions are what this preparation is designed for. A quick slap of a patch and the command word, and even the most stunned individual will regain consciousness. If nothing else, they can then be awake to see any further attacks coming.

- **Trigger:** Most commonly Command or Contact
- **Effect:** When activated, this preparation enacts the Awaken spell upon the target.
- **Required Spell:** Awaken (p. 109, *Street Grimoire*)

WATCH YOUR STEP

Inventive users can find plenty of uses for a sudden sheet of ice. From sending vehicles chasing them crashing into the streets to rendering enemies too worried about their footing to try to do anything else, the possibilities are endless.

- **Trigger:** Command
- **Effect:** When activated, this preparation enacts the Ice Sheet spell on the area.
- **Required Spell:** Ice Sheet (p. 293, *SR5*)

THE SYNERGY OF ALCHEMY AND DARK TRADITIONS

- If you can manage to look away from the cool explosions, you'll find that ultimately, alchemy is about methodology and preparation. If you can figure out how to reproduce results while cutting corners on the means of production, you have the edge. Some alchemists are willing to dive head first into the shadows of the dark traditions for any advantage. Those who practice such traditions aren't the talkative type, and most aren't willing to share their secrets at any price lest they be incriminated. So treat the information here as the rare and precious jewel it is.
- Megalith

Practitioners of the dark traditions gravitate toward alchemy, attracted to its dispassionate, results-orientated methodology of gaining power. They leverage the unique capabilities of alchemical tools and reagents to fuel their unending quests for power without the shackles of morality. In their pursuit of an exotic reagent or unknown formula, a dark alchemist will plunder a sacred burial ground, murder a kayeri for their cap, or even harvest the veins from a living adept via vivisection. These repulsive experiments have secretly led to some of the newest formulas and potent compounds and preparations that even the most law-abiding find indispensable.

BLOOD MAGIC

Alchemists who practice this dark tradition must surrender their squeamishness to forever walk in the shadows, surrendering completely to their ambition and hunger for power. Blood magicians harvest reagents through seduction, temptation, and sacrifice, making the conscious decision to trade the suffering of others for power and prestige.

The great advantage of the dark alchemist leveraging blood magic is that reagents harvested from time-consuming sacrifice work as a perfect substitute for orichalcum (see **Reagents**, p. 316, *SR5*). This blood reagent must be utilized immediately, lest it forever lose its potency. However, the nature of such a harvesting requires the dark alchemist spend three times the normal duration to prepare the sacrifice, requiring sacred alchemical compounds such as poisons and paralytics to ensure the suffering and ultimate death of their victims. Practitioners of this tradition who combine it with alchemy also learn to combine their efforts into a gruesome whole. They may create any compound or preparation to trigger at the moment of death, either of themselves or one of their victims.

Blood magicians first discovered the infamous reagent known as veins of the adept (see p. 191), which is the core reagent required for a powerful alchemical compound with the ability to completely negate drain damage. Rumor has it that the unknown alchemist who discovered this reagent willingly shared their secret with the world to fuel an unending vendetta against adepts for some grave slight.

Sacrifices may be shared among blood magicians without the dilution of the potency of the harvested reagent. A blood magician often pairs with a couple of apprentices and cultists who serve as additional allies—or in desperate times, as power sources. Together, they perform multiple sacrifices within an area to taint the mana with pain and suffering in order to synergize the reagents to their tradition. This takes repeated sacrifices and torture to accomplish, but few who are so far down the path of blood magic will flinch at such a minor requirement. They find synergy in any reagents that were once part of living, feeling beings. While they'd prefer to do the bloodletting and harvesting themselves, they will make use of what comes available. Areas of past pain and suffering are the preferred places for harvesting reagents for a blood magician.

INSECT MAGIC

Followers of the Insect Way have a single, all-important goal: to seek a place with high ambient mana, fortify it, and then summon a queen to create a hive. To achieve this end, insect shamans infect metahuman host bodies with lesser insect spirits. These infected hosts aid the shaman in progressing the goals of the hive, serving as defenders, workers, and minions of the shaman who summoned them until their queen arrives.

An alchemist who follows the Insect Way possesses an innate spiritual connection to the otherworldly mana infused within the body of an infected host. They may leverage this to quickly harvest reagents from the organs of any infected host. This process kills the host, but the harvesting process takes half the normal time. The ease of harvesting this key component allows insect shamans to make great use of such abilities when hunting for other host bodies or defending the hive location itself. These alchemists have also been taught the secrets of poisons and toxins from their insect mentor spirits. They are able to mix this mana with their own biology to turn their very blood into a potent toxin.

INSECT SHAMAN VENOM

- Vector: Contact
- Speed: Immediate
- Penetration: 0
- Power: Equal to alchemist's Magic rating
- Effect: Physical damage.
- Insect shaman venom is a toxic blood that burns upon contact with unprotected flesh.

Insect shamans rarely venture far from their hive; they remain close to keep it safe and protect it from predators. They keep a close eye on their infected hosts to ensure the population small enough to stay hidden, but large enough that they may harvest reagents at a moment's notice. The greatest advantage an insect shaman can have is time. The longer their presence goes unknown, the more powerful servants they can summon, and the more host bodies they can infect. When this leads to the successful summoning of a queen, there is even the potential of a potent spirit pact that can boost the power of an insect shaman to even greater levels.

The harvested organs of an infected host can be refined into a compound that allows an astral shaman to manifest strongly enough to activate other prepared alchemical traps. Due to the omnipresent nature of insects within their home territories, the mentor spirits of an insect shaman can grant knowledge of any area heavily ambient in mana within that sphere of influence. This again cuts down the time it takes a follower of the Insect Way to harvest reagents that are already assured to be synergetic with their tradition.

TOXIC MAGIC

Followers of the Twisted Way gain strength and power from the pollution and corruption of the Sixth World. These toxic mages seek to expand the areas ravaged by corruption through their own power, as well as by aiding those who initially created the damage. Poisoners believe they have discovered an unknown element of mana and that by spreading this pollution they increase their own power. Avengers merely lash out at the world, damaging friend and foe alike, in an all-consuming hatred spawned by the very environment that sustains them.

Toxic alchemists gain power from the tainted mana that flows through polluted areas, and their reagents reflect this benefit. They do not suffer the normal disadvantage for using tainted reagents, but instead gain a fifty percent cut to refining time when using them. When using tainted reagents, they increase the limit on any toxin- or poison-based alchemical compound or preparation by 1. These vile and twisted creations further spread the pollution and corruption for which the toxic practitioner is known. Those who combine alchemy with toxicity also find a secondary benefit unknown to any but those practitioners: They become immune to death by disease. They suffer the side effects and remain infected for the duration, but the disease itself will never kill them. The corruption they live in maintains their life on the razor's edge.

Combining alchemy with the insanity of a toxic magician is akin to giving a child a grenade. They are unflinching in pushing alchemical compounds and preparations far beyond any sane boundaries in their quest to expand areas of corruption. Free from the shackles of morality or ethics, they can develop everything from deadly poisons to plagues that ravage any ecosystem they find vulnerable. What is truly terrifying is that recent encounters with toxic magicians have all seen them interested in virus-like plagues. Imagining a toxic magician able to pervert a virus like HMHVV to their own ends is truly the stuff of nightmares.

Areas ravaged by pollution are natural habitats of the Twisted Way followers. There they make their lairs, or scour the land for reagents to use in their insane schemes. These areas are also convenient locations to test and further develop compounds and preparations, as even failures will increase the ambient toxicity which empowers the Toxic magician. Tainting these areas further also leads to increased mana levels, which make for a richer harvest when gathering reagents.

RESEARCH, RUMORS, AND LEGENDS

- I spend most of my life looking over my shoulder. I thought the horrible things I learned at Aztechnology would be enough to fuel all my nightmares. You keep running and running, and eventually you see the whole of the world, and you wish you could be naïve again. Lately, I've been taking notes of rumors and various jobs that might need an alchemist's touch. I might not live to see tomorrow, but maybe my formulas will live on. I left these secrets in care of a friend, just in case I become retired quietly in the shadows. A little knowledge is a dangerous thing. Don't let this material get you into a place you can't talk or fight your way out of.
- Megalith

PHILOSOPHER'S STONE

- Research alchemy long enough, and you'll have a slew of tales of old bastards going mad trying to locate or recreate the Philosopher's Stone. I spent a year and a half trying to crack that at Aztechnology. The corporate spooks would bring us rumors about someone making an advancement that looked promising. No one really believed it existed, but they really didn't want the competition to prove us wrong. It wasn't much different than the old days, really. You'd have academics keeping loose correspondence, confident that someone was about to figure it out and hoping it was going to be them. Not much different than your grandmother at a bingo hall, really. Eventually, I realized that being the first to shout bingo might not be the best idea. I've never regretted it. Best leave the amateurs to their game.
- Megalith

Rumors about the Philosopher's Stone have always intrigued and inspired those interested in mystic items. Alchemists who could turn lead into gold, guaranteeing unlimited wealth and the power that comes with it to whomever could possess this artifact. These stories rise and fall throughout the ages, and the cynical consider them just faerie tales. As the heightened activity of the fae has shown, sometimes faerie tales are more real than anyone could have imagined. Once more, the Philosopher's Stone has become the talk of the magical world. From corporations to runners, everyone wants to know if the rumors are true, and if they are how they can get their piece of the action.

There are a couple persistent rumors that float around about the whereabouts of this leg-endary material. The first belief is that it is an object belonging more to the fae than to the material plane. With the rise in interaction with the Seelie Court and the other denizens of Tír na nÓg, speculation is high that the Philosopher's Stone may be a faerie artifact that is secretly one of the sources of their power and wealth. So few outside the realm have any idea of what truly happens within the faerie demesnes that this rumor has gained the most traction among the cynical. If it were true, it would be one tidy explanation for the sheer amount of wealth and magical power that the faerie lords and ladies seem invariably to possess. The value of orichalcum is so high, covert trading and sales would ensure that there was never a worry over nuyen in the Sixth World.

One of the other most commonly held beliefs is that it isn't an item, but a formula; a new secret way for alchemists to refine reagents to create orichalcum. Something that corps like Saeder-Krupp or Aztechnology have been working on for decades but aren't sharing with anyone. Few would put it past a dragon to hoard the secret to a vast fortune—that's pretty much SOP for them. Yet if it were real and in the hands of one of these corporations, most feel there would be some sort of evidence—or at the very least, a patent. While solid proof has not been found, people ranging from the slickest decker to the most tradition-bound magician remain desperately curious to get their hands on any sort of clue that could lead to the stone and the unimaginable wealth it would bring.

PLOTS IF YOU HAVE AN ALCHEMIST ON YOUR TEAM:

- It takes an alchemist to discern truth from fiction when it comes to the Philospher's Stone. Mr. Johnson is looking for just such an alchemist, and he hires you and your team to investigate a lead.
- A corp alchemist in a subsidiary of the Big Ten has made a breakthrough, and she is willing to sell it to the highest bidder. Your team has a chance to get to her before she can make her auction happen.
- You have managed to come into possession of a scrap of some formula. Finding the rest may lead to a discovery that is on everyone's lips. Track down the other pieces and try your luck.

PLOTS IF YOU DO NOT HAVE AN ALCHEMIST ON THE TEAM:

- There's a run in the works. A shipment of reagents that can be used to refine orichalcum is coming into town. Hitting the shipment could net a small but tidy profit, but following it to the destination could bring in some information worth far more than a few nuyen.

- An alchemist contact is targeted by a corporation for acquisition. She doesn't want to enter the corporate lifestyle and needs any help she can get to escape their security team and take on a new life in the shadows. Get it done and she's willing to turn over a clue to a powerful artifact that has been in her family for generations.

- A Mr. Johnson who happens to be an alchemist was spurned by a partner and colleague walking out on years of collaboration, forming her own corporation. He wants to know what, if any, progress has been made and to what extent the IP of the former company is being built upon.

USING THE PHILOSOPHER'S STONE IN THE GAME

The Philosopher's Stone is an incredibly potent item that could easily unbalance a game. It is also a legendary item and quest worthy of longtime runners and agents in the shadows. Gamemasters should be careful in how they introduce the Philosopher's Stone into their game sessions. Low-level runners just starting out may be hired by more powerful agents to investigate leads, acquire reagents, or hit a corporation subsidiary for clues. More powerful runners might go after the Big Ten to get the secrets of corporate alchemy. Finding the Philosopher's Stone itself should be only used as a climactic moment, or as a reason to paint a giant target on the backs of your runners to see how they handle it. The gamemaster is free to invent their own components for the formula and should feel free to keep its creation mercurial, requiring varying ingredients and procedures in what is the antithesis of established mundane chemistry.

HARVESTING THE COURT OF SHADOWS

◦ Word has it that Tír Tairngire and Tír na nÓg have a near-infinite storehouse of unknown reagents they keep from those of us who live in the muck. I've tried here and there to make deals, do any job, or beg, borrow, and steal to gain access. Whatever the fae have in mind, they ain't sharing with the likes of us. Once they threatened to turn me in, I quit trying.
◦ Megalith

The realms of Tír Tairngire and Tír na nÓg have always been a shrouded mystery. To this day, few know of the realms these nations hide, the gateways to the planes of the true fae, which are accessible only through closely guarded and secret ways. While the masses may be unaware, the magical community, particularly alchemists, have begun to question the origin point of these reagents of legendary beasts. This has encouraged the brave and the foolhardy to begin to actively seek hidden paths into the realm of the Seelie Court. Seeking to acquire knowledge and power unseen on the earthly plane since the end of the Fourth World, these runners hope to be some of the first to explore, and exploit, what possible treasures might be found in secret forests and faerie mounds.

Already there have been documented explorations into the hidden hearts of faerie. Some few adventurous souls have made their way to the realm of the Seelie Court and survived to tell the tale. More common are the stories of those who sought and failed to find the entrances, let alone make their way into the endless forest. More common are the denizens of faerie who have begun to make their way into the material plane of the Sixth World. These creatures, some mentioned only in legend and myth, now walk among other metahumans. Tales of the Baobhan sith or the kayeri have made their way to alchemists and talismongers who lust after the possibility of trading in unobtainable reagents. Others seek these critters for experiments, wondering what might be possible with the anatomies of these beasts who have lived their lives surrounded by mana unfamiliar to the Sixth World. It is impossible to say who is the hunter and who is the hunted as both sides seek to find their own places in the world of corporations and shadows.

With the growing knowledge of the existence of the Seelie Court and the doorways that lead to their home plane, the more suspicious have begun to believe that Tír Tairngire isn't a bastion for the elves so much as a forward base. Old family lines tell conflicting stories of faerie allies from the past as well as of their alien emotions and power in battle. Very few governments are truly comfortable with the idea that the power of a hidden realm backs the growing strength of the elven nation, full of unknown reagents and powerful magic, to say nothing of untold beings that no one in the Sixth World has any idea how to combat.

PLOTS IF YOU HAVE AN ALCHEMIST ON YOUR TEAM:

- A local talismonger has come into a supply of reagents from the fabled realms of the faerie. Now strange and dangerous things are plaguing him wherever he goes. He wants to offload his inventory fast, and you may be the one to take them off his hands. If you're willing to risk the danger, and have the nuyen to pay the bill, the possibility of rare and exotic reagents could be yours.
- An elf from Tír Tairngire has a proposition. A thief has found his way to the elven realm and stolen cache of valuable seeds that may even be reagents. She wants you to hunt down the thief and retrieve her property, but she needs an alchemist to identify the missing items. Doing so could earn you an invitation to the hidden forests of the Tír.
- The opportunity to create a formula with unknown effects presents itself to the runners. The current possessor of the formula can supply the location of the reagents, but she needs an alchemist who can handle the refinement process and the dangers that come with it. If you can get it done, and survive the process, this score could set you up for some time.

PLOTS IF YOU DO NOT HAVE AN ALCHEMIST ON THE TEAM:

- An adventurer is looking for a protection team to run cover while he attempts an incursion into the Faerie plane. He's got a way in and out with the loot, but no job is done until the escape is clean. Your team must protect him from the location back to his safe house no matter what critters may try and come after him.
- One of the Seelie themselves have come

DEALING WITH FAE

One thing all the stories agree on, no matter the fable or faerie tale, is that nothing is more dangerous than making a deal with a Faerie, except breaking one. Masters of contracts and language both, they are slippery creatures who will twist, bend, and interpret any word to make it suit their whims, without violating the letter of their agreements. They can also be unexpectedly powerful allies when handled correctly. As long as you keep your wits sharp, your aim sharper, and a spell ready at your fingers, you should be fine. Success brings reward beyond measure, and failure can lead to a fate worse than death. Just another night in the shadows, eh, chummer?

to the earthly plane. She's in search of one of the more dangerous inhabitants of her realm who has escaped the boundaries and made its way here. It is up to your team to hunt this creature down and return it to the Seelie. Failure will lead to exposure, something the Seelie will not tolerate. The payoff is huge, but so are the risks.

- A fixer has had her supply of Faerie realm goods cut off from her source in Tir Tairngire. She's looking for you to investigate whether it was the elves who put a kink in her supply chain, or possibly something worse. Being the lone supplier of otherworldly goods has made the fixer rich, but some risks may not be worth the rewards.

INFECTED ALCHEMY

- I've had a good deal of complex entanglements with the Infected looking for my son. Some of them were passive, while others tried to bite me on sight. Every time I think my son has passed on, I hear rumors about Infected magicians working with alchemy. Sounds insane, right? Shouldn't be possible, but when he left, he took some of my notebooks. If nothing else, my kid had a promising future with magic. Research of this kind falls under the category of things people shouldn't mess with, lest the Almighty unleash a new plague.
- Megalith

HMHVV is something we all know about. Most of us try to avoid it, while a few seek it out, thinking the powers it brings are worth the trade-offs. They're

a minority, though; for every person looking to become a vampire, there are a dozen who would be happy to have a cure that would allow them to live a normal metahuman life. As many people seeking to perform the impossible have done in the past, some of these individuals have turned to alchemy.

Alchemy and the Infected can be a dangerous mix. Compounds and preparations can enhance the already-potent abilities of a variety of different HMHVV strains. Recently, though, there have been discoveries of compounds that are anathema to some who have contracted the virus, and possibly a dream realized for others. A formula for a particular compound is rumored to have made its way to the hands of some few runners and possibly a corporation. Reportedly it impedes the further mutation of one infected with HMHVV. Such an inoculation could be the first step in a cure for HMHVV. This could be incredibly valuable—though there are some forces, notably agents of Asamando, who would be interested in burying any such formula where it can never be found.

PLOTS IF YOU HAVE
AN ALCHEMIST ON YOUR TEAM:

- A facilitator has come forward. There's a powerful Infected magician who seeks reagents that can only be harvested in the direct light of the noonday sun. Find these reagents and bring them to him, and he'll trade secrets found in the shadows.
- Megalith, a well-known runner alchemist, has information on a possible location for

his son. If you and your team can find and retrieve him, he'll reward you handsomely with formulas and reagents he's developed in his research.
- The scion of a wealthy family has contracted HMHVV, and her family is desperate to see her condition stabilized. Conventional medical and magical assistance have failed. Her family has little hope for relief, but if her condition could be stabilized, they would pay handsomely. They'll accept treatment from any source, even an alchemical one.

PLOTS IF YOU DO NOT HAVE
AN ALCHEMIST ON THE TEAM:

- An Infected gang has kidnapped the daughter of a powerful politician. Supposedly they wish to use her for some ritual, so she's still alive—for the time being. Bring her back alive and you'll be rewarded. Save her and eliminate the vampires and you could be set for life.
- There are rumors of a stronghold of vampires nearby. The first team sent to try to eliminate them suffered almost complete annihilation. The sole survivor returned with stories of elaborate magical traps and blood-red potions that increased their speed and power. Any team brave enough to approach them in their lair could come away with a treasure trove of valuable alchemical components and tools.
- There's a bounty on vampire blood. Some say there's a corp working on an actual cure for HMHVV, and they need blood for research. If you could harvest enough, you could earn a generous chunk of change—whether the cure works or not.

ANCIENT SECRETS
IN MODERN HANDS
(CORPORATE ALCHEMY
CRACKDOWN)

> I speak from personal experience when I say that the corporations are cracking down on unaligned alchemists. We're a threat to their control. The right formula mixed with a new reagent and new brewing technique could create a compound or preparation that could change the world. Sounds great, right? Why would anyone fight that? Because the corporations don't want things to change. Profits are up. And anything outside of their

---

USING A POSSIBLE HMHVV CURE

The Infected make NPCs for any game, especially with their capabilities enhanced by alchemy or other magical skills. They can be challenging antagonists or powerful allies depending on the actions and reactions of the characters. A possible magical compound that is both addicting but also a way to stall an infection of HMHVV from taking effect is also a valuable resource to any character who may have gotten infected. Runners may also be hired to steal stores of the compound, kidnap an alchemist who is capable of creating it, or be sent out to find the reagent necessary for its production. Characters who learn this formula could even find themselves targets of similar kidnappings from desperate corporate parents who wish to save a child—or themselves.

control challenges that. If one of us discovered a simple compound to cure HMHVV, it would tank their aftercare division. Misery brings profits. The problem with alchemists is that we can share our magic. Hope is the only cure for misery.

◉ Megalith

Alchemy is the hot new research trend in corporate research, with significant funding being diverted to alchemical divisions of Aztechnology, Mitsuhama, Ares, and other corps. Companies that once focused on things like designer drugs and pharmaceuticals are now just as interested in alchemical compounds and the uses of reagents. Alchemical substances have been developed with a variety of industrial applications as corporations rush to integrate new materials into product designs. The trend has created secondary markets as the manufacturing of technological devices to aid in alchemical research and production has surged due to a wide range of efforts to cash in on the latest craze. Amidst all of this, corporate lawyers and lobbyists are working overtime seeking to secure legislation granting patent and intellectual property rights to their corporate benefactors, as corporate security is being tested by deckers looking to pry away a few secrets. Rumors of the Philosopher's Stone, the new and exotic reagents hitting the market, and espionage attempts looking to lift formulas for compounds and preparations are all indicators of the growing popularity of alchemy in the Sixth World. Where demand exists, the corps see the opportunity to make a profit. Patenting compound formulas and litigating those who might attempt to duplicate them; designing and producing custom compounds for the wealthy and powerful; and sending shadowrunners on corporate-espionage raids are all on the rise. Because of this, there has also been a corporate crackdown on all things alchemical. Agents of different corporations have begun frequenting the shops of talismongers to identify their compounds and pursue any possible copyright infringement. There is also plenty of effort going into hiring freelancers so that their ideas and creations become corporate property. The possibility of large piles of nuyen has made information on alchemy and its practitioners valuable, and so those who work outside the corporate structure are finding themselves in an increasingly uncomfortable spotlight.

Alchemists who accept corporate offers have become like songbirds in gilded cages. They are treated well, worked hard, and utterly incapable of leaving once they have signed their name on that dotted line. Some few have managed to escape, at least for now, but most are lured by the promises of an easy life without ever realizing they are signing away their freedom. Word on the streets is that many regret that decision and continually seek a way out.

PLOTS IF YOU HAVE AN ALCHEMIST ON YOUR TEAM:

- An agent of one of the Big Ten is on to your alchemist. Rumors have spread about their talent, and these agents are not taking no for an answer. Their overtures are undermining your street cred and drawing unwanted attention to some of your dealings. Flee to a new place, or crack corporate security and erase any trace of their existence. The choice is yours, but choose fast.
- A client has a corporate alchemist relative who they haven't heard from in far too long. They were supposedly working on something major but abruptly broke contact. They are willing to pay for information or contact. The more you can find out, the more you'll get paid. As a side benefit, the client could care less how you accomplish your task. There may be some clue in the alchemical notes she found.
- Your last job brought with it the reward of a new formula, liberated thanks to some creative hacking, and the corporations want it. Time to find out what it is, what it does, and why they want it before they track you down.

PLOTS IF YOU DO NOT HAVE AN ALCHEMIST ON THE TEAM:

- Ms. Johnson has a client who wants out. All but permanently indentured as a corporate alchemist, they'll do anything to escape their cage. Get in, get the client, and get out.
- When you gather enough alchemists together, there are secrets to be had. A talented decker with some on-site backup may be able to score some sweet info for sale if they can penetrate corporate security and break into a corporate alchemy lab.
- A startup corporation has an alchemical prototype that they're transporting to a potential client. The product of thousands of hours and millions of nuyen, its status as

intellectual property has yet to be legally established. The corporation is willing to take no risks with its transport and wants you as additional security as it moves. The catch is, there's a bigger corporation who sees the prototype as derivative of their work, and they're not going to leave this to the lawyers—some bigger guns have been dispatched.

CORPORATE ALCHEMISTS

Characters who are alchemists may find themselves targeted by corporations looking to recruit them. Runners could be hired to kidnap a promising researcher from one corp to another or prevent such a planned kidnapping. There are myriad ways that the crackdown on alchemy can be implemented within a game. The rumors of the Philosopher's Stone or the reagents from the Seelie Court are two ways to bring alchemists to the attention of a corporation or subsidiary, leading to a need to either escape or make a deal. No matter the power level, having an alchemist in the group or known to them as an ally offers a very easy hook into any corporate plot.

TOXICITY

ⓞ Toxic alchemists are starting to give the rest of us a bad name, feeding off the misery, and killing the world for temporary power. If you can end one of these bastards, you are doing us all a favor.

ⓞ Megalith

Practitioners of the Twisted Way are a terrifying proposition to any who hear of them. Feeding on corruption to increase their power is bad enough on its own. When you add to that the power of alchemy to refine mana to a more powerful form, they truly become the stuff of nightmares. Where most of the toxic magicians and adepts are rather conspicuous, prone to flashy spells of corruption and pollution, those who combine these skills with alchemy take what might have been a deadly but small impact and expand it into a significantly broader threat.

One particular unintended side effect of toxic alchemists has been a blessing for the corporations. By pointing out the damage they cause not just to individuals but to entire areas, the corps have been able to assure the public that alchemy

is best left to the professionals, paving the way for regulatory practices which would provide barriers to entry for smaller competitors. Furthermore, this perception has lowered public opinion of alchemy in general, making practitioners far warier of announcing their profession unless under the protection of corporate security. Chemistry done in the lab, after all, is research, but chemistry done in the basement is potential terrorism.

Those alchemists and talismongers who harvest reagents have their own complaints about Toxic magicians. Reportedly, they are the only ones who can truly gain benefit out of tainted reagents, and they aren't willing to just take the leftovers of others. They are going out and purposefully corrupting entire neighborhoods and forests to taint the ambient mana of the reagents within. This drives away competition for reagents from the alchemists and talismongers who cannot harvest anything of worth from these polluted places.

PLOTS IF YOU HAVE AN ALCHEMIST ON YOUR TEAM:

- A toxic alchemist has entered the area and begun his campaign of tainting the local ambient mana. Your team's alchemist has got her work cut out for her, as only alchemy can halt the toxic spread. If he isn't stopped and soon, there will be nothing but tainted reagents safe to harvest anywhere in the surrounding area.
- The only source of drop bear saliva in the local area has become warped and twisted by toxic energy. Find the source, destroy it, and cleanse the reagents before those who have been taking the compound to resist infection need their next dose.
- An alchemical drug has been spreading, rumored to be highly addictive while slowly exposing the user to toxicity. Your team's alchemist needs to work to inoculate the spread of those afflicted while tracking the product back to its source.

PLOTS IF YOU DO NOT HAVE AN ALCHEMIST ON THE TEAM:

- Land around an old shrine in the woods has begun to shift from a forest glade to a bog-like swamp. No one knows why, but the locals want answers. Mr. Johnson will pay you to investigate and find out what is causing it.

- Someone has tainted a shipment of one of the newest designer drugs. Instead of an out-of-body sensation, it rots the body from within, causing severe damage and possible death. A wealthy socialite recently died from it, and his mother wants revenge. She's paying fat stacks of nuyen to the person who brings her the one responsible.
- A client wants help destroying a pharmaceutical distributor who has supposedly been selling knock-offs for top-shelf prices. After the job is complete, the truth comes out that they were actually helping the community, and the client wanted them dead. Who was the client? What motive did they have to destroy hope? The answers could be deadly for all involved.

USING TOXIC REAGENTS

Toxic alchemists are not just rampaging monsters to be easily identified and destroyed. To make them true villains instead of just bad guys, consider more subtle schemes to introduce them into a game. Instead of initiating widespread destruction, have them kill off an insignificant-seeming creature in an area that turns out to be vital to the predator/prey cycle. They can sit back and watch the whole system crumble. Characters can determine how to handle such an event, deciding whether they wish to stop them, use them for their own purposes, or turn them against their enemies. These all could be viable solutions, each with their own risks and rewards. Another interesting way to introduce the concept of toxic alchemists is to slowly reduce the amount or the integrity of the reagents any alchemist in the group is gathering. Investigating why will lead to answers, followed by more questions.

THE ALCHEMIST'S GUIDE TO SHADOWRUNNING

⊘ Alchemy conjures images of nebbish scholars huddled over bubbling beakers and poring over ancient tomes. Why would a hardcore team of professionals want an alchemist on the payroll? Give me enough time and resources, and there's no telling the amount of mayhem I can manage. I've robbed corporate warehouses, disrupted bug hives, fought bloody territory wars, and not once did the other side see what was coming. Here's some tips and tricks of the trade for those of you looking to make a run.

⊘ Megalith

The basic rules for alchemy are easy to master (see p. 304, *SR5*), but the art of running an alchemist through a run takes skill and wit. Here's a series of subtle tactics and creative tricks to help any budding alchemist become a successful shadowrunner.

FINDING THE SWEET SPOT: PLANNING FOR DRAIN

Drain is the price all magicians, including alchemists, pay to pit their will against the universe. Alchemical compounds and preparations have a finite duration that depends on the Potency of the spell cast. This means anything an alchemist brews has a finite shelf life that may be augmented via special reagents and alchemical tools such as the Vault of Ages (see **New Alchemical Tools**,

p. 192). The sweet spot for a prepared alchemist is the period of time between when they have recovered from the drain of brewing their creation but before the Potency of said creation fizzles. Effective shadowrun teams work on a scheduled timeline to take advantage of the alchemist's full destructive powers.

SELECTING THE BEST SPELLS FOR ALCHEMY

The watchwords for all alchemical creations are reliability and predictability. Alchemical compounds and preparations work best when created from short-term sustained spells that you can trigger with a simple command and then leave to do their jobs, such as Antidote (see p. 288, *SR5*) or Ice Sheet (see p. 293, *SR5*).

Avoid complicated spells that require greater amounts of targeting or manipulating specific targets. Sustained spells that don't require a large number of hits are good for alchemy, since they are sustained for (Potency) minutes, giving them more time to have their effect as intended.

Alchemy requires an Opposed Test at creation, which can reduce Potency. Spell Force during alchemical creation is vital, as it defines the preparation's Magic. Many alchemists elect to overcast during the brewing process if they have the time to recover from the Drain.

Many frightening spells have a high Force requirement that makes them a poor investment for an alchemical creation. Wherever possible, it's more effective to leverage multiple low-

er-Force spells to attack others, rather than try for a single higher-Force preparation to deliver a megahit strike.

DIRTY DEEDS AND TRICKS: WATCHING THE DOMINOES FALL

Alchemical creations will always be weaker than live spells from a magician, but they have several advantages.

Unlike a magician who needs to cast multiple spells to increase the abilities of their teammates, an alchemist can prepare compounds that are ready to go at a moment's notice. Increasing the reflexes of your street samurai or granting your sniper the Sharpshooter compound (p. 197) are as simple as a command word, with the drain already handled.

Defending your home base is almost as important as going out on a run. Having a safe haven to retreat to is worth the time and effort an alchemist must expend to trap and defend. Preparations with contact triggers like Abandon All Hope (p. 198) can be set before leaving so anyone attempting to enter while you are gone suffers the effects.

Alchemy is all about preparation versus the in-the-moment needs of spellcasting. Concentrating on alchemical effects that are situational in nature ensures that even after heavy spellcasting, a magician can be useful. Alchemical Duct Tape (p. 194) to fix a getaway vehicle can be very useful at the end of a run, especially if you are suffering from drain due to spells cast up to that point.

Being aware of the different types of triggers and how to best use them in preparations and compounds is critical. Some contact triggers are not as valuable as commands or anchoring a spell to a set time delay. Setting up grenade-style traps with timed triggers will allow you to cause distractions in other areas. This can help provide a clean getaway while attention is elsewhere.

Alchemists may only activate one command trigger per Combat Turn. So plan ahead on the order in which things will be needed. Going into a run with a firm idea on how to best utilize your compounds and preparations is a major key to success.

Make use of the tools available. Having a contact poison gas ready to go in an atomizer offers you a quick reaction that doesn't require a command, allowing you to set off other preparations or compounds while still incapacitating your enemies.

INDEX

ALCHEMICAL TOOLS

Atomizer	193
Alembic	193
Athanor	193
Crucible	193
Vault of ages	193

COMPOUNDS

Alchemical duct tape	194
Astral bond	195
Astral increase	194
Baobhan's tears	195
Drain away	195
Dulled edges	195
Feel no pain	195
Force of personality	196
HMHVV II Inhibitor	196
Laminate	196
Perfect Sight	196
Sharpshooter	197
Unstoppable vigor	197
Water breathing	197

MASTERY QUALITIES

Adept Healer	31
Alchemical Armorer	31
Alchemical Bomb Maker	31
Animal Familiar	31
Apt Pupil	32
Arcane Bodyguard	32
Arcane Improviser	32
Archivist	32
Astral Bouncer	32
Astral Infiltrator	32
Barehanded Adept	33
Blood Necromancer	33
Chain Breaker	33
Chakra Interrupter	34
Charlatan	34
Chosen Follower	35
Close Combat Mage	35
Dark Ally	35
Death Dealer	35
Dedicated Conjurer	36
Dedicated Spellslinger	36
Dual-Natured Defender	36
Durable Preparations	36
Elemental Master	36
Flesh Sculpter	37
Healer	37
Illusionist	37
Items of Power	38

Mage Hunter	38
Missile Deflector	38
Mystic Foreman	38
Mystic Pitcher	38
Pacifist Adept	39
Potion Maker	39
Practiced Alchemist	39
Puppet Master	39
Reckless Spell Master	39
Renaissance Ritualist	40
Revenant Adept	40
Shock Mage	40
Skinwalker	40
Spectral Warden	40
Spell Jammer	40
Spirit Hunter	40
Spiritual Lodge	41
Spiritual Pilgrim	41
Sprawl Tamer	41
Stalwart Ally	42
Taboo Transformer	42
Vexcraft	42
Worship Leader	42

MENTOR SPIRITS

Arcana	95
Dark King	98
Death	96
Dove	94
Great Mother	99
Green Man	98
Holy Text	95
Moon	98
Oak	99
Planar Entity	95
Rat (alt)	100
Spider (alt)	100
Stag	99
Sun	98
Tohu Wa-Bohu	97
War	97
Wolf (alt)	100

METAMAGICS

Astralnaut	44
Harmonious defense	46
Harmonious reflection	46
Improved astral form	44
Noble sacrifice	46
Paradigm shift	43
Predator feast	131
Reckless necro conjuring	45
Soul tether	131

Spirit expansion: shedim | 44
Spirit expansion: UMT | 44
Spiritual sacrifice | 131
Structured spellcasting | 44
Tarot summoning | 45

PREPARATIONS

Abandon all hope | 198
Barricade | 198
Burn, baby, burn | 198
Do your best | 198
Get away from my ride | 198
High as a kite | 199
Lightning blade | 199
Noise on the line | 199
NOMW (Not on my watch) | 199
Spirit zapper | 199
Stink bomb | 199
Stop thief! | 199
Truth serum | 200
Up and at 'em | 200
Watch your step | 200

REAGENTS

Bone or hair from a baobhan sith | 188
Drake scales | 191
Drop bear saliva | 189
Ghost orhid petals | 190
Ground killdeer antlers | 190
Kayeri mushroom | 190
Organ of insect spirit host | 191
Veins of an adept | 191

RITUALS

Blood Bath | 130
Blood Oath | 130
Death Curse | 130
Forest Transformation | 52
Guardian Bond | 131
Necro Summoning | 52

SPELLS

Alter Ballistics | 51, 186
Barrage | 50
Blood Blade | 129
Blood Puppet | 128
Blood Whip | 129
Boil Blood | 125
Branch | 49
Claw | 50
Clot | 127
Comet | 50
Corpse Explosion | 126
Corpse Lash | 129
Corpse Spikes | 129
Embolism | 126

Evil Eye | 50
Giger Spit | 126
Gravity | 50
Gravity Well | 50
Growth | 49
Ice Veins | 127
Lash | 49
Multiply Food | 50
Pyrohemetics | 127
Rosebush | 49
Rupture | 127
Share Damage | 127
Slash | 49
Somatic Healing | 127
Sympathetic Reprisal | 128
Thorn | 49
Vines | 49
Viscera Web | 129

SPIRITS

Aircraft spirits | 181
Airwave spirits | 180
Automotive spirits | 181
Blood shade | 135
Bone spirit | 134
Carcass spirit | 52
Ceramic spirits | 180
Corpse spirit | 53
Detritus spirit | 53
Energy spirits | 180
Metal spirits | 180
Palefire spirit | 53
Rot spirit | 53
Ship spirits | 180
Train spirits | 181

TRADITIONS

Black Magic (updated) | 60
Buddhist (updated) | 61
Christian Theurgist (updated) | 63
Cosmic | 75
Draconic | 76
Druidic (updated) | 65
Elder God Magic | 78
Green Magic | 80
Islam (updated) | 69
Missionists | 81
Necro Magic | 82
Norse (updated) | 67
Olympianism | 84
Path of Pariah | 85
Planar Magic | 87
Red Magic | 88
Romani | 90
Shaman (updated) | 73
Tarot | 91

SHADOWRUN

BOOK OF THE LOST

NO LONGER HIDDEN

The Bastard, upright. A man in clown make-up stands in a broken skyraker window over another man on the verge of a long plummet. Near the clown's hand, a white rose. Opportunity, adventure, but also mania and frenzy. 404, upright. A woman crouches on the edge of a rooftop, holding a white rose. In the distance is the image of a woman in a red dress. Destruction, failure, collapse. Queen of coins. A woman in a red dress, lounging amidst luxury. She has material wealth but emptiness of soul. Upright, she is opulence, magnificent. Inverse is suspense, fear.

Opportunity and adventure abounds. Destruction and failure loom. Will the result be magnificence—or fear?

Book of the Lost takes the intricate art of the Sixth World Tarot and turns it into stories and campaigns for *Shadowrun* players. Full of plot hooks and adventure seeds, this book is a treasure trove of ideas, mysteries, and enigmas that can make memorable games. Open it and explore knowledge that had been lost but is now, here, rediscovered. And waiting for you.

Book of the Lost is for use with **Shadowrun, Fifth Edition**, and can easily be used with **Shadowrun: Anarchy** with minor NPC adjustments.

CATALYST
game labs

CATALYSTGAMELABS.COM